ARCHIVING

MEXICAN

MASCULINITIES

IN DIASPORA

Duke University Press   *Durham and London*   2021

ARCHIVING

MEXICAN

MASCULINITIES

IN DIASPORA

Nicole M. Guidotti-Hernández

© 2021 DUKE UNIVERSITY PRESS All rights reserved
Printed in the United States of America on acid-free paper ∞
Designed by Courtney Leigh Richardson
Typeset in Minion Pro by Westchester Publishing Services

Library of Congress Cataloging-in-Publication Data
Names: Guidotti-Hernández, Nicole Marie, author.
Title: Archiving Mexican masculinities in diaspora /
Nicole M. Guidotti-Hernández.
Description: Durham : Duke University Press, 2021. | Includes
bibliographical references and index.
Identifiers: LCCN 2020044111 (print) | LCCN 2020044112 (ebook)
ISBN 9781478013242 (hardcover)
ISBN 9781478014157 (paperback)
ISBN 9781478021469 (ebook)
Subjects: LCSH: Flores Magón, Enrique, 1887–1954. | Nadel, Leonard,
1916–1990. | Masculinity—Mexico. | Masculinity—Mexican-American
Border Region. | Men—Socialization—Mexico. | Men—Mexico—Identity. |
Emigration and immigration—Psychological aspects. | Sex discrimination
against women—Political aspects—Mexico. | Mexican-American Border
Region—Social conditions.
Classification: LCC HQ1090.7.M6 G85 2021 (print) | LCC HQ1090.7.M6
(ebook) | DDC 155.3/320972—dc23
LC record available at https://lccn.loc.gov/2020044111
LC ebook record available at https://lccn.loc.gov/2020044112

Cover art: Bracero lounging in foreground while three others look on,
Gondo labor camp, Watsonville, California, 1956. Courtesy Leonard Nadel
Photographs and Scrapbooks, Archives Center, National Museum of
American History, Smithsonian Institution.

Duke University Press gratefully acknowledges the support of the
University of Texas–Austin, Department of Mexican American and
Latina/o Studies, which provided funds toward the publication of this
book.

Contents

Acknowledgments   vii

Introduction   1

PART I: ENRIQUE FLORES MAGÓN'S EXILE
Revolutionary Desire and Familial Entanglements   29

1   Greeting Cards, Love Notes, Love Letters   35

2   PLM Intimate Betrayals: Enrique Flores Magón, Paula Carmona, and the Gendered History of Denunciation   43

3   Out of Betrayal and into Anarchist Love and Family   83

4   Bodily Harm   107

5   De la Familia Liberal   127

6   The Split   139

7   The Emotional Labor of Being in Leavenworth   147

8   Deportation to a Home That Doesn't Exist, or "He Has Interpreted the Alien's Mind"   157

   Part I: Conclusion   171

PART II: THE HOMOEROTICS OF ABJECTION
The Gaze and Leonard Nadel's Salinas Valley
Bracero Photographs 175

9   Making Braceros Out of Place and Outside of Time   185

10 The Salinas Valley and Hidden Affective Histories   197

11 Hip Forward into Domestic Labor and Other Intimacies   215

12 Queer Precarious Lives   233

13 Wanting to Be Looked At   251

14 Passionate Violence and Thefts   275

   Part II: Conclusion   283

Conclusion   285

Notes   291
Bibliography   321
Index   329

Acknowledgments

This book would not exist without the friendships and collaborations I developed with numerous people: Diego Flores Magón, Anita Swearingen, the staff of the Nettie Lee Benson Library, Juan José Colomina Almiñana, and Ausiàs Colomina-Guidotti. The Benson staff are my intellectual family. AJ Johnson, Linda Gill, Daniel Arbino, and Christian Kelleher share the love of archives that I do. They were always quick to share materials, get what I needed, and make me smile when things were not so great. I love the Benson and its collection because of the aforementioned people.

I began my work in the Flores Magón archive before it became public, thanks to my dear friend Diego Flores Magón. As I worked through the thousands of documents curated by his great-grandfather Enrique, there were loose ends and things that didn't make sense to me. As I wrote, more holes and inconsistencies appeared. On a whim, I reached out to Anita Swearingen about her grandmother Paula Carmona, the wife of Enrique Flores Magón, who had essentially been written out of PLM history. Anita's graciousness in sharing the family history is what allowed me to write chapter 2. Together, we all met in Mexico City in January 2019. The Carmonas and Flores Magóns had been separated for a century based on a political battle that ended in a bitter divorce and abandoned children. The conversation over photographs and food in Coyoacán was incredible, for history was what united us at that very important moment.

My work on the bracero program was inspired by the fact that I grew up in the heart of the program's legacy and was taught nothing about it, simultaneously elucidating my privilege as a second-generation Mexican Italian and the vast historical amnesia that took place. This was disturbing to me, and it compelled the second half of the book. Aided by numerous research assistants, I could not have completed the work without Alana Varner, Alma Buena, Christine Castro, José Centeno-Mcléndez, and Imelda Muñoz. Christine read the introduction, and I am grateful for the feedback she offered. Patrick Lawrence assisted with the translations. I also want to thank my aunt

Virginia Hernández, who provided essential information about the Salinas police force in the 1950s; my father, Richard Guidotti, for his great memory about spaces, places, and family history; and the office of the Salinas city attorney, which provided copies of numerous restrictive ordinances that governed the bracero program.

My ride-or-die crew made the last five years a little more manageable. You have no idea how much I love you all: Kathy Escobar, Lonnee Apperley, Elisa Carias, Belinda Lum, Susie Pak, Maritza Cárdenas, Eliza Rodríguez y Gibson, Domino Perez, Stephanie Quiñones, Andrew Quiñones, James Cox, Vicky de Francesco Soto, Adam Geary, Freddie Rodríguez, Luis Alvarez, Ruby Tapia, Lorena Muñoz, Tanya González, and Lorgia García Peña. I'm forever grateful to Domino Perez, who read one of the first full drafts of part II, which shaped the project thereafter. Having Víctor Macías-González at the Benson with me during the spring of 2019 was a blessing—the snark and research prodding were the best—thank you, my friend! My mentors, María Crístina García, George Sánchez, Josie Saldaña-Portillo, and Laura Briggs, have been there for me intellectually and personally—thank you. Here is where I also must thank my partner, Juan José Colomina Almiñana, and my son, Ausiàs. We've been to hell and back and are still here, thanks to Ausiàs, that little ray of sunshine. Thank you for supporting me even when it cost you.

The work also benefited from the questions raised by numerous audiences at the Ohio State University, the University of Southern California (x2), Harvard University, West Virginia University, and Kansas State University. Thanks to my editor, Courtney Berger, for standing behind the project and to Sandra Korn and Annie Lubinsky for their help with production. Everyone says that second books are hard to write, but I had no idea what I was in for with this one. I'm committed to work that pushes the envelope. But sometimes people want the envelope to stay shut. The gatekeeping has been unjustifiable. It is important, despite my experience with this book, that junior scholars know there is enough room for all of us at the table irrelevant of different interpretations. I want to express my heartfelt thanks to Readers 1, 2, and 4. You provided amazing feedback that pushed the project to be its best. I value your work and want you to know how much it means to have committed scholars make the peer-review process function so well.

I saw a *curandera* in Mexico for a *limpia* regarding health issues. She told me, "People try to attach spells that paralyze you. But you are too strong, and they merely slow you down. You keep going." After everything that's happened to me while writing this book, I have one thing to say: you all slowed me down, but I am still going strong and will continue to do so. You know what you did.

Introduction

> Yesterday morning as well as in the morning of the last Sunday, I received fruit. I am obliged to Rafa for letting me know in his note of yesterday that Tere was out of town, for I was beginning to think that she would be sick. I'm feeling fine, although my rheumatism bothers me a bit on account of last night being so cold. But otherwise I feel strong after doing some special gymnastic exercises. I wish I was as strong as I am now than when that ruffian Thompson assaulted me so unprovoked and viciously.[1]

Writing to a comrade from the Los Angeles County Jail, Mexican anarchist Enrique Flores Magón lamented much during his various stints of imprisonment in the United States. Wishing he had been physically stronger when Detective Thompson attacked him at the Edendale (Los Angeles) commune of the Partido Liberal Mexicano (PLM—a Mexican revolutionary party that opposed the Díaz dictatorship) earlier in 1916. This mundane recounting of physical weakness has additional significance. At first glance, the letter is rather straightforward—he wishes the outcomes could have been different—and is about his family, the police, his health, and his ailing body. Upon further reading, though, it raises a number of questions about Mexican masculinities and their gender formation in diaspora. For one, Flores Magón spent 50 percent of his twenty-three years of exile in US prisons. His political activities to liberate the Mexican people from the yoke of capitalism were met with hostility in the US instead of the freedom and belonging he had hoped to find.

The letter performs masculine stoicism, demonstrating to a comrade that he was indeed physically hearty and capable of surviving incarceration. Enrique idealized physical fitness as the key to thriving in an environment of police brutality. But normative masculine affect comes undone in the worry for his life partner, Teresa Arteaga de Flores Magón, showing that gender and intimate relations did indeed change in migration. Gaps in communication with intimate partners, children, comrades, and family members made migration emotionally taxing, only to be exacerbated by imprisonment. It strained emotional attachments, exposing, as Jennifer Hirsch has argued, "how women and men are motivated by emotion and desire ... but their emotion and desire must be historically situated."[2] Taken in Hirsch's framework, Enrique's expression of loss, intimacy, and lament demonstrates how deeply migration and separation, whether through imprisonment or living in a labor camp that felt like a prison, altered gender relations and expressions of gender. Although this letter to a comrade from the Los Angeles County Jail recorded the fragility of Mexican masculinities in diaspora, such fragility was a function of the intimacies that were cultivated in the face of separation and being a racial, political, and social outsider in the US. In the letter, Mexican masculinity is flexible (simultaneously stoic, visceral, fragile, and tender) and exemplifies how migrant men's intimacies also made up their lives as political subjects.

The circumstances that transformed Mexican migrant masculinities in the early twentieth century continued shifting in other historical moments as well, especially during the bracero program (between 1942 and 1964 Mexico exported agricultural laborers to the US in a bilateral agreement). Migrant Mexican men's intimacies were made flexible by migration, but the receiving society continued to express anxiety about them, particularly in northern California. The year 1956 yielded the highest number of *braceros*—literally, people who work with their arms—ever imported into California for agricultural labor. These communities felt the swell in bracero numbers, with the populations of towns often doubling overnight during peak growing season (March through October). In turn, locals responded with racist and culturally superior language and legislation to make themselves feel more American and to make braceros feel even more alien. Journalist Carlos Aniceto Gutiérrez reflected upon the impact of the 1956 bracero labor boom:

> In 1956, California farmers spent $6,000,000 in bracero transportation from and to contracting centers.... This constant current, involving millions of people on both sides of the border every year, creates all sorts of problems. "What started as an economical problem has become a social one, involving murder, robbery, narcotics addiction, prostitution and many others." Vice centers are located in or near the bracero camps. There are more than 5,000 of those camps in California and only 28 inspectors supervise them.... Fatherless children are left all over California, causing a constant increase in which the number

of cases with which social welfare agencies must deal. In 1955, eight hundred abandoned families reported in the state absorbed more than $1 million of taxpayer money.[3]

For braceros, new intimacies and gender formations generated problematic conditions for mainstream Anglo-Americans who were not in the agricultural industry as well as Mexican American cultural brokers such as Gutiérrez and civic leaders of both ethnicities. The importation of Mexican men as laborers solved an economic problem in the US but also generated a "socio-economic problem." As the Mexican American reporter Gutiérrez noted, these men were seen as a locus of vice that spread into the surrounding communities. According to Gutiérrez, their sexual relationships put a strain on the social welfare system, and his underlying message was intended to differentiate the behaviors of Mexican nationals from Mexican Americans. Instead of seeing migrant Mexican men's longing for intimacy and community as a gendered and sexualized product of segregated labor conditions, newspapers, city governments, and families (Anglo- and Mexican American alike) tolerated the bracero presence in California because the workers provided low-wage labor in a booming agricultural economy. Again, Gutiérrez was a Mexican American and did not include the perspectives of the braceros themselves, showing how the vast majority of their daily lives and newly formed masculine intimacies, emotional attachments, and a sense of loss were circumscribed, interpreted, and recorded by someone else. Not only did braceros generate a visceral emotional response from receiving communities, but their own desires to be seen as people and to be included in society as consumers with economic, sexual, and emotional desires were often at odds with each other. Mexican men's relationships with other men in labor camps prompted pleasure-seeking activity and consumer spending. Although migration reasserted the masculine privileges of mobility afforded to Mexican men at home, the racialized policing of sexuality, labor, and leisure was enforced abroad. Gutiérrez's pathological narrative produced exactly that: a wholesale rejection of bracero attempts at forging intimacies and engagement with American society. Exploring questions of masculine fragility, vulnerability, and intimacies forged as a result of a collective migration is the pathway out of the pathology narrative, especially in the context of California's Salinas Valley. One of the few glimpses we get of bracero intimate life that represent flexible ideas of Mexican masculinities can be found in Leonard Nadel's massive photographic archive, which I analyze in detail herein.

I tell these two stories and many others like them throughout *Archiving Mexican Masculinities in Diaspora* to recapture intimacy and affect as forms of history meriting documentation and interpretation. In recording these intimacies forged in diaspora from the 1890s to the 1950s, from the PLM to the bracero program, the male privileges of mobility are seen as exacerbating gender inequalities even as masculinities could take on different expressions through the migratory context. Those intimacies provided numerous configurations for masculinities built through bonds between men and their communities via out-migration from Mexico to the United States.

But even as we grapple with the idea of multiple Mexican masculinities forged in diaspora, there are political and scholarly investments in maintaining a status quo. What happens when we question these entrenched narratives? The process is unsettling, to say the least. But also, I hope, revelatory. And necessary. Because over time, the stories we tell become simplified and calcified, and they help no one. These histories must be investigated with careful precision, from different angles and fresh perspectives. Only then can we hope to have a more complete and representative understanding of the past. Here we will be investigating anew the question of Mexican masculinity. The term *Mexican masculinity* brings to mind *machismo* (I can't tell you how many times people jumped to the conclusion that this book is only about *machismo*), the concept of the patriarchal, sexist Mexican man who dominates women. But that version of the story is a simple one, painfully simple and not the reality.

I have written this book—a feminist cultural transnational history—to show that typical narratives of Mexican masculinity are often simplistic and reductive. Life narratives are far more complicated. Here we will explore the inner lives of Mexican men who were exiled and/or who migrated to the US across the first half of the twentieth century. What we find is not a single Mexican masculinity but masculinities in the plural. What we find are the various ways that the US influenced and shaped the lives of Mexican nationals within its borders. What we find is the crucial and suppressed role that intimacy, emotion, and desire played in their lives.

As we engage with Mexican masculinities in diaspora, the archives demonstrate the broader lived realities of individuals who were noncitizens within a nation that treated them as problematic outsiders. The first half of the twentieth century, the focus of *Archiving Mexican Masculinities in Diaspora*, is important because it marked the end of Porfirio Díaz's dictatorship, Mexico's social revolution, and the bracero program, which were all major factors prompting migration to the United States. As men migrated for economic and political reasons for more than fifty years, they sought freedom. They also found themselves in alienating circumstances, where their private and public lives were highly regulated by the law and the nation-state. As the archives examined in this book demonstrate, men's daily intimacies were exposed in the US and Mexico via newspapers, letters, telegrams, photographs, drawings, police reports, military communiqués, and more. Because migrant Mexican men's intimacies were under scrutiny in both nations, their political identities were shaped by this regulation. In order to understand their experiences more fully, we need a transnational approach to affect and intimacy, one where the movement of ideas, bodies, services, emotions, and goods across and between the borders of nation-states produced new forms of gender.

Because massive social and economic transformation in Mexico in the first half of the twentieth century caused migration, mostly by men, to the United States, *Archiving Mexican Masculinities in Diaspora* tracks the resulting gender transformations. It focuses on what I call *transnational masculine intimacies*, which refers to the emotional bonds and relationships that Mexican men built with other men and their extended networks during their migrations to the United States. By exploring these intimacies, we learn not only about the multiplicity of what it meant to be masculine, but we also see how diaspora shaped the idea of nation. The importance of examining the ways that gender structures and is in turn structured by transnational social ties is crucial to the project.[4] Throughout this book we will be looking at one very particular manifestation of this relationship: the versions of masculinity that existed in the transnational circuit between Mexico and California. That circuit—and masculinity itself—can be better understood if we are critical of how representations of gender and sexuality vary because of migration.

By foregrounding the power of archives, we can study ideologies circulating between 1900 and 1956 about Mexican masculinities. The collection of cultural objects about the PLM and Enrique Flores Magón, Leonard Nadel's bracero archive at the Smithsonian, the Eisenhower presidential papers, and other Salinas Valley archives make an impassioned case for taking seriously emotion, intimacy, and new masculine formations. These archives span the 1890s to the 1950s, tracking changes in how diasporic masculinity was represented and understood over time. As a result, the book commits to a more expansive vocabulary and disturbs what appear to be cemented historical narratives steeped in patriarchal nationalisms.

Mexican anarchist Enrique Flores Magón and the braceros who labored in the Salinas Valley and the archives about them represent a contradiction between emotional attachment to people and a dream that could never be realized: freedom. This book is about those attachments and their failures. Because the study is generated from archives about anarchists and braceros, we must also question the practices of archiving. The analysis focuses on the conditions and contexts of their migrations to unite the two case studies: the book contrasts and compares the migrant experiences of PLM junta members and braceros. Both studies demonstrate how the presence or absence of women in the diaspora process recast human relationships: anarchists migrated with female comrades, but braceros migrated alone. Nayan Shah has described gender and migration intimacies as disputes over domesticity, companionship, and public life, which were part of larger state efforts to regulate migrant behaviors.[5] As the United States and Mexico tried to regulate these migrants in public, their private lives allowed new forms of subjectivity to emerge. As Víctor Macías-González notes, "It is critical to consider how domestic space, households, housework and sociability"—in other words, the private sphere—provided a place for men to negotiate their roles in Mexico's diaspora.[6] Because anarchists and braceros were so heavily regulated by the US and Mexican governments, their private lives became public. Thus, by examining the intimacy analytics proposed by Shah and Macías-González, fresh perspectives about Mexican masculinities emerge.

Whereas Mexican men's migration has primarily been studied through the public sphere, my work delves into the private and domestic dimensions of migration. Part I narrates Enrique Flores Magón's intimate life and loves during his almost twenty-year exile in the US between 1907 and 1923. Part II accounts for the world that bracero guest workers encountered and created when they migrated from Mexico between 1942 and 1964 to labor in Salinas Valley's agricultural fields. These two Mexican migrant experiences vary quite a bit, yet there is much to be learned from the continuities that each cohort experienced in terms of discrimination, regulation, and the intimacies and attachments they formed despite constant policing by the state. These two cohorts of Mexican migrants are my focus for numerous reasons. First, studying the intimate lives and visual archives allows one to track migratory subjects in their affective and emotive lives across space and time. Second, the transnational nature of their lives is emblematic of the mobility—however it was policed by both the Mexican and US governments—that male subjects were afforded, despite tightening immigration restrictions in the first half of the twentieth century. Third, Flores Magón and the braceros alike were migratory subjects forged through political and economic exile. In both cases, migration was a necessity for survival, not a mobility afforded with cosmopolitan luxury. There are indeed tensions in comparing these compulsory migrations, but putting the condition of PLM political exile in conversation with the braceros' racial and economic marginalization reveals the political and ideological impetus for migration in both cases. Fourth, these national histories—of both the US and diasporic Mexican California—are histories of intimacy, where subjects forged sometimes optimistic but also harmful emotional attachments. Fifth, intimacies matter to our methodology for understanding masculinities because historicizing emotional bonds has the capacity to transform and enrich how stories of the past are told. Sixth, Mexican masculinities are highly mediated by nationalism and must be questioned. Seventh, the private spills effortlessly into the public realm with documents and photographs of varying gender ideologies that were produced by and for the state.[7] Eighth and finally, archival and visual transcripts of daily life for Mexican male migrants do not match up with long-standing, normative, and sacred nationalist forms of ideology reproduced by Mexico, Mexicanist scholars, and scholars of Mexican America. As a Latinx feminist scholar, I evaluate how intimacy and attachment are archived and how they served as quotidian forms of self-making in diaspora.

As a person who rejected the authority of the state during his exile, Flores Magón produced his own archive. Until five years ago, it remained largely a private project of the Flores Magón family. For this reason, we must also question the narrative that it constructs in telling a particular version of his family and the PLM.[8] Similarly, Leonard Nadel's photographs seem to tell a straightforward story until we start to look more closely at his archive. Nadel was a highly esteemed photographer whose work appeared in the *Los Angeles Times, Harvester News* (features photographer), *Life*, and *Business Week*. In addition, he was the official photographer for the Los Angeles County Housing Authority and was deeply influenced by the social realism of the Works Progress Administration (WPA) photos two decades earlier. In 1956 he was awarded a grant from the Freedom Fund, a subsidiary of the Ford Foundation, which sought to document the flaws of the US immigration system. Nadel spent twelve months living in bracero camps in the Salinas Valley, across California and Texas; the by-product was a series of intimate relationships that Nadel developed with braceros while he lived with them. In the end only nine of the more than two thousand photos he took were published in an editorial for *Look*.[9] Indeed, we know about the entire corpus of images because in 2010, Nadel's widow donated all of his old contact sheets, some captioned photographs, and correspondence relating to the collection to the Smithsonian. The images record the intimacy and homosocial spaces where emotional bonds were forged. Some of these relationships were sexual;

many were not. Still, the evidence presents queer masculine possibilities: the bracero program provided a less policed opportunity for those who wanted to pursue same-sex relations to do so.[10] Bracero photos taken by Nadel construct a complicated vision of the program's social-sexual legacy. The photographs of bracero daily life document how Mexican men responded to their contracted conditions in the United States and forged intimacies because of them.

I argue that because they were curated for eventual public consumption and access, both the Enrique Flores Magón archives and Leonard Nadel's archives can be read as forms of national history. With the Flores Magón case in particular, we must be attentive to the role of personal refashionings and how Flores Magón himself created suitable "histories" of the familial, and its attendant intimacies, in the construction of the archive.[11] In contrast, the Nadel photos were curated before and after the photographer's death and contain, among the contact sheets and captioned images, a biopic movie script that his widow pitched to Hollywood in the 1990s. Although the film was never made and no list of the men's names whom he photographed in 1956 is to be found—and braceros and their families may never have seen the photographs—Evelyn De Wolfe Nadel wanted her husband's radical social realist experiment to have the visibility it never achieved during his lifetime. We cannot overlook how the materials, vital records of braceros' daily diasporic lives, arrived at the Smithsonian or how they document the intimate attachments that Nadel developed with Mexican nationals in 1956.

In centering this archive, I do not argue that Nadel and his photographs were oppressive instruments of the state but rather that we should afford these documents a nuanced and attentive close reading. We should examine his artistry alongside the ideas within these images, and we should push beyond the simple notion that such documentary photographs are no more than evidence of the exploitation that braceros suffered in the US. In other words, interrogating power relations in visual records and written documents is vital to my argument, but is it never with the intention of dismissing aesthetics. We see how Nadel's photographic skill immortalized bracero experiences in a world absent of women and thus without the typical heterosexual family. In contrast to the stylized photos that Nadel took, the federal laws governing the bracero program, and the local Salinas Valley policies that guided these men and their movements, tell a very different story: their lives were highly regulated, and the men were regarded as sexually and socially deviant.[12]

In the Flores Magón archive we also see a narrative quite different from what we have come to expect about Mexican masculinity. It is easy to assume that in Flores Magón's circles, traditional family and gender ideologies were completely absent because all the people were anarchists. I question this assumption based on close engagement with long-trodden archival sources. In problematizing how Flores Magón cataloged an intimate vision of family that was at times radical and, at other times, normative and punitive, the book examines how the desire for revolution could actually be contradictory to one's own capacity to flourish. Although some see Enrique as peripheral to the PLM, he was the one who outlived everyone else from the political organization to tell the tales in the way he saw fit.[13] The body of materials narrating his place in history are evidence that a more expansive feminist accounting is sorely needed.[14] Following Roger Bartra, I demonstrate how these archival synergies of diasporic Mexican masculinity are "most effective in securing a connection between mythology and politics by means of emotion."[15] Therefore, both archives are collections of intimacy and emotion by virtue of their contents, and together they offer a plural vision of how Mexican masculinities have been made and remade through migration during the first half of the twentieth century. This book is built from what I call archives of intimacy: the records of masculine emotional bonds.

This is why we must consider not just the histories that have come before but also the visual objects that are central to their archives. Visuality is yet one more aesthetic form through which these attachments and intimacies can be understood. Depending on how an archive has been assembled by archivists, collected by family members, or used by scholars, this determines what kinds of narratives and histories are produced thereafter. Often, scholars and archivists are wedded to particular narratives and readings of documents or photographs because of the position that these artifacts occupy in preestablished histories. Emotional investment in these narratives and/or people is an attachment, which Lauren Berlant calls a form of optimism.[16] Desires form hope, and that hope generates motive to preserve particular versions of history. Hopefulness about Mexican men's migration to the US as successful or resistant locates power in the idea of upward mobility and escaping oppression.

The Mexican men who migrated hoped they would find politically freer, less regulated lives. Instead, they found different racial and ideological forms of oppression, contrary to the class-based politics of the Mexico they left behind. For example, light-skinned braceros did not enjoy the same privileges afforded to them in Mexico because they were surveilled by the state as noncitizen, temporary laborers, just like their darker-skinned counterparts. The great equalizer in their shared inequality came from being Mexican nationals, irrespective of skin color. Still, Mexican male migrants clung to the optimistic promise of freedom in the United States, even when they were imprisoned for violating neutrality laws or living in the most-squalid conditions. There was still hope. We can examine how optimistic conditions allowed men to forge relationships to one another in migration, but the intersections of gender, sexuality, and racial difference have not always been central priorities in previous analyses. For this reason, they are central to this book, most notably documented in photography. By analyzing visual documents of Mexican anarchist Flores Magón and Mexican bracero workers who labored in the Salinas Valley differently from the discursive ones, feminist, interdisciplinary frameworks demonstrate how diaspora constituted the idea of nation via transnational masculine intimacies. I not only discuss the proposition of why these two particular archives form the corpus but also interrogate their construction equally, as well as my own relationship to them as a feminist scholar. In this way no photograph or letter is taken at face value. With each object of interpretation I perform exhaustive readings of all the possible meanings and intentions. The critique and scholarly contribution are derived from the destabilizing force of Latinx critiques of gender and ideology as much as primary sources, entrenched historical narratives, and content.

Anarchist and Bracero Attachments on Paper and in Photography

Archives about Flores Magón and Salinas Valley braceros problematize the categories of human and representation, which is why this book analyzes them together. By explaining when, why, and how Mexican migrant men became threats to the US nation-state localized in California, a major engine of westward economic expansion, *Archiving Mexican Masculinities in Diaspora* traces the habitual ways that communities responded to these men. The state response was intrusion and surveillance, informing the written and visual accounts of Enrique's life in exile and that of braceros. Localized communal responses were to integrate these migrants and/or to tout their usefulness as laborers. As time progressed from the late nineteenth century to the mid-twentieth century, we see an expanded and redirected effort to regulate Mexican male migrants who were political dissidents or contracted laborers. Whereas anarchists were contained through the carceral apparatus, braceros were contained by legally negotiating the terms of entry prior to arrival. As a means of mediating Mexican migrant men's optimism about freedoms in the United States, these attachments to liberty and to one another force us to think more critically about the histories of masculinity as a product of migration and diaspora. The narratives and archives fit together along the horizon of US and Mexican collaborations in the extraction of undesirables in a Mexican economy that had no place for them (a dictatorship that crushed dissent and an underemployed workforce).

Anarchists and braceros complicate understandings of migrant streams because they forced the recalibration of racially restrictive codes and the passing of new anticommunist, exclusion, and immigration laws.[17] Although the paper legacies (archival documents, newspapers, telegrams, letters, and more) have been publicly less visible, the photographic legacies have the most impact in our visually driven culture today. Thus, I treat the visual materials as refractory aesthetic and political objects. Following Tina Campt's important work, these images of diaspora mediate the presence of a "home elsewhere, [for] diaspora is not an endless trajectory that perpetually overwrites its arrival somewhere." Visual archives document both arrival and departure as well as skillful compliance and refusal.[18] As both Flores Magón and the braceros eventually returned to Mexico after their sojourn in the US, the writings and images capturing their time in country document the hope of returning home. In part I the photographs of Flores Magón and family were a function of living a public political life. In contrast, the bracero photographs examined in part II documented and framed the ephemeral nature of intimate life. Intentionally staged and occasionally constructed images, both of Flores Magón and of anonymous braceros, straddle the boundaries between personal intimacies, public documentation, and the intrusiveness of photography. The slippage between these categories makes up much of the discussion of archiving as a political and personal act. Because the world of the photographed and the world of the viewer come into tension with each other, attachments to anarchist and bracero communities were forged daily. One of the ways that attachment is formed lies in how subjects engage the camera. A smile, in a radical political context, could be an indicator of uncontained affect or a lack of seriousness. However, not smiling could also be a response to having bad teeth as a result of poverty or an act of refusal toward the authority behind the camera.[19] A smile, in a context of joking or cajoling, such as we see in much of the bracero photographs, suggests that the images break conventions of twentieth-century Mexican masculinities, where one rarely if ever smiled for the camera. Self-representation in Nadel's bracero photographs differed drastically from Mexican norms and traditions of the proper masculine subject: *fuerte y formal* (strong and formal) men don't smile. Those traditions of stoicism contrast greatly with the scenes where Nadel coaxed his subjects into playfully engaging the camera, creating expressions of passion and pleasure not seen elsewhere. As John

Mraz has noted, the photograph is enmeshed in networks of competing interests, especially concerning Mexico and Mexican national identities.[20]

Images are fundamentally affective objects. Imbued with emotion, they powerfully draw us into a narrative, irrelevant of our attachment to the subject. There is something about the visual field, no matter who we are, that wields us into viewership. After that initial glance, if an image compels us, we come back for a second take, and a third take, and in those additional views we build an attachment to the image, however ephemeral. In some ways the power of the visual field in sculpting history, in sculpting attachment, is overwhelming. Affective relations are forged through photographs. Photographs position the subjects in their most idealized or desired state and in a form of capture. Therefore, photographic subjects are not the only things that are captured; we too are captured as we look, gaze, study, or wonder. We become a captive audience to an image as it draws us in, mobilizes and organizes our sentiments, and sways us to engage.

Particular visual archives are often cited when referencing Mexican anarchism in southern California and the bracero program to map resistant subjectivities. Historical revolutionary and bracero narratives have been reproduced by scholars such as Colin MacLachlan, who argued that Ricardo Flores Magón was "an important precursor of political consciousness among Mexican Americans."[21] Others, such as Juan Gómez-Quiñones, stated that "the PLM and the Flores Magons, in particular, have become icons who have inspired racial activists in the US and Mexico."[22] Still others have argued that Ricardo was "a worthy representative of the Mexican Revolutionary precursors"[23] or, as José Muñoz Cota explains, "within his head is all of his glory; he is above the limits of our tiny heroes in comparison."[24] On the bracero side, Deborah Cohen has argued that braceros and images of them show how they "were sent northward as heroes and received at home as 'beasts.'"[25] These bracero "ambassadors in overalls," like their PLM migratory counterparts from a few decades earlier, are celebrated for their valor.[26] Such representations revert to a discourse of heroism and recognizable exemplary political iconographies, but there is another, even more compelling way to see these images. I was first drawn to the set of images of both Enrique and Ricardo Flores Magón because of what was *not* being said about them. This holds true of my engagement with Nadel's bracero photographs. Upon seeing these bodies of work, I of course saw the lionized visual iconographies of these men; I of course saw these images as evidence of the compulsory heteronormative masculinity that had been forged in California's Mexican diaspora starting in the early twentieth century. Yet I also saw something else that was harder to put into words. Both populations were policed and heavily surveilled in intimate ways. In that surveillance a structure of feeling was created, as Raymond Williams would say; it is that feeling that I explore through the official discourse of policy and regulations, and in the popular response to such diasporic subjects.

From this surveilled diaspora, the "standard story" of Mexican masculinities is compulsory, traditional, and built on virility and excess. Anxieties were quelled by overstating virility and excess as masculine, not feminine. This normative optic for Mexican anarchists in the early 1900s and braceros in the middle of the century shows why traditional discourses framed how Mexican migrant men are typically understood. Detailed analysis of archival and photo documents reveals a different valence. The complexity of migration experiences and how they impacted notions of self are why I opt for a discussion of passionate attachments (intense emotive bonds) and their attendant optimism, tempered by suspicion of celebratory heroic narratives. Theorizing passionate attachments has the capacity to combat virility and excess as the only interpretive paradigm.

In addition to using the visual field to track masculine deviation, one of the main threads connecting these two historical moments in male Mexican migrant transnational subjectivities is the idea of desire. Mexican men are usually understood as representing racial excess in relationship to Anglo-American masculinities. This is why I centralize these individuals as desiring subjects rather than mere victims of capitalism and their supposedly own innate, uncontrollable, and excessive racial passions. Stories of desire, passionate attachment, and longing emerge as an alternative to the excessive and pathological corporeality narrated by state governments. Power relations structured the lives of racialized, sexualized subjects in diaspora, as we will see again and again, and this is vastly more revealing than any state-created narrative.

One of the major manifestations of the power relations embedded in desire is found in early twentieth-century surveillance tactics. The similarities in the use of surveillance between 1900 and 1950 are striking. Surveillance dictated how correspondence became part of the state and public domain: they were public intimacies. The hundreds of letters intercepted by intelligence agencies on behalf of Chihuahua governor Enrique Creel or those documented among braceros by Miroslava Chávez-García are evidence of this lack of public-private divide.[27] Expressions of dissent, whether with the host society for political exiles or by contractually obligated guest workers, were subject to intensive scrutiny by the US and Mexico, along with their respective agents.

Given the increased policing of labor and anarchist activists in the 1910s and 1920s, which led to deportations, the condoned use of violence and brutality experienced by this largely immigrant social movement resulted in the first red scare. After the mass repatriation of anywhere between 200,000 and 1,000,000 Mexicans and Mexican Americans during the Great Depression, a clear message was conveyed by the US government: these migrants were not permanent members of US society.[28] With Los Angeles as the hub of this removal, it is no accident that Depression-era monitoring of Mexican and Mexican American migrants in the city followed on the heels of expelled anarchists such as Enrique Flores Magón. And although *Archiving Mexican Masculinities in Diaspora* does not examine the expulsions of the Depression era, it is important to see the bracero program as an exploitative labor corrective to the mass removal of the previous decades.

The bracero guest-worker program's successful launch in 1942 was a response to the agricultural labor shortage during World War II because citizen laborers were on the war front. It was necessary because of what happened during and before the Depression; the bracero program brought back a population that had been previously expelled. A key difference, of course, is that these men came back alone; the program did not accommodate women and children. The presence of families and emotional ties would have made settlement more permanent. Initially, the temporary contracts were their own form of propaganda for the war effort and made farmers and the state content precisely because there was no long-term commitment, only minimal social integration, and no governmental responsibility to migrants without families. The way to control migrant Mexican men, or so it was thought, was to isolate and segregate them and their labor, unlike their anarchist antecedents of the 1910s and 1920s or the repatriated families of the 1930s.

Much of the book focuses on questions of state interpolation of Mexican masculinities, but another key conversation in *Archiving Mexican Masculinities in Diaspora* explores the tensions and affinities between Mexican nationals and Mexican Americans. Mexican anarchists folded themselves into the larger immigrant and Mexican American communities in places such as San Antonio, El Paso, Laredo, St. Louis, and Los Angeles. Much of this had to do with the fact that in that era, "Mexican" signaled "immigrant" and was a category viewed as part and parcel of the other mass nonwhite populations that entered the US in the early twentieth century. Mexicans were excluded from the Anglo-American dominant culture and governance to a degree that was greater than that of "other" ethnic whites, such as the Irish.[29] Thus, the possibility for seamlessly becoming part of the mass nonwhite immigrant populations, many of whom became dissenters through labor organizing during the period, made for integration of a different sort. Local and federal governments, aided by yellow journalistic reporting, feared this integration deeply. The *Los Angeles Times* went so far as to declare that the Flores Magóns, their families, and related anarchists would "with fiery utterances incite the local Mexicans" and destroy the fabric of the nation with their "vile epithets and vituperation in discussing the government of the United States."[30]

But there is something more that connects Mexican anarchist and bracero masculinities in diaspora. As a regular columnist for *Todo: La Mejor Revista de México* in the 1950s, Enrique commented on numerous social problems, one of which was the bracero program. He was an advocate for fair wages and reasonable hours for the working classes, and his later writings about the bracero program connected the PLM agenda with the exploitation of Mexican migrants in the 1950s. On September 3, 1953, his article "El fracaso de Abraham Lincoln" (Abraham Lincoln's failure) viewed the efforts of the sixteenth US president to abolish slavery as a failure given the way that Mexican braceros were enslaved through their bilateral government-negotiated contracts. Describing a bracero strike and undocumented Mexican workers in Detroit's Ford City Pickle Company factory, Enrique argued that there was and continued to be slavery in the United States: first with African Americans and then with Mexican laborers in the twentieth century. The exposé of the deplorable working conditions and strike was based on photos and letters received from Horacio Dorantes Tovar, "a serious and hard worker from a good family from Ixtapa de Sal [Edo. de México]."[31] Dorantes Tovar stated that braceros in Detroit were given "an old boat full of spider webs to sleep in that was so humid and full of rats. Using what little English I knew, I asked the patron for a habitable space but I never got it, much later he let me know that my contract said, that I was going to earn the same as the local workers and that he only paid $.75 per hour; he not only insulted me, but he ruined any illusion I might have about this place."[32] To a mass Mexican literate public, Enrique denounced the inhumane living conditions that bracero workers endured, as well as the manipulation of contract labor that allowed for their abuse. He then argued that all of Abraham Lincoln's sacrifices to abolish slave labor were a waste in light of the bracero program. Despite the lack of analysis about racial inequality as a grave difference between enslaved Africans and Mexican laborers, the essay draws attention to the plight of exploited workers in the way that the PLM did when advocating for anarcho-syndicalism in the early twentieth century. Drawing on the tropes of normative masculinities (US governmental paternalism, white growers and industrialists, and humble, hardworking Mexican men), Enrique argued that although going abroad was not ideal, staying in Mexico was a waste because of underemployment. As Mexican men went to the US to prove their merit in another labor market, however, they were displaced and disillusioned, just like their anarchist antecedents.

On December 14, 1951, this time for *El Universal*, a well-respected national newspaper, Enrique argued that "our braceros are running away from Mexico."[33] Describing disillusionment with the American Dream, he turned to the emotive costs of this migration, speaking from his own experience: "They suffer a very painful deception, because their luck does not improve upon arrival, and, at times, it gets worse. Many others return to the breast of their anguished families, called 'wetbacks' because they wander across the Rio Grande, all to introduce themselves as contraband laborers in the neighboring country."[34] Entering the immigration debate, Enrique's critique of the pejorative *wetback* centralized a conversation about race and masculinity, one that allowed such men to be exploited both in their chasing of a better life, including political and economic freedom, and for their racial difference from Americans. "I am a witness to the strong racial prejudices in the US, with their special focus on excluding blacks and Mexicans. Both are considered people of color."[35] In a rare moment of racial critique for a Mexican reading public, Enrique yoked his own emotional experience of exclusion with that of braceros in the 1950s. Equating US-based anti-blackness with anti-Mexicanness was a highly unusual critique coming from a mestizo Mexican national, for it registered solidarity instead of historical racism emanating from Mexico. Likening both to conditions of political exile because of labor exploitation, this abject form of Mexican masculinity was the result of diaspora making. In 1951 the emotive scars of exclusion, racism, and political persecution were still raw, thus linking Enrique's experience to that of braceros forced out of postrevolutionary Mexico in the 1950s.

As Flores Magón took a stand for braceros in *Todo*, the corresponding magazine covers also used comedic satire to indirectly denounce and critique the exploitative nature of the bracero program. On February 25, 1954, July 15, 1954, and July 7, 1955, the magazine featured covers with braceros (see figures I.1–I.3).

The February 25 cover uses scale to show how Mexican workers were being pushed out of the country and toward exploitative and grotesque Texas farmers as part of a larger failing Mexican economy. As the cover zeroes in on the multiple modes of corruption plaguing postrevolutionary Mexico in the 1950s, white privilege, racialization of the underclasses (including a racist portrayal of an Afro-descended man), graft, and government misspending with price inflation and price lowering are all linked to how and why braceros allow themselves to be *bien pagados* (well paid) by Texas ranchers. Desperate, comical, small, cartoonlike Mexican workers jump at the opportunity to be exploited by the Texas farmer, who is made fun of with his stiletto cowboy boots. The image depicts Anglo-American masculinities as not above scrutiny, which is juxtaposed to the infantilization of working-class, poor, and indigenous campesinos who ran toward Texans for a few dollars.

The July 15 cover, "Los apuros del bracero" (The braceros' troubles), depicts a migrant worker at a lunch counter, scratching his head about the menu in English. As he ponders the foreignness of the menu items, the real trouble is with the impatient and presumably racist white restaurant manager, who seems annoyed with not just the man's struggle with language but with the audacity to seek service in such a place. Foreshadowing African Americans' battles over lunch-counter service and the racism experienced with restaurant signs like "No Dogs, Negroes, or Mexicans," the bracero (looking a lot like Cantinflas, the beloved Mexican comedic *pelado* [street] character from *cine de oro* [golden age of cinema] films) seemingly remains unaware or willfully ignores the racist surveillance while trying to eat, in contrast to the surprised looks of Anglos eating alongside braceros on the July 7, 1955, magazine cover.

By 1955, *Todo* cartoonists represent the shock of the Anglo patron and the cook at the bracero's adaptation: he eats two meals at once, making his own huevos rancheros with chili sauce while consuming his all-American breakfast (fried eggs, hash browns, toast, and coffee). Consumption of the two meals flaunts cultural adaptation and bracero spending power. Together, the *Todo* covers and the articles by Flores Magón represent a continuum of Mexican men's disillusionment with the seductive promises of US economic prosperity and political freedom. The connection was thus an affective and experiential one between Flores Magón and the braceros documented within the pages of *Todo* and *El Universal*: anarchists and braceros were treated poorly and exploited by the United States despite the illusion of democracy and freedom.

Despite the affective, experiential, and political connections between Flores Magón and braceros, braceros had their entire presence in the US mitigated by labor contracts. Because of the contractual relationship with the Mexican and US states, deep tensions arose between these "visitors" and others of Mexican origin who were now citizens and/or legal permanent residents. These braceros were in direct competition for jobs with Mexican American agricultural laborers both during and after World War II.[36] There was one small exception. For middle- and upper-class Mexican Americans, the braceros were

FIG I.1. *Todo, La Mejor Revista de México*, February 25, 1954. Courtesy of the Nettie Lee Benson Collection, University of Texas at Austin.

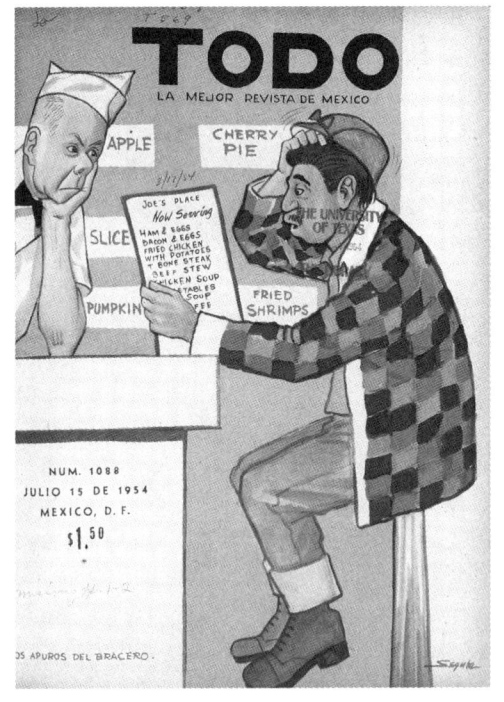

FIG I.2. *Todo, La Mejor Revista de México*, July 15, 1954. Courtesy of the Nettie Lee Benson Collection, University of Texas at Austin.

FIG I.3. *Todo, La Mejor Revista de México*, July 7, 1955. Courtesy of the Nettie Lee Benson Collection, University of Texas at Austin.

not a threat but an opportunity: they represented a source of labor in the fields that would drive profit margins for the agricultural industry. But the real social problems or tensions rested in the conflation of all Mexicans with braceros—and the analogous pejorative "wetbacks" (undocumented workers without contracts) and "drybacks" (workers with bracero contracts)—in order to describe them as noncitizens. Thus, whereas the anarchists could fold into and build solidarity with Mexican immigrant and Mexican American populations in the 1910s and 1920s, the 1950s were characterized as a time of conflict and distance between people of the same ethnicity but with varying statuses: citizens and permanent residents versus illegal residents and legally contracted laborers. The affective bonds of ethnicity and shared experiences of discrimination were not enough, especially in light of the overtly masculine migrant stream created by the bracero program.

The complexity of anarchist and bracero experiences as they were documented on paper and through images moves away from a unidirectional understanding of masculinity. From here, other models of gender-sexual positionalities emerge. Because possibilities for new relationships opened up through

INTRODUCTION 19

migration, nontraditional forms of attachment and emotion emerged in the early twentieth-century circuit between Mexico and California. The following pages provide a more in-depth blueprint for historicizing racialized masculinities and genders, beginning with the Mexican Revolution and notions of modernity as the basis for everything that came thereafter.

Part I. Revolutionary Desire and Familial Entanglements

During the presidency of Porfirio Díaz, from 1876 to 1907, a remarkable range of masculinities existed in Mexico, and particularly in Mexico City (the home of the Flores Magón brothers before they fled to the United States). President Díaz was known for his celebration of French culture and science, which included remaking Mexico City's topography to mimic the grand avenues of the French capital. Popular depictions of men during the era included dandies and individuals who engaged in sexual vice—one only need look at the Mexico City newspapers of the day, filled with advertisements to cure various sexually transmitted diseases or of scandals involving homosexuality or prostitutes. These various masculinities also reflected Porfirian values about health, vigor, militarism, bodybuilding, and the male camaraderie of the gymnasium, which all converged in the capital that formed the Flores Magón brothers as subjects.[37] Víctor Macías-González and Anne Rubenstein's book, *Masculinity and Sexuality in Modern Mexico*, demonstrates how "spatial mobility [was] a marker, or cause of modernity—[an] ambiguous and highly gendered condition" that was heightened by the Porfiriato.[38] Charting the controversy over Mexican masculinities and particular genealogies of the *macho* is the best way to discuss the history of masculinity in Mexico. In this genealogy, Andrés Molina Enriquez's 1909 study *Los grandes problemas nacionales* provides a class-based analysis of morality, masculinity, and material culture that birthed "the" national type through his discussions of the pelado. In reinforcing stereotypes about certain social groups, including mestizos and the working classes, these types dominate discussions of Mexican masculinity.[39]

Despite the dominance of the simplistic machismo narrative, a variety of thinkers have encouraged a more complex view. Robert McKee Irwin has argued that early twentieth-century Mexican masculinities carried the "gendered rhetoric of race and class shifts and twists," where "contradictions tend to go unnoticed. Gender, as a main element of the Mexican national habitus, goes unquestioned even as it becomes entangled in blatantly racist stereotypes. . . . [N]ational brotherhood came to symbolize national coherence."[40] Ben Sifuentes-Jáuregui argues that during this period, gender was described in corporeal terms and not in performatives, creating a dialectic between the body and the national imaginary.[41] Further, Sifuentes-Jáuregui states that the writing of the period used the idealized masculine body to create the nation.[42] What the virile literature of the period also records, according to Ignacio Sánchez Prado, was an anxiety generated by apertures in Mexican culture that were "feminine."[43]

Fear of the feminine shifted the direction of Mexican and Mexican American conversations about masculinity in the 1940s and 1950s. One shift was the product of Mexican Manuel Ávila Camacho's presidential campaign slogans, which were a play on his last name: "Viva el pueblo siempre macho! Y Agustín el general! Y viva Ávila Camacho y la vida sindical!" (Long live the people, who are always machos! Long live Agustín, the general! Long live Ávila Camacho and the labor unions!). Another force was filmic, originating in Hollywood, where rifle-slinging Mexican bandits represented an impediment to conquering the Wild West. Another strand, most notably discussed by film critic Sergio de la Mora, was produced by Mexicans themselves using these same stock characters with a twist: actors such as Pedro Infante immortalized the cosmopolitan nature of Mexican masculinities with buddy movies that allowed for gender and sexual transgressions among and between men.[44] These twentieth-century institutionalized forms of masculinity are grounded in gendered and sexualized national ideologies that accommodate the normative and marginalize the nonnormative.[45]

Archiving Mexican Masculinities in Diaspora considers how the interstitial experience of being between nations as diasporic subjects created opportunities for new manifestations of gender. Although scholars have debunked the idea that there is one universal Mexican masculinity, fuller appreciation of plural masculinities that these men experienced as transnational subjects is the goal. Because of these tensions about national forms of masculinity,[46] we must explain how migration shaped the transnational conversation on the subject. Scholars estimate that between 1900 and 1917, some 1.5 million Mexicans fled to the United States to escape the revolution's violence, to organize the overthrow of Porfirio Díaz, to find employment, and/or to practice their Catholic faith without persecution. Of the many who left Mexico for the US, political liberals were forced into exile because their campaigns to overthrow the Díaz dictatorship were rabidly anti-Catholic, anticlerical, and anticapitalist. All wars are complicated, and the two-decade Mexican civil war, known as La Revolución, is no exception. Although there were dozens of factions involved, and multiple phases of the war, for our purposes we can simplify the conflict as follows: it was a peasant uprising in the state of Morelos led by Emiliano Zapata and Yucatecos on behalf of the landless who were displaced by the commercialization of agriculture. Gil Joseph argues that even though most accounts suggest that the Yucatecos were more leftist, the reluctance of the elite oligarchs to join the revolutionary struggle was linked to their geographic isolation.[47] It was also a movement in the North, of wealthy elites and bourgeois landholders centered in San Luis Potosí who fought Díaz's attempts to expropriate their mineral-rich land holdings by preventing their sale to foreign industrial capitalists. These individuals were more centrist. And it was also a movement of the Constitutionalists, composed of labor activists, textile workers, and anarchists who wanted to be governed by the edict "Mexico for Mexicans." Within this final stratum sat the Partido Liberal Mexicano. By 1911, the party had split, and PLM moderates and PLM radicals were at odds about how to proceed (more-centrist liberal tendencies or anarchism) with the social and economic revolution. Thus, the Mexican Revolution was, fundamentally, three different movements.

The ideologue Ricardo Flores Magón was at the helm of PLM anarchism. Enrique, both in the historical record and the history books, is overshadowed by Ricardo. Even though Enrique is considered peripheral, his archive reveals tremendous insights about emotion, affect, and attachments in transnational Mexican intimacies. PLM members were exceedingly passionate about their politics, and the emotive attachments of those intimacies were shaped under the condition of exile. It is from this broader historical context that we move into the particulars of Enrique Flores Magón's life: as a revolutionary, a husband, a comrade, and a father. Previous scholarly accounts by Alan Knight have focused on the PLM as a marginal group within Porfirian-era politics, whereas John Mason Hart has shown that the PLM's clandestine politics represented the petit bourgeois and lower-strata discontent; both scholars produced macro-histories of revolution as ideology.[48] Other scholars have focused on how gloriously radical Ricardo Flores Magón was—and he was indeed.[49] Because I am more interested in minor actors in the grand narratives, the first half of the book explores one family's history as a way to think more broadly about ideology's capacity to shape intimacies. But I also document how ideology did not always match up with the quotidian lives of people involved in political movements. For example, the PLM preached free love as an ideology. Enrique, in contrast, chided women like María Brousse, his brother's partner, for expressing her sexual freedom openly. Although the majority of my sources come from Enrique's archive to preserve the legacy of the PLM and the Flores Magón brothers, I am critical of their content. As a result, we find that Enrique was ideologically reserved when it came to gender and sexuality. His radicalism and anarchism didn't always translate into his personal life. My research discovered that Enrique was also destroying, distorting, and purging the written record and that the newspaper essays and reports in *Regeneración* and his weekly columns in *Todo*, *El Nacional*, and *El Universal* are mediated by this practice.[50]

Amid our inquiries into the subtle realms of intimacies and document purging, however, we cannot lose sight of the very-concrete histories that make these inquiries possible. Although Enrique Flores Magón's critiques of the state encapsulate a virile masculine baroque language, that hardness is absent from his correspondence with family. Instead, virility was replaced with vulnerability, fragility, illness, loss, and doubt. What we find are intimate languages—of family and brotherhood, of vulnerability and illness and sexuality—languages where contextually specific, softened, fragile grammars are even more nuanced by analyzing homosocial spaces, encounters, and alternative family settings. I show the ways in which Flores Magón's intimate life was determined by counterintelligence, state intervention, and migration. His emotive and physical vulnerability, a tumultuous trajectory before the law and in relationship to the nation that he tried to reimagine, is not readily discerned in his public writings and speeches published in *Regeneración*. Thus, part I traces the affective threads of family, love, desire, loss, and want as the underbelly of histories of the Mexican Revolution. These divisions and fissures show how intensive feelings of love and devotion coexisted alongside and because of surprisingly severe cultures of denunciation and disavowal. As each chapter demonstrates, intimate histories were made into public histories by virtue of both the intense surveillance that the PLM experienced in the US and its own denunciatory publications.

Chapters 1–8 examine the long history of Enrique Flores Magón's inner life from his youth to his exile in the US and his return home to Mexico as a deportee in 1923. Emotional tenderness waxed and waned throughout his life, foregrounding intimacy and gender formation as cultural forces in diasporic experience. As he confronted the state, tension, and illness while doing time in the Los Angeles County Jail and Leavenworth Prison, there were few opportunities to communicate with loved ones. In disentangling how important his children and life partners were while he was behind bars, the estrangement from them centralized loss and emotional vulnerability as part of political activism. Vulnerability stood gender norms on their head through performances of so-called feminized affect and sentimentality. Engaging in what we would now call emotional labor, this was a means of parenting and mitigating vulnerability as a counter to the virile masculinity of early twentieth-century Mexican national cultures. Part I ends by examining Enrique's deportation proceedings from 1923. After all those years of optimistic attachment to the idea of freedom, Enrique had become resigned to the illusory nature of such promises. As he and the family reintegrated into the new postrevolutionary Mexico, his 1950s mainstream publications in *El Universal*, *El Nacional,* and *Todo* demonstrate why the transition back into Mexican society became a full form of integration: the reason that many historians and public commentators about the revolution's precursor movement dismiss him as unimportant or uninteresting. By his death, he was a mainstream purveyor of living revolutionary history.

Part II. The Homoerotics of Abjection: Leonard Nadel's
Salinas Valley Bracero Photographs

Part II turns to the second archive: Leonard Nadel's 1956 photo series of the bracero program. The bracero program, as we have seen, recruited more than four and a half million temporary Mexican male laborers to work in the agriculture, manufacturing, and railroad industries in the US between 1942 and 1964, filling a grave labor shortage both during and after World War II. The program was renewed several times since its initial inception because hiring temporary foreign workers was far more cost effective than hiring US workers. Terminated in 1964 because of union pressures on the US Department of Labor, the government began closing camps in 1957. One of the largest influxes of Mexican male migrants in United States history, it contracted men for short periods of time to labor primarily in the agricultural fields of California, Michigan, Texas, and Arkansas, but also in mining and railroad construction. Men went to recruitment centers throughout Mexico to secure precious contracts, often taking out loans and leaving entire families behind, all to make a living and send remittances back to Mexico. Braceros competed for contracts and endured highly humiliating forms of screening, including bodily fumigation and physical exams to detect infirmity or disability, which would in turn warrant their rejection. Recruiting indigenous and mestizo men alike, the program took in a broad swath of poor, working-class, and middle-class Mexican subjects in search of work and, in some cases, adventure in the US.

Because the program was the biggest nationalized effort to turn laboring bodies into abject bodies, part II deploys abjection to demarcate how bracero bodies were situated outside symbolic power. Following Julia Kristeva, I take abjection to describe a dehumanizing existence that was inherently traumatic. Braceros were situated outside of the symbolic order and were dehumanized, yet they continued to assert their personhood in the face of subordination.[51] But there are still key issues that emerge from Nadel's photographs. First, the photos clearly document a population and its living conditions as a space of abjection. Second, the anonymous nature of the images is linked to the exceedingly homoerotic gaze of the images. This is not to say that Nadel was homosexual; rather, I argue that what Nadel was doing with his camera, and its aesthetic but intrusive gaze, evinced the homoerotics of the exclusively male spaces he photographed. Nadel developed intense relationships with the men as he lived with them in the camps. Thus, the photographs show particular goals and desires involving the subjects being captured on film. Some readers may hope for direct evidence documenting sexual relationships between Nadel and the braceros he photographed. They will be disappointed, however, because little such evidence exists. Other readers will be disappointed by my insistence on ambiguity and say that this approach is just imposing our own twenty-first-century preferences onto the past. Yet when read through a racialized gender lens of desire, bodily intimacies and pleasures are expressed and exposed in these images. In short, Nadel's two thousand photographs contain, among other things, numerous sequences of men's naked bodies; these bodies, and their meanings, remain critically unexamined. In the Smithsonian archive where the full collection is housed, Nadel's wife, along with curators, created a "Guide to the Leonard Nadel Photographs and Scrapbooks," an explanatory text that elucidates the context and the motivations for taking the bracero photographs. Yet even this guide, situating the images in a particular "place," is rather limited (there is no list of people or places).[52] These photographs indicate not just a form of social abjection but evidence of ambiguous social relations between photographer and photographic subjects. Nadel was not concerned with preserving the names of the men he photographed. We have only a general historical context and not the specific histories of the people. The photos represent his ephemeral relationships with braceros.

Part II analyzes the homoerotics of abjection though labor and labor camp spaces (without women) as safe for exploring same-sex community formation and desire. But in upending our typical understanding I have no desire to reinstantiate a narrative of braceros as solely victims of labor exploitation, to attempt to firmly locate their position in the historical record as good fathers, husbands, and brothers, or to suggest that Nadel held all of the power with his camera. Instead, part II shows how the photos of these diasporic men register desire, self making, and longing out of the abject subject position. We might call this a particular kind of close reading: a theorization of the gestures that appear at the heart of these photographs. How can we read the photographs as traces of the multiple versions of historical masculinities that emerge from this period? Pausing and dwelling upon the conditions of production and contents dislodge images from an airtight narrative of normative masculinity accounting for how migration offered the chance to remake the self. Rethinking gender and sexuality through the Nadel bracero photographs elucidates the conditions of bracero sociality in how the photographer wanted us to see them. Similarly, I attend to the materiality of Nadel's images: the relationship between the photographer and his camera and light meter, the relationship between the photographer and the subjects he photographed, and the physical reality of the final record, printed as a photograph or, in this case, as a contact sheet.[53] The images in the Smithsonian are digitized reprints of the contact sheets Nadel used during his Fund for the New Republic grant. That transition from contact sheet to public domain has relied on particular well-circulated photographs demonstrating bracero exploitation.

Nadel's intimate photos of braceros, both in interior spaces and while at work in the fields, had different subject effects. In the fields, bracero bodies were virile expressions of masculinity. But they too were rendered vulnerable in Nadel's social realist aesthetics, which captured how they performed gender forms of compensated labor and domestic intimacies. This is why my feminist readings of these images track the aesthetic properties of an ongoing cultural conversation: how virility, fragility, and masculine excesses represented by Enrique Flores Magón carried into the bracero period but were then reframed by Nadel's photographs and the relationships he forged with braceros while living with them and recording their lives. My argument is not that Nadel was fixated on queering his subjects—that assertion would be simplistic and anachronistic. Rather, in inquiring about how Nadel built relationships with his photographic subjects and about his use of social documentary photography aesthetics, we understand cultural fears about this cohort of Mexican men as sexually and socially dangerous. The relationships built through the photographs document attachments. Negotiation before photographs were taken was a form of cultivating the self. Once snapped, the aesthetic form of the photograph documented attachments. As archives of masculine intimacies, bracero photographs also push us in a different direction: intimacies with the inanimate objects they produced. Because there is a thread of queer and feminist scholarship that argues that we must consider the other than human and the disappearance of the subject, I am also mindful that my account of subject formation is indeed grounded in humanist optimism.[54] In this way, I examine both the emergent ways that braceros were documented as subjects in the photographs as they were juxtaposed with and blend in with the inanimate objects they cultivated (agricultural products such as lettuce). My research shows that the intimacies forged in working with inanimate nonhuman objects and bracero domesticity counter the idea of virility as the only masculine subject position. Instead, intimacies and physical proximities, however orchestrated or optimistic they might have been in Nadel's bracero photographs, show emotional and physical vulnerability in the form of care work to reorient the scholarship to date.

Chapters 9–14 explore the deep historical context for Nadel's photographic enterprise: the 1956 presidential campaign, Operation Wetback, the 1956 report issued by the President's Commission on Migratory Labor, President Eisenhower's failed farm bill, and Salinas Valley policies. The regional context produced a dominant agricultural class that subjugated bracero workers in the fields, in labor camps, and in their affective relationships to the community and the US state. The subordination of difference was at the heart of policy decisions where growers narrated Mexican male migrants as nonthreatening while the local community said they were sexual deviants. Policy debates are evidence of the gender and sexual contradictions that braceros embodied. But bracero affective history complicated the male-dominated nature of the Salinas Valley's public sphere. In contrast, the bracero private sphere was filled with tasks that forged domesticity based on intimacies among and between men. Their living arrangements disrupted prevailing discourses in that the private sphere was not feminized but was made masculine through the bracero program.[55] Those intimacies are recorded in Nadel's photographs of men and document how attachments to one another or to their property were codified through physical violence and emotional closeness in these socially isolated communities of Mexican men. Part II's conclusion meditates on violent attachments to bring the book full circle, moving from the optimism of hope and freedom to its opposite extreme expression.

Archiving Mexican Masculinities in Diaspora takes its theoretical and methodological cue from transnational feminisms and Latinx studies because of the way that it analyzes the expansion of gender and sexual categories in migration. Specific historical moments from the early to mid-twentieth century (Mexican anarchist activity in Los Angeles and bracero laborers in the Salinas Valley) and specific places (Los Angeles, the Salinas Valley, Mexico City, and rural Mexico) form the backbone of the book, where masculine subjects were produced in spite of or because of the state's domination of transnational migration and transnational networks. When analyzed as a historical continuum, six decades of evidence from the two case studies demonstrate the ways in which Mexican male bodies have been historically defined as racially excessive. The anarchist expulsions of the 1920s and the bracero migrations in the 1950s demonstrate just how entrenched narratives of lionized heteromasculinity were and how they continue to overdetermine early twentieth-century migrant men as political, gendered, and racialized outsiders. At the same time that both populations sought freedom from oppression in the US, they encountered a very different gender, racial, and political landscape than they anticipated. All of them traded in the currency of emotion as expressions of self and community. In some cases they worked around these set ideologies; in other cases they were violently policed by them. The tension between the freedom that anarchists and braceros sought and what they actually experienced in the United States builds an affective history of Mexican masculinity in diaspora. These complex masculinities in diaspora, in both Enrique Flores Magón's life and that of the Salinas Valley braceros, show why affective flexibility, in conjunction with a series of well-grounded feminist readings, further explains the dialectic of fragility versus virility and how all the in-between emotions or affects and subject positions matter. These are key—though often overlooked—elements of transnational Mexican national cultures. The book provides students of gender, race, and sexuality tools that might chip away at totalizing and limiting national modes of storytelling. My hope is that this model can push Latinx and Mexican studies to be more cautious and flexible in their approaches to masculinity and sexuality, to be more thorough in the discussion of migration as an affective process of subject formation, and to help us consider how histories of discursive attachment, visual attachment via photography, and ephemera must always be read with skepticism.

PART I. ENRIQUE FLORES MAGÓN'S EXILE
Revolutionary Desire and Familial Entanglements

Introduction

When Porfirio Díaz's dictatorship began to lose ground in the 1890s, it was in large part because of his own programs. Díaz's project of privatization of public resources made a very select class of Mexican bourgeois men and their families rich, but the majority of the populace faced poverty, illiteracy, land displacement, and a clamping down on intellectual freedoms. Díaz fancied himself as fatherly patriarch and guardian of the nation during his thirty years in office, but the indoctrination of proper capitalist masculine subjects was incomplete, providing the aperture for others to challenge state power.

In an oft-cited 1908 interview with James Creelman of *Pearson's Magazine*, the seventy-seven-year-old Díaz described the role of democracy in the Mexican nation in terms that bespoke confidence, even as they betrayed underlying vulnerabilities: "I have waited patiently for the day when the people of the Mexican Republic would be prepared to choose and change their government at every election without danger of armed revolutions and without injury of national credit or interference with national progress. I believe that day has come."[1] Just three years after the organization of the Partido Liberal Mexicano (PLM) by a group of Mexican liberals and anarchists, Díaz avowed his brand of democracy had staying power.

Yet Díaz appeared to have little confidence in the majority of the Mexican people. He went on to describe Indians as having no natural interest in governance, suggesting that they had become a hazard to patriarchy whenever they ceased being subservient: "The Indians, who are more than half of our population, care little for politics. They are accustomed to look to those in authority for leadership instead of thinking for themselves. That is a tendency they inherited from the Spaniards, who taught them to refrain from meddling in public affairs and rely on the Government for guidance."[2] Almost congratulating the Spanish who "taught them to refrain from meddling in public affairs," Díaz makes a nature-versus-nurture argument about the distinction between inherent and cultivated Indian docility. Given that Western Apache and Yaqui Indians were communities that indeed interrupted and destroyed capitalist advancement, he responded to the challenge of governing indigenous peoples by reasserting the need for a strong, patriarchal nation.

Díaz's fatherly benevolence, self-aggrandizement, and overconfidence in his version of democracy were the very things the PLM had come together to fight against. Although the PLM was one of the many, many factions with ambitions for Mexico's future, its extensive network in the US to raise funds for its planned revolt contrasts greatly with the dictatorship's designs. Magonistas were just one very small fraction of the 1.5 million Mexicans who fled to the United States between 1910 and 1917, during the Mexican Revolution's most bloody and violent phase. Indeed, Díaz's claim that democracy would take hold "without danger of armed revolutions and without injury of national credit" may have been an allusion to his 1903 efforts to arrange for a judicial decree ostensibly banning Ricardo Flores Magón from publishing in Mexico.[3] After the seizure of the printing press owned by *El Hijo del Ahizote* on Calle Republica Colombia in Mexico City, Ricardo escaped to Laredo, Texas, in early 1903, and Enrique joined him in St. Louis, Missouri, later that November. With the Flores Magón brothers publishing from their exile in St. Louis, Díaz could continue to govern "without injury." This unspoken animosity about competing notions of governance and free speech tells us that critique of the patriarchal father was injurious to Díaz's national body politic. To question the father was to be a bad child.

Nevertheless, the bad children were undaunted, and they would devote their lives to overthrowing the fatherly patriarch from afar, in spite of the

FIG PI.1. Enrique and Ricardo Flores Magón in the Los Angeles County Jail, 1916.

severe punishments they would suffer. Even after the Magonista anarchist revolt of June 23, 1908, was foiled, failing to bring down the Díaz regime, they continued their struggle for the liberation of Mexico in the ideological realm. Ricardo Flores Magón was imprisoned three times for violating neutrality laws. Brother Enrique, the subject of the first half of this book, served time first in the federal prison at McNeil Island in Washington State (1912–14) and then again in the Los Angeles County Jail (with Ricardo), followed by another incarceration at McNeil Island and then a transfer to Leavenworth (1918–20).

Ricardo was always referred to as the lead *vocero* (spokesman) of the PLM, which left Enrique playing perpetual second fiddle to his brother. Yet he was no less interesting. As a noted anarchist critic of the Díaz regime, he too endured the emotive and physical burdens of leading a political life, along with corporeal punishment. The complexity of Enrique's intimate life, laid bare by state interference, locates him as an exceedingly complex masculine subject.

Ricardo and Enrique Flores Magón have been lionized as the quintessential icons of the normative, anti-dictatorial masculinity of the period. Images like the one in figure PI.1 continue to be appropriated by communities on both sides of the US-Mexico border. As figures of revolution, dissent, and masculinity, the brothers and their sense of new national possibilities stood in direct contrast to Díaz's claim that he had "waited patiently for the day when the people of the Mexican Republic would be prepared to choose and change their government at every election."[4] Patriarchy's implacable grip on the republic was completely challenged by photos like this one, where revolutionary men such as Emiliano Zapata, Francisco (Pancho) Villa, and the Flores Magón brothers are represented as normatively masculinized sources of social and intellectual change.

In the image of Ricardo and Enrique Flores Magón in the Los Angeles County Jail in 1917, the focus is on Ricardo. Away from the center, Enrique looks into the center of the photo. The photo is an apt metaphor for Enrique's role in the ideological or demagogue-making histories of the PLM: he was peripheral to it, in Ricardo's shadow. But if we take the marginal position in the visual field as a starting point for this history, Enrique's look into the frame diminishes the temporal and emotive distance, inviting us to plumb the depths of his complicated subject position in history. When Enrique looks beyond the frame, he invites us into a different history copiously documented in its own course, on its own terms, and with some major self-serving historical revisions. But there is also something invasive about this photograph, for it symbolizes just how much their lives were intruded upon as political dissenters.

Even as the shot focuses on Ricardo, it is the periphery that propels our attachment to the margins as viewers and students of history. It is the visual field that most poignantly registers defiance, fierceness, and dissent, especially as Enrique looks beyond the frame. As a form of national allegory, Enrique's story is fractured and was revised by his own hand. Much like the Mexican nation during this time period, his narrative is a reflection of how individuals responded to the Díaz dictatorship. In this light, his history can be understood only from within the perspective of nation. As Fredric Jameson writes, "One of the determinants of capitalist culture ... is the radical split between private and public, between poetic and political, between what we have come to see as the domain of sexuality and the unconscious and that of public world classes, of the economic and of secular and political power; in other words, Freud vs. Marx."[5] The split between these two positions becomes naturalized: the libidinal versus the psychoanalytic. And yet this is not the case for reading Enrique's life. The private became public because the state needed to probe and put asunder alternative national imaginations and familial formations because of their capacity to destroy capitalist patriarchy. Enrique's life story is all about self-narration as national allegory of heteronormativity in the PLM Los Angeles–based movement for independence.[6] As a penumbra of revolutionary consciousness, my Latinx feminist readings of Enrique's history and archive problematize narrow understandings of national formation and masculinity more broadly seen in canonical Mexican revolutionary histories.[7]

Thus, in the chapters that follow I trace the affective threads of family, love, desire, loss, and want as the messy underbelly of transnational histories of the Mexican Revolution. The chapters analyze letters between Enrique and his multiple familial and political interlocutors from his childhood in the 1880s to his deportation from the US back to Mexico in 1923, along with the accompanying photographs, newspaper coverage, drawings, and oral histories. One is struck by the sheer volume of documentation, its meticulous curation in the face of so many migrations and moves, let alone the fact that Enrique had, in true nineteenth-century intellectual fashion, beautiful literary skills in English and Spanish and could read and occasionally write in Catalán, German, and Russian: all the key revolutionary languages of the time. Although networks of fraternity and family were stretched by anarchism and intensive emotional attachments, these reconfigurations of relationality were some of the few spaces where emotional vulnerability, melancholia, loss, love, and attachment to compatriots, partners, and children could be expressed, especially when betrayal and denunciation entered the picture. Other works, such as Claudio Lomnitz's *The Return of Comrade Ricardo Flores Magón*, have finally taken on the question of love in the lives of Enrique and Ricardo. As Lomnitz writes, "Love, conjugal love, was more important to them, both as an ideal and as a daily practice. . . . Such emotional intensity, in which love and the cause were inextricably intertwined, seems to have been present in many intimate friendships. . . . In relationships like these, trust was such that anything might be sacrificed for the other."[8] Lomnitz argues that none of these ideas of love were competing but were in fact complementary to the social isolation of living a politically committed anarchist life. My work takes these notions of love and their complicated entanglements as the central historical thread of Mexican masculinity in diaspora. As a historical actor, Enrique Flores Magón mapped affective meaning through social networks. Affect was grafted onto cultural practices that contained and reproduced gendered and sexualized forms of power relations.

In reading these archives by and about Enrique Flores Magón, *Archiving Mexican Masculinities in Diaspora* problematizes what constitutes truth and explains what it meant for family intimacy, personal desire, love, and social revolution to be in the public domain: property of the state and not private. In other words, I read transnational voyeurism and counterinsurgency activity as a disruption of what was viewed as nonnormative, antistate reproductions of intimacy. Manipulations of intimacy, both by the state (US and Mexican governments) and by Enrique and his circle, resonate with, question, disrupt, and reproduce these supposed deviant and criminal figures as impediments to capitalist reproduction. Because Porfirian Mexico crumbled under the strain of civil war and the US's simultaneous bolstering of its own alien-exclusion laws, I argue that we need to move away from the lionized, static representations of Enrique as a secondary foil to Ricardo's hypermasculine, sexy revolutionary subjecthood and see them together as vulnerable subjects, both physically and emotionally. By taking intimacy seriously and theorizing through the idea of the masculinized Mexican and US nation-states, the possibilities for historicizing how masculinities are archived and to what end emerge. Although the majority of previous historiography has been ideological in scope, my aim is to provide an affective narrative. Moreover, the event-like nature of the revolution contributed to why Enrique was a central figure who generated hostility on both sides of the border. Part of this has to do with power relations of gender and sexuality but even more so with the complicated familial networks and histories explained in this first part of the book.

Chapter 1

GREETING CARDS,
LOVE NOTES, LOVE LETTERS

From the time he was a small boy, Enrique Flores Magón (April 13, 1877–October 28, 1954) cultivated a sense of poetry in his life. Those poetics, inscribed to his mother on scrap pieces of paper, on the backs of greeting cards, and eventually in longer poems and essays, are what would make him a *vocero* (voice) of the Mexican Revolution in exile. We must consider these early declarations and poetic acts as part of a longer tradition of literacy and poetics in the Flores Magón family. Enrique was influenced by the Romantic poets of the late eighteenth and early nineteenth century, and those influences are evidenced in a lifetime of writing. Blocked from access to power by the Porfirian *científicos* despite their role as part of the petit bourgeoisie, Enrique responded with poetry. His letters, political tracts, newspaper articles, cards, and love letters all display intra-poetic dynamics in dialogue with texts of love, longing, and loss that predated his Mexican revolutionary existence. With a literary style that used hyperbole to drive home the intensive sentiments conveyed by the texts, Enrique's writings are affect-laden documents that perform proximity in light of the physical and emotional absences he experienced throughout what eventually became his life of exile. Mimicking the baroque style of the period, the density of his poetry and prose, even in childhood, was representative of something much bigger.

At the age of ten, Enrique sent a greeting card to celebrate the birthday of his mother, Margarita. That Margarita, then his brother Jesus, then his first partner, Paula, then his second partner, Teresa, saved the tokens of love and affection to his mother from when he was a young boy tells of sentimental importance and levels of emotional attachment conveyed with such documents. It also speaks to a tremendous sense of privilege because he and his family saw themselves as historical actors with a history to be documented and preserved. Given the multiple moves from Mexico to the US, to Canada, through the US (all over Los Angeles), and back to Mexico, the cultivated sense of self represents a historical subject position worthy of preservation. Such sentiment was cultivated by Margarita, perhaps in motherly attachment, but more so as evidence of historical embeddedness. As Justin Akers Chacón argues, Margarita "envisioned her sons becoming leaders who could advocate for the marginalized."[1]

Part collage, the card showed an angel (clipped from a magazine) adorning a self-drawn hearth with a bottle of wine (see figures 1.1 and 1.2). It demonstrates the emergence of love, joy, and a poetic soul in childhood. The placement of a found object (the *angelito*), along with Enrique's own drawing, "involves the interaction of aesthetic, cognitive, emotive, mnemonic, ecological, and creative factors in the seeking, discovery, and utilization of found objects."[2]

In addition to the found objects, we see urns similar to those that line Paseo de la Reforma, which was designed in the 1860s, holding cacti and strings of lanterns. The combination of French-inspired Porfirian stateliness with modern and pre-Columbian symbolism in this childhood devotion to his mother uncannily assimilates national symbols. Reflecting on his desires prior to becoming a revolutionary, Enrique noted that when he went to school, he wanted to be a painter, a sculptor, and a musician, ambitions to which his father, Teodoro, firmly objected.[3]

Margarita saved the birthday cards, letters, and report cards (Enrique always had perfect attendance), showing her sons the value of their drawings and written words. That cultivated sense of subjecthood carried over into how Enrique, Paula, and Teresa carefully curated their family's legacy: they preserved everything they deemed important. The archives preserve a keen sense of irony and humor that formed part of young Enrique's budding social critique. His lifelong project of collecting documents of his family's history includes public critiques of the dictatorship, writing, and ephemera from his student days. But there are also concrete moments where the archival materials have been destroyed for the purpose of making sure that he could be enshrined into the history of Mexico as a precursor: he guaranteed that his historical legacy was as one of the intellectuals who fomented what would eventually become a full-blown revolution in 1910.

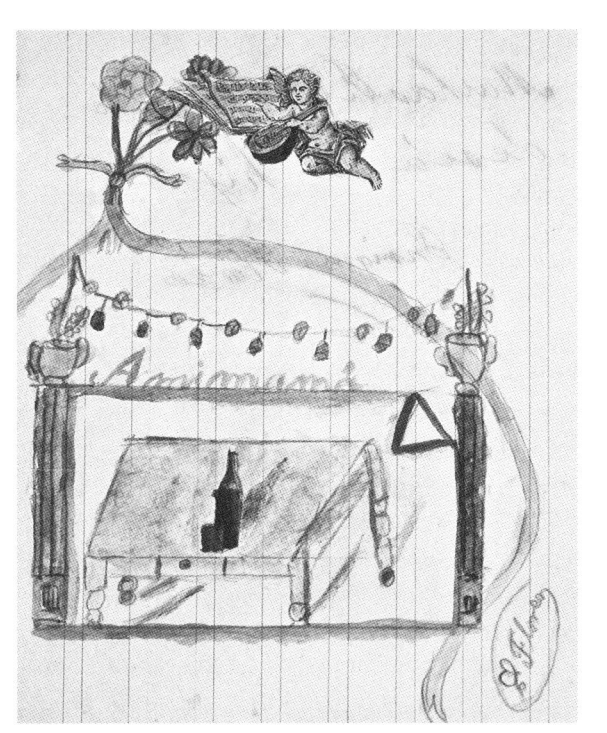

FIGS 1.1 AND 1.2. Carta de Enrique Flores Magón a Margarita Magón and verso. Courtesy of Casa de el Hijo de Ahuizote.

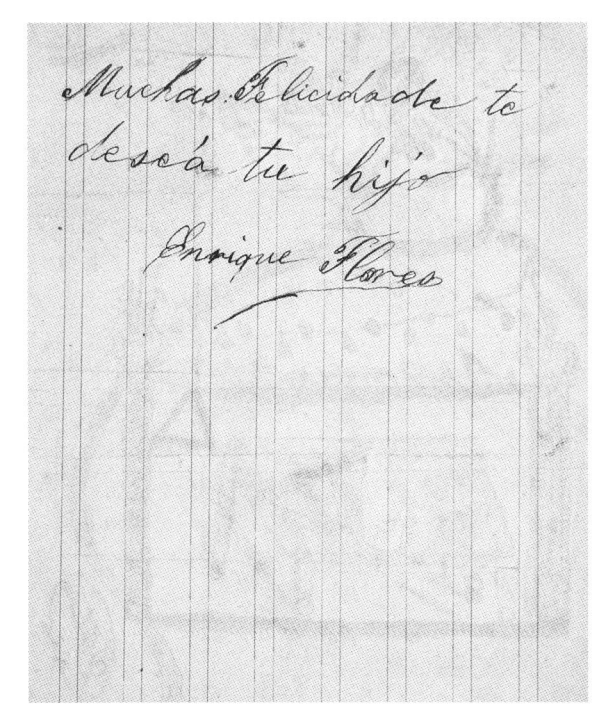

For example, in a typed 1899 letter to the Mexico City office of registration for bicycles, he informs the *funcionario* that he had sold "the Maroa bicycle, 'Porfirio Díaz' under license number 3333 and had purchased another Maroa brand bicycle, Cleveland, on which I have placed a license plate that read 'Porfirio Díaz.'"[4] The thought of Enrique riding a registered bicycle around Mexico City named Porfirio Díaz, especially in light of Jesús and Ricardo's anti-reelectionist activities and 1893 imprisonment as students in Belem, solicits a chuckle. To ride the dictator over rough streets was to metaphorically beat him into the ground. That Enrique traded in Porfirio for another newer or more modern "capitalist dictator"—President Grover Cleveland, who aided Díaz with economic support for his regime—doubles up on the meaning and humor conveyed by the similarity in the replacement. Substituting hard-ridden bicycles named Porfirio and Cleveland for an imagined violence that one would only love to commit against these capitalist dictators mobilizes the metaphor that they are mere machines of modernity that people ride in pursuit of material accumulation. Thus, the proximity of the two dictators and two metaphors, dictators as bicycles, extracts its humor from the allusion and implied knowledge that one would need to see this as satire, and not the work of a young Mexican man who simply adored Porfirio Díaz and Grover Cleveland. Context is everything, and perhaps Enrique wanted to get caught mocking Díaz and Cleveland, but he counted on the funcionario not reading the letter this way and, as such, saved this documented pleasure of mockery in his personal archive.

Although he would become more prose-driven later in life, Enrique's youthful work shifts to a poetic mode of seduction that draws from ideas and images of nation. In an undated essay titled "Unavoidable," Enrique called upon a poetic image of Mexico as a means by which to name the nation's violation: "Political and social freedom, by taking possession by force of the land for the care and benefit of all, regardless of sex, race or color," was then fomented by how "we strive to take possession of the land because we understand that the source of wealth is the land. On the land grow the fruits, grains, vegetables and plants to feed us; on the land are the woods that give us fuel and lumber; on the land are the rivers to generate life and power; in the bowels of the land are the great stocks of metal, stones and coal. From the land comes life itself and the means to make it beautifully livable. We understand that he who owns the land owns everything else and that, therefore, is thoroughly free."[5] This recitation of the land's bounty and a slight nod to private property as an ownership of "everything else" quickly turns to what happens when beauty is under siege: "Tyranny and slavery breed revolution, armed revolution, most unavoidably, regardless of our own [text illegible] tastes."[6] The tyranny of capital, authority, and the Church—the hallmark critiques of the PLM junta's ideological stance—is wrapped within beautiful lines of verse, repetitively extolling the land's virtues like that of a lover, a kind of seduction that draws you in closer and closer only to slap you in the face with tyranny and the need for armed revolution. In the seductive quality of Enrique's verse, when taken alongside the platonic notion that "speeches and speech making serve as a veneer for the more important substructure, a façade for the more subtle and significant undertaking—the construction of extended metaphors about the erotic nature of communication," we see the ways in which writing about revolution was erotic in nature.[7] It appeals to our sensibilities about the beauty of nature as something withheld or held captive by tyranny, so as to make one want it all the more. The erotic nature of extended poetic metaphor moves the soul to desire the land and thus desire freedom.

This baroque prose is emblematic of what has been called the genre of Mexican virile literature. Robert McKee Irwin has argued that the debate around this body of literature indicated that "masculinist participants in the debate favor a socially conscious literature that supports class struggle, or at least a gritty social realism that contests the aesthetic elegance and elitism of *modernismo*, [so] throughout the debates *virile literature* remains a rather nebulous notion."[8] This vagueness, posited in normative gender language, regards the feminine as bad and the masculine as good. But McKee Irwin does not attend to the prose's density. Reinforcing a compulsory heteronormative masculinity masked any vulnerabilities like espousing weakness in moral character. But even in the baroque density of Flores Magón's lifetime of writing, lamentation and vulnerability do seep through the cracks of virile languages of nation in the institutionalization of revolutionary projects of modernity. As Esther Gabara argues, "The formulation of revolutionary popular culture had to be masculine and had to be taught to the uneducated masses."[9] That normative masculine quality is what defined the "good literature" of the period.

Framing good and bad literature through gender ultimately explains why Enrique continued to use this baroque, masculinized style of writing and why critics and historians have classified him as a heterosexual man's man. Virile discourse would be inherited by those left behind, solidifying an unquestioned claim to nationalized forms of masculinity. Incarceration also shifted feeling and emotional attachment to a heightened crescendo that standardized PLM writing conventions. With every letter and article written by Enrique and Ricardo each time they were in jail or prison, their frail health and the distance from family made them politically and emotionally vulnerable, something that the state implicitly wanted. Such sentiments were only exacerbated by the distance from family, comrades, and their beloved newspaper, *Regeneración*. The brothers responded with rage, alienation, and even misogyny. As the following pages will show, baroque writing was about an excess of feelings and sentimentality, enunciating a masculinist and virile form of revolutionary discourse that deployed feminized emotional tactics as well.

State Surveillance and Intimacy

The degree to which the Porfiriato collaborated with Mexico-based and US-based law enforcement agents and spies created a vast surveillance mechanism. The very letters, newspapers, and documents that passed through the respective Mexican and US postal services to communicate PLM activity or to let loved ones know of senders' whereabouts were often already read by the government before they reached their final destination. For example, a rousingly pro-PLM letter from Heliodoro Olea dated February 5, 1906, never made it to the junta in St. Louis. Instead, it ended up on the desk of Chihuahua governor Enrique Creel, mostly likely because Olea said that "without a farce of an election Enrique Creel would have left millions on the table from when he was governor!"[10] Statements like these, considered the most inflammatory and antigovernment by the Mexican ruling class, were either withheld or copied and then sent to the intended recipient. They were also held as evidence of sedition. Therefore, the paper trail in official Mexican state archives such as the Archivo General de la Nación or Secretaría de Relaciónes Exteriores demonstrates the scale to which the Porfiriato and subsequent governments during the revolution depended on what Ranajit Guha has called the "prose of counterinsurgency."[11]

The volume of these records is striking. The Mexican government took great pains to have every intercepted letter transcribed and typed. Personal letters were often relatively transparent in communicating love, family, and community values, even if they did contain requests and coded messages. But the more-political letters, those directly related to the Mexican Revolution, were often written in code. The Mexican government worked to crack Enrique Flores Magón's coded alphabet for such correspondence.[12] Much capital was spent on deciphering these messages, demonstrating the degree to which the Mexican and the US states, along with the Furlong Detective

Agency, wanted to terminate their activity and, by extension, terminate the PLM activists' lives. Kelly Lytle Hernández argues that these state practices represent eliminatory projects of settler colonial regimes, designed to cage dissidents in the early twentieth century, particularly as responses to accelerated dispossessions of workers and indigenous people in Mexico more broadly. People like Ricardo and Enrique Flores Magón and the PLM membership were "race rebels and unlawful border crossers [who] constantly upended subjugation, exclusion, and removal, as did the many queers and deviants who lived within the formal racial boundaries of the settler community but refused to perform its sexual, social, and political reproduction."[13]

The Mexican state's obsession with the PLM and its tracking of and intrusion on all the daily minutiae of junta life force us to think of this intensity as a form of optimistic attachment that was violent. The PLM was interested in creating a completely new system from the vantage point of diaspora, but the cost of its attachment to freedom was to have its members' lives laid bare by the state in daily communication. By questioning state power in early twentieth-century North America, the PLM, along with trade unions, and insurrections, made state projects of caging and incarceration a normal practice. It also reminds us of just how political poetry and prose could be.

Chapter 2

PLM INTIMATE BETRAYALS

Enrique Flores Magón, Paula Carmona,
and the Gendered History of Denunciation

From boyhood into adulthood, Enrique's baroque language and sentiments permeated his writing. Whereas chapter 1 focused on Enrique's development into a conscious revolutionary subject aware of his place as a historical actor from a very young age, this chapter shifts our attention to the ways in which these practices of sentiment, affect, and style carried over into his marriage: It also explores the hidden history of his first wife, Paula Carmona, to examine Enrique's misogyny following the divorce from her. Although this chapter won't go extensively into the role played by his second "wife"— partner and comrade Teresa Arteaga de Flores Magón—I will briefly discuss the "transitional period" between the two women and the two overlapping partnerships because there were multiple relationships among and between Flores Magón, Arteaga, and others, reflecting the ethos of free love as a tenet of anarchism, but this too is complicated in Enrique's case. As Emma Pérez has argued, the PLM's gender ideologies, like Enrique's, were contradictory despite the group's leftist ideology, which surprisingly did not guarantee women's emancipation.[1] Few people know about Enrique's family life before he formed a partnership with Teresa Arteaga. He had another family with his first wife between 1909 and 1913, which he disowned. He erased this fact in his two as-told-to autobiographies (1958 and 1960) and multiple newspaper accounts written in the 1940s and 1950s, raising some questions: Why he would do this? What insights can we gain from this perspective? By untangling the complicated history of overlapping and/or consciously forgotten familial relations of anarchist Enrique's exile between 1907 and 1914, we see how women's histories of supposed betrayal had no place in the revisions necessary to make foundational narratives of self and nation in early twentieth-century Mexico. This chapter counters masculinist national histories of the Mexican Revolution by examining Enrique's destruction of almost all evidence of Paula's existence and that of their three children—Margarita, Práxedis, and Demófilo—except some writings from the *Regeneración* newspaper.[2] Paula kept a few photos and drawings from her marriage to Enrique, but it is highly likely that after their split she also destroyed letters Enrique had written to her.

Because the chapter focuses on gendered notions of betrayal, my work aligns with feminist scholarship like that of Emma Pérez, Gabriela González, and Cristina Devereaux Ramírez, arguing that women's proto-feminist expressions were through the prism of political responsibility in encouraging men to take up revolution.[3] When Paula was seen to have broken with this convention while Enrique was in prison, their family and marriage were dissolved. As González notes, what they "failed to acknowledge was that patriarchy, not capitalism, had been the longest and most enduring oppressive ideology for women."[4] The way that Paula Carmona and her children were treated by the junta illuminates the power of gender ideology despite the espousal of gender equality for women within the PLM. As Pérez argues, PLM leaders believed in the "natural order" of sex between men and women, that equality was possible but only when women pursued their natural roles as mothers and wives.[5] They also were to assume the role of activist and *compañera* (intimate partner), which explains why Enrique and the PLM describe Paula's position as an act of betrayal: these were the two roles that women in the party were supposed to assume simultaneously, in effect expecting more of the women than the men ever would of themselves.[6] The PLM depicted Paula as a betrayer of Enrique by associating her with her father, Rómulo Carmona, whom they saw as the main traitor in the PLM junta. Even though the PLM created spaces for new sex-gender roles, the excommunication of Paula, her children, and her father from the party and Enrique's life and history suggests that assigned sex roles were traditional, warranting punishment if strayed from.

Enrique's personal history is tempered by public lies and revisionist histories. His 1958 autobiography states that he married Teresa Arteaga in 1905, when in fact he married sixteen-year-old Paula Carmona in 1909.[7] At that time, Teresa was married to Santiago Beleno Villapando; census data indicate that they were married in 1900. Thus, Enrique blurred the historical facts to create a more palatable history worthy of enshrinement as a revolutionary precursor.[8] Although some could argue that this moralizing stance about marriage and the boundaries of relationships within the PLM defies the anarchist principles of free love, there is much evidence in Enrique's denunciations of Paula that suggests he was far more traditional about gender ideology in practice than in theory. Given that Paula and Enrique's baby Demófilo was born just as his father began serving time in McNeil Island Federal Penitentiary in July 1912 and they violently split in May 1913 before he was released from prison in 1914, it is as if Paula and their daughter, Margarita (born in 1910 and named for Enrique's beloved mother), son Práxedis (born in 1911 and named for Enrique's beloved comrade Práxedis Guerrero), and Demófilo (born in July 1912 and died in December 1912, whose name was the Greek term for "love of the people" and also the name of an exile newspaper published in Mexico)[9] never existed in most histories of the PLM.[10] I've unraveled this story using newspaper articles, census data, photographs, and oral histories, and I have extracted Paula's history from these sources, showing how PLM women's life narratives are tied to the culture of denunciation. And although such misogyny should be viewed as gender essentialist under the traditional rubric of Mexican masculinity, we should think about it as an expression of violence and vulnerability. But in order to understand the affective weight of this relationship for Enrique, we need to know more about Paula and their children.

Paula Carmona's Life in Brief

Paula was born in Banning, California, to Rómulo and Desideria Carmona-Robledo in 1892. Paula's family was involved with the Flores Magóns from very early in the Mexican Revolution, the family living in El Paso, Texas, as early as 1896. By 1902, when she was in the fifth grade attending the Alamo School, the family resided on Campbell Avenue. Her father was a grocer.[11] In December of 1903, Paula participated in the school Christmas exercises for the city of El Paso, reciting "The Snow Birds of Xmas"[12] (see figure 2.1). The family was good at documenting its presence in the world with photography. Both Rómulo and Paula were highly proficient with cameras, and this photo of Paula at the Campbell Avenue house charts Rómulo and Desideria's daughter's growth into adulthood. In her teen years, Paula took up photography as a hobby and also played the piano. Literate in Spanish and English, she read and wrote reflections about those readings regularly.[13]

As part of that cultural literacy, Rómulo was working with the very strong PLM community of Magonista clubs while they lived in El Paso and was

FIG 2.1. Paula
Carmona on
Campbell Avenue,
1901. Courtesy of the
Swearingen family.

the founder of the Santiago de la Hoz Liberal Club.[14] In June 1905 Ricardo Flores Magón received a wire from Rómulo stating that Chihuahua governor Enrique Creel was plotting his arrest.[15] Rómulo was a trusted confidant and informant for the PLM junta and was being spied on by Governor Creel and the Furlong Agency. On March 16, 1906, Ricardo, Enrique, Juan Sarabia, Trinidad Salcedo, and her small son Adolfo (with Trinidad most likely following Ricardo for romantic reasons) left for Toronto from St. Louis.[16]

By 1905, the Carmona family had moved to South Stanton Street in El Paso.[17] Whereas some historians claim that Rómulo had fled Durango to escape persecution in the spring of 1906, census records indicate that Rómulo and Desideria had been in the US long before Paula was born in California

46   CHAPTER 2

FIG 2.2. Paula, Desideria, and Rómulo Carmona in their El Paso bookstore, 1905. Courtesy of the Swearingen family.

in 1892.¹⁸ Their bookstore, where Rómulo distributed propaganda and anarchist publications, was quite successful in El Paso (see figure 2.2). This early image of twelve-year-old Paula with her parents in their bookstore documents the family's role as purveyors of ideas. When Paula worked in the bookstore while not attending school, she was exposed to the anarchists and their ideas as they came through the door.

Some members of the junta were in St. Louis, Canada, and New York, and Rómulo was a frequent correspondent who provided information about the conditions at the border. He reminded the leaders about how advantageous El Paso was to their revolutionary designs. Rómulo also provided reports about new recruits to the liberal cause and worked with cross-border allies in Chihuahua. On June 22, 1905, Ricardo noted that he had received both a letter and

PLM Intimate Betrayals   47

telegram from Rómulo. Demonstrating the intimacy of their relationship, Ricardo discussed how he and Enrique were consulting lawyers about the Mexican censorship law's effectiveness in the US, signing the letter "I thank you so much for all of your attention, and remain a friend who truly loves you."[19] Their relationship, though infrequently documented in copied letters apprehended by authorities, suggests that Ricardo, Enrique, and Rómulo were in contact and shared extensive junta intelligence. When Ricardo was fleeing authorities in Canada, Rómulo knew where to send letters to him, signifying the level of trust between them. In a letter on June 30, 1906, Rómulo stated that El Paso would be an ideal site for the junta because "here there are various railroad lines and all of the population is from Texas, New Mexico, Arizona and California . . . and it is ideal for attacking C. Juarez."[20] Acting as military strategist, Rómulo also made sure to disparage Porfirio Díaz, indicate his organizing work with Lauro Aguirre, editor of *El Democrata*, and provide a warm hello to Enrique by the letter's sixth page.[21] Such long letters by Rómulo built trust and intimacy between the men, and this was important to their being able to operate the junta from Canada. By September 1906, the PLM had moved its headquarters to El Paso.[22] Paula was a mere thirteen years old. Rómulo continued his role as a confidant of the Flores Magóns, distributing newspapers and propaganda for the PLM in El Paso and later through his La Aurora bookstore in Los Angeles. Rómulo and other PLM operatives had an established cell of more than two hundred persons in El Paso.[23] He also distributed a number of El Paso–based propagandistic papers, including Lauro Aguirre's *La Reforma Social*; *La Democracia*, edited by W. Tovar y Bueno; and *La Bandera Roja*, edited by Rafel S. Trejo.

Rómulo was arrested as one of the El Paso PLM lieutenants on October 19, 1906, for attempting to incite armed insurrection.[24] He clearly had designs for being a heavy in the PLM and sought proximity to Ricardo and Enrique. Once the junta moved to El Paso, Rómulo had an opportunity to prove how useful he could be to the cause. They were close comrades, and he facilitated contact between the El Paso liberal clubs at the behest of the Flores Magóns.[25]

Enrique had substantial contact with the Carmona family while he passed through the El Paso community because Rómulo was central to the junta. Although the Mexican government believed that Lauro Aguirre and W. Tovar y Bueno were the leaders of the El Paso cell, Rómulo maneuvered to become closer to the junta leaders during their stay. The best way for Rómulo to further broker his access to the cultural and social capital of the Flores Magón name and reputation was through his daughter.[26]

By late 1906 or early 1907, the Carmonas and Enrique and Ricardo had relocated the PLM cell to Los Angeles. A 1907 report from Enrique Creel's intelligence files listing PLM dissidents to be targeted indicated that Rómulo lived on Avenida Street.[27] Many scholars state that Ricardo and Modesto Díaz took to hiding in Rómulo's previous residence on San Fernando Street in late October 1906.[28] Enrique followed Ricardo's footsteps to the Carmona home after a stint working as an electrician in the Singer building in New York, arriving in October 1907.[29] He took over secondary editorial duties at the Los Angeles–based periodical *Revolución* with Práxedis Guerrero while Ricardo was in prison.[30] In August 1907, when Ricardo, Librado Rivera, and Antonio Araujo were apprehended by the Los Angeles police, Rómulo wrote to Manuel Sarabia stating that eight thousand Americans and Mexicans were protesting their arrest and the $3,000 bail set for the three of them. Deploying excessively sentimental language to communicate the gravity of their incarceration, Rómulo wrote that "an immense number threw flower bouquets at the prisoners. The people must collect money and send it. Move the press and create protests and demonstrations. We can sustain their lives and avoid their deaths with the community's exuberant exaltation."[31] Imitating the flowery language of revolution made popular by Enrique and Ricardo, Rómulo cemented his relationship to the junta by supporting the main actors in fund-raising. He was also a link to the PLM cells in Texas, given his previous role in organizing in El Paso. After this correspondence, Manuel Sarabia wrote to a contact in Austin and to his brother Tómas Sarabia (Henry Max Morton), stating that Rómulo would serve as a go-between with Jesus Rangel in raising funds in Texas to be put toward their bail.[32] Trusting Rómulo and his word meant that he indeed was an integral part of the Los Angeles PLM junta operations.

Ricardo, Librado, and Antonio remained in custody despite Rómulo's exuberant efforts to raise funds for their release, but this activity pushed Enrique underground and into the Carmona home. Enrique arrived in Los Angeles in November 1907, most likely with the help of the Carmonas. Claiming that he had just arrived from New York, he "used his last twenty-five cents to arrive at a comrade's house, essentially as an incommunicado prisoner for 8 months."[33] Rómulo also hid Enrique in his home for eight months between 1907 and 1908: a letter from Ricardo to Enrique confirms this.[34] Enrique had become part of the Carmona household.[35]

Just after the family attended the rousing Grand Mitin de Simpson Auditorium gathering on November 26 with eight hundred other Mexicans, socialists, and anarchists urging the release of the three prisoners, Enrique began to focus on other things.[36] A December 1907 sketch of Paula by Enrique intimates that their courtship began when she, looking mature for her age, was fourteen and he was twenty-nine (see figure 2.3). As stated in chapter 1, young Enrique was a prolific sketch artist, poet, and letter writer.

In putting that romantic sensibility into the practice of drawing Paula as a token of love, the sketch also documents how Enrique had interests outside of his supposed participation in the ill-fated July 1, 1908, action in Palomas, Chihuahua.[37] On July 17, 1908, Fernando Maetus, *jefe político* (political boss) of the Bravo region in Juarez, discovered an envelope on the person of El Paso merchant Benito Solis that contained several letters penned by Enrique. His conclusion: "Enrique Flores Magón is in El Paso Texas, hidden in a house of confidence, making a call to all anarchist liberals, exploiting their temperament assuaging them to enter México to serve in the carnage and his anti-patriotic and crazy plan."[38] Although it has been verified that Guerrero did indeed participate, it is unclear if Enrique actually did, for his conflicting accounts state that he was there, whereas others argue that he wounded himself so that he would not have to join the group of eleven men who attacked Palomas.[39]

By August 1908, Enrique, Guerrero, and Carmen and Teodoro Gaytán moved on to Albuquerque for the fall.[40] For the winter of 1908 they then moved on to Arizona. But Enrique told *El Demócrata* in September 1924 that he immediately returned to Los Angeles and was "prolongedly and completely hidden in the Carmona home for eight long months to avoid capture by the secret service," roughly August 1908 to May 1909.[41] Because Enrique was in the Carmona household, he had a chance to see Paula on a daily basis before she became his life partner. The two surviving sketches of Paula (1907 and 1909) and deliberately shooting himself in 1908 bookend Enrique's shifting priorities: love of a woman and love of the revolution.[42] As one of Ricardo's former comrades, Nicolás Bernal, stated of Enrique at this time, "He didn't figure in the history because between 1907 to 1910 he was lost from political activity."[43] Perhaps a dig at the fact that Enrique prioritized his budding love interest in Paula Carmona, Bernal characterizes Enrique's role in the PLM as minor compared to that of Ricardo.

Both sketches (see figures 2.3 and 2.4) demonstrate the romantic sensibility and love that he much earlier communicated to his mother with greeting cards and drawings. The sketches document his absence. This tradition of sentiment was part of his means of communicating his attachments to the young Paula, destined to be his partner. For the 1909 sketch, the dedication reads "My first work in color, I dedicate lovingly to my much-adored wife, little Paula."[44] The *cariños* (indulgences of love and spoiling) were not wasted. They exemplify creativity as an expression of love and longing for

FIG 2.3. Pencil sketch of Paula Carmona by Enrique Flores Magón, December 15, 1907. Courtesy of the Swearingen family.

FIG 2.4. Watercolor sketch of Paula Carmona by Enrique Flores Magón, January 28, 1909. Courtesy of the Swearingen family.

each other, what Ana Rosas has called the capacity to "experience moments of love wherever" through objects such as photographs and drawings.[45] But because Paula saved these sketches, we should also consider them traces of what Tina Campt has described as the ways in which images become "sites of articulation and aspiration; as personal and social statements that express how ordinary individuals envisioned their sense of self, their subjectivity, and their social status; and as objects that capture and preserve those articulations in the present as well as those for the future."[46] The sketches articulated love and aspiration, attachment and family formation, a way for Paula to imagine herself as a young woman betrothed to an important Mexican revolutionary thinker. No doubt, their time together in the Carmona home produced an intensified sense of intimacy, which is documented in the carefully guarded sketches. Because the sketches were optimistic documents, they record how Enrique imagined Paula and his future with her.

Moreover, because Enrique's sketches were saved by Paula, they evince an emotional fragility. To show affections through sketches complicated the ways that masculine revolutionary diasporic subject formations and emotional attachments were tenuous at best. This expression of emotional vulnerability was in stark contrast to what the Flores Magón brothers projected through their insurgency activities. The sketches bracket Enrique's stay in El Paso during 1908, when he and Guerrero were to orchestrate an attack on Las Palomas Chihuahua. As the sketches defined the distance between Paula and Enrique during his absence in the name of the PLM's armed struggle, his return to their relationship and marriage was articulated through the freestanding cardboard cutout of two hearts together with a dedication to Paula that she tore off, but her age of sixteen years, nine months, and ten days (as of July 28, 1909) remains scrawled in Enrique's hand (see figure 2.5).[47] The level of attachment expressed through a homemade cutout further demonstrates just how invested Enrique was in documenting his emotional bonds with Paula. These forms of emotional labor document just how adored Paula actually was and how both individuals imagined their relationship through the sensory. Moreover, in demonstrating Enrique's emotional investment in this romantic relationship, the person for whom the sketches were drawn and the heart cutout were made could envision herself as a subject of revolutionary love and femininity: feelings that she could touch and remember upon each encounter with the objects. Overall, these documents of intimacy counter Enrique's revisionist narratives in the biographies that state he married Teresa Arteaga in 1905. Instead, he was engaging in artistic productions signifying his love for Paula Carmona.

FIG 2.5. Handmade heart cutout made by Enrique Flores Magón for Paula Carmona, July 28, 1909. Courtesy of the Swearingen family.

By 1910, Rómulo's Los Angeles La Aurora bookstore had become a successful brick-and-mortar enterprise, selling thousands of books, newspapers, and magazines (see figure 2.6). The literate public of Spanish speakers in Los Angeles was rather large. Rómulo was quite an astute businessman, making his money by importing Spanish-language books for pennies on the dollar and selling them at a markup. He regularly advertised in the PLM paper and donated money to the cause. The first Los Angeles issue of *Regeneración* appeared on September 3, 1910, and Paula's father was using the alias Pilar A. Robledo to advertise in the paper for "Libros Casi Regalados."[48] Carmona's advertisement occupied two full columns on page three of the reinauguration of the paper. He did not waste time in establishing himself as a PLM distributor and supporter.

Paula was sixteen years old and Enrique thirty-one when they became life partners in 1909. Rómulo approved of the union. As far as records indicate, they were not legally married but referred to themselves as being married, which goes against anarchist principles of free love. She had her first baby, Margarita, on January 2, 1910, just a year after they were "married"

FIG 2.6. Rómulo Carmona in La Aurora Bookstore, Los Angeles, California. Courtesy of the Swearingen family.

in San Francisco. Their contacts in San Francisco were with the Schmidt family, where Katherine and Matthew, he notorious for being connected to the bombing of the *Los Angeles Times* building in 1910, put Ricardo, Enrique, and Paula in their Temple of Labor circle.[49] In fact, from the time that both Ricardo and Enrique were in San Francisco, Kathrine Schmidt sent checks of $10 to $100 in support of the PLM cause.[50] Enrique, Paula, and eventually baby Margarita lived in San Francisco roughly from June 1909 to September 1910. Enrique's 1958 autobiography makes no mention of Paula or Margarita but states that he held two jobs while he lived in San Francisco, first as a manual laborer at the American Can Company and second as a mechanical supervisor in charge of thirty-six heavy machines.[51] They essentially waited in San Francisco while Ricardo finished serving his sentence in the Florence (Arizona) Federal Penitentiary. With Ricardo's release in August of 1910, Enrique's family returned to Los Angeles in September to resume publication of *Regeneración*.

In the pictures of baby Margarita (Maggie), she is a brown cherub with full cheeks. Paula, in another image (see figures 2.7 and 2.8), looks ecstatic to be a mother—she will be pregnant again with Práxedis in 1911—and one-

FIG 2.7. Margarita Flores Magón, ca. 1910. Courtesy of the Swearingen family.

FIG 2.8. Paula Carmona de Flores Magón, Margarita Flores Magón, and Clarita ca. 1911. Courtesy of the Swearingen family.

year-old Maggie bounces on her leg. The image conveys typical PLM representations of motherhood as central to the future of the movement. The pleasure expressed on Paula's face exhibits adherence to this gender ideology: motherhood-fomented revolution. By this time, they are back in Los Angeles, because Práxedis was born in the city. Rarely did Mexican women smile in photographs, as we can see from her compañera Clarita, who looks stern and almost regretful for being in the picture's frame. Perhaps baby Maggie would not sit still for long, causing Paula to smirk and grin. She was nineteen in this image and shows the delight of motherhood and marriage for a young wife "interpellated by forms of familial attachments that resonate" in the photographs as evidence of PLM intimacies.[52]

A family photo of Enrique, Paula, Margarita, and Práxedis from 1911 shows Paula leaning and resting her hand on Enrique's lap while they hold the two babies (see figure 2.9). Enrique physically leans in to Paula, showing a desire for proximity that goes beyond simple affections in a photograph: theirs was a love ever so worthy of physical and emotional documentation. These attachments ultimately demonstrate just how emotionally and physically committed they both were to this union, even if the photo was a performance of PLM gender ideology of masculinity and femininity. As Nicole Hudgins has argued, family portraiture was a means of building a visual sense of one's own past, including women's ability to exert their subjectivity by capturing it on film. Further, she argues that "standard of neatness and, if possible, elegance, optimized the photographer's results."[53] This domestic portrait is the only surviving evidence of them as a family, representing neatness and elegance, simplicity and humility, attachment and emotion. The photograph is its own form of propaganda in promoting the idealized liberal family in anarchism: a father, a mother, and two beautiful children. It was a heteronormative family as well. The affective register of this family portrait, in its total erasure from ideological histories of the PLM, cements a narrative of the ideal revolutionary family, one where Paula was dependent, rearing children, and occasionally writing for the movement's main organ, *Regeneración*. Such portraits of family seal the record of marital relations, documenting domesticity despite the anarchist beliefs. When they said they were married, such a statement went against anarchist principles of free love—marriage and their brand of anarchism both reinforced the PLM's gender ideologies about women's role in the revolution through the family.[54] The radicalism of the male leaders did not move far beyond traditional views of women.[55] Because the image was taken just prior to Enrique, Ricardo, Librado Rivera, and Anselmo Rivera's arrests in June of 1911 for

FIG 2.9. The Flores Magón de Carmona family (Enrique, Paula, Margarita, and Práxedis), 1911. Courtesy of the Rosello family.

violating neutrality laws, the picture functioned as a memento for Enrique to focus on his young family during political strife.

Early in her marriage to Enrique, Paula had a role in *Regeneración*, the PLM newspaper. Historians such as Gabriela González credit her, along with other Magonista women writers and journalists such as the Villarreal sisters, Blanca Moncaleano, Margarita Ortega, and Rosaura Gortari, as the feminist arm of the movement.[56] Her writings demonstrated the early twentieth-century women's rights discourses espoused through the traditions of political motherhood and family building.[57] Paula wrote a manifesto titled "Que luchen," in October of 1910, urging Mexican mothers to take up the struggle:

> It is good that we, women, Mexican women, speak. Those that have a family must fight against oppression and exploitation so that their children do not become slaves. Comradas, Mexican Mothers: push

your husbands into the fight. To do it this way, they will understand the dignification of the man through his labor that you have instilled in your comrade ... we often have the guilt of preventing men from taking part in great battles for liberty, without thinking about how it degrades the man as it degrades us women, because slavery does not dignify, misery does not elevate character for our own humankind.[58]

This piece was written a few months after the birth of Margarita, when Paula was a mere seventeen years old, and it codified her role as a PLM mother and visible figure in the movement. As a young mother and revolutionary subject arguing that one's children shouldn't be born into economic slavery, her words pushed women to urge their husbands to join the anarchist movement. Misery doesn't elevate character; fighting in the struggle for proletarian motherhood does. As a rhetorical remonstration from which women claim their public role as mothers, Paula performed idealized PLM gender ideology through her writing.[59] Her role can thus be seen as an originary mother of the PLM movement. Her words demonstrate how women were politicized within the context of a male-led nationalist movement.[60]

Rómulo also publicly pledged his undying support of the PLM within the pages of *Regeneración*. In addition to his monthly contributions to fund the paper, he wrote the following on January 1, 1912:

> I donate the sum of fifty pesos to show my monthly support of sustaining *Regeneración* instead of giving a peso a day since the 31st of December last year. . . . Against the wind and storm we must defend our ship's advancement against the black sea of egoism of those who falsely call themselves liberals, who have converted to the hopeful politics of el Chato la Laguna which makes them happy. I reject those farcical patriots and have accepted completely the liberal idea of protest to defend until the last moment of my life. I don't possess illusions of that the triumph of the Social Revolution will be tomorrow or past; even if I can't see it, it is simple that my children will. While I can, I fill myself with pride for the cause whenever possible. Permanently protesting with my words before the enemy, I loudly yell Long Live the Social Revolution![61]

As Rómulo declared his love for the cause via monetary contributions, the junta gladly applauded his solidarity within the pages of the same issue. He also resorted to the masculinized baroque prose of lament and loss by pledging his undying love to the newspaper and the social revolution. Rómulo's public propaganda reinforced his centrality within the PLM movement and in the good graces of Ricardo and Enrique. Such discourse also bolstered Paula's political capital in the sense that Rómulo could be publicly perceived as the one who taught his daughter to abide by anarchist principles from an early age. But the fact that he calls the PLM movement a social revolution also raises doubts about the limits of his radicalism. So too does the fact that he announced a second branch of his bookstore, La Aurora, would open in El Paso in March 1912.[62] For the Flores Magóns, the revolution was not just a social cause; it was completely structural in an upending of moral standards, capitalist exploitation, property rights, and the church.

When Rómulo declared his undying love for the social revolution, he also publicly pledged affections for his son-in-law and daughter as part of public discourse in the newspaper. Paula, as the mother of Enrique's children and through her writings in *Regeneración,* showed that her loyalty to Enrique was beyond reproach. Publishing partner William Owen, editor of the English-language section of the paper, wrote to Enrique in August 1912 to discuss an attempt by the Industrial Workers of the World (IWW, with its members referred to as "Wobblies") to interfere with the PLM and the paper, and he comforted Enrique that "you must rest assured that, to my conviction, at least, everyone here is perfectly loyal and doing the very best he or she can."[63] Remarking upon Paula Carmona and Conchita Rivera's loyalty to their husbands and the movement in the face of a thwarted political and moral takeover, he stated,

> I.W.W. men, whose absolutely rotten record I found out in five minutes, were the main advisers, and the absurd confidence placed in them threatened, for the moment, lots of damage. The men in question—I am quite convinced—were after whatever money there was in sight, free meals, chances—they thought—of picking up women, and the gratification of their burning desire to make trouble. Nothing in that sort of thing, and I have been glad that your wife and Mrs. Rivera held themselves aloof.[64]

At this point in time, Paula could be trusted, and her fidelity, along with that of Conchita, provided support to resist the advances of ill-intentioned Wobblies seeking to move on the offices and women linked to the PLM for sexual satisfaction, monetary gain, and personal debauchery. They were the perfect revolutionary wives and mothers who formed the moral core of PLM gender ideology, so much so that when Enrique and Ricardo were convicted on June 22, 1912, "the women of their party who have been in daily attendance wept quietly."[65]

Paula's political efforts were all the more gallant given that she had a baby son, Demófilo, just a day after her husband was sent to prison on July 7. The Spanish version of Demófilo's birth announcement is far more poetic than the English. "Un revolucionario nuevo" states the following:

> In solemn moments, when our valiant brothers were serving time in McNeil Island Federal Prison, where they have been recused from society for 23 long months, only for loving liberty and consecrating their lives for the true emancipation of humanity, the Monday of this week, at 2:30 in the morning a future revolutionary saw the light for the first time as the son of our beloved brother Enrique and his companion Paula. Our cordial congratulations for the parents of this little comrade and that the circumstances in which he came into the world where his father serves with much bravery and for his time, that this little creature continue the beautiful work began by his father.[66]

Enrique never saw the baby because of his sentence. Paula had a family picture taken on August 27 so that Enrique could see his baby son (see figure 2.10). She looks mature for her age: a young mother raising her three small children while her husband served time for the anarchist cause and violation of neutrality laws. In terms of gender ideology, the image also documents how it was "far more challenging for women than for men to survive under capitalism" because proper motherhood required having access to resources.[67] With Enrique in prison, the ideological work of the photograph stages motherly suffering as part of giving one's life to "the Idea." The image also performs a kind of emotional labor in absence, as Ana Rosas has argued, that gave the incarcerated Enrique glimpses of the children during "the most challenging moments in the family's history."[68]

As a celebration of proletarian survival, Demófilo's joyous birth was again noted in English a week later in a nondescript fashion in "Yet Another Rebel": "Born July 8, 1912, in Los Angeles to Paula Carmona, wife of Enrique Flores Magon, a Son. Dr. Juan Creaghe, who was in attendance, reports both mother and child as in the best of health. We can wish the latter no better luck in life than to develop into as brave and honest a man as is his father."[69] Baby Demófilo was the hope that buoyed Paula and Enrique's relationship while he was in prison. Demófilo was seen as an extension of his father's anarchist character and legacy. Still, Paula continued her activities for the movement as part of the female supporting cast of the newspaper, as did her father with his donations and the distribution of the paper through his bookstore. Rómulo continued to purchase advertisements in

FIG 2.10. Portrait of Paula Carmona de Flores Magón, Margarita Flores Magón, Práxedis Flores Magón, and Demófilo Flores Magón, August 27, 1912. Courtesy of the Swearingen family.

the paper up until the week before the junta began to denounce them both in May 1913.

But tragedy struck the young family in December of 1912. In the obituary titled "Un rebelde menos" (One less rebel), the editorial staff states that

> resembling the sadness of a mother the day she has to deposit in mother earth what nature gave to her as the fruit of her womb: a beloved being: Demófilo Magón. The father of the dead child, Enrique Flores Magón, partner of Paula Carmona, as parents of the newly named rebel saw 1st light on the 8th of July past, they should have been together to share

the pains and pities before the little body of their beloved son. But this did not happen: because the BAD and CRIMINAL SOCIETY of the U.S. prohibited as much the father as the young innocent, to hold him in his father's arms, just like he should have received his tender son, with caresses and longings of his father; even for a moment and you Demófilo with a fever that snatched your existence in the middle of this criminal and egotistical society, you have been liberated later than the rest of bandits of power, you would have sunk in an unclean cell, actually the way your father has. Oh! Vile society, the men of law; how many criminals are present; you are the only ones responsible. Paula Magón gives thanks to the comrades that had the good will to help her with the cost that originated in burying the baby.[70]

Sentiment and excess permeate the obituary to mobilize the proletariat masses to mourn baby Demófilo. That loss also reveres the proletarian mother for her suffering at the hands of capitalist evils. By blaming criminal society for incarcerating the boy's father, the *Regeneración* editorial team turned the responsibility onto the state for depriving a freedom fighter of his parental rights. Idealizing the Carmona de Flores Magón family's public loss, the pain endured by this particular family seeped into the households of other PLM members.[71]

Enrique never saw baby Demófilo because of his prison sentence, which made the sting of the death doubly felt. It was a tremendous loss for them both and for an entire transnational network: if the chosen son of the revolutionary leader was vulnerable to death, so too were all of them. Their poverty was also noted in the obituary, for members of the Los Angeles PLM cell contributed money for the baby's burial. Moreover, the fact that all three children were born so close together placed undue emotional and physical strain on the young Paula Carmona. Emotional and financial instability led her to rely on her parents for economic support while Enrique was in prison. She was also expected to rely on anarchist networks to help raise her family, both politically and financially.

Nonetheless, it appears that Paula threw herself into revolutionary work after the baby died. She allowed *Regeneración* to publish a letter written to her by Enrique from prison. Exposing the intimacy between Paula and Enrique in the name of informing the public of denied parole, the letter appeared in the newspaper in March 1913:

My Unforgettable Paula—now is the time to give you more bad news: This morning we were called, Ricardo, Anselmo, Librado and I, before the Director's desk to consider liberty on parole and Mr. DeLan,

Prison Superintendent and, at the same time, part of the Department of Justice, who came from Washington D.C. notified us that we should not dictate ourselves to the idea of liberty on parole as prisoners in McNeil Island. In few words: I want to say that we will not be liberated at the end of this February but on the 19th of January in 1914.... DO NOT STOP YOUR PROPAGANDA WORK in favor of our unconditional and absolute liberty.... I wanted to write about family matters, but for this time only they permitted me to write this special letter, because of the generosity of the prison head Mr. William F. Muehe. Given regards to all from all of us. With unending love for you, I remain always your loving companion in life. Enrique.[72]

This is the only existing letter that Enrique wrote to Paula, and one thing becomes clear: his love and adoration of her are as plain as day. Enrique publicly pledged his undying love to Paula in the pages of *Regeneración* just two months before the "betrayals" that would cause their marital split. In terms of gender ideology, the letter performs loss and longing as a form of masculinity, while Paula is represented as the perfect mother of the revolution by not sacrificing her propaganda work. While reporting on their release date, the letter's closing reaffirms Enrique's deep attachment to Paula. Publication of the letter signaled that lavish expressions of sentiment were appropriate to a family man of the revolution, an affect that carried over in his propaganda rhetoric for the freedom of the prisoners and of his México *querido* (beloved) from the arms of tyranny.

In the same issue, it was advertised that "Paula Carmona, companion of Enrique F. Magón is interested in collecting funds for the 'Casa del Obrero Internacional'" and has "organized a BIG DANCE for Saturday 1st of March in one of the biggest dancehalls in the city of O.I. The dance begins at 7pm. We congratulate our enthusiastic comrade for her interest in supporting our urgent work. Price of entry: men $.50 and women free."[73] Despite the original enthusiasm by the organizing junta, this support of the Casa del Obrero Internacional would be the undoing of Paula and Enrique's relationship. At this point in time, the dance was still considered a fund-raiser for the release of Enrique and comrades, as well as for the new headquarters of *Regeneración*. It was a welcomed form of political activism. When her father and the known anarchist Juan Moncaleano brokered the $10,000 deal to eventually buy the Casa del Obrero property for the *Regeneración* headquarters, residences for workers, a school, and a salon to hold events, the organizing junta didn't see anything wrong with this. By February 22, 1913, the move had been made, and the new offices were located on Yale Street in Los Angeles. But the junta had not foreseen that Moncaleano and Carmona would unsuccessfully try to take over the newspaper along with the Casa del Obrero. The March fund-raiser, while seeming innocent at first, became the final breaking point that fractured the junta because events like the dance were seen to individually benefit Rómulo, Paula, and Juan. Even if Paula's fund-raiser was for the Casa del Obrero, once the junta found out her father's designs to seize the paper, her support for (or failure to oppose) her father's project nullified anything she had previously done and counted as a form of gendered treason.

"The Betrayal"

It is important to note that what the PLM claims that Paula did, or did not do, is dependent upon perspective. From Enrique and the PLM's perspective, the Casa del Obrero Internacional real estate transaction was the key issue that led to a series of emotional and personal betrayals, most notably by Rómulo and his daughter. But from a feminist perspective, Paula didn't betray Enrique; she was a young woman with two small children and no income. Enrique could not support his wife or children from prison, so what should Paula have done? Thus, we must critically examine the following narrative for how it stages Paula's activities as betrayal when they actually were more a function of being a dependent.

When it was made known that Rómulo and his accomplice wanted to take over *Regeneración*, a family came undone, and the PLM loyalists went on the offensive. Because these were considered to be acts of political treason against both the PLM and Enrique's fragile masculinity, the editors of *Regeneración* (Antonio de P. Araujo, T. M. Gaitán, Blas Lara, and others) unleashed the power of public shaming and denunciation to utterly and completely sever ties with the Carmonas and to symbolically sever Enrique's marriage while he was in prison. According to a June 21, 1913, exposé titled "Perfiles negros. Los criminales" (Dark profiles: The criminals), written by junta loyalist and *Regeneración* editor Araujo, Carmona and Moncaleano's real intent was to take over the newspaper and abscond with the donated money. The article quotes a letter from Pedro Rincón Gallardo to Rómulo describing Moncaleano's proposal that they use the money donated for the center to build themselves homes on land acquired in Santa Paula.[74] I extract the second half of Paula's history from this evidence, showing that women's betrayals are secondary or invisible within masculinist histories of the PLM. Commencing what Claudio Lomnitz has identified as a form of PLM direct action (against Carmona and Moncaleano's failed attempt to get control of the newspaper) called the Judas Cycle, "a vehement discourse of betrayal within the inner circles," the politics of exposure and humiliation became the mode to punish deviators who betrayed, especially if they were romantic partners.[75]

From June 7, 1913, to January 31, 1914, the editorial team mounted a flat-out exposé of Paula, her father, and Moncaleano. They published what were supposed to be authentically translated telegrams of the disagreements between Enrique and Rómulo Carmona. Carmona, in turn, deployed his daughter to telegraph Enrique while he was in McNeil Island proposing that Carmona and Moncaleano should take over the paper. But the paper's editors never actually published these telegrams, and readers were to take their word for it that Paula was threatening and quarreling with Enrique while he was in prison. In a telegram from Pilar A. Robledo (i.e., Rómulo Carmona) to Enrique that was published, Paula and the children were used as bait. It stated: "REGENERACION is on the eve of death. Send me forces, put me in charge, and buy a printing press. What do you prefer more, your friends who put you in prison, or your wife and children?"[76] Enrique was so lathered up by the threat that he saved an original clipped copy of the newspaper that reprinted the telegrams as evidence and a reminder of the vile nature of the betrayal.[77] Paula's loyalty, just like her chaste morality mentioned by Owen in 1912, went to the wayside as she was most likely forced to side with her father and not Enrique. Raising two small children alone during the prison sentence could not have been easy, nor could recovery from the death of a baby. Paula relied on her parents during this time. The denunciation and termination of the marriage were, as Gabriela González has stated, a way to discredit Paula's "political voice and her right to participate in public debates."[78] In retrospect, her political voice as a mother was sacrificed as the primary concern centered around her father financially supporting the children whom Enrique had left behind while in prison. She had no choice—she was twenty-one years old.

A column, simply titled "Paula Carmona," was a scathing attack on the mother of Enrique's children and his soon-to-be former wife:

> Comrade Enrique Flores Magón writes us from McNeil Island, informing us that his marriage with his former partner has been dissolved. Paula Carmona, showing strange and unfair behavior, deserted her husband while in the grip of tyranny at the time, the tyranny that has him imprisoned. Paula Carmona is the daughter of Rómulo S. Carmona, or Pilar A. Robledo, the individual with whom the so-called

"libertarian" Juan F. Moncaleano tried to rename REGENERACION. To avoid future mistakes, we warn all comrades that Paula Carmona is no longer a part of and has no more participation in the movement, and that she does not support the Mexican Liberal party along with her father and the infamous Juan F. Moncaleano.[79]

According to the editors, Paula committed an act of political and personal betrayal, irrespective of the fact that she was left to raise her children without resources. They highlighted Paula's allegiance to her father and not to her husband. Moreover, in his failed attempt to take over *Regeneración*, Rómulo, according to the junta, traded her family to become a power broker in Ricardo and Enrique's absence. Whatever motives Carmona and Moncaleano may have had, profiteering was one of them, according to Araujo. The editorial group was fearful that if Carmona and Moncaleano got control of the newspaper, they would stray from PLM ideologies, use it to serve their own egos, and then take the money and run. Thus, the editorial board of *Regeneración* accused Paula of abandoning her husband and his political cause because she was linked to her father's political aspirations. Because of this, Paula was considered to have betrayed not only Enrique but also the movement's gender ideology about motherhood and revolution. As a result, Enrique telegraphed her in June 1913 from McNeil Island stating, "Since today 1913, we are divorced, you and I."[80]

Trustworthiness was of monumental importance to the PLM and the Flores Magón brothers' understanding of what constituted moral character. Trust meant putting your life on the line to protect the welfare of others. Betrayal of trust was also a violation of PLM gender ideologies about womanhood and motherhood. Because her actions were labeled by the junta as a betrayal of her life partner, her father's attempt at sabotaging *Regeneración* while the Flores Magóns were serving time was sold to the PLM readership as the Carmonas and Moncaleano undertaking personal monetary gain from a project that was sustained by a transnational network of workers who could barely themselves spare money to support the paper. Such violations of the trust relationship to extract monetary gain, even at the nuclear and heterosexual familial level, posed a huge threat to their children and the PLM network by damaging their credibility with workers.[81] It was a threat to Enrique because he was incarcerated and had absolutely no control over his family situation or his wife. The newspaper was in damage-control mode, serving its own cause and disregarding how Paula and the children would be hurt by the lifelong family separation.

To repair that credibility and mount the social capital embodied in the Flores Magón name, Araujo's "La campaña contra *Regeneración*" went so far as to publish the telegrams, in Spanish and English, that both Pilar Robledo (Rómulo Carmona) and Paula sent to Enrique while he was in prison:

> Los Angeles, Cal., Ap. 9, 1913: Ricardo Flores Magon companions: McNeil Island. Gaitan and Lara want papers offices changed. Make substitution with Pilar A. Robledo, Juan F. Moncaleano and Pedro Soto Ramírez. Answer to buy printing shop. PILAR A. ROBLEDO.
>
> Los Angeles, Cal., April 19, 1913: Ricardo Flores Magon, McNeil Island. Knowing your silence is answer, I annul my former telegram but wait consequences because I will fight Gaitan, Lara, Cordero and the fatal woman. PILAR A. ROBLEDO.[82]

Such evidence mobilizes truth in disclosure, putting the documentation of anger and hurt out in the open, which overexposes the violation of trust to the point of no return. The telegrams also document just how authoritarian Rómulo was, ordering Ricardo and Enrique to act because they were at a disadvantage while in prison. Labeling Carmona and Moncaleano as criminals for their willful deception, Araujo's June 7 article followed the telegrams with his explanation of the perfidy they reveal:

> Robledo's telegrams, or that of Rómulo S. Carmona, reveal the decision that Carmona and his accomplices made in seizing REGENERACION so that the "leader," maverick Juan F. Moncaleano, would remain as the mastermind of the situation, supposing that Robledo, because of his dealings . . . could not assist with the management of REGENERACION. The phrases "buy a printing press" are the incentive with which the self-interested Carmona believed would engage the comrades at McNeil Island, and the last phrases of the second message threatens a defamatory campaign just because comrade Ricardo Flores Magón did not give up his desire of making the vulgar Moncaleano owner and head of REGENERACION. . . . [T]he ambitious ones who desired to unleash their unhealthy passions found in comrades Teodoro Gaitán and Blas Lara, adamant defenders of the cause, the impregnable barrier that blocked their passage. . . . For today, we are satisfied with having thwarted the conspiracy of these reptiles that were threatening the newspaper to a greater degree than the persecutors from a capitalist gang.[83]

The telegrams, as presented in the pages of *Regeneración*, identified a fivefold threat: Carmona and Moncaleano attempted to undermine Ricardo's claim as editor, they attempted to damage Ricardo and Enrique's reputations as revolutionary leaders, they destroyed Enrique and Paula's family, they attempted to undermine the cause for worker liberation, and they threatened the jobs and stability of the Los Angeles junta that worked on *Regeneración* while Enrique and Ricardo were in prison. The baroque language uses the ideology of gender, but this time about masculinity, calling Gaitán and Lara valiant defenders of the cause and calling Moncaleano and Carmona reptiles. The harsh sentiments of denunciation that even if, as Gómez-Quiñones states, were a function of PLM factionalism, are nonetheless brutal in their critique.[84] Dramatized, baroque, sentiment-laden language was meant to incite political action so that PLM members would feel empowered to excommunicate the Carmonas, and it was indeed emotionally painful for all involved. Even though Rómulo was a regular monetary donor to *Regeneración* and distributed copies from his Aurora Bookstore as Enrique's father-in-law, it did not matter once he had betrayed the junta.[85] If anything, it was a way to distance the PLM from a dishonest but astute businessman.

But we should also be wary of these claims of financial impropriety and misuse of the PLM reputation, for Lawrence Douglas Taylor notes that the $25,000 raised to support the Magonista insurrection in Baja California during 1910–11 "disappeared because of the financial incompetence of the junta, and above all, Enrique Flores Magón, the treasurer of the party."[86] So although the PLM junta historically had money problems because of mismanagement on the part of its main leaders, those earlier mishaps were erased by the betrayal for monetary gain on behalf of the Carmonas and Moncaleano. In between the original denunciation printed by Araujo and the article "Perfiles negros," a letter from Pedro Rincón Gallardo to Rómulo was printed, describing Moncaleano's proposal that they use the money donated for the center to build themselves homes on land acquired in Santa Paula. Thus, irrelevant of her prior fidelity and PLM loyalty, twenty-one-year-old Paula could not break with the authoritarian hold of her father, leading to the split and harsh denunciations by Enrique and his PLM circle.

Because *Regeneración* publicly laid bare the supposed treason, members of other PLM groups from Texas began to write their own denunciations of Paula Carmona, Rómulo Carmona, and Juan Moncaleano. Because the culture of denunciation within the Mexican Revolution and PLM in particular was so strong, the demonstration of support for Enrique and Ricardo came in the form of anti-betrayal vitriol. Two PLM chapters from Gonzalez, Texas, and Maurin, Texas (the latter group including one female chapter secretary as signatory), mined the Spanish language for all its capacity to discursively decimate the traitors of their beloved brothers in struggle, the anarchist principle of family, and the movement more broadly. "La protesta contra la conducta mezquina de Moncaleano, Carmona y Cardenas," by El Grupo Regeneración Bandera Roja, centralizes their betrayal of ideology and the cause: "We, members of the group, who fight to recognize neither power nor proprietors, protest against all those who by means of tricks and combinations try to divert and stain our cause."[87] Mobilizing the notion of willful defamation as the cause of total rejection of private property and authoritarian power, the Gonzalez group, with fifteen male signatories, named its allegiance to the PLM and its principles. Furthermore, these masculine performatives of honor and dishonor, represented in Carmona and Moncaleano, identify lying and abuse of privilege as a cost to the worker: "Additionally, to the group sending out their call to all others who gather in Texas to protest against the individuals that want to seize what belongs to the workers. We can never allow the sacrifice, safety, and lives of those who give themselves over to the blossoms of the struggle, to remain in the hands of the ambitious . . . they scream with us, and we with them: Bread, Land, and Liberty."[88] Ambition, like lack of consent, was an ideological betrayal in anarchist circles. This made the Carmona group all the more dastardly for its willful embrace of accumulation of wealth with the paper and a move away from the struggle to liberate Mexico. These poetics of denunciation evoked an unjust snatching of life from "those who give themselves over to the blossoms of the struggle to remain in the hands of the ambitious" and put forth a visual image of fragile, flower-like beauty being destroyed by the crushing hands of authoritarianism and greed. Such poetic texture lends an even greater force to the discourse of denunciation, for it posits the depth and density of the loss in rejecting traitors. Betrayal, in poetics, is a tragedy that the González Bandera Roja group captures perfectly with its floridly worded treatise on behalf of the worker and its testimony to Enrique and Ricardo's honorable conduct. These were fights over the gender ideology of the PLM and "real" anarchist revolutionary masculinity. Even though the takeover was incomplete, the auxiliary groups continued to denounce the traitors.

Paula S. Torres, from Maurin, represented El Grupo Regeneración Feminino Aspiraciones Libres, who also denounced the PLM traitors: "With all the energy against the ambitious and wretched conduct of Juan F. Moncaleano and Carmona, because we have assembled under the banner of Land and Liberty with the purpose of putting an end to the system of masters and when aforementioned individuals try seizing REGENERACION, a newspaper that in part sustains this group shows enmity to the cause we pursue and their sympathy for the system of owners."[89] Although there is no direct gendered discourse of women attacking Paula, a collective sense of gender-sexual servitude (masters) forms the basis of their critique. Both groups frown upon ambition, so women must unite under the banner of *Tierra y Libertad* (land and liberty) to end authoritarian capitalist master-slave relations. Their deep identification with *enmistad* (frenemy) energies in the fierce persecution of those who attempted to rob the newspaper that politically and intellectually sustained them showcases the impact of anarchist ideology on women's groups and how they conceived their potential liberties through literacy and activism in central Texas. Moreover, being sympathetic to the master-slave system as Moncaleano and Carmona had shows how these savvy readers of *engaño* (deception) naturalized betrayal not only as an innate characteristic of women but also of morally weak men. Read doubly, their lack of sympathy for the power hungry and the ability to stand up to authoritarianism indirectly reflect poorly on Paula because her father's authority took precedent over her own or that of her husband: she had no choice when raising children alone. These were two competing forms of patriarchy. When the editorial group stated that "to avoid future errors, we advertise to all of the compañeros that Paula Carmona does not have any singular participatory role in the movement any more that sustains the PLM, and neither does her father," they publicly sever her family ties, humiliate her, and ostracize her for political betrayal based on gender ideology.[90]

Enrique's colleagues continued the humiliation by defending their own masculine authority in "Perfiles negros. Los criminales":

> We used to say that Moncaleano is a slave of the most depraved desires, as to compel comrade Enrique Flores Magón to withdraw his trust from our brothers Gaitán and Lara, he influenced Enrique's ex-comrade, Paula Carmona, to accuse this prisoner at McNeil Island under so many and small pretexts, knowing that in order not to lose her and his young children, Enrique would do whatever Moncaleano and Rómulo wanted, and the only thing that the criminal Moncaleano achieved was breaking up comrade Enrique's home and leaving his children as orphans without a father. Enrique would never have allowed REGENERACION to remain in the hands of criminals.[91]

Based on this article and without other evidence, we are forced to take the word of Gaitán and Lara about Paula's bickering telegrams that made Enrique turn against them. Their position relies on gendered conventions of masculinity and femininity to exonerate Enrique and blame Paula for emotional weakness at the behest of Moncaleano and her father. Because of the distance between Los Angeles and McNeil Island and because of the small children Paula was caring for, she never visited him in prison. There is no evidence of Teresa Arteaga visiting him either, but his 1958 biography intimates that she wrote to him frequently during this incarceration.

Although Paula and Rómulo would receive the blame for the breakup of Enrique's first family, the previously cited article, written on June 7, 1913, by Araujo, says it was Moncaleano's direct manipulations of Enrique while he was in prison that led to such chaos and betrayal. It all started with Moncaleano mobilizing his anarchist credibility in Colombia, Spain, and Cuba as a means of discrediting editors Lara and Gaitán in the absence of Enrique and Ricardo. Small notes sent by Enrique's father-in-law, including one published in the article threatening to fight Lara and Gaitán for control of the paper, all raised Enrique's doubts about his comrades. When coupled with what Araujo describes as quarreling with his wife under small and ridiculous pretexts, this amounted to an all-out coordinated assault on Enrique's core values: family and freedom of press. Extolling the role of being *padre de familia*, Rómulo and Moncaleano had essentially robbed Enrique of the things that gave him hope in light of his prison sentence. And while Araujo does not say that Enrique was duped, he does go as far as to indicate that Enrique was manipulated through his intense emotional attachments to his wife, small children, and the paper, making him highly vulnerable given the physical distance from the situation at hand. Considering *Regeneración*'s consistent financial deficit and history of fiscal mismanagement, it is clear that obtaining the social capital and mobilization of the Flores Magón brothers' reputation was the goal in Rómulo Carmona and Juan Moncaleano's failed attempt to take over the newspaper and in the Casa del Obrero real estate transaction. Araujo laments that the only real outcome was the violent breakup of Enrique's home and the intentional orphaning of his children. Only authoritarians would commit such deeds by exploiting emotional and familial connections, and because neither Enrique nor Ricardo could leave their beloved paper in the hands of criminals, Enrique instead sacrificed his children to the "young mother" who "had been criminally manipulated and ripped away by her father."[92]

According to particular interlocutors of the history with the Carmonas, Enrique believed that Rómulo was the author of the telegrams. He could not understand why Paula would write such a thing. Once Enrique believed that Paula authored the line about preferring the movement over his wife and children, her father's betrayal and her disloyalty became something beyond repair. Although Enrique was the one who voluntarily separated from Paula for political reasons, some chroniclers of the history state that she was the one who barred him from seeing his children and that she abandoned him.[93] Nonetheless, with his release from prison in January 1914, Enrique printed his own denunciation of his former wife and her father. Ethyl Duffy Turner summed up these cathartic losses about family quite well: "The world he had left behind had changed with the same dizzy rhythm as always. Both Enrique and Librado had lost their wives."[94] Conchita contracted cancer and died, and Paula supposedly committed the ultimate sin by choosing her father's greed over her husband and the junta.[95] Duffy Turner focuses on the fact that they "lost" their wives, one to illness and the other to political treason. Tita Valencia goes so far as to say "Las esposas de Enrique Flores Magón y Librado Rivera, mueren durante la estancia de los revolucionarios en McNeil" (The wives of Enrique Flores Magón and Librado Rivera died during their imprisonment as revolutionaries in McNeil Island).[96] The word *lost* indicates something out of one's control, or victimization, yet Enrique indeed had a choice in the matter. To write that she was dead is a lie. What gets lost in all this talk of dead and lost wives is Enrique's siding with the junta family in the face of Carmona's accusations about Ricardo embezzling money from the paper. This was a way to make Carmona and Moncaleano's planned takeover of *Regeneración* the main reason for the breakup of Enrique's family.

Along with Valencia's claim that Paula died, both suggest the effectiveness of denouncement in the PLM orchestrating Paula's social death. That this statement about her being dead was published by Mexico's Secretaría de Gobernación demonstrates just how invested people were in erasing Paula Carmona from PLM history: the state was willing to endorse lies as official history. But when PLM operative José Guerra's article "La revolución en el sur de la republica" appeared on July 26, 1913, he also further indicted Paula, stating that when he was in Mexico,

> In the capital . . . what I did was send something to Paula Carmona's address, but the messages never arrived to the junta again, and well, Paula Carmona appropriated them, all of them, of the ones written in Mexico one half were sent to the junta and the other half I sent to El Paso Texas. I did this because I believed I could confide in the honored Paula Carmona because she was supposedly the wife and companion

of comrade Enrique Flores Magón and never could suspect that all the fruit of my labor where I risked my life or how I related information through this joke of a woman who was in cahoots with or could be influenced by enemies of REGENERACION. . . . Upon my return to Los Angeles, I presented myself in the house of Romulo S. Carmona to get the communications that I had sent to the junta back but because of the conduct of his daughter Paula Carmona and he finally negated that they had ever received them.[97]

Guerra again instrumentalizes Paula's conduct regarding the relay of junta messages as an act of betrayal. By calling her a joke of a woman, he questions her capacity as a formerly trusted and revered intimate partner to make fun of her and her father. When Guerra, according to his public account, went to the Carmona home, both Rómulo and Paula denied ever receiving the messages. Given that they had already been excommunicated from the junta, these mischaracterizations of Paula's extrication from the PLM and her husband's life locate power in Enrique's denouncement. By completely discrediting Paula, the public provided Enrique with the capacity to narrate history for his own benefit and that of the PLM.

In the transition between Enrique's family with Paula and his family with Teresa Arteaga, I want to discuss a poem drafted on the back of a formal letter to *Regeneración* subscribers, where Enrique sketched out a short verse of lament and loss. With no date on either the poem or the letter on the reverse, the economized use of paper reveals thin resources, "¡Claro, corazón!" is a poem that discusses emotional losses with great detail. It's refrain, "Lloro y lamento / Cry and lament," is followed by the lines "Clearly, your pains, your sadnesses. From your bitterness, you suffer now. Clearly, dear, I have my doubts. Cry to my heart! Cry and lament. / My sadness absence / My sick desperations, terrifying / Cry my dear, cry, cry. / such that your punishment is active. You lament so loud and louder, oh / I never your pity and humble imploring / Before the after the others / the fair strength / Coward! You briefly appear, cowardice! And cry / Well from your platitudes and your love, quiet heart, that fails to cry."[98]

Because the poem was written on the back of a letter signed by Anselmo Figueroa as editor of *Regeneración*, it had to have been written between 1910 and March 1915. Figueroa died in June 1915, and the paper went on hiatus from March to October of that year. A narrative of suffering, it was most likely produced as a transitional piece between Paula's betrayal and Enrique's relationship with Teresa. If we read the poem as a kind of doublespeak, with two subjects of loss, then "the punishment" that one most highly regrets is both the betrayal and loss of the first wife and children and the lament it caused with the second life partner. Given the ways in which Enrique portrays Teresa in his autobiography, the second reference to writing "pity and humble imploring / Before the after the others" demonstrates his penance to her, of sterling character, uttering "Coward!" to himself under his breath. This marks the end of the poem. Because the poem names the quiet heart that fails to cry because of cowardice, it posits a victim who has lost affective resonance with the pain after so much loss. But there is a crossed-out stanza that raises further questions about the love object of this poem:

> Until I face my punishment of the greatest kind,
> and I ask your pious and attentive forgiveness
> and with my humble imploring early in the morning,
> with this just force that no one can take from my beloved
> fall like bricks, coward! And cry
> below the planets and without words, my beloved heart be pierced with arrows.[99]

This last, crossed-out stanza focuses on self-flagellation and suffering on the part of the author. Unlike the pain of loss or inability to cry because of cowardice in the previous stanzas, it appears that Enrique thought twice about ending a poem that engaged in such emotional punishment as a form of penance for harming his beloved. So if Enrique is the victim of both Paula's deception and bad-faith gestures toward Teresa because they were both married while he was first involved with her, it makes sense that half of the poem is crossed out: it insufficiently addressed two people at the same time and was ineffective at capturing the complex emotions of attachment, detachment, loss, and self-castigation that marked his personal experience of family.

But this transitional poem with two subjects of love and lament—Paula and Teresa—marks a kind of shift in consciousness, documented via *Regeneración*'s obsession with monetary transparency following the embezzlement charges against Ricardo.[100] Enrique was clearly in a relationship with Teresa by the printing of the November 28, 1913, issue of *Regeneración*, where the editors documented that she received "$2.50 medicina para 'Teresa V. 'Magón,' compañera de Enrique." Whether to justify the expense for the newspaper or an actual confirmation of their romantic relationship, there was a political and personal reason to continue denouncing Paula, her father, and Moncaleano: Enrique's own honor and pain made it necessary to create distance between them. The official announcement of the split with

Paula first broke in June 1913, and Teresa was using Enrique's name in November, which means that he could have been involved with both women during his prison term or that he was at least in communication with Teresa while in McNeil and formalized their relationship before his release on January 19, 1914. In either case, we see that Enrique was deeply committed to the political cause and that even though he was in a marriage with Paula and his last child with her had died only six months before, it did not take long for him to separate from her and form a new relationship with Teresa. Because of their political circles, there had to still be some form of contact, either between the two women (Teresa and Paula), Rómulo and Enrique, Paula and Enrique, or members of the junta and his ex-wife and children. Los Angeles was big, but in these political circles, it was not that big. Enrique publicly took up with Teresa, who was a well-respected figure in the PLM community. Forming a new partnership with Teresa resuscitated his tarnished reputation. In order to publicly sever any conflicting ties, Enrique denounced Paula in January and February 1914, immediately following his release from McNeil Island.

The denunciations of Paula and her father don't actually name them directly. In both instances, Enrique's virile words represent a baroque density of sadness, loss, and rage. In this light, understanding these denunciations through Mary Kay Vaughan's assertion that "we need to look at gendered violence as part of Mexican political culture as it was constituted across space and time" is of the utmost importance.[101] Enrique wrote the following in "¡Viva la anarquía!":

> The fetid halo of slander further poisoned the bad air of my cell and the cowardice shackling my hands, it collected heat and whipped me in the face. And slandered, cursed, insulted, and backstabbed by those who I thought were my friends and comrades and who, on the contrary, knew to take advantage of my absence and the impossibility of defending myself to rip out my heart destroying my home and making orphans of my ill-fated, gentle children out of vengeance for not enlisting to be an instrument of ruinous passions and of bastardly ambitions, I return once again, as I say, bringing in my saddlebags new disillusions and new disappointments along with my broken health, lightened of flesh, and combing more silvered threads among the curls of my black hair.... Back, I am among you, chained brothers: and so I send you the most cordial greeting, I spit at the snout of the despicable imbecile who thought his plots could corrupt me, that in his impotence,

his anger, and his spite, rallied fools against the beautiful fight that on Mexican land sustains the proletariat, and moreover taints and hurls everything onto my clean name and places discord in the middle of my home. I have suffered like never before in my life, and I am ready once again to rise to the challenge.[102]

Purloined sadness and rage pervade "¡Viva la anarquía!" The poetics of betrayal are again operationalized to clear Enrique's name with his pen. Performing disdain to make the severing of his family and victim status credible, Enrique diverted attention away from his other relationship with Teresa. Like a haunting residue in his prison cell, slander violently slapped him in the face. The violation of expectations and values, by both Paula and Rómulo, turn suffering into a baroque language of unethical violations of person and soul. To expose the soul and degree of loss, which includes orphaned children, Enrique publicly performs masculine vulnerability that was only exacerbated by incarceration. Furthermore, the unspeakable sex-gender content of his interpretation shows the fragility of the boundaries between intimate sexual relationships and intimate comrade relationships: just because one was related by blood or had children with a person later discovered to be a traitor meant that the betrayer was essentially dead. Such trauma floats in the prison cell as much as it floats in discourse or the psyche, and it exposes the depths of Enrique's personal losses as a performed self-flagellation and suffering. This affect of violence marks the existential aftermath and remorse that come with making what now appear as bad-faith choices of trust in the wrong comrades.[103] But it also defends the misogyny as a necessary form of gendered discursive violence. In performing those emotions that come after the loss of family and trust, the call for anarchy to live on takes the passionate connections of love from the past and oversteps them to pursue, even more fervently, an anarchist future where authoritarianism is extinct.

But the aftermath of Enrique's familial and psychic losses, including the death of an infant child, lingered even after he forged a new family with Teresa and her five children. In the title of his short story or fable "Los 'huérfanos,'" the quotation marks tip off the reader that these orphans are not exactly abandoned by their father. When the four-year-old girl protagonist, exactly Margarita Carmona's age in 1914 at the date of publication, asks her mother why her father has left, the mother replies:

> Oh! That Father was not there nor would return again, because the ruinous passions of exactly those same ones who should have watched over the well-being of that innocent four-year-old child, had crimi-

> nally ripped her away from her father, along with her gentle little brother and the young mother. Because of the authoritarian father's brutal command and the passive obedience of a weak daughter, she unfairly abandons the partner that loved her so much, she loved them so dearly, and so longingly kept them by her side.[104]

Domesticity is torn asunder by an authoritarian father and a daughter who cannot contest his power, clearly representing Paula and Rómulo. The narrator genders the domestic and innocence to erase the violence of Enrique's words.[105] In other words, pastoralizing domesticity and portraying Paula's father as a despot conceal the narrator's later discursive violence in misogyny and sexism. His veiled representations of Margarita, which I will explain later, are the site of this concealment.

In "Los 'huérfanos,'" the children continue life without the guidance of their father, and the criminals who created their orphan status only continue their wrath with dirty, hateful lies about their father. They were like "savage plants; without cultivation, without solicited care," and when passing into adolescence, the young, attractive girl becomes swept up in the bad anarchism of

> free love: bestial love of Priapus that did not even respect naïve childhood because in their immense shamelessness those fauns would describe as "pure love," which led her to give into the impulses of her prematurely awakened nature by the lasciviousness of a celebrant satyr of that so-called "free love" and went on to add to the pile of cadavers of syphilitic girls thrown by the thousands onto slabs of dissection halls, after which the he-goat, once satisfying his appetites, would abandon her, defenseless because of her inexperience against the harshness of accursed bourgeois society, prudish and selfish.[106]

To move from a domestic scene of a patriarchal father's authoritarian violence featuring a four-year-old political orphan to a scene of syphilitic cadavers of adolescent girls who could not resist free love because of bad rearing and naïveté is to blame her grandfather, the immoral decision maker over his grandchildren, and by extension her mother for the girl's sexual downfall. For the mother, by virtue of separating from her beloved partner at the request of her own father, has morally left her daughter unguarded and filled with bourgeois ideas of egoism and self-indulgence.

Although this is an anarchist tale of what goes awry when children are wrongfully alienated from their fathers, the special position of the daughter in this story is one of disease and predestined sexual betrayal on account of her mother's disloyalty to her husband and the loyalty to her father. But what is even more important is that the PLM was supposedly advocating free love and practicing it in their Edendale commune. Enrique staunchly opposes the practice in "Los 'huérfanos.'" The thinly veiled slander is not just an attack on the Carmonas but is also a moralizing diatribe against free love. Intrinsically, because of her sex and because of her mother, there was no other way to be except a sexual and social traitor. Cutting close to the bone in predicting the potential moral-metaphorical downfall of his own children, Enrique's fabled orphans, when female, are misogynistically portrayed as corrupt because of an inherited sexual and gendered propensity to obey bourgeois fatherly authority. And if we turn to his daughter Margarita's actual life history, by 1930 she was twenty years old, living with her mother, stepfather, and stepsiblings, and was waiting for her husband to return from the navy.[107] She never became a fallen woman but went on to have two children and was married for forty-five years to the same person. Nonetheless, there is a disjunction between the utter sadness and utter violence expressed in "Los 'huérfanos.'" The tension in the moment where the father moves from being a memory to being completely absent wreaks revenge on the girl's body, condemning her to death, sexual decay, and deterioration of all kinds. It laments Enrique's incapacity to shape the girl's gendered morality as a patriarchal father.

The son, on the other hand, has the good fortune of meeting what the narrative describes as "a true anarchist, an old friend of his father, of the unjustly abandoned father and from him he learned beautiful egalitarian ideas."[108] Such privilege, while represented as completely innocent and by chance, epitomizes core Mexican cultural values about masculinized forms of moral superiority while highlighting feminine Malinche-esque tendencies for betrayal and deception. But the solution to all of this is true anarchy and the dissolution of Church power, the equilibrium that could liberate the young woman just as much as the young man in the destruction of bourgeois society. That just and free world would be without

> famous priests of "pure, pure love," who whored girls out at a young age; where the beloved little sisters of the others, educated, rationally, not by milkers of anarchy, but by the true anarchists, reach their full development and conscientiously seek the satisfaction of their needs when their nature demands it; where the authoritarian and brutal father would no longer exist and relinquish his position to the consent-

ing man who understands and practices the great respect that a father owes his children, given that he forces them to be born without their consent; where the daughter laden with tender progeny and isolated by inevitable circumstances from her partner's support, saw herself forced by economic issues to slavishly obey with shameful weakness, the autocratic orders of a thoughtless and anarchist father.[109]

Almost a word-for-word transference from the previous editorials by Araujo and Enrique's own January *testimonio*, the fable replays the scenario of his betrayal by Rómulo, who used his daughter and Enrique's children as bargaining chips in a personal quest for power. Deflecting the sexual prostitution of young girls onto the Church instead of their mothers thinly distanced the story from Enrique's personal narrative. He again criticized free love, stating it was the undoing of young innocent girls and daughters, propagated by male milkers of "true anarchism." The irony here is that Enrique was not a true anarchist either; he was against free love except when it suited his own needs and desires. Enrique relied on the same metaphors he used to critique dictator Díaz's stranglehold on Mexico to suggest that his former father-in-law also subscribed to brutal authoritarianism. He also questioned Rómulo's commitment to anarchism, indicating that he was not "true" but was a "milker" of ideology. Thus, Enrique, through "Los 'huérfanos,'" blamed Rómulo to justify the abandonment of his wife and young children and to reinforce the PLM cause. However, the similarities are uncanny. How did Enrique reconcile the hatred of Rómulo to justify the misogyny related to his ex-wife and young daughter when anarchism supposedly allotted a place for women within the PLM and his heart?

In contrast to Enrique's representation of Margarita, Práxedis Carmona was a student at Long Beach Junior College who graduated in 1933 and served as the president of the International Club in 1931 and was part of the college Y Club—he indeed was an educated man just like his father.[110] Thus, based on the forgiveness granted to the son and not the daughter in this fable, anarchism did not readily translate into a feminism that treated women as sexual equals. Instead, when women strayed from the PLM gender ideology of being supportive wives, mothers, and daughters to revolutionaries, they were condemned as disloyal.

As "Los 'huérfanos'" and the editorials "¡Que viva la anarquía!" and "Paula Carmona" demonstrate, there was indeed a sexual and gendered double standard for women whom junta leaders believed had betrayed the movement, especially if they were the intimate partners of junta leaders. Sexuality and sexual denigration in immoral behavior were used by the junta, most notably Ricardo and Enrique Flores Magón, to further condemn those who had emotionally hurt them most.[111] In a later interview, such disdain is further directed at Paula and Rómulo by Nicolás T. Bernal, when he stated that "Paula divorced Enrique, forced by her father, who sold her to a Japanese owner of some vegetable gardens in San Pedro, not far from Los Angeles. Just like that, Enrique never saw those children again."[112] Paula's family, on the contrary, states that she was not trafficked but met her second husband in 1914 while they were both working at a hotel in Los Angeles. Carl Nakashima's naturalization papers state that they married on March 3, 1914.[113] After they married, they ran an ice cream shop called the Bon Ton at the Long Beach Pike until the sugar shortage of World War I. They later bought land in Long Beach and discovered oil on their property, which explains the ongoing PLM disdain for Paula because she married a Japanese capitalist—she was politically dead to them.[114] Nonetheless, the PLM supporters narrated what happened as a personal betrayal for political power to configure these intimacies within racism. Paula never had a chance to tell her side of the story, and we should take PLM representations of the betrayal as evidence of their capacity to control a particular historical narrative about revolutionary masculinity and its potential vulnerabilities. Bernal's exaggeration represented the core of the PLM's beliefs about authoritarianism, while the anti-Japanese racism toward her immigrant husband only demonstrates just how loyal PLM members were to Enrique, even long after Paula and Rómulo left the movement. Nonetheless, what Enrique and colleagues narrated as a betrayal was still an example of how women's political and sexual potency, just like Enrique's 1913 "divorce" from Paula (represented as obedience to her father), demonstrated the shifting standards of what constituted PLM anarchist women's belonging. Paula's family further stated that she married Carl of free will and had the blessing of her father, especially after Enrique abandoned her and his children for the cause.[115]

After publishing his denunciations of Paula, Enrique and the PLM had moved on from the Carmona family's betrayal of the PLM, even while he was still in prison. But there still was residual resentment toward the Carmonas and lingering effects from Teresa's first marriage to Santiago Beleno Villapando. Enrique and the PLM's denunciations were published well into Enrique's relationship with Teresa as evidence of his total separation from his former wife, their children, and her father, in addition to his complete destruction of the evidence of their existence. Paula moved forward as well, becoming a woman who raised her eight children, six of whom would be interned during World War II with their father.[116] Nonetheless, to erase the existence of Paula, Práxedis, Margarita, and Demófilo Carmona de Flores Magón is to rewrite Enrique's life partnership with Teresa Arteaga de Flores Magón as what Doris Sommer would call "foundational fiction": "Even when things end badly . . . the infallible justice meted out produces a kind of readerly happiness derived from satisfaction with the book's and the country's, narrative logic."[117] The rewritten life story in the 1954 biography *Peleamos contra la injusticia* hands down a judicious solution for the Mexican nation that makes Teresa Arteaga the originary mother of the revolution, not Paula Carmona. When one looks closely, however, there are crags and fissures in that foundation: the mother of the children named for revolutionary figures Margarita Magón, Práxedis Guerrero, and the *Demófilo* newspaper are as absent from Enrique Flores Magón's life history as is their absconded mother Paula Carmona.

In her later life, Paula refused to speak about her marriage to Enrique and what happened, which has made the history very one-sided up to this point.[118] Instead, the nationally endorsed revisionist history posits Enrique as *padre* of the nation, *padre de familia*, with six children and Teresa as the inheritors of the revolutionary legacy. As the first person to write about the Paula Carmona biography in intricate detail, I, as Olcott, Vaughan, and Cano have also argued, am not surprised that what has come before shows how "patriarchy is nothing if not an endless strategy of concealment."[119] This history has been sitting under a misleading, state-endorsed masculinist narrative of triumph all along that Enrique himself altered to his benefit. To conceal a history of women and nation within the PLM, there must be lies to sustain it.

Chapter 3

OUT OF BETRAYAL AND INTO ANARCHIST
LOVE AND FAMILY

The transition to a new, public relationship with Teresa Arteaga was documented in *Regeneración* in November 1913, even though Teresa's husband was dying at the time. In this chapter I detail Teresa's life history as a means of understanding both her role in the PLM and Enrique's transition to new forms of attachment and desire after his first marriage dissolved. In this context, I explore how debt and intimacy were forms by which the public-private divide did not exist in their relationship. It weaves in and out of Teresa's biography as a way to contextualize how she and Enrique, despite their relationship beginning while they were married to other people, attempted to forge the perfect family of love and respect bound in equality. And although living in the Edendale commune aided their intimacies, problems with fully embracing free love as a part of communitarian life surface in the archive. Their correspondence and his writings in *Regeneracíon* during this time period lead one to question the stability of their relationship, but we must also pay attention to how the interspersed conflicts about freeing the Texas Thirteen complicated their march toward idealized anarcho-familial bliss. These complicated familial and romantic entanglements, alongside the political and gender ideologies for which Enrique lived, created a highly mobile and flexible notion of family, sexuality, and emotional attachment, both to people and ideas.

Teresa Arteaga's Life in Brief

Teresa Arteaga was born on November 7, 1880, and died on August 31, 1963, both in Mexico City. When she arrived in Los Angeles, she immediately connected with María Brousse, the sister of her mother, Adelaida Brousse. Given María's immigration history, it is likely that María's and Adelaida's families reunited in 1901.[1] The 1910 census states that Teresa's first husband, James (Santiago), arrived to the US in 1888, and Teresa arrived in 1898. They were married in Los Angeles in 1902, when she was twenty-two years old.[2] But there is also evidence that would suggest Teresa married Santiago on account of family pressures.[3] In a 1914 letter in which María offered to help Teresa find work in Los Angeles, María says to give kisses to the children, her sister, and Santiago (which meant Teresa's first husband was still alive), although she says nothing of Enrique despite the 1913 announcement that Teresa was already his *compañera* and using his last name while he was in jail.[4]

These were unconventional women for the Progressive Era. They were not bound by white Protestant ideas of controlling passion; instead, their extended notions of politics and family mapped their networks differently. Some of them, like María Brousse, were deeply committed, like Emma Goldman and her anarchist comrades, to free love. But in the case of Enrique and Teresa, it's a bit more complicated. I've intentionally separated the chapters on Paula Carmona and Teresa Arteaga, subjects that are thinly represented in PLM historiography compared to male counterparts, despite the fact that the bulk of Enrique's life and correspondence were with Teresa, focusing on both PLM activities and the family they shared. Even Emma Pérez's excellent chapter on PLM third-space feminists in *The Decolonial Imaginary* mentions Teresa only in a cursory manner, compared to the actions of her aunt María. In line with María, they were "revolutionists, activists, and journalists," but because of the direct action María took with Ricardo, Teresa, like Enrique, is relegated to a secondary historical role.[5] Teresa was nonetheless essential to this affective history and to the PLM more broadly, which is why the transition out of what Enrique and the PLM articulate as a betrayal into idealized family and love hinged on her and her children.

In a 1901 letter to Adelaida, María states that she left her two children (Lucía and Pedro)[6] with her so that María could pursue political activity. She remarks that her landlady, Sra. Blanco, was constantly complaining about the fact that she was an unwed mother and harboring Ricardo in her house—clearly this annoyed María enough for her to complain about it to Adelaida.[7] In the same letter, she sends love to Teresa, Santiago, and the family. Given the unconventional standard María set with her relationships and network-based child rearing and given that Teresa's mother, Adelaida, migrated without her father, Pasqual, Teresa witnessed the various ways in which relationships and families could be made.[8] Those examples authorized unconventional notions of family, which included anarchism and some gender flexibility. A January 23, 1913, letter from María to Teresa says to give regards to Santiago and her sister Adelaida.[9]

Exactly when Teresa became a widow is unclear. The November 28, 1913, issue of *Regeneración* announced her as Enrique's compañera, yet a March 20, 1914, letter from Lucía Norman to Teresa discusses that Santiago is so sick that he is unable to work, meaning that Teresa and Enrique were involved while her husband and the father of her children was dying.[10] This would have been a normalized relationship under the banner of anarchist free love, and in one letter Enrique explains how impossible the situation was, for he loved Santiago like a brother but that other women got in the way.[11]

Nicolás T. Bernal, a friend of Ricardo, says that Santiago died in 1915 but that Teresa's involvement with the PLM, and most likely that of Santiago, started in 1905.[12] Enrique claims that Teresa became interested in the PLM upon discovering an issue of *Regeneración* in 1904 in the port of San Pedro.[13] This was shortly after she had married Santiago. By 1905, she had answered a call to help sustain the paper. With this account, Teresa boasted that she had the original issue of *Regeneracíon* in her archive.[14] Upon joining the junta in 1905, Teresa began running messages for the Liberal Party and, according to Enrique, saved his and Ricardo's lives multiple times.[15] Enrique's 1958 autobiography states that Teresa was a messenger for Ricardo, working under the name Teresa Tellez, to protect the family while he conducted other activities in Los Angeles.[16] Both Teresa and María participated in the anti-reelectionist campaigns and drummed up socialist support for the PLM.[17] Enrique also stated that Teresa agitated for his release from McNeil Island when he served time there from 1912 to 1914 while he was still married to Paula.

In her marriage to Santiago, a cook, Teresa had six children: Esperanza, Hortencia (1901–6), Estela, Santiago, José, and Pedro. Esperanza married and died in Los Angeles; Santiago, the oldest of the boys, died in a transit accident in the streets of Bucareli. He was still alive and living with Teresa and the rest of the children according to the 1920 census.[18] With Enrique, Teresa had one child, Enrique Jr.

Trouble in the Commune, 1914–1917

Before Santiago's death in 1915 and after Enrique's release from McNeil Island on January 19, 1914, Enrique; Teresa and her children; Ricardo and his partner, María Brousse; Lucía Norman and her boyfriend, Raúl Palma; Blas Lara; Librado and Conchita Rivera; and other anarchists rented five acres of land at 2325 Ivanhoe Avenue, moved the *Regeneración* offices there, and called the commune Edendale (now Silverlake and Echo Park).[19] Situated among a large artist and communist community, it became a haven for the radical Left in Los Angeles. As Daniel Hurewitz notes in *Bohemian Los Angeles*, sleepy and small Edendale became a hotbed of alternative notions of family created by artistic, radical, sexual, and political activity, and it became the gay-infused Silverlake area in subsequent decades.[20] It was also home to a number of Hollywood movie studios because of its geographic seclusion.

Similar to its peer commune founded by the Flores Magón socialist ally Job Harriman, Llano del Rio, the Edendale commune came to fruition in 1914. Ethyl Duffy Turner documented that the location was within a eucalyptus grove with many fruit trees, sheep, goats, and chickens. It was rather pastoral, with about a dozen men and women living in the commune.[21] However, Enrique's autobiography states that a total of thirty-six people lived there: ten male laborers and the rest women and children.[22] It was a modest place, with small dwellings and the *Regeneración* offices in two small *jacales* (shacks) in the *bajío* (lower part) of the property.[23] These poor dwellings contrasted greatly with the stately mansion of female impersonator and film star Julian Eltinge, who built his villa on Edendale Ridge.[24] The members of the commune often shifted housing arrangements across buildings in order to protect them from outside attack.[25] They used their dog, Teodora (named after Ricardo and Enrique's father), as a means of protection, for she was not only their pet but also the night watch when various people were spying on their political activities.[26] Enrique noted that he slept with a Winchester .30–30 rifle on his nightstand and could hear the smallest movement because their lives were so highly surveilled.

Working and living communally, they were close to Keystone and Paramount, some of the first movie studios in Los Angeles. With these ultimate markers of capitalism standing ironically nearby, they cultivated the land and sold vegetables in Plaza de Olvera in downtown Los Angeles (La Plaza de los Mexicanos). Connected by the streetcar line, the area afforded tremendous mobility to PLM political activities around the city. Their ideology was based on anarcho-communism and creating an ideal society outside of capitalism. Such communes also advocated giving up personal property, which was already in alignment with the PLM exiles, for Ricardo argued that they should "kill the right to private property."[27] Historian William Estrada notes that the PLM collective adhered to communal and sexual equality, enlivening their struggle with public dances, *mitins* (political rallies), publishing, picnics, musical concerts, dramatic readings, and selling their farm produce.[28] The daily rhythms of communal labor had to be established, and each person had to contribute to the ongoing life of the commune. In 1946 Enrique noted that "in our colony, we worked for the benefit of all, in common, and principally to maintain our beloved *Regeneración*. Ricardo my brother, Librado Rivera and José Flores and myself, worked the land in the hours when it was not hot; and when the sun heated up Ricardo and I dedicated ourselves to writing articles and correspondence . . . while the rest dedicated themselves to printing or working on circulation for the paper."[29] As the men of the commune engaged in manual and intellectual labor, the women and children engaged in reproductive labor. Even though the political project was grounded in the idea that one could create space for the comingling of personal passion, political activity, and sexuality, gendered divisions of labor remained intact.

To demonstrate the level of sacrifice that was made on behalf of workers by PLM junta members in the Edendale commune, Enrique later explained:

> The comrades of other races and other nations, that came to visit us in the commune we had formed in Los Angeles California always expressed enormous surprise to find us living in such vile misery, making a life out of constant sacrifice, all to sustain the newspaper: to the point that we, on occasion, would go out and work or we worked cultivating the land so that we could earn money and not be weighted by the newspaper, we maintained the custom to put all the earnings of the hands of Librado Rivera and he distributed it equally between all the houses that formed our commune, the small money we earned, cutting expenses to the bone so that we could permanently and always open the coffers to sustain *Regeneración*.[30]

Although the commune was a space for families, those families worked in dire poverty for "the Idea." Putting the newspaper before their own material comfort meant that everyone in the commune was dedicated to sacrifice as the ethos of practice. Edendale provided PLM members a chance to practice anarchism in raising children, so they thought they were training a new generation of leaders ensuring longevity and self-determination as a political act. This had a definite impact on Enrique and Teresa's children, for many of them disidentified with the PLM struggle later in life because they were so poor, even if their family benefited from the prestige and social capital derived from it, which I discuss in chapter 7. The children took up middle-class lives far distanced from the enforced poverty they grew up in.

Geographically close to downtown Los Angeles and its Mexican communities, the commune's members tried to make their agricultural designs and the men's manual labor funded their existence (Enrique worked for the Van Vorst Manufacturing Company, *Regeneración*, and the movement). They collectively worked the land and their newspaper in line with their revolutionary ideologies. At the time, the family consisted of Teresa, five children, and an "uncle," which was Teresa's dying husband, Santiago.[31] Nonetheless, a cultivated sense of sacrifice for the workers' cause dominated Enrique's writings during this period, along with his sacrifice for love and family. In many instances, those concepts could not be separated. In fact, there was a real *mando* (a mandate, almost religious in nature, though anarchists are atheists) or innate sense of sacrifice to the point that death was a natural part of people's destiny who belonged to the movement. Sacrifice was a normalized perspective of self-determination sought by Enrique and his circle. And this carried over into the profundity of his love letters to Teresa Arteaga, but even this should be examined closely, for their relationship was uneven. For example, a letter dated 1914 and typed on *Regeneración* stationery demonstrates the intersectional nature of sacrifice and love. The letter was written before the July 4, 1914, edition of *Regeneración* was printed—he would author three articles for the issue. After being unable to focus on his work, he wrote the following:

> I set, well, aside, my slave chains of liberty, and even that if for a moment, to soothe my conscience, and also to quiet that little square letter from last Sunday. It is true, my life, what I told you in my previous letter: I love you. I wish you could see into the depths of my heart that you could read even my smallest thought, that my yearnings, my aspirations, my desires, are those of you being my dear life partner, the beloved little treasure whom I support in the bitter hours of life, and who gives me enough strength in turn with her coveted charity and her loving attention.
>
> I want, Tere of mine, that you and I join our lives together, for our experience of what the world serves us to understand each other better, to identify with each other more until our two aspirations, desires,

and hopes come to form a single aspiration, a single desire, a single hope; that of being united forever, devoted to each other and always affectionate, attentive, and caring, and loving.[32]

Poetics and passion dominate the correspondence. The repetition of diminutives (*cariños*) closes the physical distance between Teresa and Enrique even as they are living together. The anaphora only heightens the sense of passion: the desire is for the two of them to become one body, one heart, one aspiration, and one hope. But this is not a joining that relies on an institution like matrimony. Rather, it is a desire for proximity that is political in nature. As a "slave to liberty," Enrique's devotions to country, cause, and Teresa are one and the same. He is a willing slave to justice and a relationship that is attentive and fortifying. Instead of delineating Teresa as a mere object of desire, he locates her in a shared poetic vision of the future, a desiring subject in her own right, unified through those "chains" of the revolution. Pleasure is realized in the expression of mutual love, mutual proximity, and an about-face from female passivity. Here, identification is about equality, not female passivity or masculine domination. Enrique is the nervous one, the one who dreams from the bottom of his heart.

Although the family life and marriage mandated by the state were far too invasive for their anarchist sensibility, Enrique's separation from Teresa and her children always produced a longing for connection and, I would argue, a desire for a normative home life. Teresa's mandate, in turn, was a responsibility to the revolution as mother and activist. The flexible nature of the commune made free love an option. Having a compañera (partner) and activist relationship with Enrique while her husband was dying had an effect on those times of separation and their interactions as a blended family. At times, their correspondence admonished other anarchist unions, often referred to as a "free love marriage . . . in accordance with the anarchist decree" that made all notions of unconventional family politically uneven.[33] In fact, one could argue that this tension with anarchist ideology represents what Sonia Hernández has called the "modern domestic language to define the new . . . modern Mexican woman from both sides of the border. Gender inequity remained, but was framed in a new modern context."[34] Even though the PLM and Enrique advocated for women's equality in the PLM movement, the personal letters, as they responded to conflict with his chosen partner Teresa, were laden with tension. The desire for a normative home life as a domesticated form of femininity and masculinity for two activists, despite the publicly espoused radical family, shows inconsistency in how they practiced sexual and gender relations.[35] Given the transitory nature of his constant movements to evade authorities or his absences because of work (Enrique often worked long hours at a nursery doing manual labor in La Puente),[36] longing for a normative home life was a logical response. This was counterintuitive and contradictory to their critique of women's inequality under capitalism and the eschewing of marriage (a form of slavery).

In the same letter, Enrique wrote the following:

> I dream of a happy home, tranquil, honored, in which to find yourself as my dear companion whom to love with every fiber of my being, and to be loved by, whom to care for, and from whom to be cared for, whom to coddle and from whom to be coddled.... And I dream, I dream a lot, so much, my darling Terita; so very much!
>
> It is enough to dream of that joy—(I do not know what to say, if by disgrace or by fortune)—I am a dreamer, and for this reason I possess a ridiculously romantic soul. Hence comes so much longing to be by your side. And hence comes, perhaps, that I am a fighter; well—being romantic, I am terribly sensitive, and because of this, I cannot turn a blind eye and instead remain at eye level with the miseries, anguish, and pains of those from below.[37]

Stating that he is a dreamer four times in two paragraphs, the desire, whether for disgrace or fortune, is to be at her side in a tranquil, honored, shared home. Counter to the *ama de casa* (housewife principle) of elite Porfirian women of the early twentieth century, this is a home imagined with Teresa not as the center of feminized reproductive labor but as the center of love. This letter emotionally labors to construct and maintain a family in a moment of physical absence. And that such acts like *mimados* (coddling or spoiling) move a bit outside the bounds of communitarianism preached by the junta, they produce an emotional and sexual force that is unbounded by the discipline of institutions. These private mimados heighten the emotional attachment and baroque nature of the prose in expressing modern anarchist love. Coveting the intensity of the relationship, Enrique still cannot disengage from the fact that he is "at eye-level with miseries, anguishes, and pains of those from below."[38] The vexed nature of desire for freedom of *los de abajo* (those from below) and desire for romantic love are constantly negotiated and debated in letters to Teresa. They are what Kelsey Williams has called "the dynamics of desire and arousal that can result from oppression and domination."[39] In linking his desire for Teresa with the anguish of the proletariat, a dramatic tension is mounted in causality with oppression. In other words, the oppression that the junta organizers, the working classes, and those repressed by the Porfiriato in Mexico and abroad experienced intensified their passions, sexual desires, and role as agents in a struggle against tyranny. To love with intensity and passion was an affront to the contained sensibilities of a crumbling capitalist state of traitors who sold their souls for commerce and the sacrificing of the lives of their fellow countrymen. Emotion was the currency the junta traded in, not material objects. Emotion was the ultimate anticapitalist expression because it did not have material value in the marketplace.

But their unconventional relationship was complicated by the fact that Teresa's husband was still alive. Early in the letter, Enrique states this:

> My darling, for you I have come suffering by natural evolution. The story is short. My sympathizing first; thus, neither you nor I were free and therefore, my sympathy for you could not go beyond what happened, a simple friendship. Even though I would have been free in that I would have dared loving you, if it had not impossible to avoid it, I would have prevented you from knowing, not only because I loved Santiago fraternally as a good comrade, but because I maintain and profess that a true anarchist must never concern himself in the slightest with the cost of the sadness of a third person.[40]

Although Santiago was both part of their circle as a comrade and dying, Enrique described his love as an inevitability, like an extension of anarchism. The logic demonstrates that even though both of them were "unavailable" (in partnerships with other people), the intimacy forged in the anarchist sense allowed Enrique to love her, and it helped their intimacies if Santiago was a believer in free love.

Using excess and sentimentality in proclaiming the romantic love part of the cause, Enrique's discourse justifies their intimacies even though her husband was still alive:

> Time passed. I saw you again. The good comrade he was, and happy, since he had returned to our Mother Nature what she had lent him. But you, all alone, without your companion of your soul, without the moral support of a man that would understand you and adore you, came to this city. I saw you crying; it was here in María's kitchen. You were laughing, spirited and strong, but when you were reminded of your neglect, poor little thing! Would you see the heartbreak that entered me as well? And something else entered your soul in those moments:

in those instants, that empathy had turned into merely friendship, opened a wide groove in my heart, and the hand of your pain planted the seed of love those tears of yours were the fecundating risk that made the first bud of love arise.[41]

In recounting the story of their love and partnership, this letter is slightly different from the many others written over the twenty-plus years of exile and incarceration. Addressing Teresa as a comrade, the retelling of their early encounters in María Brousse's kitchen casts them as being founded upon an anarchist platonic admiration for the cause. For a woman about to be widowed with five children of her own, the junta and commune were spaces of unparalleled intimacy and interaction because of dedication to the cause and the outside surveillance of the group. At the same time, women like Teresa were often confined to secondary roles in the movement because of the domestic mandate that Hernández has framed as a form of anarcho-syndicalist modern femininity. Public ideologies drew women like Teresa into the movement and perhaps were the point of attraction, but they were still marked by "a gendered rhetoric whereby women were promoted as partners, supporters, *compañeras*, but not as individuals capable of independent action."[42] Enrique's intensive expressions of emotion, while tracing a genealogy of comrade relations that became romantic love relations, differentiate their union. The letter is nevertheless evidence of Teresa's taking independent action to separate, distance, and critique the inequity of their relationship. It is also evidence that Enrique still suffered from his severed relationship with Paula Carmona.

The kinship and intimacy shared in these circles, argues Claudio Lomnitz, was expressed in nicknames and created a sense of family and affection among the comrades.[43] And perhaps those intimate ties that lingered from the fallout with his ex-father-in-law and ex-wife, expressed in the 1914 letter, were too much for Teresa to bear in building a family with Enrique. Thus, this letter represents the desiring position to be "the dear companion of your soul." By reproducing the patriarchal language of gender differentiation, they redefined notions of romance and anarchist attachment. Enrique provided a historical narrative, from his perspective, with expressions of early intimacy to show a budding attraction that could be furthered only by making the desire about ideas and not corporeality. He conjoins what Pérez has identified as activist and compañera.[44] Without discussing his own body or that of Teresa, another body is incorporated into the discourse, that of Mother Nature, and perhaps Santiago's corpse. The inclusion is curious.

In stating that "he had returned to our Mother Nature what she had lent him. But you, all alone, without the companion of your soul, without . . . the moral support of a man that would understand you and adore you, came to this city. I saw you crying," Enrique articulates major losses. Subtly gesturing to Santiago's dying marks a deep emotional shift. Mother Nature was going to or had taken something borrowed from them. Given that the letter has no date, the reference to something borrowed or taken could refer to comrade Santiago's life or a miscarriage, and however much Enrique loved or adored Teresa and her children, she was alone when the loss happened.

Just six months after his release from McNeil, a July 1914 photo of them with Teresa's son José is evidence of moving on (see figure 3.1). The photo focuses directly on Enrique and José's closeness, but it does much to demonstrate Enrique's role as a father. It also documents their relationship while Santiago was dying. This family snapshot serves as both an intimate portrait and a highly public document, deeply meaningful to those involved but less transparent to peers or the government.[45] The photo, like the letter, was unusual, especially given that both were living in a North Los Angeles commune together when they were produced. It projects what Campt has called "an affective material practice that constructs and reproduces family not necessarily as it was, but rather as it would like to be seen."[46] Given that the photo was snapped in 1914, before Santiago had died, the vision of Teresa, Enrique, and José as a family projects a continuous narrative of their partnership that makes them the originary foundational couple of the PLM.[47] It also displays anarchist, comrade familialism as a shared political unit of care. In other words, this photo imagines them as a family before they were actually a family or, rather, while they reconfigured their families together through the ideology of the Edendale commune. With the communal living, whether Santiago had knowledge of the romantic relationship or not, they are a family by virtue of their anarchist ethos and in the way this image operates. This letter, like the photo, had a much greater significance than simply supporting Teresa in their shared loss. That Santiago's death could have made Enrique so distracted from work that he wrote a letter despite cohabitating with someone speaks to the separation experienced through the labor of revolution and his absence. His role as a "man that would understand and adore her since she made the sacrifice of moving to the city" acknowledged Teresa's physical, emotional, and familial sacrifice in uprooting her children to create an intentional anarchist family. Moreover, he acknowledged her crying not as feminine excess but as a real expression of warranted grief.

FIG 3.1. Teresa Arteaga, Enrique Flores Magón, and José Beleno de Flores Magón, Bonnie Brae Street, Los Angeles, July 1914. Courtesy of Eugenia Flores Magón.

From the letter, it appears Teresa had thought about leaving Enrique and the cause:

> With an honorable bunch of young players, I tell you that I am fully convinced that no one will be able to dispute the affection I have for you; I want to tell you that no one will have enough power to take away my love; NO ONE. I have surrendered myself to you. Trusting in your honor, I have deposited in your dear hands my sensitive and affectionate heart and I only dare to beg of you, my adored Tere, that you do all that is at your part, everything that you can to conserve it always. I plead to you like this because I do not want to lose you, little darling of my soul. I feel that my life is tied to yours, my happiness founded in yours, my entire being strongly bound to yours, your love forming a part of me, and losing you would be to me a severe blow, terrible, annihilating.

Begging for acknowledgment of the depths of his love, Enrique reinforces the idea that no one but he has sufficient love for Teresa. But what would make her doubt such love? Given the bohemian and transitory life in anarchist circles, love relations were not based on fidelity, yet the tone of this letter would suggest fidelity was at issue. At this juncture, given Santiago's death, or a miscarriage, the *golpe rudo* (rude awakening) of being emotionally abandoned, why did this require three typed pages of eternal love and devotion? In depositing his heart with Teresa, other physical transgressions could be transcended. If infidelity, overwork, a pregnancy loss, or Santiago's death was a by-product of separations and sacrifices embodied in the suffering of giving one's life to the revolution, this letter demonstrates the great lengths that Enrique went to in salvaging the familial and filial relationship with Teresa. It depends on the feminine capacity to be a forgiving and supportive compañera and also on the condition that his passionate words were enough to ease any tensions.

Family, whether anarchist, national, or nuclear, however anticapitalist Enrique might have been, was of the utmost importance in convincing Teresa of his dedication. His words demonstrate how principles of women's equality were a mere theory and did not apply equally to junta leaders in their partnerships:

> I want, in the end, beloved Tere, that in your dear little heart you dedicate a little place beside the love that you have for Adelaida and for our young sons, not even give shelter forever, if it is possible, to the great affection and sincere and honest love that I feel for you, and I will

know, helped by you, how to make it everlasting forever, and forever dedicated to no one else but you.

Locating dedication in the family and through bonds of love for their children or her love for her mother, Adelaida, Enrique asks for space in her heart, suggesting that he was at least, for that moment, shut out of Teresa's affections. It also shows how he relied on romanticism to reconcile misunderstandings and past wrongs.

Enrique's 1914 letter petitions for her divine and mortal intervention of honest love, vowing dedication to her alone. This is counter to the idea of free love preached by most anarchists of the period in southern California.[48] With the same baroque prose, the argument is given one last big breath in the closing paragraphs of the love-and-forgiveness manifesto:

> What I have told you is adjusted to the truth. I do not know how to swear, given that I am not religious but I preserve in my life two things that are my pride: my mother and my honor. And so, by the sacred memory of my mother, I assure you that I have spoken with sincerity, honesty, without duplicity, without bringing a heated end. I respect, like I say, my honor, and for that cause, I add ultimately, not even playing, do I give my word of honor falsely under oath. Take, well, today, my word of honor that I am sincere in expressing to you my feelings, and that, upon asking you as I do, with all the strength of my being, that you be my life partner, I do so because I am convinced that I will know how to love you forever and be completely faithful forever "as best as I can be, that is, be a good man, so far as my defects of being human allow me; but I will always do everything possible to be as perfect as a human being I can be."
>
> If regrettably, you were not to believe me in my words, or that, at the very least, you were to have some doubt, I place in you my life as a fighter to guarantee that I act honorably towards you. My life is under public dominion; I can say that I have no private life, the acts of my life that are not unknown by anyone.
>
> Additionally, with my constancy in the struggle, I will guarantee constancy in my love for you. The unwavering will to face the dangers of death, incarceration that undermines my health or the miseries and endless persecutions to serve an Idea guarantee for you, and our unbreakable love. I will love you always.

Even though the entreaties are "adjusted to the truth," the prose is tremendously doubtful, overemphasizing the depth of commitment and love. Despite the declaration "I preserve in my life two things that are my pride: my mother and my honor," it might have been too much. There is nothing equivalent, culturally, to swearing on the grave of a venerated mother of Mexican revolutionaries. Invoking Margarita Magón's memory is the ultimate gesture for cementing the sincerity of Enrique's word. But taking into account his past history of altering documents about his previous relationship with Paula, we have to question his motivations with Teresa as well. By juxtaposing the memory of a dead mother with honor, Enrique mobilizes some of the most potent and sacred symbols possible for a Mexican anarchist deploying masculinist rhetoric of vulnerability and valor. Approaching the apology without malice ("sin llevar un fin torrido"), the appeals don't actually apologize but instead defer to future behavior, where he is "as best as I can be, that is, be a good man, so far as my defects of being human allow me; but I will always do everything possible to be as perfect as a human being I can be," relying on redundancy to reinforce that he means what he says.

Enrique asks for Teresa to take him at his word. If there were other women in the picture, which commune life would have dictated, then he would absolutely need to defer to future behavior as the salve. The circular logic of the letter does not rely on sensual femininity or female subordination but heightened masculine repentance, sentimentality, and vulnerability. Enrique again returns to the struggle for freedom and its link to the struggle that is the relationship with Teresa: "With my constancy in the struggle, I will guarantee constancy in my love for you." And even because their separation of an emotional nature was related to the revolution taking precedent over the family, the interjection of another person in a sexual encounter, a miscarriage, or the death of a spouse, Enrique cannot imagine his life with Teresa without the revolution. The intensity of experience, proximity to death and incarceration, poor health, and a lack of privacy, all for the sake of an "Idea," made all worth living for. Once more, there was no such thing as a private life with him because every movement, every intimacy, every desire was basically under scrutiny and observation because of his politics and history of contesting the Díaz regime: he was spied upon constantly. Thus, to declare "My life is under public dominion; I can say that I have no private life, the acts of my life that are not unknown by anyone" is to complicate the notion of intimacy as a public one. Whereas the demands of having a family and an intimate relationship in an anarchist framework should have been communal, Enrique's entreaties to Teresa desire a more private, intimate, and unmonitored relationship. The lack of privacy and the openness of the relationship also suggest a strategic cue to maintain silence and secrets, as much as permitted, within the structure of the family and the movement. Although the letter is a private declaration to fix any ill will, misconception, sexual misstep, or loss, it nonetheless is always already compromised by the heightened context of surveillance that made intimacy almost impossible for these noncitizen Mexican revolutionaries. The "Idea," though noble, carries with it trauma and loss, and the potential for a future filled with more losses, including loss of love and self. The circular nature of the arguments in this love letter gain force when contextualized in the appropriative power of surveillance and its ability to destroy trust, love, and the "Idea."

Layered with the atonement letter to Teresa is a love poem, doubling the emotional labor to maintain his family and sustain the PLM movement. The time line for the poem falls within the fierce and intense dedication to promoting the freedom of the Texas Thirteen on Enrique's part, dated July 5, 1914, the day of the Gran Mitin at La Plaza de los Mexicanos in downtown Los Angeles. "Como a Nadie" has six four-line stanzas:

Tere, my Tere, beloved Tere
The darling yearned for by my heart
My heart loves only you
I adore you with unparalleled passion

Triumphant over all women
Victory touched your palm
Love no longer exists for other beings
Beyond you, inside my soul

You suffered last night, from your eyes tears
Rolled down your beloved cheeks
I also suffered, if you would only see how much! . . .
How much I suffered, my beloved dear Teresa

Your tears fell, drop by drop
Until filling my heart with pain
Instead of ending on a high note
Bitterness presided over our dinner

But it was not in vain, my dear Teresa
The pain our beings suffered
Well today I can say without falseness
That who I have loved the most, my dear good, is you

> I can tell you now honorably
> Without my lips being stained with lies
> That no one have I loved so profoundly
> Whom my soul loves, desires and breathes.[49]

Of note is the metaphorical contest over Enrique's heart in which Teresa was the triumphant victor above "todas las mujeres." Though metaphorical in quality, sexual encounters with other women were almost certain given the communal living arrangements guided by free love. Given the previous letter of atonement, it appears that free love was available to men like Enrique until Teresa threatened to leave him. As Pérez notes, "These anarchists sanctioned free and spiritual love" but had a restricted vision.[50] Returning to the notion of intensified sensation and desire attached to the Flores Magón brothers, it made Enrique and Ricardo objects of attraction within PLM circles. Thus, the interpretive possibility of what unknowingly is "de la victoria te tocó la palma" (a touching victory for her hand) is, if read in reverse, a contest. To be the victor implies competition. Competition implies multidirectional desires and being a love object for many. This poem extends the apology of the previous letter, but it does so on a tenuous foundation by foregrounding a battle between women over Enrique or, at minimum, evidence of multiple sexual partners. But this appears to be the last battle Teresa won in terms of Enrique's heart; all the letters after this one indicate a solid emotional foundation and no other external sexual relations. And even though the poem references a terrible dinner because of another woman in the commune, Enrique and Teresa had moved on from this period of intimate strife: Santiago's death, the other women, and imprisonment to work for a common goal of an anarchist life in the Edendale commune. As they struggled with ideas about gender ideology, sexual fluidity, and collective responsibility in the commune, those ideals were tested in Teresa and Enrique's intimate partnership.

With the crisis behind them, Teresa sent a letter to the Chicago-based Bureau of Mushroom Industry and received an emphatic reply on June 12, 1915. Addressed to Teresa V. Magón of Los Angeles, and no doubt referring to a newspaper advertisement from 1915 that guaranteed fast profits and immediate crops, the intimate conflict of 1914 had been resolved: the evidence is in Teresa's continued use of the last name Magón without hesitation. The letter explains how success in the mushroom industry is so simple that women and children can do it. However, the most important part of the gimmick is that the mushroom spawn needs to be purchased from the

Bureau of Mushroom Industry. General Manager E. E. Hiss, who signed the letter, stated the following:

> We suggest that you send for 25 bricks, per $600 and sufficient for a bed of 200 square feet, or say 10 × 20 ft. You will be surprised at the profit made possible in a small bed of this size. With every first order of spawn we will supply an illustrated instruction book, "The Cultivated Mushroom," which contains expert information as to every step to take from making the bed to marketing of the product—how to sell, where to sell.... For making money or adding to your income, the small capital necessary it has no equal anywhere. This is the best time to start a mushroom business, any time is a good time.[51]

Although this letter might seem unrelated to Enrique and Teresa's intimate lives after their 1914 struggle to maintain their relationship in light of public and private pressures and losses, it marks a key moment in Teresa's enterprising spirit to support the cause: providing for the family. For a woman who was functionally literate in Spanish and English, such efforts meant taking risks and investigating economic opportunities for the junta.[52] A resourceful woman in her own right who raised five children with very little monetary support, Teresa's letter to the mushroom company demonstrates a desire to quickly derive profits from the Edendale farming commune. The economic circumstances of the commune were quite dire between December 1914 and October 1915, so the information from the mushroom company clearly did not help their cause. Pérez notes that the farm work was shared at the commune, but there is also evidence of a division of labor where men wrote the articles for *Regeneración* and women cooked, cleaned, and rolled the newspapers for distribution.[53] Thus, the mushroom scheme was a means for Teresa's children to eat because *Regeneración* fed the mind and not their bodies.

Public and Private Debts

Because gender ideology was a double standard for the men and women in the PLM junta's leadership, it did not stop masculine privileges from being exercised on Enrique's part. In between Teresa and Enrique's conflict about the stability of their relationship in the letters, photo, and poetry from 1914, he wrote fervently for *Regeneración*. Labor distribution in the Edendale commune may have been unequally divided, with the men doing the writing and women doing everything else, but debt weighed heavily on Teresa and Enrique's union and the lives of Teresa's children. For the July 11, 1914, printing of *Regeneración*, Enrique reported a deficit of $1270.23 after expenditures and income.[54] Several issues went unpublished in August and September of 1914, most likely because of insurmountable monetary debt and the emotional debt that Enrique was paying to Teresa and the family to make up for straying. Time had a monetary trade-off: one could expend time working manual-labor jobs to support the family and the newspaper. Given that the paper was at an economic standstill despite having the intellectual brainpower to produce material, Enrique's focus could naturally shift to paying off his emotional debt to Teresa. Private love was linked to publicly held debt. And although they wanted to maintain some shred of privacy, the public nature of everything they did, including shared debt, was heavy. In this issue, as in all the other issues, the *Regeneración* editors plead with the reading public:

> We hope that all comrades will do everything on their part to kill the deficit, sending their donations during this month, and coming August and September. This campaign to kill the deficit must be undertaken with determination and enthusiasm by all those who love honorable work and without fear of this newspaper. Let us be supportive, united, let us uphold REGENERACION, we will not let it die.[55]

The July 4, 1914, issue of *Regeneración*, for which Enrique produced three articles, tells of the broader political context for the tensions between him and Teresa. In addition to the fund-raiser on the US's hallowed Independence Day in Santa Paula, there was another "Gran Mitin de Protesta" slated for July 5 as well.

In preparation for the post–Independence Day "Gran Mitin de Protesta," Enrique and Teresa's relationship was tenuous at best. He was trying to hold together his intimate partnership at the same time he was trying to "kill the deficit." Both of these emotional labors were taxing and stood in stark contrast to the abandonment of Paula Carmona and his children from the previous union. In rectifying such guilt by doubly committing himself to fidelity to his life partner and his PLM-*Regeneración* families, the fury of political activity at this moment created a deep tension between Enrique's private obligations to his nuclear family and his public obligations to liberating the Texas Thirteen. With the activities in support of liberating the twelve PLM Texas Mexicans and one Wobbly conspirator who left Carrizo Springs to enter Mexico, much was afoot in the Los Angeles PLM cell. Although many considered it a pretext for their arrest, the thirteen men were chased by four law enforcement officers, who killed Silvestre Lomas with a bullet to the head. Sheriff Eugene Buck and Deputy Candelario Ortiz were taken prisoner as the men fled to Mexico. Met by law enforcement, they surrendered at Caponez and were supposed to return to Carrizo Springs. While they were sleeping, a group of vigilantes fired on them, hitting Juan Rincón Jr. The vigilantes were said to laugh while watching him die. The deputy was killed, and the prosecution targeted Jesús Rangel, Eugenio Alzalde, José Abraham Cisneros, and Charles Cline as responsible for the deputy's death and sought the death penalty by hanging. From September 13, 1913, onward, they were held in the San Antonio jail for speaking on the economic emancipation of workers. The group was celebrated by Emma Goldman's radical magazine *Mother Earth*:

> [The group was] known to every Mexican worker of the south. By their daring and devotion, they have endeared themselves to these workers. These cases offer the first opportunity that the American labor movement has had to give a practical demonstration to the Mexican worker that the American worker is not indifferent to his Mexican brother. . . . Right now, the strength of the Building Trades organization on the west coast is seriously endangered because of the influx of the Mexican worker who can do the unskilled work of the concrete worker, etc. Unless these men are organized and brought in, and made part and parcel of the American labor movement, the strength of those organizations which have been developed as a result of years of struggle is, in danger. . . . These cases offer the opportunity to make the Mexican worker realize his class solidarity, not as a Mexican worker, but as a member of the great international working class, and offer the opportunity to make the state of Texas realize that down underneath the surface of apparent social apathy and social indifference there is a great mass of workers whose demands for social justice must be heeded.[56]

That *Mother Earth* embraced the cause of the Texas Thirteen was an opportunity, especially for *Regeneración* and its editors to build cross-racial solidarities in the workers' struggle. Enrique demonstrated his renewed commitment. With early twentieth-century worker migration and upheaval because of the Mexican Revolution, the workers who could be "part and parcel of the American labor movement" were essential to unionization efforts and anarchist ideological wins against the capitalist state. Universal worker ideology incorporated the threat of Mexican scab labor taking the jobs slated for collective bargaining agreements into the IWW fold. And because, as

Emma Goldman noted, the Texas Thirteen were known to every worker of his race in the South, this was a ready-made galvanizing blueprint merging the interests of Mexican-origin and Anglo-origin anarchists and unionists. Even though the IWW only sent funds to defend Charles Cline, he was sentenced to life in prison while José Rangel was sentenced to ninety-nine years in prison, only to be pardoned in 1926. Thus, the mitin hosted by the PLM in La Plaza de los Mexicanos of Los Angeles represented a public occupation of space, doubly signifying the ways in which the oration by Blas Lara and Enrique was an ideological pursuit that allowed workers to celebrate and come together because of their oppression. While these efforts did not deliver their comrades to immediate freedom, the fervent public performances on behalf of their jailed brethren further illustrate the tensions between Enrique's private debt to Teresa and his public debt to the PLM and IWW.

Enrique's English-language column for the same issue elaborates on the Texas Thirteen's state. In "Educators and Warriors," he wrote the following:

> The Mexican Liberal party is both educator and warrior. It gives an Idea to the Mexican proletariat and, at the same time, induces him into action. An Idea, without action, is a dead useless one. Rangel, Cisneros, Alzalde and the other ten Mexican comrades who are now imprisoned in the Texan jails—unjustly charged with murder and facing the gallows or long jail sentences—are active members of the Mexican Liberal Party and therefore, are class-conscious workingmen who, either by means of the press, the word or the action, were exerting themselves to awaken the unconscious Mexican working men and to orientate them toward the conquest of their emancipation. For that reason, they were marching to Mexico to fight for Land and Liberty. . . . [N]ow in jail, after two of their comrades were brutally murdered—Silvestre Lomas and Juan Rincón Jr.—were arrested, maltreated, tortured and finally placed in jail under the elastic charge of constrictive murder.[57]

In characteristic fashion, ideas and action are treated as proper nouns. Despite the masculinist rhetoric of warriors, the role of the PLM as educator is gender neutral, subscribing to the ideology that all are included in the struggle. The ethnic-racial Mexican proletariat was represented to an English-reading public in this section of the paper, and as translator, Enrique argues that the masses of "class-conscious workingmen," embodied in the Texas Thirteen, must be primed into action like a sleeping giant. To dream of revolution is nothing without action, and like his peers at *Mother Earth*, Enrique mobilizes the context in favor of the Mexican cause, the Mexican worker in the US, the racism experienced, and inclusion into a broader US milieu of workers' rights.

In "Silencio liberticida," which is the original Spanish version of the column cited above, he argues for undoing the tension between supporting local workers' rights and the cause of the Mexican Revolution. They should not be at odds:

> Silence concerning the Mexican Revolution continues in the workers' press, the workers of the world will be caught unaware, without knowing why the Mexicans fight with weapons in hand, unaware of the economic and social drama developing in those regions, without knowing that the Mexican's fight is their own fight, and easy they are, therefore, of being surprised by the capitalist press, stirred up in their patriotic feelings and converted easily into cannon fodder, into material willing to go to conquer Mexico for their owners to rivet the chains of his brothers whose worthy and virile example should be followed by the proletariat of the whole world, to conquer by force of arms what will never be given up willingly by the powerful: Land and Liberty.[58]

This sharp critique of the press's capitalist-driven nature for workers in the US and Mexico relies on ideological imprisonment. For *tierra y libertad,* the PLM's ideological slogan of land and liberty, necessitated that all workers unite against their oppressive conditions and for the liberty to the Mexican people. To stand by and be silent was to make your comrade "cannon fodder" or was "to rivet the chains of his brothers whose worthy and virile example should be followed by the proletariat of the whole world." To do otherwise would be to conquer Mexico and its three enemies: capitalism, the Church, and authority. Calling on the workers to read between the lines, Enrique's return to the PLM slogan is a shift away from overzealous patriotism, a masculinist demand to be prepared for fighting in a world that counts on proletarian docility. To further communicate the passion for the cause for the English-speaking public, a final note punctuated the column: "Clean-cut revolutionists like our comrades in a Texas jail are badly wanted in the Labor movement. Therefore, let us not let them be hanged."[59] To say that the Texas Thirteen were "clean-cut" was to make a moral argument about the value of workers' lives and their salvation as honest men. Enrique's dedication to freeing the Texas Thirteen had an impact on his relationship with Teresa, making his debts to her all the more heavy. While there is little evidence of changes in the divisions of labor in the commune, as he and the men worked fervently on the paper while the women engaged in reproductive labor, each dedicated his or her life to the movement and the communal vision. For Teresa, that meant raising five kids in community and repairing the relationship with Enrique. For Enrique, it meant preserving the masculine privileges of intellectual and ideological labor alongside working in a nursery in La Puente for wages.

As Teresa's biography demonstrates, her relationship with the PLM predated her romantic attachment to Enrique. Although some may find fault with my method of excavating a reading of her position from Enrique's correspondence to her, these are some of the few pieces of evidence that articulate her role as political subject, revolutionary mother, and gendered patriot in freeing the proletarian masses, which included her own children from her first marriage to Santiago Beleno Villapando. Staying in the commune and staying with Enrique despite conflicts was an emotional and economic risk, so much so that the letters, poems, and photographs document the fragility of their relationship. Their relationship is further evidence of how women were expected to endure more than their male counterparts, including putting up with their sexual and emotional transgressions and "party expectations as catering wives and companions."[60] Thus, although Enrique and Teresa's emotional labor to repair and maintain a family in light of their political struggle was difficult, we still cannot ignore how the division of labor changed somewhat with the second arrest of Enrique and Ricardo in 1916.

Chapter 4

BODILY HARM

The 1916 arrest and June trial of Enrique and Ricardo for mailing "obscene literature" provide the basis of this chapter. By detailing the arrest, their time in the Los Angeles County Jail, and the aftereffects of these actions on body and soul, the chapter demonstrates how fragile emotions and bodies formed the core of PLM ideologies about masculinity and suffering at the hands of the state. The role of psychic pain and suffering ultimately represents hidden affective history during this key period in PLM history. Enrique and Ricardo's performances of gender in the courtroom and through press representations of them also point to the level of fame they had achieved, which in turn furthered the bodily harm committed against their person by authorities.

At the time of arrest at the Edendale commune, Enrique charged that he had been badly beaten by the mob who accompanied law enforcement: "The arrest of the Magons was accomplished by federal officials and others near Los Angeles at a country plant where the paper was printed. Expecting difficulties with the arrest, a large posse was sent to the scene. The two Magons submitted to arrest without a fight but charged afterward that they had been beaten while the arrest was being made. The printing press was confiscated, the Magons were tried and convicted after Enrique had recovered from his injuries."[1] Enrique and Ricardo were not above being subjected to vigilante violence. They faced the same local posses and law enforcement operations that tormented the US-Mexico border throughout the Mexican Revolution, extending border space into Los Angeles proper.[2]

From the *Regeneración* eyewitness perspective, the story of their apprehension by law enforcement provides a different narrative regarding Enrique's physical harm:

> At four in the afternoon, about twenty dirty law enforcement officials came to our offices, rifles in hand, with an arrest order for Ricardo and Enrique Flores Magón. The charge against our dear brothers is for circulating obscene literature in the mail. We already know that obscene literature is the honorable fight that *Regeneración* has been doing against the operators. The esbirros [pigs] were not only happy with the arrest of our unyielding fighters, but they also intended to assassinate them with the slightest movement. Enrique was hit and his head badly injured. As the group who witnessed the facts, without being able to save our honorable fighters, we energetically protested against such abuses committed in the country of "freedom." The Editorial Group of *Regeneración* asks all the world's workers to join in a single unanimous voice of protest ordering the immediate release of Ricardo and Enrique Flores Magón. Everyone get to work! Send funds for the defense, in the name of Enrique Flores Magón, box 1236, Los Angeles, CA.[3]

According to Teresa and other members of the extended anarchist family living at the Edendale commune, Enrique's grave head injuries were inflicted by J. G. Thompson, assistant to Detective Mariscal, who administered a pericranial pistol whipping.[4] When preparing for the trial, Enrique noted that he wished he had been doing more gymnastic exercises when Thompson attacked him so that he would have better sustained the blows with less arthritic pain.[5] Ethyl Duffy Turner states that "the women from the liberal colony flipped through the newspaper uttering insults at the police. They already had known the women should suffer again: experiencing the fight so that they take back the accusations, exorbitant finances, months in jail, a farce of a process, the prison."[6] As Duffy Turner notes, the reproductive labor of being a woman in this anarchist commune was twofold: one had to do the domestic labor to keep it going, one also had to earn wages outside to support those living within it while male leaders were in prison, and one had to perform excess emotional labor in helping the PLM's chosen family stay together in the name of "the idea." Regarding the PLM women's experience of the attacks on Enrique and Ricardo, the Spanish edition of the *El Paso Morning Times* reported that "a group mixed of fifteen men and women rushed inside the room to avoid the Magons being taken out of the office. But they were rejected by showing them firearms."[7] So not only were productive and reproductive labor foisted onto the women of the commune despite supposed liberal gender ideologies practiced by the PLM; they were also put in a position of physically defending their leaders and subjecting themselves, along with other men, to bodily harm enacted on behalf of the state.

The mixed-gender group interfered with police procedure, protecting Enrique and Ricardo with a sense of urgency: it was already clear that the event would lead to brutality. Committed to anarchist principles, the commune members were well aware of the potential for state-sanctioned violence against them. Their moral mandate outweighed the psychic costs of violence, especially on the Arteaga-Magón children who were present to witness their father/stepfather's and uncle's injuries and confrontations with the law. Furthermore, the fact that Enrique's family, both nuclear and anarchist, witnessed his beating explains why his daughter Esperanza came on May 16, 1918, to his workplace in tears to announce that he had been sentenced to Leavenworth.[8] These violent encounters with law enforcement wreaked havoc on the emotional lives of the children and the commune members equally.

Witnessing the violence made emotional attachments all the more valuable, especially when Enrique and Ricardo lived the bulk of 1916–18 in the Los Angeles County Jail. Emotional attachment served as sustenance for a prisoner and their family alike. And these inherently optimistic attachments sustained the Edendale group while their leaders and intimate partners were in prison.[9] Much of the correspondence during this time emotionally labors to maintain interest in the children and a sense of family in light of physical absence. Enrique also documents how revolutionary masculinity was reinforced by serving time in prison. In a February 19, 1916, letter there are two inscriptions, the actual letter and an annotation that was written afterward, where Enrique reflects on his arrest and beating. In addition to assuring Teresa that he and Ricardo were among friends in the jail, he asks about Esperanza, tells her to make sure to let Santiago and Pedro know that he received their messages, calls Santiago "grandecito," and says that the bag of paper in the house could be useful to him and Ricardo. Never forgetting the minor quotidian details of being a father, the *cariños* such as *grandecito* describing both Santiago's adult demeanor and his physical growth, or addressing Teresa as "Mi Querida Teresita," use compassion, love, and warmth to close the emotional and physical gap. As efforts to manage the family as patriarch from afar, the letters maintained contact seemingly so that they would not move on without him as life partner and father. Enrique also asks that Teresa send his shirts that were gifted by Betancur, a PLM friend, and reminds that she not forget to bring paper.[10] To stay connected with the world outside, comforts such as a shirt and paper to write provided essential material contact with objects that convey memory and personhood. After all, emotional and material connections are cut off while people are in prison, so these petitions, while small and quotidian, along with expressions of affective attachment, show the emotional labor of maintaining family and politics. Even though Kelly Lytle Hernández demonstrates that the open-air steel bars of the LA County Jail allowed the incarcerated to communicate with passersby in the alleyway, there was still much emotional labor to be performed by Enrique in light of the fact that his children and life partner were on the outside, left on their own to continue the business of the PLM and the day-to-day work of surviving as a family.[11] Whereas one reading of these actions could be described as emotional connectedness, the converse reading would be to examine his maintaining of fatherly authority as an assertion of patriarchy.

The description of the Magón plight took on epic proportions. As "Shall Free Thought Be Throttled?" states, the witnesses were "unable to save our honorable fighters" but urge energetic protest against abuses committed in the "land of liberty." It is further repeated that Ricardo and Enrique were gratuitously and viciously assaulted in their offices and beaten badly, with Enrique requiring treatment at the emergency room, and since then, "they lay behind bars in the County Jail of this city."[12] To demonstrate the indignity of the assault, a PLM group from Tampa, Florida, showing the geographical breadth of the network, sent a letter rallying the troops around Enrique and Ricardo's physical assault by police: "Hereto a persecution campaign on the Mexican border has been undertaken, and the writers of *Regeneración* the brothers Ricardo and Enrique Flores Magón have been the last and bloody victims. A large police group brutally raided his office; they tried resisting, with the result of Enrique Flores Magón being barbarically beaten and his head badly destroyed."[13] Satirizing the uneven nature of justice, to claim Enrique and Ricardo as "our irreducible fighters" uses excessive survivalism and masculinities in the face of extreme physical violence to mobilize the masses against such injustices.[14] In some ways, Enrique's disfigurement, which I will explain later, left him with bodily reminders of his suffering and sacrifice. Excessive force and brutality against anarchists and Mexicans during this historical time period were common. Lytle Hernández further demonstrates that in the practice of human caging in Los Angeles, brutality and elimination were at the core of police strategies of containment.[15] Thus, to call on all workers of the world to mobilize on behalf of Enrique and Ricardo, from LA to Tampa Bay, made the urgency of state violence all the more politically potent: Enrique was targeted by the vigilantes because his name was on the masthead as editor, and this in turn justified the anarchist response to totalitarianism all the more.

The time that elapsed between arrest, trial, and sentencing uncovers the grave nature of Enrique's bodily injuries, which were cataloged with great detail in his 1912 intake form from McNeil Island and the second intake form from the same prison in 1918. When incarcerated in 1912, he weighed 152 pounds and had black hair with "Scars: ½", dome of the head, 2½" above right ear, ½" inner surface right buttocks. . . . Upper right first molar and upper left molar missing." By the time he arrived back at McNeil Island on May 21, 1918, his hair had turned "iron grey. . . . Teeth—all upper right back teeth and all upper left 1st and 2nd molars missing [front]—Upper right bicuspid and lower left central and lateral incisors missing. . . . Scar ¾" long and ⅔" long and ¾" long left side of head—Scar 1¼" long front of right forearm—Scar ½" long outer side of left wrist—Scar ½" long front base of left thumb—Scar ½" long palm of left hand—Scar ½" diameter between buttocks—Scar ½" long upper inner left buttock."[16] In the years that had passed after his first arrival at McNeil, Enrique had gone completely gray, lost thirty pounds, lost more than half of his teeth, and accumulated six more scars, especially on the hands, arms, and head. Signals of blunt-force trauma, poverty, and lack of medical care manifested the physical costs of the PLM struggle on Enrique's body. The fiery performances of revolutionary masculinity had been replaced with physical frailty and damage.

These were not the first signs of the wearing, physical toll of revolutionary agitation. In the speeches at the Silver Swan Hall held on September 19, 1915, just following their first release from McNeil Island, a muckraking columnist remarked that "both Magons appeared emaciated yesterday, and had evidently lost much of the fervor which characterized their previous disturbances . . . should their talk be taken too seriously, steps will be taken at once to return them to their resting place."[17] After serving their twenty-three-month sentence at McNeil for breaking neutrality laws, their bodies showed the consequences of poor prison conditions on their health. Enrique's 1958 autobiography insinuates that they were poisoned while in prison.[18] The columnist also notes that their intensity had been reduced as a result of being physically worn down and that Enrique "spoke for thirty minutes trying to lash the audience into a fevered heat. Those present brought their wives and the wives brought their children, and the children brought their voices. At times the speakers were compelled to stop until the united squalling was appeased by food for that purpose." Poking fun at Enrique's slower than usual "Mexican-Spanish phrases of the virulent description and seeking to inflame their hearers to deeds of immediate violence," the author represents the scene as a farce of misplaced radicalism, misinterpreting the communalism and familialism of anarchist solidarity as a crowd of misbehaving children and adults.[19] He goes further, making fun of the fact that Enrique and Ricardo, along with Blas Lara, would have to pause to wait for wailing children to be appeased with food, thus undermining their masculine prowess and revolutionary fervor. If read against the grain, however, stopping so that children might be calmed amid a fiery tirade against capitalism was an exercise in restraint, a desire for an audience to follow along, and a potential lesson from which workers, wives, and children could all benefit.

While they were awaiting sentencing in the Los Angeles County Jail in 1916, English-language reports detailed Ricardo's emotional decline. Diagnosed with neurasthenia, Ricardo's psychological disorder of chronic fatigue and nervousness with symptoms of headache, insomnia, and irritability caused by emotional stress and trauma compounded his already-diagnosed diabetes. Though represented by the press as a ploy for leniency, the medical prognosis was submitted to the court by their lawyer, J. H. Rickman, with an opinion by Dr. N. K. Noon. Meanwhile, the headline "Ricardo Magon Feels Nervous" serves as a smear in its own right, framing excess sentiment as a form of feminization and emasculation to derail a public political figure whose intense rhetorical presence was nothing short of electrifying. In contrast, Enrique is represented as the site of masculine rationality: "Enrique Flores Magon, the brother, is not troubled with nervousness, and is apparently willing to remain in the County Jail until the trial for the pair the 31st inst."[20] Given Enrique's head trauma from the arrest, it may in fact not have been physically possible for him to object and express dissatisfaction with his imprisonment in the way that Ricardo was openly painted as a nervous nag. In both cases, the press takes aim at disassembling their masculinities by evoking disabilities, which, in turn, were feminizing. But this also was an opportunity for Enrique to position himself in the spotlight that Ricardo regularly inhabited.

Enrique's private correspondence with friends is contradictory on this point. In an English-language letter to Rafael B. García, he mentions that he "eats just to not starve but changing what I eat. This way, that terrible pain in my stomach has been subdued already to a great extent and it comes but once each two or three days. Therefore, don't worry about me. I hope to keep afloat and even regain some of my lost muscles and strength, enough to undergo the five years in the Penitentiary to which I am already sentenced beforehand in this Land of the Free."[21] Their vows of poverty as anarchists make the abovementioned fast all the more normalized, except that he doesn't eat because of a developing ulcer. As he privately mocks the US justice system, Enrique uses humor to defuse his body's increased frailty. Constantly reassuring comrades and family members through his correspondence that his body was in pain but not frail—"I feel well and strong after doing some gymnastic exercises"—even as he notes that his stomach and arthritis are acting up, Enrique performed masculine normalcy about health and wellness to family members. The reassurance not to worry operated as a form of masculinized stoicism. At the same time, given that Teresa was experiencing headaches, he asks that the money that would have been used for his own spectacles be diverted to Mama Lola for "my dear old lady's eye glasses," orchestrating the finances and economy of care with their utterly limited resources. Depending on Teresa's labor to support the family while Enrique was in prison meant that every dime was necessary to maintain the well-being of those outside. But even in this way, Enrique orchestrated his authority and intentions from inside the jail cell.

In contrast, Enrique's untroubled countenance in the face of trial and in spite of grave injury reversed the public perception of the brothers' masculine behavior. Enrique was now the perfect masculine subject in self-composure, while Ricardo had become the *descompuesto* (messy one) in his excessive expression of uncontrollable emotion in the face of imprisonment. Such a retreat into emotional weakness was the antithesis of earlier demands for liberty that the Flores Magóns were famous for. Characteristic of what Shelly Streeby has described as "the sensational mode [that] dwells on outrages done to bodies and often refuses the closure that sentimentalism strives for, where characters are reconciled with society," the war on Ricardo's nerves and on Enrique's body was not reconciled but totally at odds with the judicial system that jailed them.[22]

Within their own community, Enrique and Ricardo's health was represented as equally fragile after their stint in the Los Angeles County Jail. Juanita Arteaga wrote in March 1916 that "they, for their shaken health, need to be free; but they prefer, that first we attend to the newspaper . . . we have to make special efforts in order to keep 'Regeneración' alive, and to save our brothers. . . . Let's do it! They sacrificed themselves for us. Let us sacrifice ourselves for them!"[23] Again, sensation forces us to dwell on bodily clues, affect, suffering, and trauma, the very stuff that constituted their sacrifice for the paper and Mexican freedom. The sustained outrages against their bodies by the state, and even discourses that discredited and undermined their being, principles, and writings, centralize direct action in emulating their sacrifice to alleviate physical suffering. The forceful nature of the exclamation points visually mobilizes affect and sympathy to their side, conveying emphatic anger, agreement, and passion for their long-suffering bodies.

But bodily harm was not Enrique's only concern. The brothers and their attorney, Kirk, had other ideas: they were to establish that they were innocent, and Enrique expressed concern that Kirk did not understand "we are politically persecuted and that, therefore, as in other accusations before, the authorities shall use all trickery and chicanery they would command to have us convicted and railroaded." While the press represented Kirk and Rickman as anarcho-socialist radicals, the doubt about their true understanding of the trial's political stakes, based on a long history of persecution both in the US and Mexico, was something that concerned Enrique very much. He was so worried that he closed the letter with Kirk's last-ditch trial preparation attempt to "see you all right away, for he wants certain assistance that only you, our wives, and friends outside could give him."[24] Perhaps a plea for character information, simply details of how the paper was mailed, or their conduct as *padres de familia* (heteronormative fathers), the idea that friends and family would be called to provide context for the lawyers demonstrates that every shred of evidence, including witnesses of the original arrest and attack at the Edendale commune, ultimately demonstrated how difficult the defense would be.

Enrique was the first witness called to the stand for the defense, where he testified that "he was a journalist and editor, and that he was connected with the management and control of Regeneracion." By deflecting attention away from Ricardo, Enrique was to share the burden of the indictment. Notably, "the courtroom was crowded with friends and sympathizers of the Magons, but every man was searched for guns before being allowed to pass through the doors. The best order prevailed. When the court adjourned some of the spectators rushed forward to take the hands of the defendants but the crowd was pushed back by the police, who accompanied the Magons to the County jail, after both men had been fervently kissed by their wives and children."[25]

Despite the fact that the press consistently labeled the Flores Magón brothers as hell-raising reds, it is interesting to note the ways in which their families are located within the scenes of the law being meted down upon their antidemocratic, propagandistic activities. These men were indeed celebrities in local union, socialist, and anarchist circles and thus merited a crowded courtroom of previously convicted Wobblies, including IWW members such as Alexander Berkman, who had spent eighteen years in prison for the attempted murder of steel magnate Henry Clay Frick. In the company of their anarchist community, those friends and sympathizers provided comfort to Teresa and her five children, and María Brousse and her daughter. In true anarchist spirit, none of these women, labeled by the press as the wives of Enrique and Ricardo, were married, and the fact that the press imposed the logic of nuclear family onto these common-law unions mobilized moral sentiment for their plight. The "fervent kisses" intensify the staged courtroom drama, magnifying their celebrity and the emotional attachments: separation through imprisonment could not destroy the bonds of love; it did the opposite, intensifying the affective response to loss in the name of an anticapitalist political cause.

Women Anarchists Go on the Offensive
for the Flores Magóns

As a result of the trial and Enrique and Ricardo's stint in the Los Angeles County Jail, the women in the family went on the offensive, buoying *Regeneración* and publicly defending their innocence. The March 18, 1916, edition of *Regeneración* is filled with articles by Estela Flores Magón and Juanita Arteaga, Lucía Norman, and Teresa V. Magón. In fact, Estela and Juanita took up a good amount of space with their writings while Enrique and Ricardo were in prison between 1916 and 1917, often informing the anarchist and labor publics of their conditions while incarcerated, their contributions and sacrifices for the revolution, and their health. Like revolutionary female journalist peers such as Juana Belén Gutiérrez de Mendoza and Sara Estela Ramírez, who used "mocking, grassroots, and angry ton[es] that soared off the page, affecting and arousing the emotions" of those who read their writing, the Flores Magón and Arteaga women deployed similar strategies.[26] No records exist for Juanita, but Estela was nine years old at the time of the 1916 publications. Enrique confirms the documented ages of the children from the 1920 census in his autobiography by stating that Esperanza was thirteen at the time of the May 16, 1918, Supreme Court rejection of the appeal, which made Estela just nine.[27] In addition, the 1920 deportation proceeding documents note the children's ages as fifteen (Esperanza), thirteen (Santiago), eleven (Estela), nine (Pedro), seven (Jose), and three (Enrique Jr.).[28] This means that even if the oldest daughter, Esperanza, was using the name Juanita as a pseudonym and Estela was actually writing, they were very young to be published writers. Estela, Esperanza, James (Santiago), and Pete (Pedro) could read and write, but only Estela, James, and Pete attended school. Judging from the letters that Estela and Esperanza wrote to Enrique while he was in Leavenworth (1918–21), it is highly unlikely that the girls mobilized such vehement defenses of their father and uncle in the press. Thus, one has to believe that the articles published under Estela's name and Juanita's name were covers for Enrique and Ricardo.[29] During his 1911 stint in the Los Angeles County Jail prior to serving his prison sentence at McNeil Island, Enrique admitted that his pseudonym during that time was Rosa Mendez. He used this pen name to inspire women to join the PLM and engage in fighting the social revolution.[30] Because juveniles could not be prosecuted as adults under the Espionage Act and other anti-anarchist and anticommunist legislation of the early twentieth century, writing under the names of his children or the fictitious Juanita afforded some protection. And given her anarchist commitment to the movement, Teresa's previous risks and sacrifices with her children would probably have her agreeing with Estela writing or with using Estela's name.

With Estela and Juanita dominating the pages of *Regeneración* while Enrique and Ricardo were in jail, Teresa took to the public arena in their defense as well. Managing *Regeneración* from within the jail, Enrique encouraged her to continue the work. On February 27, 1916, he reassured her with "now, what you all need to do is be confident in yourselves, in your own ability and; what angst! Although it leads you to comment, you are all the more-ready than a cheeky person to not skip the line although you do not follow the same. Move forward, brothers!" Asking her not to be bogged down by the large task of continuing publication, he encouraged that she and the comrades rise above what they've experienced. Moreover, Enrique closes the letter with "Tere my dear for [*sic*] and my poor Tere. My love for my kids. The intended states he loves you all."[31] In collapsing love for the movement together with love for his family, affective bonds propelled the paper and the family through crisis, exhorting direct action: direct action that Teresa would take.

In her writing debut, Teresa penned an article about Margarita Magón. As a "simple venerable woman" who was a sterling example of "proletarian mothers," Teresa proclaimed, "with such a lioness, it is no wonder she had such cubs." Dramatizing a mother's influence for the revolutionary cause was something that Teresa had to perform both to cultivate the efficacy of the movement in Enrique's absence and to position herself as a public thought leader, very similar to the posture Paula Carmona took in her *Regeneración* writings as well.[32] Like other Mexican female journalists of the era, such as María Gutiérrez de Mendoza, Teresa was "an embodiment of her discourse, which makes clear that she was living what she wrote."[33] And because of her embodied writing, Lomnitz notes that Teresa's literacy was uneven in Spanish and English, and her limited correspondence reflects this because she often had Esperanza or Rafael García respond to Enrique's letters.

Nonetheless, even if it received heavy editing by the collective, the article is identifiably hers as it sticks with a subject she knew well—the veneration of a revolutionary foremother as told to her by Enrique—for Margarita had died long before the two of them met. Margarita Magón's energy in the face of danger, her honorable character, and her quest for justice made her a champion of her children and the poor. The article was placed strategically on page 3 next to a large advertisement for the Gran Mitin Internacional, where Teresa V. Magón and Raúl Palma, Lucía Norman's boyfriend, were the top-billed Spanish speakers for the event, along with Sam Adkinson in English and Chaim Shapiro in Hebrew. This was one of Teresa's first appearances without Enrique.[34] To make Teresa's role in the movement readily recognizable, the advertisement in the English section announced her appearance as Mrs. Enrique Flores Magón. Because it was dubbed an international meeting with three languages featured in protest against the persecution of the anarchist fighters Ricardo and Enrique, it was a big step for Teresa. Although her performance was described by *Regeneración* staff writer Remigio Guevara in terms of "valiantly defend[ing] our companions and was also greatly applauded," it was Raúl Palma who brought down the house with his "virile and eloquent elocution, even for those who did not speak Spanish!"[35] With this feminized public debut, Teresa's role as mother, compañera, and woman did not match the speech acts of her male public counterparts. With bias in how gender influenced anarchist public speech acts, it is highly unlikely that Guevara would have detailed the content of her speech anyway, given that three-fourths of the article is dedicated to the men who took to the podium on the same night. Out of respect for Enrique and Teresa's more public role cultivated since 1914, these genuflections to Enrique's compañera frustrate gendered notions of equality within the Los Angeles PLM anarchist circle. Even in the highly valorized form of direct action so prized by anarchists, her contribution is muted compared to others, especially Palma. This must have stung given that once Enrique was in Leavenworth, monies raised for his, Ricardo's, and Librado's defense were misappropriated: "Raulito and company were using it for booze and withheld the balance."[36]

The other form of work that Teresa took up was as a surrogate or messenger on behalf of Enrique and Ricardo. As Enrique noted in his deportation proceeding transcript when asked who helped run *Regeneración* besides Ricardo,

  Q: Your wife also assisted you?

  A. My wife also assisted me.

Bodily Harm   117

Q. Their views are with you?

A. Identical to mine, all of them.[37]

Thus, Teresa's surrogacy, even in the later years, extended from her experience running the paper and total alignment with Enrique's anarchist ideologies and, at the time, those of Ricardo as well. Such ideological alignment, whether actual or a performance in the deportation proceeding, further reinforced the notion that women in the PLM were activists and compañeras in supporting the men. Enrique argues that "they believe that it is not convenient to let the propaganda of our dear ideals die. They also believe that for dignity, it is necessary to keep the newspaper running, now that the wild bitch of capitalism, the Authority, wants to kill it. Receive through my conduct the brotherly love that Ricardo and Enrique send you."[38] By making Teresa's public role as wife and mother primary to her testimony (even though they weren't married), she conveyed tenderness as a surrogate for their love of the paper, the workers, and their supporters. As a mother figure, she extended commune labor by infusing the same sentiment into the PLM's gender-progressive political activism. Moreover, taking advantage of Teresa's strengths as a long-standing member of the movement, worthy of Enrique's trust because of their union, she controlled their message while in prison. Whereas Enrique and Ricardo focused on how they were being heard in the courtroom or from their jail cells, Teresa's public speeches and running of the paper blurred the public and private realms between individual and political surrogacy. With Teresa connecting their message to the public, she domesticated the ways in which these men were represented, converting them from rabid anarchists into men of reason.[39]

Distinct from the muted success of Teresa's public speech, the written tribute to Margarita F. Magón, and appearing as a surrogate in print for Enrique and Ricardo while in jail, Juanita Arteaga's critiques of the justice system in the United States were most blunt in their political jabbing, with a consistent mockery of "due process" and the vile treatment that Enrique and Ricardo received while in prison. Never lacking in what we would now identify as "feminist" critical self-reflexivity (even if it was Enrique or Ricardo actually doing the writing), she wrote the following on April 22, 1916:

> For more than two months our comrades Ricardo and Enrique Flores Magón have found themselves deprived of the relative liberty that "we enjoy," us who live outside of the jail; two months being sick and when they most need loving attention from their life companions, the brutal

hand of bourgeois injustice keeps them far from these necessary attentions, separated from the beings that love, subjects to the torture of not receiving the comforting visit of their friends, locked up being two keys like savage beasts in narrow iron cages, to tell the truth: that Wilson and Carranza are working together because this old trickster promised his wingman from the White House to reestablish the same conditions in Mexico that exist under the Díaz regime.[40]

Appealing to emotions of loss and infirmity, Juanita foregrounds the glaring disparity between the relative freedoms enjoyed outside of prison and those of Enrique and Ricardo in jail. Even indicting herself for enjoying such limited freedoms, she zeroes in on how emotionally impoverishing jail was for two men whom the arbitrary bourgeois system had separated from their life companions, particularly during a time of illness. The emphasis on emotion and the need for domestic relations of caring echoes reform movements of the nineteenth century, but this time in an anarcho-syndicalist context. On the one hand, depicting the two men as physically compromised by police brutality demonstrates a kind of masculine weakness rarely articulated for Mexican men. Their frailty without love, care, or friends close at hand solicits political action on the part of the readership. On the other hand, compromised health and lack of access to health care or family care double down on the argument that the bourgeoisie deprived the proletariat freedom fighter from his right to health and family at all costs. Domesticity was the salve for healing wounds, improving health, and righting moral wrong, but that requires sacrifice by all. Such a narrative centralizes women and children in providing that care, an extension of PLM gender ideologies about women's revolutionary labor as that of maintaining the family and communalism. Blaming Presidents Woodrow Wilson and Venustiano Carranza for treating Enrique and Ricardo like savages in iron cages, under two forms of lock and key for pursuing freedom of the press, Juanita Arteaga pulls no punches in arguing that the leaders of North America are no better than dictator Díaz.

Performing Affect

Essays by Estela Arteaga, Teresa's middle daughter, deployed radicalism most directly, with confrontational and internationalist tactics. Her work was discursively in line with the confrontational tone of other Mexican women during the period.[41] In the article "El jurado falló en contra de los hermanos Magón," she stated that the jury had predetermined the verdict. Describing the testimony of Lucía Norman, who was her older peer by thirteen years, Estela wrote, "In the room was our young comrade Lucía Norman, daughter of Ricardo's partner and who he had adopted as a daughter years ago and Lucía also loves Ricardo with the endearing love of a daughter. The prosecutor, creating cruel luxury all the while knowing that Ricardo is sick, and on the edge of the tomb, he had the diabolical ideal to torture the father by forcing the daughter to sit and testify against her own father!"[42] Relying on the relationship between public sentiment and familial bonds, Estela uses sympathy for Lucía Norman, making her seem young and emotionally frail, forced to testify against the father who had loved her so. Such emotionalism and empathy with Lucía and Ricardo's plight are yoked in a way that parallels what Karen Sánchez-Eppler has called emotions and tears that "designate a border realm between the story and its reading, since the tears shed by characters imitate an answering moistness in the reader's eye."[43] And although the description of Lucía Norman is not of shedding tears but being on the verge of tears because of her courtroom dilemma, the reader is drawn to the bodily sensations of struggle, loss, and strained parent-child bonds at the hand of an evil juridical and capitalist system that misunderstands their values. In true formalistic representation of the revolutionary period, these writers made sentimental and sensational appeals as they translated political and economic struggles into melodramatic narratives.[44]

As opposed to Ricardo and his grave state of health, the mainstream press and Estela represented Enrique as perfectly rational throughout the trial. If Enrique was the author, it again was an opportunity for him to displace Ricardo as an ideological leader of the movement. Contrary to the extreme emotion framing Lucía and Ricardo, Enrique was emotionally contained. Moreover, he orchestrated his dominance on the stand during the trial because of Ricardo's health. In a letter to Rafael García, he noted, "I told Kirk to see Ricardo, for we shall depend on his health condition, for I do not want my brother murdered forcing him to the strain of the trial if he cannot stand it."[45] Enrique's time on the witness stand was a masculine display of affect to indicate mastery of self in contrast to Ricardo's frailty. Such a strategy is about efficacy in storytelling, a means of holding the attention of the audience, something for which Ricardo was known for, more so than Enrique, making this trial testimony all the more crucial because he verbally represented both of them. But their decision to lean on Ricardo's health condition gave Enrique all the more credence in delivering a masterful performance and to center himself as a main actor in this long history of masculinity and "the Idea" of revolution. That he drafted the speech several times in Spanish and English prior to and after the trial and reconstructed it from memory shows the high-stakes investment in Enrique's one chance to address the court:

> During his testimony, Enrique searched for and took advantage of the only opportunity that he had to present our fight and our ideals, so as to actively denounce the constituted authorities as longstanding conspiracy of tenacious persecution of which both brothers have been the objects for a long time. On that topic, Enrique improvised a discourse that pronounced with such simplicity, repose, and tranquility, that more than on the defendant's bench, he appeared to be in a dissertation room, developing and defending our beloved anarchist communist ideals . . . with serenity and good manners, [he] recommended to the prosecutor that he calm down and appease his anger, if he wanted his words to be easily understood and answered. The members of the jury and the public laughed openly for the good lesson that the defendant Enrique taught the prosecutor so that the enormously fat butterball that constitutes the body of that loyal guardian of the institutions returned to his seat, and due to the rage of seeing himself humiliated by the serenity of the defendant, he ended the interrogation.[46]

Claiming Enrique as the *portavoz* (spokesman) of the movement that *Regeneración* represented, the author of this passage, if Estela, does not claim Enrique as her father. Instead, a distanced form of inclusive objectivity pervades the description, much like Enrique's detached performance. That is, the author uses the "our" to represent a community of shared ideas delivered via Enrique. He was merely the medium. Nonetheless, to "improvise a discourse . . . pronounced with such simplicity, repose, and tranquility" was not what actually happened. The performance on the witness stand, something that any trained and educated man like Enrique would know and anticipate, was calculated to be pitch-perfect: there are two copies of the speech in his archive. What is naturalized by Estela Flores Magón was actually cultivated precisely because Enrique was educated in a way that the proletarian masses that he spoke of and spoke for simply were not. To represent the testimony as organic is to locate Enrique's speech acts in the *pueblo* (the community). Repose, tranquility, and simplicity are desensitized emotional strategies that run counterintuitive to all radical perceptions of anarchists and the Flores Magón brothers in particular. Even within the context of the first red scare that underpins Enrique's testimony, he nonetheless relies on his expertise as a trained elocutionist, expansive reader, and restrained speaker to elicit a particular response from the judge, the jury, the prosecution, and his comrades in the courtroom. The laughter in response to his speech indicates consensus that the performance was effective in undermining the authority of the state cross-examiner. Laughter signals an alignment of thought and an established relationship in constructing shared meaning and public feeling. He therefore mobilized normative masculine cues to centralize the political performance of his testimony.

Serenity and good manners are tools of the educated and the middle class. Turning this discourse onto the prosecutor, the power of interrogation is flipped. The courtroom was one of the battlefields, much like the arena of public speaking, where Enrique had mastered discourse and self-composure in appropriate moments, questioning the official's ire and calmly entreating him to behave with the proper comportment expected in a courtroom. In true *Regeneración* rhetorical fashion, brutal sarcasm and humor temper the scene of Enrique's humble (*humilde*) performance of serenity with an interrogation of the prosecutor's excesses, including his body. Because of his unruly body and unruly affect, unlike that of Enrique, the discourse of white supremacy is reversed with razor-sharp precision to galvanize the idea that Mexicans, in their thoughts, bodies, and words, can indeed expose the flaws of a judicial system persecuting anarchists out of rage and passion instead of rationality and law.

Continuing with the same affect of excess and emotion in describing the prosecution's closing arguments, Estela further mounts sentimentality as a strategy to expose the 1916 trial's injustice:

> The prosecutor ended the session with new intemperate shouts, such that it did not take much for the public to go silent. The prosecutor yelled and debated so much like a lunatic, in his desire to defame our ideals and to his counsel, sweating and panting. After letting out his venom, he collapsed into the seat as if it was covered in butter. There our dear brothers spoke, perhaps for the last time in their lives, given their declining health it is likely that they will die there, far from their own loved ones, within the thick walls of the penitentiary.[47]

Estela describes the closing arguments as nothing short of a desperate emotional tirade outside the bounds of rational law. She again uses physical excess and insults by describing the prosecutor as yelling at the top of his lungs to defame anarchy, a humpbacked, uncontrollably sweating ball of lard sitting in his seat and spitting venom. Such a portrayal of authoritarian white masculinity is very much in line with the visual representations of empire, capitalism, and their agents during this time period, especially in newspapers such as *El Comillo Público* in Mexico or the IWW's *Industrial Worker*.[48] Disgust for a disabled and diseased body was the affective response solicited by the writing about the prosecution to expose moral corruptness.

In stark contrast, emotional sentimentality closes the article, drawing the audience back to the Flores Magón brothers' unnecessary suffering. A dramatized departure, as if on their deathbeds like Little Eva in *Uncle Tom's Cabin*, their diminished health guaranteed that a prison sentence was a death sentence. Their broken bodies in the courtroom of public opinion evoke what June Howard has called "the spontaneity, the sincerity, and the legitimacy of an emotion" in bolstering an authentic connection to the political and emotional losses that would come with conviction of the "beloved brothers."[49] Although I am not a believer in authenticity, it nonetheless serves as an affective political strategy in centralizing the Flores Magón bodies and the public's attachment to them. They are treasured objects/subjects, and the sensation capitalizes on their physical vulnerability as a prelude to death. Such embodied thoughts—from shivering at the potential loss of the brothers' lives, the greasy prosecutor's overemotive rants, or the courtroom drama itself—all give way to a physically felt sense of belonging and involvement.[50] On June 22, 1916, Enrique was remanded to three years in federal prison and Ricardo to one year and a day because of his failing health.[51]

Juanita Arteaga's and Estela Flores Magón's articles evidence the familial nature of *Regeneración* and its political satire of sentimentality in times of crisis. Whether pseudonyms or the actual named authors—remember that Estela would have been nine years old at the time these articles were published—the emotional result served a dual purpose. Such affect is evidence of how sentimentality mobilized the PLM politically. First, a child could not be arrested for violating neutrality laws or mailing unmailable materials, or violating the Espionage Act of 1917. Second, and this is important, yoking sentimentality and emotion with female authorship, while problematic for the essentialist nature of the claims, could deflect attention away from the possibility that Enrique and Ricardo were writing as Juanita and Estela while in jail. It also provided the opportunity to mobilize sentiment, feeling, and emotion for themselves directly and not just for the anarchist movement and Mexican independence they championed. Third, if Enrique was writing about his own performance, it gave him the opportunity to state or overstate his importance on the witness stand. Because the articles were an open forum from which to mourn their own losses and separation from family, using female authorship disseminated public feelings on their behalf without compromising their masculinity. Given the volume of publications I've read written by both Enrique and Ricardo, and Estela and Esperanza's letters, I am inclined to believe that the two men took on these names to write without being detected.

Fame, Attraction, and Courtroom Dramas

Press coverage of Enrique and Ricardo's sentencing appeals was steeped in the language of fame and attraction. On June 23, 1916, the *Los Angeles Times* described the scene:

> A packed audience-room greeted the sentencing of the famous trouble-makers. A score of officers were scattered throughout the crowd, but there was no outbreak of any sort. But few Mexicans were present. Before passing sentence Judge Trippet said it was not a question of free speech and free press, but "the right of the government to preserve itself against insidious attack...." Enrique Flores Magón then rose and asked that he be given an opportunity to read a paper he had prepared on the justice of this punishment, but Judge Trippet would not allow him to do so, saying that "this was no time for a speech."[52]

On the heels of Ricardo's third conviction for violating federal law and Enrique's second, the familiarity that the Los Angeles press had with their cause is striking. The *Times* calls them "famous trouble-makers" who again dominate the court, despite the fact that the occasion is their own sentencing. Although the judge described the sentence as a nation protecting itself, Enrique tried to take the space back from the law in what the headline calls a "martyr pose." Rising to read a paper after sentencing, the martyr pose, and an audience all suggest a level of performativity in these public mobilizations of affect toward the brothers and their cause. Enrique had clearly prepared for this moment, to speak publicly after a sentence that he surely knew would direct him to federal prison, and in front of an audience that was not majority Mexican. This was a pro-labor, pro-PLM, pro-anarchy audience that cheered and recognized his celebrity as something to mobilize around. Enrique was willing to challenge and interpret the "justice" of his punishment, to literally talk back to the state after it had handed down the final word. Such defiance, especially in the face of the clear racism in press coverage ("there was no outbreak of any sort. But few Mexicans were present"), was a chance to mobilize defiant masses to come together in solidarity. That was the real problem with their celebrity and charisma. It didn't matter that "few Mexicans were present" and that there wasn't a violent outbreak. The problem was that Enrique's "stump speech" had the potential to mobilize the social and racial cross-sections within the courtroom and beyond.

The speech, documented but not admitted as evidence, was performed in such a manner that it brought the room to hinge on every word, according to the *Regeneración* editors. This was partially caused by the fact that Enrique composed numerous drafts of the speech in Spanish and English before delivering it, and then he reconstructed what he said in a later document for his own records.[53] It passionately argued that his conviction would stand as a symbolic sentence of all the men and women who work against tyranny, plutocracy, authority, and the Church. He made explicit transnational connections between downtrodden laborers fired upon and murdered in strikes or worked to death in Louisiana, Colorado, West Virginia, Yucatán, Valle National, and Cananea, and the indictment of capitalism that "when the conditions of the proletariat become unbearable, they rise in revolt."[54] Citing Jefferson as the original anarchist of the United States, Enrique further argued for a broad context for their political activities:

> The world is our country and all men are our countrymen. It is true that, by birth, we are Mexicans, but our minds are not so narrow, or vision not so pitifully small as to regard as aliens or enemies those who have been born under other skies. . . . The court may choose between law and justice. If you send us to our graves and brand us once more with the stigma of felons, we are sure that history will reverse the sentence. She will be marked indelibly the forehead of Cain. Let the court speak! History watches![55]

With a universal call to workers, he agitated for justice, not corruption. But we must also question whether or not Enrique was the one to report about his own courtroom speech, as he often did in other contexts, aggrandizing his performances. If the speech was the center of attention, why did the press focus on the fact that in the afternoon, "friends of the Magons packed the courtroom," where Ricardo received roses from Lucía Norman, "who will be the especial object of the attentions of the police today when the verdict is returned" as a precaution by federal officials to prevent riots? If Enrique were the focus, why are Lucía and Ricardo the ones being surveilled? It seems that the highly militarized courtroom was guarded by deputy marshals, circulating "among the crowd of Mexicans and local 'Reds' who are expected to be on hand to greet the Magons in case the government fails to convict" because Ricardo and Lucía had the most potential to react violently to the sentencing.[56] Described as a "sensational scene on the occasion of conviction," it did not result in the court ruling in their favor.[57] There was no riot despite the socialist-anarchist population in the audience and their excessive anti-American sentiment. The preparations for an overflow of sentiment and rage nevertheless exposed the state's view of immigrants, and Mexicans in particular, as incapable of containing their base bodily reactions.

With their lawyers filing an injunction, they appealed the conviction to the United States Supreme Court on July 3, 1916, and bail was posted at the amount of $5,000. It was covered by Mary E. Clark and CWR Burns. Enrique was met by "a delegation of Los Angeles Socialists" who "cheered Enrique Flores Magón when he was released." The headline also uses a pejorative: "Socialists Cheer as 'Red' Gains His Liberty."[58] In the lead-up to what would be the height of the first red scare (1919–20), using the slur "red" was a shorthand for identifying and condemning radicalized anarcho-communists. Those cheering Enrique Flores Magón's release were indeed a threat to national security during World War I, and the sentence of three years in federal prison was thought to be light, according to the *Los Angeles Times*. But those cheers of positive socialist and anticapitalist affective expression represented the core of a communal ethos at the center of the Los Angeles anarcho-socialist circle's politics. There was something energizing and mobile about a small victory like being released on bail, or being sentenced to three years in prison instead of twenty years. The delegation's celebration venerated the sacrifice made by intellectuals so that they could publish, agitate, and spend time with comrades and family. And even if their celebration was overinflated by the yellow press to demonstrate their anti-American sentiments gone wild, the excess emotional display demonstrates an improper masculine affect that was racialized differently. Moreover, that the anarchist masses could celebrate small victories demonstrates how even in the face of bodily harm that was to curtail the movement, survival itself was cause for celebration.

Chapter 5

DE LA FAMILIA LIBERAL

Behind the scenes of courtroom dramas, and between the 1916 trial's end, sentencing, and appeal, Enrique Flores Magón Jr. was born on March 17, 1917, just nine months after Ricardo and Enrique were tried and released on June 20, 1916. With a focus on family in light of the impending prison sentence, this chapter elucidates the gendered imperatives and nuances of being "de la familia liberal," or part of the PLM's liberal family. Though seemingly incorporating feminist ideals through notions of family, the PLM nonetheless romanticized heteronormative family and women's traditional roles.[1] As women within the junta organized and challenged men's ideas about them, *Regeneración*'s "Liberal Family" column suggests that such creativity in asserting their rights and interests was overshadowed by patriarchy.[2] Under Enrique's editorship the newspaper took on a renewed interest in family networks, almost as if to mourn his own losses, while downplaying the birth of his and Teresa's only shared biological child. This focus on children and family was influenced by Enrique Jr.'s birth.

Enrique Jr.'s birth was a testament to the family's endurance during Enrique's incarceration in the Los Angeles County Jail. Teresa had a network of supporters during her pregnancy, including Kathrine Schmidt of San Francisco, who was affiliated with the Labor Temple. Remarking upon the pregnancy, Schmidt

[w]ant[ed] to say a few words about your sweet little Theresa [sic]: I told her, Enrique that she need not make any preparations for the little

newcomer expected. As we connected with the League will consider it a great privilege if we can prepare the little layette. I am just dying to make baby clothes, and this will be my one opportunity. We are taking just as much interest in this little newcomer as you people are. Also, Enrique, I want Theresa to go to the hospital and have the attention of a good physician and a competent nurse. You know the little girl has been under an awful strain for many months, and she will need the very best of care. To begin with, it will be rather inconvenient for her to be there at home while she is confined to her bed. At a hospital, she will be kept quiet, the children will not be there to annoy her, and under all circumstances, I think a good hospital is the only place for people when they are ill, don't you? . . . I want Theresa to make her own selection and I would rather it be some place other than the County Hospital. I want her to have a good Dr. one who can converse with her in her language, as it will be easier for them to understand each other so you people can attend to it, and I am going to attend to the financing of it. We will prepare all the little clothes—everything— so Theresa need not bother about anything.

Kathrine Schmidt was the sister of Matthew A. Schmidt, who provided the dynamite to the McNamara brothers, who blew up the *Los Angeles Times* building in 1910. A part of Emma Goldman's circle, Kathrine's group was used to raising money and support for socialists, anarchists, and their families when they were arrested by the police. Kathrine worked for years as the San Francisco office manager for the International Laborers Union. Because she had never married and dedicated her life to union politics, the arrival of the "little newcomer" in her extended anarchist family was all the more exciting. A degree of benevolent paternalism was evident in her desire for Teresa to deliver the baby in a hospital, despite the fact that her previously delivered six children had been born at home. Yet Kathrine wanted to help financially, which was something the Flores Magóns actually needed at the time. The diminutive "your sweet little Theresa," although misspelling her first name, communicates a level of intimacy, solidarity, and family that crossed racial lines in the name of gendered expressions of care and politics that originated when Enrique had lived in San Francisco with Paula eight years earlier. Schmidt's correspondence often laments Enrique's losses and sacrifices in light of the cause. Later letters catalog deep sympathy for their suffering and poverty: "Hope Tere has regained her strengths and that you too are feeling better. Get as much rest as you can. This everlasting struggle to keep body and soul together does not give any of us a chance to lay down . . . just give 'our baby' a great big love and kiss from Matthew and me and receive of love to all of you."[3] She also sent Tere used clothes and money via parcel post to help out while Enrique was in Leavenworth.[4]

While Kathrine's racial benevolence and anarcho-socialist support of Teresa and Enrique's family in times of crisis were helpful, there was another form of familial benevolence expressed in *Regeneración*'s "De la familia liberal" column. Announcements of the births and deaths of children connected their transnational network through affects of loss and hope. It was customary for columns to display a masculinized tender form of revolutionary love for family, not through nationalist expressions but for anarchist conceptions of partnership and child rearing that contested capitalist exploitation of the proletariat. The anarchist collective at *Regeneración* understood the fragility of family in light of such political and legal struggles and often published *felicitaciones* to comrades who had children: "We sent our congratulations to all of the friends mentioned earlier, mostly because their homes now enclose an illusion and a hope more about not dirtying their little children by bringing them to the religious trickster."[5] Well wishes to four PLM comrade families after the birth of their children demonstrate a tenderness and value for family in light of the political struggles and sacrifice. As a patriarchal form of tenderness, these masculine expressions of emotion contrast greatly with the PLM's fiery political protest. In this instance, children represented hope for the future. The possibility of not having their homes monitored by the state is what they fought for, as the child was an innocent figure untouched by corrupted power. It is the tenderness expressed for newly born children by protecting them with anti-religious ideology in the PLM circle of comrades that captured Enrique's emotional labor.

For example, the September 1, 1917, issue managed the tension between joy and sadness quite graciously:

> There have been a significant number of births: Floreal, son of Antonio and Lola Betacur, Puente Cal., 12 August. Floreal, a boy born to Asunción and Elisa Martínez, Los Angeles June 10. A boy to Apolonio and María Rivas of El Paso Tex.
>
> The deaths that we have to note are the following: Pablo Zamarripa, Leigh, Okla., died on 21 June. Saturno Escobedo and Juan Correa, Johnson, Ariz., victims of a mining accident. Pedro Hernández, La Cañada, Cal., died in August after falling from a mare that released itself from the carriage that was heading to a propaganda meeting. Teresa

VA Magón met Florencia Hernández, widow of Pedro in El Monte and gave her the following assistance: Fermín Galván, 50¢; Refugio Solano, $1; Ramón Tenorio, 10¢; Juan Pelty, 50¢; Pilar Valdez, 50¢; Silvestre Jarmillo, 25¢; Gregorio Teos, 25¢; Anecleto Seañes, 40¢; Felix Zamora, 20¢; Gumersindo Valenzuela, 25¢; Cristóbal Dominguez, 20¢; Juan Morales, 10¢; María Rivera, 10¢. Those who want to help the widow can do so by contacting Florencia Hernández, 2130 E. 8th St., Los Angeles, Calif. [6]

Most notably, two families, one in Puente and another in Los Angeles, named their sons Floreal, for the eighth month in the French Republican calendar (each month had the name of an agricultural plant or domestic animal). Using the Latin root word *flos*, the parents separately studied the French Revolution to arrive at a name with such significance. Their learned choices as conscious revolutionaries used naming to signal their intellectual reach within the confines of an anarchist and socialist movement that the public represented as unreasonable and violent. To make the opposite clear, their children symbolized the revolutionary potential of education and being learned. As editor, Enrique took pleasure in announcing the well-thought-out naming practices of the children born of PLM comrades who made public their political choices.

"De la familia liberal" also marks losses that were to be mourned on behalf of the network. Expressing sorrow and loss for Pablo Zamarripa of Oklahoma, Saturno Escobedo and Juan Correa of Arizona, and Pedro Hernández of California demonstrates the vastness of the PLM network and the value of comrades' lives. In particular, the deaths of Escobedo and Correa, who perished in an accident in the Johnson Camp mine (sixty-five miles east of Tucson in the Dragoon Mountains) presented an opportunity to lament the losses of unorganized Mexican wage laborers who continued to work in subpar conditions long after the Cananea strike of 1906.[7] Although the Cananea strike was successful in shutting down mines and bankrupting their owner, Colonel Green, the resulting massacre of the protesting Mexican workers did not necessarily improve the wage and living disparities that existed as a vast gulf between Anglo workers and the underpaid Mexican workers. Public acknowledgment in *Regeneración* of the bodily sacrifice by Escobedo and Correa mourned another labor struggle and loss, linking them to the martyrs of the 1906 strike: they were enshrined in a fleeting history of Mexican miner sacrifices at the hands of American capitalism. Given the ephemeral nature of newspapers, the one-sentence tribute to their lives was quite fitting for a proletariat that was rarely recognized as historical actors of consequence. It creates an affective register of melodrama that drew the PLM membership into a critique of the state. Moreover, mourning was a form of contesting state power.[8]

A similar and more solemn tone mourned the loss of a man who was clearly a close comrade: Pedro Hernández. While he was loading a wagon with propaganda for a meeting, the mare bolted, and Hernández suffered a fatal blow to the head. The level of care with which Enrique documented the lament is further registered in the list of thirteen comrades who donated money to support Hernández's widow, Florencia. Also of note is the fact that Teresa helped collect the donation money. At this time, Hernández was thirty-seven and was listed in the 1910 census as a head of household (occupation: laborer). He was a resident alien, as was Florencia Tomellino, then thirty-five.[9] Curiously, Pedro is listed as white and Florencia as a mulata and lodger. That the census enumerator listed Florencia as a lodger without an occupation would suggest that an interracial common-law partnership was unimaginable. Given that Florencia was an Afro Mexicana, the racial signals may have prevented the enumerator from seeing the two as partners, especially because Pedro is listed as white. Nonetheless, by the time of Pedro's death Florencia was, according to the PLM publication and Enrique and Teresa's outpouring of sentiment, Pedro's widow. The $4.60, or what today would be about $110, was a crucial amount to help Florencia cover Pedro's funeral costs and her living expenses after his death. If she was still not in the labor force and was a *comadre* (feminist comrade) of Teresa's, the money was raised for Florencia because she dedicated her time to PLM activities and the junta while Pedro's *yugo* (yoke of manual labor) supported their existence.

The thirteen comrades who contributed the money for Florencia were part of the El Monte circle of PLM supporters, and their donations represented the anarchist principle of action over social and economic condition. This form of mutual aid and sharing demonstrated the ethos of the El Monte anarchist group Luz Libertaria, including several of the donors such as Seañes, Valenzuela, Teos, and Dominguez.[10] As guests of honor at their benefit picnic, Enrique and Teresa intended, along with their El Monte comrades, to "activar la propaganda" (activate propaganda) in favor of the movement. This allowed Teresa to collect on behalf of their La Puente neighbor Florencia and her deceased husband and, moreover, raise money for *Regeneración* in solidarity acts that bolstered PLM morale.[11] Here, anarchist expressions of communal loss became actionable through the monetary support of a socially marginalized, Afro Mexicana destitute widow, Florencia Hernández.

To name Florencia, Pedro, and their supporters is to mourn the dead as a member of a community and keep the struggle alive by envisioning him as part of the family.

"De la familia liberal," then, became a space for the PLM, at Enrique's initiative, to mourn, commemorate, and celebrate the lives of its members across their networks. These gendered nuances of what constituted anarchist notions of family were again bound by emotional ties. It was a place to document small victories and hope, including those personal gains, however few. The February 24, 1917, column read as follows:

> Last January 5th, Luz was born in the home of our friends Dolores Villanueva and Pablo Díaz de Delvalle Tex. On the nights from the 3rd to the 6th of this January, two little children were born, one boy and one girl, who will be called Germinal and Consuelo, respectively. Their parents are friends of Camile and Rafaela Nevares de Somerton Ariz. These three friends, by being children of conscientious parents, saved themselves from the foul baptismal waters and from being seen as foolish in the eyes of the judge. Pascual, the youngest son of Francisco and Altagracias Betacur de Puente Cal, and Salvador, son of Francisco and Concepción Chavarría, passed away from this city. If they had been bourgeoisie children, they would still be alive; but their parents are proletariats who did not have the necessary resources to save their own loved ones.[12]

Enrique's recognition of the births and deaths of beloved children born to Mexican-origin proletarian parents was quite the opposite of his fervent critiques of the state. His column exhibited the consciousness that came with being estranged from his children with his ex-wife, Paula Carmona.[13] With Teresa's five children, whom he adopted as his own, Enrique celebrated birth in an economy of scarcity as a way to contest state power and reinforce the idea of family and reproduction as key to the movement, however nationalist, patriarchal, and gender normative it might have been. Reproducing the liberal family was proof that the network, beliefs, and values of anarchism would live on in the lives of these children. The tender emotion of joy, juxtaposed with the "children of conscientious parents" whom the PLM must save "from the waters of baptism and to be registered as sacrificial lambs in the judge's books," represented secularized child rearing in a community of likeminded people who knew that the state needed to recognize their births but also that the church did not grant salvation. In a tongue-and-cheek dismissal of the state, the PLM calls for collective action in the expansion of the liberal family. And little Salvador and Pascual, lost to parents because of infirmity, became baby martyrs in the recognition of their parents' deep emotional losses of their beloved children at the hands of a capitalist system that could not provide them health care.

Just like the death of his own son, Demófilo, in 1912, the losses of infant children had special significance for *Regeneración*'s editor. Enrique's critique—"if they were children of the bourgeoisie, they'd still be alive"—staunchly and emphatically blames class inequality as it intersected with ethnicity (these were all Mexican-origin, US-born children) for the loss of Salvador and Pascual, who, just like Luz, Germinal, and Consuelo, represented utopian possibilities for the future and the chance for creating a better world.[14] The sentiment mobilized through the babies just born or those who no longer exist draws upon utopian politics of survival to both celebrate and mourn as part of the PLM cause. For the future of the PLM, according to Enrique, was one that included children as autonomous critical subjects socialized through the cause for justice of workers, their Mexican comrades, and the extended networks into which they were born.

The "De la familia liberal" column on March 24, 1917, announced the deaths of several comrades across the US Southwest. While Juan L. García died in February, it was only nine days after his young daughter Ninfa Martínez died. This double tragedy spurred Enrique to rant about the exploitation García's widow faced in burying her family in Uvalde, Texas:

> His partner and three more young children survive.... The local priest of Uvalde Texas was befuddled because although he demands payment for each burial in the vault that belongs to everyone, Juan neither paid him anything nor accepted his hypocritical services. That priest will need to work in order to eat. What a poor guy! Tranquillo Hernández, a man from Como Tex., ceases to exist. Juan Torres, Bernardo González, Sesideio Cruz, Eugenio Galván, Kelly and Juan Hernández loaned his partner and five orphans solidarity from what they could.[15]

Lost comrades meant fewer anarchists to spread the work of the movement. Moreover, calling out church corruption attacks the hypocrisy of religion in the US. Mourning these losses collectively reveals absence as a form of political motivation and was the tender form of masculinity acceptable in this context.

In a separate section titled "Nacimiento," an announcement was made: "In the home of Teresa and Enrique Flores Magón a baby boy was born on the 17th of March."[16] Contrary to what Kathrine Schmidt wanted to provide or impose for the baby's birth, or the announcement for Demófilo, who died five months after his birth, Teresa and Enrique welcomed their only biological son into the world without fanfare and with a home birth. Contrasting with the way that Enrique publicized the deaths of comrades, the case of Juan Martínez and the death of his small daughter, and the situation of Tranquillo Hernández's widow and five orphaned children, this is a clear moment where Enrique heeded the warning of his letter to Teresa back in 1914: the birth of their son was intentionally made minor news compared to the losses of their compatriots. Contextualizing the birth of Enrique Jr. as a private matter worthy of protection was for the safety of the infant as much as it was a fulfillment of the promise of "a happy, tranquil, honorable home, where you can find yourself, my partner, to love and be loved, care for others and be cared for, spoil someone and be spoiled" made in that 1914 letter of apology. Baby Enrique Jr. represented hope for the future of the movement and their family, and they shared the birth with national comrades but kept the details private, given their confrontations with law enforcement, Mexican state-sponsored spies, and the desire for *un hogar felíz* (a happy home). The humility of the birth announcement prioritizes the losses of comrades who have left behind partners with orphaned children of the PLM cause. Instead of mobilizing the famous emotional heft for which Ricardo and Enrique were known, the editorial team notified the network of the birth without hyperbole. They strayed from the heightened sentimental discourses that marked the births and losses of other PLM children because it was a safety issue. Especially given the fact that later that month the *Los Angeles Times* openly stated that "a special watch will be placed upon Ivanhoe, the small Pacific Electric power station on the Glendale route, where the Magons have established an anarchistic colony," the surveillance was redoubled in light of the 1916 conviction.[17]

Instead, the emphasis is placed upon lost proletarian children and their dead parents as a means of making something creative out of something so negative: Mexican working-class motivation for continuing the struggle against capitalism. After the deaths of Juan and baby Ninfa Martínez, "De la familia liberal" identifies a network of supporters. Similarly, that Juan Torres, Bernardo González, Sesideio Cruz, Eugenio Galván, and Kelly and Juan Hernández all made monetary contributions following Tranquillo's death is a record of what David Eng and David Kazanjian see as "what remains of [loss], by how these remains are produced, read and sustained."[18] The melancholic record of collective and community lament created the momentum to activate PLM networks in hope that more laborers and their small children would not die because of poverty: this was another form of propaganda. The stakes of making such losses and their economic, political, and emotional costs representable were necessary to forge the community "De la familia liberal."

The September 12, 1917, issue was the last one edited by Enrique leading up to the denial of the case appeal by the Supreme Court. The "De la familia liberal" section featured an update on Ricardo and Enrique's case. Although this was the last display of Enrique's tender expressions toward PLM families, the editorial about their case works with the fervor of discourse in defense of their innocence and persecution. By writing themselves into the heart of la familia liberal, they mobilized sentiment around their plight. Their lawyer, J. H. Rickman, had recently informed them that the appeal would go from the San Francisco appellate court to the Supreme Court, which took ten months for a final decision. The appeal date in the appellate court was postponed several times in order to produce satisfactory evidence for conviction and to buy time for the federal government. Although they were both able to post bail, they were still significantly short of money to pay their legal fees, filing fees, and document costs. Making an appeal to their anarchist circle, Enrique wrote the following:

> Without use of hypocritical modesties, we believe that our services to the proletariat are still useful; and more so currently than the tyranny that claims to prussianize this country. Such a conviction makes us wish for freedom more than in any other circumstance. And with the belief that other ladies and gentlemen share the same opinion, I propose the following fundraising plan, that can be carried out by the groups as well. September 23rd is approaching, which is the anniversary of our manifesto from September 23, 1911. For that day, you can organize a mitin, a veiled dance, or dance-like meetings; it being a Sunday is good because everyone is free from the daily slavery of work. With such dates, more than providing a moment of happiness, they will generate propaganda and our defense as well, if the agreement is accepted that one half of the acquired funds goes to the benefit of REGENERACION and the other half to our defense. This way we are helped two-fold: being free for a few more years and securing our combat weapon, REGENERACION stays alive to push the fight for land and freedom forward. My initiative is still standing. The ladies and gentlemen of good will that accept it and wish to practice it, surely put yourselves to work with determination.[19]

In line with typical PLM practices, the dance or mitin turned sadness into joy and joy into a fund-raiser. Such suggestions posited fun and amusement as sites of pleasure that were tethered to anarchist goals of land and liberty on the day free of slavery: Sunday.

This wish for freedom, for a proletariat that could enjoy the fruits of its own labor, was also evinced in the public speeches that Enrique made in 1917. In a joint public appearance, when Enrique Jr. was a mere six months old, Enrique and Teresa were honored guests at the September 15 Club Hidalgo celebration of the 107th anniversary of Mexican independence. In what is now Huntington Beach, the land tract where they spoke was originally part of the Rancho Los Alamitos land grant in Wintersberg, California. By 1910, the land was a major agricultural hub for growing alfalfa, celery, corn, beets, onions, potatoes, and lima beans, a process that included Japanese and Mexican immigrant laborers and their families. It was an important natural site of intervention for Enrique, Teresa, and the PLM network because the California Vegetable Union was the selling agent for various producers, including the Orange County Celery Growers Association and the Poultry Association. The ten to twelve boxcars of celery shipped each day from the Smeltzer and Wintersberg stations brought in twenty-five-cent-per-dozen bunches, with the season ending in April.[20] Beet production was at peak, with eighteen to twenty-five boxcars leaving from Wintersberg daily. It was described as a "region of hardworking, prosperous people, big crops, bright prospects and hasty pudding roads," and Mexican workers migrated between various ranches in the area to work in bean threshing in one season and beet harvesting in another, with company stores in each community controlled by the growers, the clergy, and the landowners.[21]

In Wintersberg, Teresa and Enrique were hosted by Mateo Ortega and Cresencio Ramírez. They presided over the celebration, where Enrique and Teresa were "directing the word in concurrence with the patriotic fiesta and dance to commemorate the 107th anniversary of Mexico's Political Independence." The paper excerpted Enrique's speech for the readership with a solidarity call to the "Compañeros y compañeras de Miserias." The end of his speech was the most telling aspect of Enrique's further absorption in anarchism:

> That country does not belong to us, it is not ours, but rather it belongs to the Terrazas, the Creel, the Otis, the Hearst, the Escandón, the Iñigo and Noriega, the Rockefeller, the Pearson, the Carranza and the Madero and other scoundrels who, with help from the government and

with cheap methods and even with the use of brute force and murder, individual or in mass, they have taken over the land that, by natural law, is a common inheritance of everyone. . . . We do not call ourselves children of that venerable elder, Hidalgo, if we do not have the value of continuing his work, however cut short by accidents in the fight. The Mexican Liberal Party is fighting to finish the work set forth by Hidalgo, expropriating the land and everything else that exists for the benefit of the people; its members, making propaganda from their elevated anarchist ideals, which are love, brotherhood, and justice for everyone, or fighting in the Mexican battle fields to the virile cry ¡Viva Tierra y Libertad! They are making an effort to finish Hidalgo's work, to conquer free access to land and to establish a new society in which we all stop being the shearable herd of today and we become the free men and women of tomorrow. As long as we are not working in this way, we must stop fooling ourselves screaming "hurrah!" to a country that is not ours, but actually for the rich, and let us stop tricking ourselves in dreaming about freedom when in reality we are more slaves than ever before.[22]

While Enrique lectured about the grand history of Padre Hidalgo's work to secure Mexico's independence from Spain in 1821, he demonstrates how it has been disgraced with monopoly capitalism under the Porfiriato. Calling on these agricultural workers in Wintersberg to truly be the children of Hidalgo, they must unseat the corrupt landowners in Chihuahua (Terrazas and Creel), US venture capitalists making money off of the proletariat and/or benefiting from land gifts made by Porfiro Diaz (Rockefeller, Pearson, Hearst and Otis),[23] and the newly emerging PRI presidents (Carranza and Madero). Citing a false sense of patriotism, the speech at Wintersburg calls on the working classes of men and women to seek Mexico's freedom and their own. Enrique's Wintersberg speech outed US-based land barons like Hearst, among others, to illuminate how the working Mexican people were deprived of land that belonged to them. This joint appearance and their speeches marked a shift from Enrique and Teresa operating as a political unit that privileged their family first and foremost. By linking their role in the PLM to the ideals of Hidalgo, independence, and the liberty still sought by the members and workers they addressed, their political attitudes shifted how things were done publicly. "De la familia liberal" also reflected this familial sentiment as a concrete way for public expressions of tenderness, family ties, and the transnational value of the lives of workers and their offspring. An extension of Teresa and Enrique's work as a unit, the column, along with their joint public appearances, marked the beginning of the end in the deteriorating cohesiveness in the PLM in anticipation of an ideological split with Ricardo. In a letter at the end of 1916, Blas Lara wrote to Ricardo from Fort Bragg, explaining that he was leaving the *Regeneración* editorial collective because Enrique was a "busca-pleitos" (troublemaker).[24] Privately, and in response to Lara, Ricardo noted that Enrique had separated from the group by late 1917, but he did not publicly announce this until 1918, despite the fact that the July, December, and October issues of *Regeneración* were published. In a June 28, 1917, letter from Ricardo to Enrique, the tone is not of two brothers having an ideological split; rather, the letter speaks of quotidian things such as Ricardo's health, María, and what to publish next in the paper.[25] Unlike with the culture of denunciation that we saw with Rómulo and Paula Carmona, the lack of emotion announcing the brothers' split is silent about painful emotional realities.

Chapter 6

THE SPLIT

By February 9, 1918, Ricardo resumed his editorial duties of *Regeneración*, with his name back on the masthead for the two final issues. Accounting for the leadership shift, the newspaper announced that "colleagues José Flores, Trinidad Villareal, Rafael B. García and Teresa and Enrique Flores Magón have left the editorial group of REGENERACION, due to a lack of mutual understanding amongst themselves and those who stay with the group with regard to the fight. The people that left are not going to abandon the fight for our honorable anarchist ideals, as they have a firm purpose in continuing it with their strengths and possibilities."[1] In reality, they separated because Ricardo decided to support Lucía Norman's boyfriend, Raúl Palma, in his murder trial, and the others disagreed.[2] Enrique had long harbored animosity toward Palma and was troubled by Ricardo's blind faith in him, and some suggest that this was a pretext to leave the junta. Nicolás Bernal coupled this split with Enrique's flawed judgment in trusting the Carmona family as further evidence that he was never committed to the revolution and wanted to be a leader separate from his brother. Bernal also noted that Enrique split with Ricardo not because he wanted to but because Teresa forced him to.[3] And in the last issue, a paltry two pages, the editorial group, with some exasperation, had to remind the readership of the change: "Once again the following colleagues no longer belong to the editorial group of REGENERACION: José G. Flores, Rafael B. García, Trinidad Villareal, Enrique Flores Magón y Teresa Magón. All related correspondence should be sent directly to Ricardo Flores Magón."[4]

To disassociate both Enrique and Teresa from the editorial collective shows how much had changed in their relationship and in women's participation in anarchist structures. The fact that Ricardo addresses Teresa's departure, even if symbolic, marks a changed understanding of her role in the movement as an author of the struggle for direct action against tyranny. As with the public appearances Enrique and Teresa made in El Monte, La Puente, and Wintersberg between 1915 and 1917, the shift in how they approached their participation in the movement was mandated by the 1914 letter and poem of atonement: the agreement put family first. Such public displays of their unity in the movement place Teresa and Enrique on equal terms, even if only to visually mark their chosen family and radical action simultaneously. Nonetheless, the split from the *Regeneración* editorial board, though vaguely represented as a difference of opinion on how to carry out direct anarchist action, was never fully articulated by either Enrique or Ricardo in print or publicly. In 1918 Fernando Palomares wrote to Enrique:

> As a permanent member of the grand Mexican Liberal Party, knowing you as Ricardo—I feel hurt and it hurts me philosophically to see you—you both <u>divided</u>. Everyone is surprised and absolutely confused—they say if it were a political question, he would not miss the street comments filtered by the patriot Don Jesús Flores Magón—in the end what happens that dried fruit with no seeds is part of the Villista journalists that got together to make trouble. Would it not be possible for you and Ricardo to speak again?[5]

Palomares makes this request a second time, as if his expression of heartbreak over the brothers' split was too much to bear. These expressions of homosocial love as a form of philosophical standpoint, a way for brotherhood to return to its original state, exemplify how male-male forms of privilege make agreements about the sense of self.[6] In other words, Palomares cannot imagine his love for the cause without his love for and the love between the Flores Magón brothers. Extolling Ricardo's virtues as a revolutionary, while framed as an attempt to win Enrique over, backfired and generated resentment, even though Palomares wanted desperately not to squander the twenty-plus years of his life dedicated to the PLM and the brothers who stood together steadfastly in the cause. He even goes so far as to blame Jesús, their brother who left the movement years before. Although Palomares's alienation and sadness dominate the letter, he does not withdraw his love or support from Enrique and Ricardo. Instead, he held out hope that they would reconcile in the name of the party, a desire for renewed homosocial forms of camaraderie and love. It didn't happen.

The split also marked the end of the Edendale commune experiment. By the time of Ricardo's death, María and Lucía were living on Fargo Street in Silverlake while Teresa and Enrique's brood were living at Exposition Boulevard with Rafael García in downtown Los Angeles.[7] Upon his death, Ricardo's body was shipped back to Los Angeles before it went to Mexico City and was at the Alvarez and Moore Funeral Home in Echo Park. After the *Los Angeles Times* reported that "the Scorpion," Ricardo's code name, was laid in state at the Brees Brothers Mortuary on South Figueroa Street, his coffin was marched through the Plaza de los Mexicanos and then back to Mexico City for his interment.[8] The geographical distance between each faction of the family in the city could not be any more indicative of the wide chasm that had grown between the two brothers. Given that María and Ricardo introduced Teresa to Enrique and that Teresa was María's beloved niece, the pain of the political separation cut deeply because this was a family schism times two. The conflict was not even resolved with Ricardo's death. Even though, as Lomnitz explains, María tried to control all the funeral arrangements as a means of generating cultural and social capital for herself and Lucía from Ricardo's death, Enrique ended up arranging the memorial service.[9] Correspondence with Rafael García shows that Enrique was the one actually negotiating with the Mexican government and various labor organizations to bring the body first to Los Angeles and then to Mexico: he even selected the order and content of the memorial program. Bernal discredited Enrique's participation in the memorial or planning, stating that his efforts had nothing to do with the national railroad union negotiations in repatriating Ricardo's body.[10] Balking at María's public performances of stoicism as Ricardo's widow, Enrique was flustered by her mobilization of sentiment using his brother's memory to gain political capital.[11] At one point he had thought to cremate the body and donate the ashes to the Liberal Party, but María Brousse and Fernando Palomares went to the mortuary officials to block cremation and burial in the United States.[12]

Whereas cremation was an affront to the capital and legacy imbued in Ricardo's corpse, María's anti-American and anti-Enrique sentiments determined the burial arrangements. While Ricardo's body waited in the mortuary for transit to Mexico in December and January, reports did not mention her vigilance. What got noted by the press, as Ricardo's body lay in state while in Los Angeles, was Enrique's vigilance: "Some time was passed at the bier by a brother, Enrique Flores Magón, who recently was released from the Federal Penitentiary on McNeil Island, Washington where he was imprisoned for a similar offense and who is under bond pending a review of the department of labor at Washington D.C. of deportation proceedings against him."[13] And even though the facts about where Enrique served his time are incorrect, the article nonetheless notes his loyalty to Ricardo, even if it was a mere performance after their severe break in ideology and family. It does not mention María's loyalty. This may explain why Ethyl Duffy Turner later notes, without a hint of irony, that the 1923 publication proceeds for Ricardo's *Verdugos y víctimas* were directed to Jesús, the other brother accused of betraying Ricardo, and to María Brousse, with the aid of José Vasconcelos.[14] For even though they had split ideologically, Enrique would not sell his brother's memory. He would instead sell his own, in the form of unreliable and overstated recollections in two autobiographies in 1954 and 1956 and a series of high-profile newspaper articles published between 1950 and 1954.

Moreover, whether it was produced while Enrique was serving time in Leavenworth or while they were together, his communication with Teresa regarding Ricardo is telling and often contradictory. While in Leavenworth and hearing about Ricardo's twenty-year sentence, he wrote, "Have read Ricardo got 20 years, Rivera 15, and María's arrested. It's a heavy blow to them."[15] With some compassion, despite the split and the hostility, Enrique acknowledged how the sentence affected Ricardo's health. Self-reporting by both Ricardo and Enrique to law enforcement authorities on December 18, 1918, stated that "Enrique Flores Magon was formerly associated with his brother Ricardo, and Librado Rivera, in the publication of the revolutionary anarchist newspaper, 'Regeneracion' in this city and now the brothers are bitter enemies," representing the split and the ways in which they were differentially treated in federal prison.[16] At other times, Enrique disdainfully refers to encounters with Sifuentes, his code name for Ricardo in the letters. After Ricardo approached him in December 1919 in the dining hall with the greeting "Manito," Enrique griped to Teresa that such actions were the result of mistaken intimacy between the two brothers. That this occurred right before Christmas suggests that big brother took liberties that Enrique would not tolerate. He referenced the slight he felt about Ricardo's ego and fame. He asked Teresa, "How can anyone tolerate that kind of thing?"[17]

Even in correspondence with Rafael de Lara early in the Leavenworth sentence, it was clear that Enrique had moved to extricate Sifuentes further from the party but that de Lara did not agree: "We have taken good note and considered your proposal about getting the signatures regarding Sifuentes, and while it appeals to us all, after receiving the prevailing sentiment, owing to their conviction, of he being regarded as a martyr, we unanimously saw at once that this is not the proper time to propose this, even with those comrades who are close with us."[18] Clearly, a faction of the PLM was tired of Sifuentes and wanted to make a change, but the political stakes of making a move against Ricardo would have further jeopardized the loyalty of comrades, even if they agreed that Ricardo was part of the problem. But such a move would have made Ricardo an even more powerful political martyr, something that Enrique was bitter about. Those closest to Enrique even made fun of Ricardo. As García wrote of Ricardo, "The 'pelado' is getting more and more 'wicked' all the time; you ought to see him walk now, he is a wonder, and walks like a general."[19] Part mockery of Ricardo's increasingly disabled body because of illness and his portly stature, part critique of his perceived authoritarianism, being a *pelado* is really about being totally screwed physically and politically. It recognizes how reduced he had become, and the mention of his state, was, at minimum, comforting to Enrique.

But letters indicate that the children and others in the political circle were somewhat unaware of the split, and neither man forbade contact while they were both in prison. The split's blast radius depended on who the people were in their circle. For example, a 1919 letter from Kathrine Schmidt to Teresa says, "Hope Enrique and Ricardo keep up their spirits—they are so wonderful," demonstrating that even their good friends, Matthew and Kathrine Schmidt of the San Francisco union and anarchist circles, had no clue about their fighting.[20] Limited knowledge of the split ensured continued monetary and emotional support for the PLM leadership and their families while in jail.

Esperanza noted in a 1919 letter that "we received a letter from my uncle and he sends regards for you. He doesn't know the news yet. Today we are sending him the medicine which grandma left to him because he has the same sickness [kidneys].[21] Despite the split, Esperanza and the family continued to care about Ricardo's poor health. That Adelaida's medicine was shared with her sister María's partner demonstrates that the feud was really between Enrique and Ricardo, and perhaps María. Although, a few days later, a letter from Esperanza provides Enrique with María's address, presumably assuming his intent to write to her because of Adelaida's death.[22]

Even in Enrique's deportation proceedings, there is a kind of doublespeak evident in the testimony surrounding his brother in Leavenworth:

> Q. Do you know if your brother has been served with a warrant under deportation proceedings?

A. I do not know. I have very poor means of communication with him, because he is in another cell house and it is very seldom we meet. It is very difficult here to come together.[23]

As Enrique narrated his separation from Ricardo to Leavenworth prison officials, this stance was not always reflected after he was released from prison on September 10, 1920. The feud between brothers had a tremendous impact on them and their intimates but a more limited impact on their broader PLM circle. While Enrique was awaiting deportation and Ricardo was still serving time in Leavenworth, William Owen wrote from England, "I have not written to Ricardo, for really I do not know how to write a letter that can pass the authorities. I am most sorry to hear about his failing eyesight. Please give him my warmest affection, as I give it to you and yours."[24] This final signature note with well wishes signals two possible things: despite their shared indictment for mailing obscene material, neither Enrique nor Ricardo ever told Owen of the depth of their emotional separation as comrades and brothers, or by 1921 Enrique was on slightly better terms with Ricardo. Either way, it is clear that the people who wrote to Enrique about Ricardo's health and death also had limited knowledge of their split.

Nonetheless, the blood feud continued for many years. María Brousse's censored letter to Francisco Aconte Acasio on April 10, 1918, disavows Enrique and, by extension, Teresa, arguing that *Regeneración* and the movement were "sustained during many years by the brain of Ricardo and not through any influence of Enrique." She also denounced Enrique's former father-in-law, Rómulo Carmona, along with Juan Sarabia and their elder brother, Jesús, to link all of these individuals as evidence of how "Ricardo's ideals are far superior to Enrique's" or the other men who were co-opted by subsequent revolutionary and postrevolutionary Mexican presidential administrations.[25] María advanced the idea that Ricardo, not Enrique, was the brains of the PLM by bringing up bad decisions and poor judgment on Enrique's part, especially related to the Carmonas and an interview he gave in *El Democrata* in 1924 citing his relationship with them. The fact was that María and Enrique both profited from being spokespeople for the PLM after everyone else had died. She went on tour, gave interviews, and collected funds for the cause and her interests into the 1930s.[26] He wrote several columns for *El Nacional, El Universal*, and *Todo* between 1944 and 1954, reminiscing about Ricardo as a leader and an intellectual. They were essentially competing for who could legitimately lay claim to the legacy of the PLM and who could monetize proximity to Ricardo.

To drive home the depth of the feud further, María publicly slandered Enrique while he was on a propaganda tour through Mexico. After his release from a Puebla prison for inciting anti-Obregón riots in 1923, which I discuss in the subsequent chapter, she made sure to publish further indictments of his character. *Excelsior* carried exclusive coverage of the prison release:

> The agent of the Federal Public Ministry of the state of Puebla, who knows about the practiced proceedings against Enrique Flores Magón for slander to the President of the Republic and to the National Army, I communicated today by telegram with the Attorney General of the Nation, I who following his instructions of said district court, ordered to suspend the case, remitted the proceedings to his study with the same attorney, to the effect of working on this case with all justification suspended at the consideration of the First Magistrate.[27]

In rebuilding his Mexico-based credibility as a radical union leader, Enrique's arrests, like this one in Puebla, where the state called out the National Guard, represented an affront to Ricardo's memory according to María. But the state did call out the National Guard, which means he was taken as a serious political threat to Obregón's postrevoluntary Mexico. Even the English-language section of *Excelsior* called Enrique a "red labor czar," and the military was preemptively deployed in anticipation of the strike he was to lead that following Monday.[28] Nonetheless, María's dismissive tone in the *Excelsior* editorial countered and undermined the ways in which Enrique and Teresa launched themselves back into radical, "red" circles of Mexican political life. Accusing him of mobilizing Ricardo's memory at the expense of the workers, her insults were designed to undermine Enrique's political credibility and boost her own. As she stated, "It is truly painful for me, that I witness the agony of a stoic man, who offered his life in the interest of an ideal redeemer, looking later like an individual with impunity and with the memory of the sacrificed." Deploying the same excessive emotional loss that was required of a grieving widow, María's performance enshrined Ricardo as the picture of perfect suffering for an idea he would not abandon. Their collective suffering, and that of the workers, was in great contrast to Enrique, for whom "reliable records exist showing that that individual committed the crime attributed to him. And what, should the Mexican workers show off their wellbeing and that of their families and cause the damages of a strike, by going out to defend a delinquent, who exploits and deceives them?"[29]

Calling her brother-in-law a self-serving, antiunion delinquent who took advantage of a worker's strike inflicted great public harm on Enrique's political reputation. That *Excelsior* would print such a denunciation just two days after Enrique was released from jail by a federal judge in Puebla shows that María was not the only one who wanted to undermine his comeback, especially because he was agitating with workers in the textile industry, which was dominated by men.[30] The government targeted the Puebla appearance, as did María, because of masculinist forms of union militancy that Enrique reinforced with his speech. National interests were at play, even if the alliance to bring Enrique down stemmed from the blood feud with Ricardo. It was now being mobilized on a grand scale with Ricardo's body of ideology as the national battlefield. A presidency was at stake. Not only did María call herself "María B., Viuda de Flores Magón" to the interviewer who wrote the piece, but much later in her life, on a border crossing card in Nogales, Arizona, she signed "María Brousse, Vda de Magón," to verify her identity and listed General Magaña, governor of Michoacán, as the friend who vouched for her.[31] The insults about legacy, credibility, and revolutionary prowess went both ways, while María continued to mobilize Ricardo's legacy as Teresa and Enrique built their own. Thus, the private and public culture of PLM denunciation had a long life.

Still, the February 1918 *Regeneración* split surely exacerbated Ricardo's alienation from PLM comrades, further fracturing the junta. Although María did not call Enrique a traitor, she insulted him with the greatest insult she could find: she called him a fake leader. In her defense of Ricardo's deepening anarchist sentiments prior to death, she called Enrique intellectually and politically bereft in order to rationalize the separation. María's rage about who controlled Ricardo's legacy was at issue. Teresa and Enrique's separation from the writing circle of anarchist family was devastating but was deemed necessary in light of the impending imprisonment and the fact that they did not agree that Raúl Palma, Lucía Norman's boyfriend, was innocent of murder. María Brousse's rage, its own affective excess of detachment, demonstrates her dedication to the movement, Ricardo, and her sense of loyalty as a core value. In pitting the competing interests of the sisters-in-law (Teresa was also her niece) and comrades in arms against each other, the letter shows that women who had the most intimate ties to the junta were key players in the circulation of propaganda and gossip. Ironically, this letter was used to indict María on conspiracy charges on July 12, 1918, when a bench warrant was signed for her arrest.[32]

Chapter 7

THE EMOTIONAL LABOR OF BEING IN LEAVENWORTH

Although the split between Ricardo and Enrique was privately waged on the page and in prison, there was another struggle Enrique engaged in: the emotional labor of preserving his family when he began serving time in Leavenworth. On December 18, 1918, Enrique was transported from Los Angeles with a group of land speculators found guilty of fraud to McNeil Island in Washington.[1] One month later, he was transferred to Leavenworth because of overcrowding. He was in Leavenworth from 1918 to 1920. The US census for 1920 states that he was forty-nine years of age, his race was white, his status was married, and he could not read or write. His occupation was listed as a nurse, and he had worked in a hospital. However, his autobiography states that he worked translating in the hospital because he knew so many languages and was trusted by the chaplain. Enrique also worked in the mailroom at the recommendation of prison guard McIntyre.[2] On the intake documents, Enrique's occupation is listed as "journalist," with Teresa V. Magón as his wife and six children (four boys and two girls), not including the children he had with Paula Carmona. Teresa and her children were living at 914 East 52nd Street in Los Angeles, which was different from the 1920 census's recorded address of 1120 E Street. They were rather transient at this time, given their precarious economic situation. Teresa had frequently worked in orchards picking fruit for wages to support the family,[3] and she returned to work, including a stint in street vending immediately following Enrique's incarceration at Leavenworth with comrade María A. and daughter Esperanza on Central Avenue in Los Angeles "to send what help I can to mamá."[4] The emotional explanation of helping a sick mother primarily justified the work, which included taking baby Enrique with her. In 1918 all of the children were fourteen years old or younger, and Esperanza, the eldest, worked in the informal sector or in temporary jobs to help out, despite the 1920 census noting that none of them had an occupation.

And while the children and Teresa labored externally to keep the family afloat, Enrique struggled in Leavenworth on his own. In his letters to the children and Teresa, he mobilized every shred of emotion enabled by language to express his sense of family and assert his presence in their lives. Even before incarceration at Leavenworth, he privileged personal needs over the movement in 1918. Because of the impending prison sentence, spending time with Enrique Jr. and with the larger family took precedent. Lament and love dominate Enrique's prison correspondence. For example, in a September 9, 1919, letter he writes individual notes to each of the children:

Mi Chatita linda:

Cannot find words to express my joy by receiving your letter . . . that you all don't forget poor old Daddy, and I feel gratifying love from your letter knowing that you're a chip off the old block when you say "but all of us will resist until our hopes come true!" That's my babe! = O, yes, when I'm out, I'll go with my hair turned all white. . . . Receive many, many kisses all over your dear little face and the love of your daddy . . . that begs you to always be good, [illegible] and helpful to mama. Bye, bye baby mine! My boy James—Believe me, seeing that your letter brought a ray of sunshine into my cell, you all are not still able to realize how much I love you and how sappy I feel by my situation from you and [illegible] shine to me. Glad to hear that you help mother. It is the proper time for you all to be kind to mama and to always do your best to help her the most and to be contented and happy. Thank you, my little man, as the oldest of my sons, have the duty to teach with your good example for your younger brothers to be good to her and to behave honorably. = Take as a point of honor, all the time to go out and play before you are the given as a help to Tere = Esperanza tells me you are going to look for work. I wish I'll be out as more of you had to work being still so young, but since it is unavoidable to go out my dear. Be careful my boy in the kind of friends you may make in your surroundings. Never pay attention to what they might want you to do, always listen and [illegible] ask mother, follow her advice. She knows the world better than any of you and so she will tell you all, my children, what would be best for any of you to do [*page torn*] you will be kept out of trouble. . . . Esperanza, my little señorita. Hah! You go so well when I call you that name. Well, then, get out of the house on your horse and better be simply my Esperanza. That sounds better than señorita, for the good for nothing daughter of a bourgeois. She who just likes to be a pretty little animal that passes her hours in front of the looking glass, a mere parasite that does nothing useful. So, dear, as [*sic*] fine to be a señorita if you don't want to be a pretty but useless [illegible] animal = As I say to James, am sorry you have to go to work being so young. But being it unavoidable, since I am helpless to help you and provide for your wants, and that all the weight of the house has fallen on the shoulders of our Florito alone, I only wish that the appetites that burden you are vast, I recognize how difficult it is to fulfill, for they falter on the sweat of the old as much as the young proletariat. Still such injustice shall end someday. = In the meantime, my darling, take good care of your mother. Make a point of honor to make yourself respected for everybody. To this effect ask the advice of mother and follow it to the letter, you are young now, and have more opportunity to come in contact with people of age. I must say, is the most dangerous for either a boy or a girl, for there may come mistakes that afterwards may pain and ache your heart. So, to avoid any pain and sorrows, trust in mother and have her be your confidence as if she was your oldest sister and bosom friend. Trust her. What she also knows from her life shall benefit you. Do not trust your own wisdom, dear, you are too young to know anything. You shall need to be guided, trust mother. = Don't send the slippers. Hold them to help, I did not care much to ask for them, but know that these are the only reasons. Floritos, this is not a good use of money and I don't want slippers, they are not allowed. I want only undershirts, neck ties, and my watch. If only I could, have my James to hug, dancing and all his stunts. = But this cell is not same. = Shall you really want my picture? Shall ask the Warden about it. I hope you all mind the already [illegible]. Avoid Sad times. Put up a fashion. Pleased mama received my letters of the 7th and 10th of the month. Love to all of them. Greetings to the friends. Mama did not write!! Give her my kisses and heart. Caresses for you all my children. And for you, my dearie, kisses, hugs, and love. Be good, eh?

> Your old daddy,
> Enrique Flores Magón.[5]

Economizing his space in parenting from afar, Enrique insisted that the children always support their mother and revere her in a way that alleviated her emotional and financial burdens. On the one hand, he praised Estela for being a "chip off the old block" for enacting a resistant subject position in line with PLM ideology. On the other hand, his articulation of anarchist morality for Estela and Esperanza, so that they didn't become useless bourgeois female slaves to the looking glass, was Teresa's labor as much as it was that of the girls. She was the model of femininity and loyalty with her ongoing sacrifice to the family and her political beliefs. The time Enrique spent on jokingly chiding the girls about becoming "señoritas" was a sexist double standard that the boys, especially Santiago, who was the eldest, were exempt from. Being a good little man, or being obedient and supportive, is not the same as being sexually chaste and avoiding self-indulgent femininity. Although the language is less harsh than the echoes posed in "Los 'Huérfanos'" about Margarita and her mother, Paula, we still see patriarchal anxiety about unprotected daughters who even with their devoted mother's presence are far from their father.

Equality in parenting appears with the lament about early entry into the workforce, something that the anarchist circle fought to repeal: childhood laborers and unfair wages were one of the main points of agitation. Thus, the painful economic reality was that the eldest children had to forgo schooling in order to eat and pay rent, which explains why Enrique asked that they not send things like his slippers. He urges Floritos not to spend his hard-earned money on such frivolities. Throughout his stay in Leavenworth, his prison records indicate that they ignored his entreaties when they could afford it and sent the slippers, among other creature comforts such as soap, shoe polish, paper, ribbon, chocolate, pencil protectors, flowers, fountain pens and ink, cherries, raisins, nuts, birthday cakes and cards, a mirror, a handball, baseballs, pipe cleaners, witch hazel, razors, cigarettes, books, a violin, and a pillow.[6] The many objects sent to Enrique signaled a level of care and sacrifice, a kind of emotional labor that let him know he was loved in absence. Small treats like nuts and raisins, despite his bad teeth, were pleasures that the family knew he would appreciate.

English-language correspondence with the older children demarcates their US Latinx subject position, all born in Los Angeles and all schooled there. He also made fun of himself, using gringo-speak in the letter's closing, using "dearie" to address Esperanza and signing off as "your old Daddy," for prison and his inflamed teeth and rheumatism had indeed aged him significantly. Moreover, the fact that Enrique was allowed to correspond on Leavenworth Post Office letterhead indicates a level of privilege that resulted from his cultivated relationships with prison personnel who recognized his intellectual talent early in his stay. He also knew the limit of these privileges and thus used the precious space on the paper as prudently as possible, using "=" to indicate a transition.[7] That literacy in multiple languages allowed him to be a broker outside of his cell was significantly noted in a letter where he told Teresa how much he misses her and about his progress: "On the 29th of last May, they changed my job. I was passed from the Library to the Doctor's Office, in the hospital. It is more of an achievement, as it is one of the best jobs here and it's better than the Library, mostly because one is more independent and the food is better. Here for the first time . . . when I arrived here I weighed 125.5 lbs, yesterday I weighted 135 exactly." While he intellectually benefited from the library and contact with other comrades, there were physical advantages to working in the hospital. A major benefit was his vastly improving health. His education, both formal and informal, brokered a better position within the prison structure of work—he continued to teach Spanish classes for the inmates with both jobs.[8] By creating an emotionally and politically enriching life-world behind bars, Enrique more frequently joked with Teresa in his letters, asking, "You also don't stop reading, huh?"[9] Finding humor in the incarcerated space, and maintaining a family bond through loving reproaches and jokes were vital means of shoring up family and intimacy in spite of physical separation. Emotion was the currency that made Enrique feel like a father and partner from behind bars at the same time that he improved his structural position within the penitentiary.

Enrique's emotional labor, through writing or making objects such as identical purses for the two oldest girls, served to constantly remind the children to avoid becoming bourgeois subjects of waste. Instead, it was vital that they should always help their mother in his absence. In October 1919 he requested that a picture be taken to send to Teresa for her birthday in November. Although the request was first denied by the warden, it was resubmitted and approved on November 8.[10] "The approval for One (1) only photo to be sent to your wife" gave him a way to connect with them, updating both physical and emotional forms of attachment through the visual field. Enrique, like Ana Rosas's female informants during the bracero program who stayed behind in Mexico, used studio portraiture as a mechanism to cultivate "emotional investment," where love became a resource to combat separation.[11] And even though the studio of the federal penitentiary served as backdrop and limited self-expression, the gift to Teresa, given the number of requests he had to make to the warden, was nonetheless a determined, good-faith effort to surprise his spouse for her birthday.

Similarly, in a letter to Esperanza, he lovingly yet heavy-handedly reminds her, "To you my daughter, just like I say to the rest of my children, I pray you never stop helping your mom with anything possible and in the right way. Be good with Tere; I will value it. My regards to all my friends. And for all of you my vigorous affection. To my Tere a thousand loves. To the rest of my children many kisses and affection."[12] Using diminutives to signal emotional care, he begged that they help their mother. With Estela, Santiago, and Esperanza in the workforce along with Teresa, they had enough income to support the three younger children while they finished school, but the help Enrique referred to was of an emotional nature. Contrasting with the previous letter he wrote to Estela and all the children in English just weeks earlier, the insistence of communicating in both languages showed Enrique's desire for them to continue their learning and linguistic dexterity of their bicultural upbringing. Never forgetting the community of comrades who emotionally and financially supported his family while in jail, Enrique's remarks of love to family, Teresa, and friends recognize how networks buoyed the family in his absence. And in case that Teresa could not, because of her limited literacy, read his previous letters, he reminds Esperanza to give her a thousand times his love.

The children also cultivated family in Enrique's absence. Baby Enrique Jr. was only a year old and teething, and in a note to Enrique, Esperanza remarked, "Here we are all well since you left and mama has been alright. Just baby is kind of cranky on account of his teeth, he has two of them." In these lines she accomplishes several things at once. First, she updates her father on baby Enrique's growth and his moods in light of his teething. Second, she identifies the demands of having both adult children and a baby in the household, plus their grandmother and Flores, the close friend who helped pay rent and take care of the family in his absence. And third, and most importantly, Esperanza thoroughly assumed the role of mediator by writing letters the most regularly of all the children. A few weeks later she notified him that both she and James were looking for work and constantly mitigated Teresa's sporadic writing by taking matters into her own hands "so as you wouldn't be in worry."[13] Often acting as a surrogate for Teresa in writing, Esperanza's consistent short notes and longer letters communicated that Enrique "receive many hugs and kisses from mama."[14] But most importantly, she performed extreme acts of compassion with her writing and sent objects of sentimental value: "I enclose a little curl of your baby, Enrique."[15] Although the letter's salutation is "Dear Enrique" and the baby is his, and not her full brother, Esperanza deeply understood how a lock of the baby's hair would affect her stepfather. The emotional closeness and slight detachment indicate some strain in how her biological father died and how and when Enrique stepped in to parent. But when read another way, Esperanza may have said "your baby" to remind of the bond between them despite his incarceration, but it also indicated emotional distance. Still, such mementos of baby Enrique's growth symbolically aided imagined and real closeness to the baby and family he left in Los Angeles. They also provided a kind of presence in absence in that physical objects like a lock of hair or letter were surrogates for actually being there witnessing the baby grow his first teeth or take his first steps.

When Teresa did write to update about the quotidian aspects of their lives while Enrique was in Leavenworth, the comments were sparse. For example, in the postscript of a letter dated July 2, 1918, she wrote, "Baby is all right. He is walking by cue [sic]."[16] Between Esperanza's lengthy updates about baby Enrique Jr. and Teresa's sparse correspondence, they both juggled the competing interests, emotional labor, and information priorities in letters to Enrique. Baby Enrique was always part of the letters because he was the most hopeful part of the reports. Teresa also worried that the mementos or the letters would not arrive. On July 26, 1918, she asked "Did you receive the babies [sic] curl you never mention it in your letter?"[17] Even with her limited correspondence, Teresa labored intensively to remind Enrique that the objects and letters would keep him close to baby Enrique Jr. and the rest of the children. The sense of loss was overwhelming, especially given that this was Enrique's fourth child (Margarita, Práxedis, Demófilo, and now Enrique Jr.) whose infancy and toddlerhood he missed because of being in federal prison. Though not replacements for actually being there, the "Idea" and going to prison for it were sacrifices tempered with letters, small gestures, and physical objects of emotional value.

These letters continued until his release on September 10, 1920. Right before the completion of the sentence, the family sent a suitcase with one suit, one pair of suspenders, two pieces of underwear, two shirts, and a towel.[18] Even if Enrique was a shadow of his former self, with scars, missing teeth, and less weight, he wanted to look like himself upon being released. This was a form of grooming and personal styling that indicated, even though the institution was to politically wear him down, that he and his family clearly understood the stakes of self-representation: it helped him feel like a person in light of his political persecution. The family, in turn, was willing to make that monetary sacrifice to get him the objects that made him feel like a man and a person upon his release from prison.

Enrique's emotional labor was part of his public writing while in Leavenworth. For example, in an article from the Leavenworth prison magazine *New Era*, his writing also bears similar baroque and sentiment-laden hallmarks in the description of the fandango, or "Mexican Kaleidoscope or the Dance." In it, the main characters, Mr. Smith (an American) and Teresa (no doubt a loving double homage to his life partner and comrade in struggle), are in a small community in Mexico where a fandango is about to take place. Teresa is a master dancer; Smith is a befuddled onlooker mesmerized by the context of the dance and the ways that movement draws him into the scene. At the story's climax,

> New airs begin to be played by our faithful friends, the musicians, new figures are cut by the maiden's feet, again high pitches of whimsical metric comes forth, once more the vivacious feet go here and there making figures while keeping time and dreaming their accompaniment to the music on the *tarima* and in all the while the glass of water without a single drop of it being spilled, remains tightly fastened on the head of Teresa until the last figure is made when the music stops once more all of a sudden; a surprising feat accomplished by Teresa by keeping her head constantly plumb by the help of her flexible waist, of her undulating hips, her nimble legs and her delicate feet. Again, the house goes wild with enthusiasm; and again, a new surprise is in store for Smith, who thinks that Teresa must be all in by now because she remains with the glass full of water on her head while one of the men stretches a waist-band across the *tarima*, Teresa stepping on the middle when the music starts again with new airs.[19]

In a fast-paced narrative that uses the tarima of *son jarocho* (Afro-Veracruz folk music) as its rhythmic background, Teresa's dance reveals Mexican character to be a mixed race, for the history of this form of dance is a combination of the Spanish-Caribbean Son, Afro-descended pounding of the feet on the tarmia (cajon de tapeo), and indigenous vocal traditions. As Micaela

Díaz-Sánchez and Alexandro D. Hernández have argued, this musical form evolved from "rhythms once performed on hand drums [by slaves, which] were reconfigured to the lower body. The legs and feet replaced the percussive movement of the hands and the tarima were percussion, which shaped the *zapateado* (percussive dance) of the son jarocho in particular, but also of México's *son* music in general. Those who sang, played, or danced banned *sones* were punished and jailed during" the colonial period.[20] And thus, Enrique's tale of seduction through fandango can be read two ways: first as a narrative of the three cultures and Afro-Mexican social and cultural practice through a homage to a sexually empowered and fully self-possessed female subject like Teresa, or second as an essentialist account of Afro mestizas as the ultimate site of sexual energy and seduction in a predominantly mestizo world with an Anglo-American suitor. This contrasts greatly to a somewhat racist report from Ricardo, when he wrote to Enrique in 1899 from their father's estate in Oaxaca, cataloging the black population as degenerate because of their wild howling and singing.[21] That the title character is named for his beloved Teresa Arteaga, who served as the archivist of his legacy by saving his letters while in exile, suggests that the homage uses Son Veracruzana and Afro mestizo cultural forms of sexuality and bodily sovereignty as an imagined anarchist treatise of women's embodiment and self-possession. Teresa is skillful at cutting, having "vivacious feet that go here and there making figures."[22] And it was far more poignant to introduce the fictional Teresa while incarcerated in Leavenworth because it expressed his imaginative capacity every time he represented or engaged with the living Teresa and his family through letters. The ability to dream familial, conjugal, and comrade love into being from inside the walls of a prison aptly expresses "concentrated human passion," as Ethyl Duffy Turner described it.[23] In other words, the concentrated and confined nature of incarceration and exile compounded the sense of loss at the same time that it cultivated memory, desire, and imaginative capacity.

From the letters to family to the "Mexican Kaleidoscope" piece in the prison magazine, these archives of emotional labor demonstrate just how invested Enrique was in preserving his family in his position as father. Incarceration was designed to completely cut the prisoner off from the outside world, but his correspondence and parenting from afar, though reproducing gendered double standards and patriarchal gender norms within an anarchist framework, nonetheless helped to preserve his family during the absence. Christina Heatherton has shown how the Flores Magón brothers used Leavenworth as a kind of radical university for war dissenters, union organizers, foreign-born radicals, and black militants, demonstrating the imaginative and creative capacities cultivated by a life of the mind in a space that was supposed to prohibit it.[24] In this vein, Enrique also cultivated family and his own masculinity despite his confinement.

Chapter 8

DEPORTATION TO A HOME THAT DOESN'T EXIST, OR "HE HAS INTERPRETED THE ALIEN'S MIND"

After all of his emotional labor to maintain his family via letters and handmade objects of affection, Enrique was finally released from Leavenworth in 1920. In March 1923 Enrique and his second blended family were deported to Mexico. The deportation was normalized in the context of a 1920s national wave of removals and also voluntary returns by Mexicans to their home country. Natalia Molina and Shelly Streeby, among others, have shown how mass Mexican and anarchist deportation was part and parcel of a US crackdown on immigrant dissidents and what eventually became Depression-era "repatriations" of returning people to their native country, despite the fact that many were US citizens—the Flores Magón children fell into this second category as the US-born children of immigrant dissidents.

Knowing that the end of his time in the US was near, Enrique lamented to Rafael García that he didn't want to accept money from the workers to help pay for his family's return to Mexico: "I do not want ties nor for them to be obligated to strange elements of our class. I was born poor, I have been poor, I am poor, and poor I want to be always. In other words, I was born a proletariat having my life dedicated to the proletariat cause. I do not want to have friends other than proletariats and those that loyally recognize at least the injustice of our cause and who fought for it with sincerity and hunger."[1] With the poetic eloquence that characterized his writing, foisting his poverty onto the impoverished workers who supported him was not an option. And despite the fact that his family once owned an estate in Oaxaca, he claimed that they had always been poor. The "Idea" meant poverty, a sentence he willingly accepted. Moreover, Enrique simply wanted to be free to return to Mexico, without attachments and obligations. Taking the money of workers also meant obligations that he seemed hesitant to absorb in the wake of his removal: he wanted to be free like the workers who offered to help. Being designated an alien dissident was enough without burdening the workers on whom the PLM had relied upon in the past for their survival.

The time leading up to deportation was marked by multiple INS investigations. US authorities were constantly looking for an excuse to remove communist and anarchist activists in the 1920s. Part of the title of this chapter, "He Has Interpreted the Alien's Mind,"[2] is a quotation directly taken from Enrique's deportation case file. What does it mean to "interpret the alien's mind," and that of an anarchist alien no less? According to Mae Ngai, the term *alien*, especially during the early twentieth century, always signaled that which belonged to another person or place, or simply a noncitizen, who is unassimilable. Part a consequence of racial exclusion under the law and part a historical phenomenon of conquest and immigration, the construction of the alien preconditions foreignness as a default. Racialization and exclusion are rarely discussed in this part of the book because of Enrique's education levels and mastery of discourse, but he was still Mexican, and his race and color were classified as Mexican by the McNeil and Leavenworth penitentiary authorities, along with the Department of Justice, which ultimately informed the notion of "interpreting the mind of the alien." This represents the intersection of racial difference and ideological difference. Add on the fact that the alien was a criminal alien with an intent that goes beyond being illegally in country, and the notion of the alien's mind becomes a question of both ideology and the intent to enact the ideology. Evidence of anti-US ideology was what inspector R. A. Scott looked for. In other words, intent to do wrong already undermined any kind of valuation Enrique brought to the table as a laborer, for example. A precursor to what Ngai further calls "the illegal alien as impossible subject," because the person represents a problem that cannot be solved, the claim of interpreting the alien's mind usurps the rationale of the individual and projects state concepts about permissible forms of citizenship and belonging onto the testimony, irrelevant of its actual content.[3] Fodder for what became the 1924 Johnson-Reed Act, Enrique's alien mind was a problem because he, like most Mexican anarcho-syndicalists, had a long record of direct action in favor of deposing the dictator Díaz and his successors, along with a history of writing propaganda, and because "his acts in the United States are more than enough on which to judge him."[4]

Inspector Scott's arguments from prisoner file number 5486/116 are wrought with an overconfident tone, in which the interviewer had the capacity to interpret from "what was said, what he should have said. He interpreted from what the alien said he meant, what he should have meant." Such omissions, the idea that Enrique would have things to hide in this proceeding, constitute a complex and somewhat incorrect reading, given that his crime was for speaking too much about his indictments of capitalism, authority, and oppression. He had already served time in McNeil Island and Leavenworth and had lived in the US for almost twenty years at the time of deportation. The alien had in fact come to know the system and its laws so well that he had become deeply enmeshed in society. This was indeed a problem for the state. Investigator Warren Long stated that "you are informed that an additional charge other than that contained in the warrant . . . this being that you are an alien anarchist."[5] Enrique replied, "No." Introducing this new charge in the deportation proceedings created another category, indicating a sweeping change in anarchist deportations of the 1920s.

The press also had a way of linking forms of racialization, exclusion, and this new category of alien anarchist to justify Enrique's removal. Calling him a "Mexican Red," the *Los Angeles Times* on October 12, 1922, detailed the charge of distributing seditious works at the Italian Hall on Macy Street in 1921. Notably, the article states three times that Enrique "made his residence here" in Los Angeles and was sure to remind the readership of his original 1912 conviction, when "anarchists caused sensational scenes at the Federal Building here. Lucille Norman, stepdaughter of Ricardo, made a savage attack on the police who were taking the brothers to the County Jail, and radicals, both Mexican and European immigrants, were loud in their support of the prisoners throughout the prosecution."[6] The previous history of anarchist agitation deemed Enrique Flores Magón and family worthy of deportation.

In conspiring to encourage young men to evade the Selective Service Act and the original charge of mailing offensive materials, Enrique's deportation case was built on seeking refuge in the US. His formal contact with the Home Colony anarchist collective of Tacoma while he was in McNeil Island was admitted as evidence for the state's case documenting his inability to quit illicit activity, even while serving time in prison: "It was from this colony that the visitors to the Magon brothers, Zen Zogg, and other anarchists confined to the prisons at McNeil Island that came, and these visitors kept the anarchists inside in touch with the outside world and their 'comrades.'" The problem was thus that men like Enrique could not stop being anarchists while in prison, could not stop their antistate activities. They were depicted as having an incessant, fanatical need to continue their critiques. Defense of such ideas carried through to his last moments of contact with the US state, when Enrique insisted that his writing and work, the very things for which he was convicted, were not "'obscene.' That is the wrong word. That is why I appealed the case. It is wrong to call it obscene when it is revolutionary." With this extreme rejection of what the state and its actors would say were semantics, Enrique negates the idea that anarchism and his beliefs were obscene or lewd. Arguing that "I have the perfect right to think what I want as long as I do not commit a crime. An idea is not a crime,"[7] Enrique pushed back against the criminalization of discourse and instead appealed to American free-thought values. The idea of revolution should not be punished as a crime. It was free speech.

In a prior deportation case that was dropped in 1920, Enrique interviewed with immigration officer Long, making the following claim: "Madero and myself came together and used our force to overthrow Díaz."[8] This statement would have been found obscene by his brother Ricardo. Eliminating his brother from the narrative and dismissing their ideological split with Madero when he came to them in 1913 to have Ricardo become his vice president, Enrique locates himself in Mexican revolutionary history by overemphasizing his individual action. And this claim, when he was finally deported in 1923, would eventually usher Enrique tenuously back into the Mexican nation, but eventually with a pension and a position as a *funcionario*. A foreshadowing of what was reported in 1923 as "many of their [the Flores Magóns'] political followers are said to occupy a high place in the Obregon administration," there was a practical side to such claims in that one had to avoid death and feed the family.[9] But this was also a jab at his elder brother, Jesús, who had stayed in Mexico, ceased his revolutionary activity, and become part of the eventual PRI machine. It is also evidence of the lies Enrique told about himself in the service of politically motivated historical revisions.

The true danger of immediate deportation would be this:

A. If I were deported, I would be shot down.

Q. You feel certain that if you were deported, you would be arrested?

A. I feel certain of the fact.

Given this sense of life-threatening danger if returned to Mexico, Enrique noted that he had not renewed his citizenship, so "I have no country." In some ways being stateless bolstered anarchist masculinity through absolute and cultivated defiance. Such defiance signaled how rooted he was in ideology and yet outside of Mexico's early years of postrevolutionary rebuilding. In the final questions of the interview, Enrique's responses were quite telling:

> Q. Have you any further statement to make to show cause why you should not be deported?
>
> A. If I am not allowed to remain in this country, I should like to go to Russia, together with my whole family.
>
> Q: In the event that you are ordered deported, you feel that it would be the wish of your wife and family to accompany you?
>
> A. They would wish to go with me.[10]

After being in US penitentiaries and evading authorities for more than twenty years, why would Enrique want to stay in the US or go back to Mexico? Turning to Russia and its recent revolution as an alternative to returning to Mexico and facing death was a not-so-surprising option. Russia was more ideologically familiar than the Mexico that had expelled him or the United States that had persecuted him: the imagined Russia represented the anarcho-communism to which he had committed his life for the past thirty years. Emotionally and politically, Russia symbolized optimism in the face of impending deportation and/or death in Mexico. He further argued that "I am perfectly sure that among the Mexican people whose traditions, etc., are much similar to the Russian traditions and customs" would be grounds for his preference for "the soviet form of government."[11] To make cultural value judgments that parallel one another, between Mexico and Russia, was to link their internal proletariat struggles for equality through revolution. Once more, although it would be completely alien to all six of his US-born children, his decision that they and Teresa would accompany him to Russia demonstrates that even though in prison and on the verge of deportation, Enrique was the family decision maker who argued that the cultures and desires of the peoples were similar and familiar.

His violation of the 1918 Immigration Act for trying to overthrow the government was wielded as the primary grounds for his removal as an alien anarchist. Because of his celebrity and/or infamy, the public followed his case closely, noting that as the hearings occurred, "Enrique Flores Magon has grown grey since his last appearance in local courts, and his mild manner is contrasted with his one-time bluster."[12] No longer a desiring subject or desirable subject, Enrique's age and tonal resignation indicate how brutal incarceration was and how poor his health had become. His "bluster"—his indignation, aggressiveness, and ineffective stance against state powers—was affectively absent. This court performance was the direct opposite of the 1916 stump speech, for he was no longer the "raging red radical" the *El Paso Times* painted him to be in its October 13, 1922, editorial that relied on previous physical memories of the staunch anarchist. Yet the same piece proclaimed that "his style has been cramped badly by the persistence of the United States and Mexico, in jailing him at frequent intervals. . . . Magon has been in and out of our penitentiaries ever since 1908 or 1910. His company isn't particularly desirable. There is no reason to keep him as a steady, non-paying boarder."[13] With a caustic and dismissive tone, the editorial painted Enrique as a freeloader with no contribution to be made to society, thus reinforcing violent anarchist alien masculinity tropes. Making fun of the fact that Enrique no longer acted freely as he did previously, the author called out his stylistic physical and vocal self-representations of public appearances past to mock the present. A knock at the previous investment in dapper dress and fancy oratory, the shift in masculine presentation denotes aging, deterioration, disability, and resignation for a man who had never been resigned to anything.

As a diasporic masculine stateless subject, Enrique and his affect registered resignation after being persecuted for decades because of his ideas, justifying the mockery of his style and weathered attitude. This question of style was further taken up by the *Los Angeles Times*, which remarked that "the acknowledged 'Communist-Anarchist' (so he styles himself) shall be sent back to Mexico."[14] Using style (physical, vocal, emotional, political) to yoke race, masculinity, and self-representation gets at the core issues of embodiment and how Enrique's performance of the anarcho-communist standpoint changed over time. The oppositional position of "communist-anarchist" had become anti-American after World War I. That style was linked to a sustained criminality and negative racialization because of the "three previous terms in the penitentiary" and spending the majority of his time behind bars. There was no sentimentalism here for family or political dissidence in the face of potential assassination. Instead, intellectualism was circumvented in the name of good old Mexican criminality and being a jailbird. He was an "undesirable alien," one whose race, demeanor, anti-American (anticapitalist) rhetoric, and excessive red masculinity all contributed to the public sentiment that deportation was a forgone conclusion.[15] Enrique had his chances to reform in the penitentiary. Instead, his ideological style, previously blustery enactments of defiance, and racial predisposition as radical performativities left the state no choice but to protect itself. Because he was a vulnerable subject, style was again mobilized to express Enrique's nonnormative affect.

But the state examiners understood the complexity of Enrique's anarchist style and performativity, so much so that the previous deportation request by A. Caminetti, commissioner general, was canceled on April 14, 1920, by Louis F. Post because of the discrepancies inherent in the word *anarchy* and the imminent danger that Enrique would face if deported. Enrique's idea "favors the American theory of peaceable government by the majority. To deport a believer in government, because he calls himself an anarchist, would be as absurd as refusing to deport a believer in 'anarchist propaganda by deed' if he called himself a Christian."[16] But this plea for political refugee status did not hold, as the 1923 deportation demonstrates. As early as 1921, Frank M. Sturgis of the Department of Justice wrote to the Leavenworth warden for Enrique's mug shots because he had reignited his radical activity after serving time.[17] Los Angeles–based immigration officials requested the deportation, with the final hearing occurring in 1922–23, "alleging he was an undesirable alien, because of a campaign of anarchist and communistic propaganda" carried out after his release from Leavenworth.[18] With these officials reverting to state discourses of undesirable aliens, Enrique and his second blended family were nonetheless granted return to Mexico City and left without being remanded into immigration custody. Being allowed to return to a somewhat fractured social network in Mexico City and without state violence structuring the deportation was an acknowledgment that he was not a physical danger to the populace or a flight risk with six children and a wife in tow. It was also an acknowledgment of class privilege, given Enrique's position as an intellectual who chose to live in poverty.

But the silence and the solemn style that was cramped in the Los Angeles federal court did not stand once the family crossed the border. When they arrived at Juarez after crossing the international border in El Paso, three hundred people gathered to listen to Enrique's fiery homecoming speech at Plaza Juárez. "The Mexican flag is the emblem of the wealthy who oppress the poor and hold the land in a steel grip," he shouted to the group, declaring that "the red and black was his emblem."[19] Announcing his arrival and a career of continued agitation on behalf of the workers, this strategic return to bluster could not have been better calculated. For Teresa, "Mrs. Magon made a short talk for woman's suffrage. The audience gave the speakers a loud applause." This appearance was almost overshadowed by a fight between the speaker and a Juárez resident, at which point "Mr. Magon called the police and ordered the heckler taken away, declaring he was 'drunk.' The police obeyed."[20]

Social orchestration, vibrant PLM networks, and a police force that saw Enrique and Teresa as legitimate speakers with the right to talk freely and unmolested in public show how one's style can be uncramped with a context change. With a magical crossing of the border, however hampered by the political persecution and physical violence and poverty suffered in the US, their pleas for women's suffrage and distrust of the Mexican flag registered normatively because El Paso and Juarez were historic PLM hotbeds of activity. Teresa's speech was in line with what Jocelyn Olcott has identified as the ways in which "well placed Mexican women argued strenuously for women's suffrage, land and labor rights, and even mothers' wages" to identify their place in the newly formed postrevolutionary state.[21] A bloody revolution had passed, with power still consolidating itself, and their speeches confirmed Enrique and Teresa's joint leadership, with their children as witness, in the Mexican nation's future. Radical talk finally had a place, at least upon initially crossing that international border they had so feared just twenty years earlier. The prodigal family had returned with children from two families bearing the Flores Magón name, providing a different vision of modernity and gender forged from anarchist strife (see figure 8.1).[22]

But the Juarez scene was not as disorderly as the newspapers suggest. There was plenty of time to take a family picture with the Juarez chapter of the IWW before moving to the Mexican interior. The defiant poses of Teresa, Enrique, the workers, and the children are directly in contrast to the analysis of abjection that Shelly Streeby posits in her reading of a predeportation photo. Streeby argues that the family's humility and poverty register abjection in another photo from this same time, but this image with workers who immediately recognized the Flores Magón family, their sacrifices, and their centrality to national revolution and reform is quite defiant.[23] The contrast between the two images is striking: one evokes humility and the other defiance. As a photo documenting the return from diaspora, the image is, as Tina Campt argues, "a performative practice that enacts complicated forms of social and cultural relationships." The antiestablishment tenor of worker anarchists with beloved leaders and their children suggests that the nation, at least where the proletariat and anarchists were concerned, was ready to receive them and document their return (see figures 8.2 and 8.3). Following the fiery speech, the IWW of Juarez led a procession through the streets. Photos documenting the event depict Enrique's mood as rather somber. He performed solemn affect of the return's mixed emotions after decades of exile. He appeared pensive, with blurred worker masses in the background, the sense of photographic capture willed and welcomed. As evidence of the "relationship between the experience of migration and the . . . feeling in these images," the images from Juarez exhibit sober and stoic

FIG 8.1. Enrique Flores Magón, Teresa Arteaga de Flores Magón, Enrique Flores Magón Jr., Estela Flores Magón, José Flores Magón, Pedro Flores Magón, and Santiago Flores Magón. "Group of Fellow Workers and the whole Magón Tribe after our reception Meeting on March 4th, 1923, at the Constitución Plaza, Juárez Chi. Mex, when we crossed the line into México the day of our deportation from the Land of Freedom for Wall Street and San Quentin for the Rebel. We spoke from the music stand (or kiosko) in the back." Courtesy of the University of Washington Special Collections, Industrial Workers of the World Photograph Collection. Photographer: Estudio Villegas. UW11042.

affective performance.[24] The Juarez stop marked what eventually became an extensive propaganda tour that resuscitated Enrique's and to some degree Teresa's roles as intellectual leaders in Mexico, calling for unification among labor struggles, organizers, and suffragists. These images centralize the Flores-Magón brood, along with the Mexican IWW, as the heart of national politics. Ideologically, the images legitimate their legacy, especially given María Brousse's public attempts to question Enrique's revolutionary credibility. His return to Mexico soon led to arrests and activism, including a Red and Black demonstration that turned into a riot in Juarez on March 22,

1923, where several people were wounded and his potential presidential candidacy was discussed,[25] and a June 13 arrest in Santa Ana Chiatempan, Tlaxcala, along with Spanish anarchist Maria Belen de Sarraga, for being alleged agitators.[26] With Enrique labeled a socialist and labor leader, these further arrests and harassment also affected Teresa and Enrique Jr. as they went on the tour. In his 1954 autobiography, *Peleamos contra la injusticia*, Enrique reestablished activist credibility upon touching Mexican soil, which allowed the authorities to punish him for past offenses and also paved the way for his role in the Mexican state as a precursor of the revolution.

Enrique continued to bolster his credibility and reputation by securing a government pension under President Miguel Alemán and by writing columns for mainstream magazines such as *Todo* and *El Universal,* and the Department of the Interior official newspaper, *El Nacional*, between 1945 and 1953, often singing Alemán's praises. Reflecting on everything from the Haymarket riots to the Mexican Revolution and his role in it, from elegies to his dead brother Ricardo to solidarity, he was positioned as an authoritative historical commentator. Although he claimed to be a humble and truthful servant to history, comparing his narratives with what actually happened on the ground reveals discrepancies. Not only was his seven-year stint as a regular social commentator evidence of how he parlayed cultural capital into a return to journalism, but it was also a chance for him to revise history as he wrote it. Despite the earlier misogyny expressed toward his ex-compañera Paula Carmona, his 1946 article about his life riding the Edendale tranvia with his life companion, Teresa Arteaga de Flores Magón, displayed a staunch gender critique: "We learn, also, that respecting the woman, as our partner and not viewing her as our miserable slave, that we can slap or drag like a horse, to which many people say 'fine,' which echos like a cavern in almost all of our community."[27] In later life, and because of his partner's dedication to him and the cause, his gender critique of women's equality shifted greatly. His masculinity, as a narrator of history and Mexican public cultures, was staked on his advocacy for those less enfranchised than he: the poor, the worker, women, and even Jewish people. Thus, as Enrique Flores Magón wrote his way back into Mexican society, he also used the position of political critique and advocacy as a form of masculine privilege.

His columns reminded the audience that he had been a political prisoner. From that vantage point, Enrique reconstructed a notion of revolutionary masculinity to compete with that of his brother Ricardo. When narrating their release from McNeil in 1914, his March 20, 1946, account centralizes his role as a natural orator. He, Ricardo, Anselmo Figueroa, and Librado Rivera

FIG 8.2. Enrique Flores Magón, Teresa Arteaga de Flores Magón, Enrique Flores Magón Jr., Estela Flores Magón, Esperanza Flores Magón, José Flores Magón, Pedro Flores Magón, and Santiago Flores Magón in Los Angeles on the day of their deportation, March 1923. Courtesy of the University of Washington Special Collections, Industrial Workers of the World Photograph Collection. Photographer: Estudio Villegas. UW11043.

FIG 8.3. Enrique Flores Magón holding the red flag, Ciudad Juárez, Chihuahua, Mexico, March 4, 1923. Courtesy of the University of Washington Special Collections, Industrial Workers of the World Photograph Collection. Photographer: Estudio Villegas. UW11038.

were hosted by the Seattle chapter of the IWW on their two-month speaking tour on the way back to Los Angeles. Calling himself an "obligated orator" because he was the only one who had a command of the English language, it was his responsibility to convey the gravity of their incarceration at McNeil and create solidarity between the PLM and the IWW despite the fact that he "had never spoken in public before." Reflecting on his speaking debut, he embeds the remarkable nature of the performance into the narrative: "I mounted the discourse for two hours, but when I wanted to conclude my remarks to the public, they began to protest because there were details they wanted amplified, small details dissected. And so I passed two more hours answering questions and more questions until the public was satisfied with all of the facets of our Mexican social revolution of 1910."[28] The epic description of his performance does several things in terms of historical memory about the PLM. It displaces Ricardo as the main orator of the movement. It also posits a natural aptitude for public discourse in English, centralizing his physical stamina despite just being released from federal prison. Finally, in terms of masculine virility, the description of his impromptu oration normalizes his masculinity away from the emotional fragility and psychic instability of his time in McNeil, for this was when he split with Paula and was separated from his small children. Instead of representing loss, regret, or sadness, Enrique used the opportunity in *El Nacional* to normalize his masculine performance as exceptional.

In one column called "¿Amargados?" (The bitter ones?), Enrique detailed the pacts he and Ricardo made to suffer on behalf of workers in freeing Mexico from the yolk of capitalism. Cataloging the years of political persecution, emotional suffering, and starvation, Enrique answered typical questions that he was asked by the public:

> Don't you feel disillusioned? Don't you feel alienated before the ingratitude of Mexico that didn't recognize your sacrifices? . . . There was no reason for disillusionment. Since we entered the struggle—Ricardo and I responded—we knew that the road would be harsh, full of pain and vicissitudes, as well as mortal dangers. . . . The proof is that the majority of the revolutionary precursors save a very few, live in misery. The majority, are older than sixty years old and have to continue working in order to live. Effectively, I am not "bitter." I see all of it a kind of naturalness.[29]

The naturalness of suffering and sacrifice was a twofold representation of revolutionary masculinity bound to a vow of poverty. In suffering for the masses, they came of age and became men. And, as men of a certain age (Enrique was sixty-nine when he wrote the article), he locates himself and the other precursors as men who have to work in order to survive. Survival was something that he and Ricardo had become accustomed to. Although some might see having a regular column in *El Nacional* as a privilege and luxury (it was), his authority as a revolutionary precursor was what allowed him to work as a journalist until his death in 1954. Thus, the lack of bitterness can be read doubly: it was an expression of masculine stoicism in the face of extreme hardship and an indirect acknowledgment of the fact that his suffering as a precursor did provide some privileges. Despite the moral pain and vicissitudes of sadness and suffering, Enrique emerged from his historically reflective writings centralizing his masculine pain and displacement.

Part I

CONCLUSION

"Enrique Flores Magón died on the 28th of October 1954," states Ethyl Duffy Turner's closing remarks in her history of the PLM.[1] She says everything and nothing after her account of the ideological measure of the PLM's main figure, Ricardo Flores Magón. Enrique remains the secondary figure in the PLM, along with his brother Jesús, who betrayed them and the revolution for a family life and a position in the government. But Enrique's footprint in history was a bit larger than scholars have previously suggested. He was eulogized in Mexico in places such as Ciudad Juarez, where the press stated that "the death of Enrique Flores Magón signifies the loss of one of our most intrepid and stalwart fighters. . . . It was impossible work, toppling a dictatorship. . . . It is impossible to negate his decisive role as an initiator of the revolution however effusive it might have been."[2] Contrary to a mere death date provided by Duffy Turner, Enrique's vast correspondence and meticulous archiving of his own materials, along with those of Teresa Arteaga and Paula Carmona, demonstrate how, from a very early age, he understood his role as a historical actor and subject. His life and letters were of value enough to cultivate them, along with his ideas and family, in perpetuity, except where Paula, Práxedis, Demófilo, and Margarita Carmona were concerned. But we also have to take into account that he expunged things from his records and the narrative of revolutionary masculine subjecthood that were damaging to his emotional countenance and reputation. What we can learn from Enrique's life is that the great losses he and his immediate family experienced were a result of his ardent defense of Mexican freedom through anarchist modes of direct action. That "Idea" of freedom and masculinity produced by it, as I've accounted for throughout part I, was driven by a deep need for loyalty coupled with ever-increasing suspicion of others.

Enrique's love letters, personal losses, long-suffering body, and mobilization of sentiment, including the split with Paula Carmona and resulting loss of three children and the second partnership with Teresa Arteaga, are often ignored because they simply don't fit with a history of revolution. These were the elements that rendered him emotionally and physically vulnerable: a threat to traditional narratives of Mexican revolutionary masculinities. These expunged histories—of his own volition and by historiographers themselves—are quite messy, both politically and emotionally. The anarchist stance and cause were intertwined with all forms of intimacy, often intensifying homosocial and heterosexual forms of love and loss. Thus, in addition to the familial love letters that form the backbone of Enrique's archive, we have treatises of seduction penned by the same author in the name of the revolution, and letters to and from comrades expressing love in exile as an act of politicization. When paired with the dissolution of his first marriage to Paula, the idealized family and life-partner relationship he created with his second compañera were all the more noteworthy in tracking the history of affect that underlies the gallant PLM narrative. His relationships with Paula and their children, and Teresa and her children, were stretched to the limit and, in the case of Paula, completely destroyed by what he and the PLM perceived as betrayal. Moreover, the deep expressions of love and loss, be they about completely severed family ties or in the face of serving various prison sentences, demonstrate very flexible notions of Mexican masculinities that were at times tender and at other times excessively and strategically sentimental, misogynist, and brusque. Protection of the "Idea"—that is, anarchism—often trumped or reinforced gendered performances in familial contexts. The "Idea" necessitated that one not stray too far from ideology. Even though the PLM and Enrique were supposed to be free-love and gender-equality advocates, the archival materials suggest that they were more interested in preserving their own masculinities and masculine privileges in the movement than in women's equality. With the intimate partners of PLM leaders such as Enrique, there indeed was a double and more harsh standard about toeing the party line in the name of the "Idea."

The visual aspects of the archives examined herein—photographs, sketches, and found object art—illuminate and materialize affect.[3] Affectively, the image texts interspersed throughout part I illustrate the ways in which Enrique drew people to the cause and drew them into his circle of confidants and family relied on various forms of masculine performatives to sway and mobilize intense desires for proximity and closeness. They also suggest that family formation was worth documenting and was vital to his cultivation of home in an alien land. The ideological work of the images in creating a historically embedded masculine subject cannot be underestimated. As ideology was cemented through photographs of his two families, Enrique, Paula, and Teresa cultivated emotional forms of attachment through strident discourses defending anarchy, opposing Mexican proletariat oppression, and exposing the poverty that Mexican workers and their children faced on both sides of the border. These foundational principles were executed and documented through images of family, discourses of critique, and sketches of loves lost. Such love for his fellow workers, their children, and his own family is most ardently mapped in the pages of *Regeneración*. However, those intense desires could occasionally be mobilized in the opposite direction, in vile hatred and denunciation of those who he represented as betraying him, such as Paula and his children Práxedis, Demófilo, and Margarita, whom he never saw again after their split. However, this too is debatable based on the evidence presented herein. Those moments of human vulnerability, of lashing out with misogynist rants and public humiliation, were part of how the PLM did business. The ability to denounce and destroy those closest enforced the party line.

Over the years, Enrique's relationship with Teresa was self-narrated as an idealized form of love and family: a form of emotional labor. As late as 1946, long after the family had been deported to Mexico, Enrique extolled Teresa's feminine virtues in the context of revolutionary ideology: "For the use and benefit of those who think a woman involved in revolution cannot be a good wife and much less a good mother, I think it's best to intimate that she always conserved her femininity, while also attending to our home and taking care of our children until each one left our home."[4] Knowing his audience, for *El Nacional* was the official newspaper of Mexico's Department of the Interior, Enrique used the weekly column to write and rewrite the history of the PLM and social revolution in Mexico. He broke a few rules of anarchism, first calling

Teresa his wife, which was antithetical to the idea of marriage as slavery for women. He also spoke to gender-normative ideologies about womanhood and the domestic sphere, stating that women's revolutionary activity did not prevent them from being good mothers and wives.

The commitment to the struggle, shared poverty, and emotional losses was daunting, but Enrique's revisionist histories reinstate a normative gender order as he reflected on the past. Both he and Teresa had experienced the deaths of children and state violence being enacted in front of their children, which set the tone for what was, in correspondence, represented as undying faith and love. And although it was a heteronormative relationship, Teresa and Enrique's rocky start (they were both still married to other people when they made commitments to each other) and their anarchist beliefs worked together to forge a nontraditional family, including Enrique's own memoirs, which rewrote history as it was to represent them as a traditional Mexican nuclear family with a marriage that did not happen in 1905. The intensity of these emotional attachments demonstrates the power and costs of living a public life in the name of anarchism and freedom for the Mexican people.

The collective emotional labor of the families, and Enrique in particular, used sentimentality, feeling and excess, and material tokens of affection to sustain patriarchal visions of family and ideology during Enrique's various sentences in county jails and federal penitentiaries. Those affective excesses used circuits of desire and attachment to produce social subjects differently.[5] Therefore, this work moves away from the lionized, static representations of Enrique performing hypermasculine revolutionary subjectivity and sees him as a vulnerable masculine subject, both physically and emotionally, producing a disruptive and fragile position. The arc of Enrique's emotive history resonates within this most capacious approach to an intricate and intimate family history of revolution. As we look back to the frame of that 1917 Los Angeles County jail photo, we understand why the diasporic subject almost cut out of the frame invited us to look. For what is on the periphery allows us to see a different history altogether.

PART II. THE HOMOEROTICS OF ABJECTION
The Gaze and Leonard Nadel's Salinas Valley
Bracero Photographs

The bracero program recruited more than 4.5 million temporary Mexican male laborers to work in the agriculture industry in the US from 1942 to 1964. This program represented one of the largest influxes of Mexican male migrants into the United States, and it also was one of the biggest binational efforts to turn premodern laboring bodies into abject bodies. There is a long tradition of bracero scholarship, in both Spanish and English, most notable in the work of Ernesto Galarza, research director of the National Agricultural Workers Union. His report, *Strangers in Our Fields* (1956), took a documentary approach, as did most of the texts of this era, demonstrating the failures of the bracero program in its promise to protect the rights of workers and a lack of compliance with the contracts on the part of both the US Department of Labor and the growers who hired them. Esteemed Los Angeles–based photographer Leonard Nadel embarked upon documenting just how bad the conditions were for braceros. Galarza's report, which made its way into the White House for then president Eisenhower's consideration, tracked dependence on the labor of "Nationals."[1] But we must also remember that the report followed on the heels of the 1954 implementation of Operation Wetback, which used special tactics to curtail illegal Mexican migration by those who were not officially accepted into the bracero program. Galarza demonstrated that the program was "a mainstay of certain agricultural operations," representing 75 percent of the labor force in California alone during 1955.[2] Even so, the primary focus of the document was to catalog "grievances of Mexican Nationals arising out of violations of their rights."[3] In doing so, Galarza inadvertently set the tone for how subsequent historical scholarship about the bracero program would document Mexican nationals' experiences in the US fields as victimization and suffering.

More recent historical scholarship by Mireya Loza, Ana Rosas, and Deborah Cohen has parted with this trend, instead showing the complexity of these mass migrations. Rosas and Cohen rightfully include the gendered dynamics for men and women in the breaking up and remaking of the Mexican family and of sexual and gender roles. Loza and Rosas also detail the role of citizenship and the modernizing impulse inherent in Mexico's shipping off poor rural men to the US and the implications of the program for the Mexican middle and upper classes on both sides of the border as they reaped tremendous benefits from financing bracero migration and the provision of services to the migrating populations. Rosas looks at women's roles, writing them into the history of reproductive and emotional labor in the bracero program.[4] Loza discusses the political organizing and conditions, with a focus on "deviance and defiance," even gesturing to male-male sexual relations within the context of labor camps in her fantastic oral history, even though she does not theorize these queer moments in depth.[5] She explores how braceros have since politically organized regarding monetary compensation for wage theft and also a recuperation of their rights as citizens. Overall, bracero scholarship focuses on questions of nation, citizenship, modernity, the fracturing of the Mexican family, migration, and its damaging effects on all of these structures of meaning and sociality.

In addition, most studies of the bracero program suggest that the Nadel photographs were published in Galarza's *Strangers in Our Fields*. They weren't. Nadel was inspired by Galarza's pamphlet and therefore retraced his steps by receiving a grant from the Fund for the Republic, a left-leaning nonprofit created by the Ford Foundation. The Fund for the Republic tackled controversial issues at the time, and the bracero program was one of them. To bolster the fund's investigations into immigration policy, Nadel's project was to create what Richard Stevens Street has described as a visual counterpart to *Strangers in Our Fields* as evidence of exploitation and squalid living and working conditions.[6] These photos are often taken as transparent truths of what really happened to the laborers in their migration routes and while in the United States. Although it is indeed true that the Nadel photographs documented grower policy, poor living conditions, and suffering, it is also somewhat problematic to allow his particular angle on the visual field to determine truth so completely. In the same way that Nadel flattens out nation and specificity based on a visual narrative while aestheticizing poverty to sell the story of the "drybacks" (another uncritically used derogatory term to describe legal Mexican labor in the 1950s), I suggest that a more attentive reading reveals clues and details about region, race, intentionality, and forms of desire and attachment. Galarza urged Nadel to treat the photographs as propaganda, capturing suffering as the endgame.[7] And Nadel was tasked with knowing and recognizing suffering based on his left-leaning political beliefs. Particular images from Nadel's social-reformist photographic exposé show that "policy is as much an artistic endeavor as it is a bureaucratic enterprise."[8] It also forces us to question "how sexual norms uphold themselves to constitute and regulate hierarchies of humanness as they work to unsettle those norms and the default humanness they uphold."[9]

The goal of the following chapters is to raise questions about the context, subjectivity, and temporality of Nadel's photos and the subjects that compose them. No scholar, to my knowledge, has inquired about Nadel's feelings, desires, or positionality in relationship to the bracero photographs he took in 1956, especially because he often lived in the camps with those he was photographing. He did indeed develop familiarity with the subjects and, in some cases, intimacies and attachments. Although critics have stated that his work was on par with that of Dorothea Lange for its powerful capacity to provide a strong emotional response to the conditions of farmworkers, and I'd agree, it still doesn't erase the sense that the political mandate of these images necessitates an analysis beyond their aesthetic greatness. As numerous scholars of photography have shown, a "photographer's power to redraw the line or blur the distinction between happening and trace, aesthetics and politics, or . . . spectatorship and performance, stems from [photography's] constant renewal of an original prolepsis and an original temporal transgression."[10] This idea of prolepsis, or anticipating and answering objections in advance, is key, for temporality and location ascribe or detract meaning from the bracero images in their universality. Further, there is indeed a tension between the happening (what braceros experienced) and the trace (the documents that were left behind). The photos stand as the site where the photographer's intentions met those of the men being photographed. One critic described his style as follows: "a gently intruding lens that focused warmly on human relationships."[11] Despite the fact that Nadel himself grew up during the Great Depression and clearly identified with his subjects as he photographed them, the intrusion factor is derived from the chasm of racial and cultural difference in the bracero photographs. Although the photos are compassionate, there is a stark set of issues surrounding contracted, racialized, noncitizen poverty. Still, cataloging by both the Nadel estate and the Smithsonian Museum of American History built a universal narrative, as did repeated use of particular bracero photographs in scholarship thereafter. Nadel built a narrative of suffering that others could identify with. He called it "selling the picture story." These photographed frozen moments in time disrupt the narrative of braceros in the project of modernity to reflect, if anything, a further entrenchment of social and economic inequality.

Nadel took his work seriously, following the men from the time they left their homes in Mexico's *bajío* (Central Mexican states: Aguascalientes, Jalisco, Guanajuato, and Querétaro) to the processing centers in Monterrey, Nuevo Leon; Empalme, Sonora; and Calexico, Baja California; and then onto the buses and into the labor camps. As he traveled more than five thousand miles to "sell the picture story," he lost any sense of neutrality. His highly subjective approach was steered by his social values of documenting the lives of the less fortunate in society, despite being a highly sought-after commercial photographer.[12] Reflecting upon his career, Nadel said, "Without feeling that emotion, my photography wouldn't say anything." He did not specify the exact emotion he experienced when with braceros, but he defined his work by its capacity to create affective attachments and build relationships of an emotional nature. This was furthered by the fact that he often got to know his photographic subjects. He continued: "I like to share the experience of those whom I'm photographing. I want to be close to them. I'd never use a long lens. If I'm too far away, I don't feel it."[13] To achieve a form of intuited emotional responses, Nadel required physical and emotional proximity to those he photographed. If he didn't feel the emotional connection, he knew that he was not close enough to his subjects. Like an ethnographer, often living with the men in the camps, he retraced the steps of Galarza's work as a part of a California political mandate to document the filthy and substandard quarters. He was seasoned in the field, having served as a World War II combat photographer, slogging his way through the Pacific war front with the US army.[14] He knew what poverty, war, and abjection could do to people and thus committed himself to the bracero photographs as a form of social justice in exposing exploitation. In his essay

"The New Role for the Photographer," Nadel argued that "the conditions I had witnessed stirred me deeply. I felt that it was as much my responsibility to help 'sell' the picture story. The new role of the magazine photographer is to make such worthwhile projects more widely read and its human content enlivened by the visual impact of a sensitive and honest portrayal."[15]

In the summer and fall of 1956, his mandate was to provide that evidence of immigration's adverse effects on braceros. He wasn't simply interested in documenting the backbreaking field labor but was "attentive to the broader rhythms of life outside work."[16] He also emotionally connected with braceros because their experiences, like his own, reflected the impoverished neighborhoods where he grew up in New York City during the Depression. As he remarked, "There is a natural affinity between these environments and the places back East where I spent so many years." In this way he received much criticism from growers who claimed the images were biased and distorted.[17] But although the images were circulated to a congressional committee investigating the program and some of the content was very strong, they did not achieve wider notoriety. Even as Nadel's intention was for social justice purposes, "selling the picture story" commodifies the bracero visual archive in a way that unsettles the altruistic political narrative of the photographs. He actually had to fight with *Look* magazine to finally get a measly four pictures printed along with a story in 1957. As Nadel wrote to a friend in Mexico City, "Everyone feels that the photographic documentation will serve to accomplish something constructively in spotlighting the violations and improving conditions both in Mexico and the United States."[18] This constructive documentation for social change was always tempered by emotion and the desire to connect with those being photographed. "I just don't grab a camera and start shooting. I take time to relate . . . to elicit some kind of response from them. It always starts with a conversation. I try to get to know what they're doing and how they're feeling."[19] Nadel articulated the mediated nature of his interactions with the subject before he began taking shots. He cultivated relationships within particular contexts to emotionally connect. These politics of empathy in representation are what drove him as a photographer, carefully choosing not just what to shoot but how to elicit the most affect from the subject and, in turn, positioning the camera in a way that centralized compassion as the key emotion as much as possible.

Yet Nadel's bracero catalog is curious. Repetition of single-subject photos, as Bajorek suggests, reveals more-sustained or apparent traces in their repetition and, therefore, create meaning at both aesthetic and political levels.[20] Nadel's particular politics as a child of the Depression governed why the photographer chose for some individual men to be photographed in two to ten images in series or to repeat certain domestic, intimate, or labor scenes from multiple vantage points in his photos. Contrary to the previous scholarship, these chapters argue that the archive demonstrates that he developed emotional relationships with the braceros he photographed. The gaze lingers upon them because of the development of rapport. Instead of claiming that these documents merely show men suffering, going through a screening process, or being fumigated or taking a shower, I suggest that the trace has a political content and intentionality that is both homosocial and homoerotic. In fact, the bracero program, as a federal policy, was built on queer notions and structures. It forced Mexican men in the bracero program to adopt and internalize new forms of domesticity. As bachelors, they could achieve privacy and autonomy from the family. There were no wives, families, or children, which formed part of the program's ideology. The program offered a way to document how men lived in poverty with one another and without women. Because of the bracero program's design, they performed the invisible work of domesticity, much like gay couples in the US and Mexico, including food preparation and feeding, kin work, interaction work, consumption work, emotional work, and household-status-presentation work.[21] Braceros were doing double duty in their gender work, legislated by the state, in the absence of women. The demand for their labor power infantilized them and made them nonthreatening to Anglos, as well as forcing new forms of domesticity.

Thus, Nadel's perspective, much like the historiography of the bracero program, represented two competing national narratives of suffering, on the one hand, and compulsory heteronormativity and domesticity on the other. A queer reading becomes a way to rectify the national project of modernity with quotidian same-sex relations and domesticity, which were institutionalized through the program. By reading the homosocial and homoerotic with the ways in which braceros are lionized as heteronormative subjects who suffered, we not only see the attachments and new masculine gender formations among and between braceros but also account for those relationships that Nadel developed with his photographic subjects. They developed, in essence, a repertoire of same-sex relationships and domesticity as a result of the bracero program policy.[22] The shift from the regimes of racialized feminized labor to shifting gender-labor paradigms produces an alternative to the idea of the Mexican macho steeped in patriarchy and privilege. Instead, when read closely, the alternative reveals queer potentiality.

My argument and methodological approaches in these chapters move away from the most publicly known bracero pictures, which show them in concentrated masses, awaiting selection at recruitment centers, where they were subject to bodily inspections and fumigation with toxic chemicals before entering the US. Another swath of visual images represents the quotidian nature of their lives upon arrival to the US: their disciplined labor in the agricultural fields, always subject to the whims of their employers or their domestic spaces and limited leisure time. While all of this is certainly a part of the Nadel Smithsonian archive, my work takes three very different approaches. I am most interested in the photos that did not make it into the public archive of bracero suffering and attempt to explain why this is so. Further, I reread many of these stock photos for the ways in which they register the body as archive of shame and abjection: a feminized and uncertain boundary of horror and fascination, threatening that which exists outside of it. Stock photos were, and continue to be, put to use as evidence of bracero suffering, compulsory heteronormativity, and poor treatment, strengthening their impact in claims for bracero reparations because of that abjection.

In addition, Nadel's personal archive and Nadel as a person, as much as the braceros that he photographed, are the main actors in this part of the archiving Mexican masculinities story. I write an affective history of practice embodied in the photographs and the relationships established between and among men. And although the images construct bracero personhood, there is a way in which readers of the Nadel archive have underestimated the inhumane conditions of what has become a highly and occasionally uncritically cited body of photographs. Finally, because the photos were taken in 1956 in places such as the Salinas Valley, the San Joaquin Valley, the Imperial Valley of California, and the Rio Grande Valley of Texas, one needs to be mindful of how the local and national worlds of receiving communities responded to the men, Nadel, his photographs, and how the larger political landscape functioned as an affective archive.

Nadel documented to decry the exploitation of braceros with his camera. Thus, I have selected images that are both somewhat normative and that also stand out in their relative positioning in the catalog series imposed by the Smithsonian Museum of American History. As Sontag argued in *On Photography*, "Both the order and the exact time for looking at each photograph are imposed; and there is again in the visual legibility and emotional impact." Further, she argues that photography conveys the ways in which one "put[s] oneself into a certain relation to the world that feels like knowledge—and therefore, like power."[23] We can glean that the photograph, in and of itself, is an object that imparts knowledge of self to the world or to an imagined self in a particular moment frozen in time. The imagined or aspirational self, in photography, extends beyond state expectations for those men who came to the US in the bracero program. The historical narratives provide very limited, top-down expressions of the imagined self, but examining the gestural pushes against the will and power of being nonnormative: they refuse to be what the camera asks them to be, docile and nondesiring. Plus, these photos also traveled and have had quite a life after they were initially produced. Sontag reminds us that questions of legibility and emotional impact are just as crucial: how the photo is read and by whom and when seem doubly important. Thus, taking these ideas about epistemology and reading practice together and the fact that Nadel's photographs were produced for the Fund for the New Republic, I explore how power, legibility, and desire get configured in producing an abject subject in relationship to the nation-state, be it Mexican or American.

Taken in sum, the photos clearly document an abject population as a threat, a site of masculinized-feminized horror and fascination, while the living conditions mimicked that abjection in the spatiality of power relations of transnational capitalism. Second, the setting, context, place, or space of these photographs is not necessarily known without intimate knowledge of the program or the landscapes themselves. This tactic is both universalizing of "the" bracero experience at the same time that it denies the personhood of those being photographed. A lack of clear locality lends disorder to the visual archive of bracero suffering and further suggests that there was a reason to keep these geographies and the bodies that inhabited them anonymous. Nadel created propaganda types through physical proximity in the images themselves despite concrete indicators of who these men were or where they were photographed. In essence, the lack of context further alienates the subjects from the national landscapes. From them, we glean how sexual and gender relations in bracero communities shifted by reading the bodies as physical texts.

This second part of this book analyzes what I am calling the homoerotics of abjection in Nadel's 1956 photographs, using queer theory and feminist methodologies to closely read how they display and register desire, sexuality, and longing out of an abject subject position. I focus on how Nadel's realist photographic experiment was designed to document a population and its living conditions as a space of abjection on the one hand and, upon close reading, as a divergence from the compulsory narrative of heteronormativity on the other. Because the collection of two-thousand-plus photos made its argument of universal abjection by keeping these geographies and the bodies that inhabited them anonymous, they essentially created an archetype of universal labor exploitation, or what I refer to as the *archetype of bracero public suffering*. Nadel did not record the names of the men he photographed in any of the scrapbooks, captions, or contact sheets he produced for the Fund for the New Republic. Because we do not know their names, this anonymity and abjection, I argue, were produced through the intense feelings of attachment generated in the photographs and because of the physical proximity with these subjects as he took the pictures. Thus, we don't see pure victims, but engaged subjects in an exchange, in a series of glances and attachments. The photographs indicate social abjection as a multidimensional ambiguous longing for and by the individuals in the photographs. As Sharon Patricia Holland has argued in *The Erotic Life of Racism*, "Racist practice does limit human desire by attempting to circumscribe its possible attachments."[24] Knowing how racism delimits attachments, the queer diasporic possibility of these photos is mobilized by the ways in which braceros chose to meet the longing documentary gaze with their own desires. The queer diaspora framework explains how the Mexican national subject position shifted and was remade through sexuality and race in migration.

Nadel's latent homoerotic gaze created—because of those emotional attachments he forged—an out-of-place framing and cross-temporal context. That cross-temporality and lack of geographic context capture longing for and by the individuals in the photographs as they look back: there were indeed just as many willing subjects as there were unwilling subjects in the photos. Queer diasporic possibility, or rather pushing back against the blanket heteronormative scripts of bracero migrants, is also mobilized by the ways in which braceros in the photos chose to meet the longing homosocial documentary lens of the camera with their own desires. As Robert McKee Irwin argues, "Even the most macho visions of lo Mexicano have their queer elements," and the return of the gaze with longing and desire was one way to thwart the imposed narrative of the family, the nation, and the normative.[25] When prioritizing desire, sexuality, and longing, we can read these photographs in the ways that Gayatri Gopinath has proposed, as a way of registering a queer diaspora, and what this tells us about the affective and emotive registers of men who traveled, worked, loved, drank, and gambled together in highly homosocial and potentially homoerotic spaces. With this approach, bracero photographs serve as traces of other historical registers of masculinity contesting written national scripts of machismo as the only way to be a Mexican man in the 1950s. We can see these images taking "accidental encounters ... [to] produce pleasure and affiliation, which then produce more encounters and more pleasures."[26] If, as Lauren Berlant explains, "immigration discourse is a central technology for the reproduction of patriotic nationalism: not just because the immigrant is seen as without a nation or resources and thus as deserving of pity or contempt, but because the immigrant is defined as *someone who desires America*," can we think through these images as sites of desire for the nation and desire for the bracero and his body simultaneously?[27]

Chapter 9

MAKING BRACEROS OUT OF PLACE
AND OUTSIDE OF TIME

The Nadel photographs cannot be accurately understood without recalling that they were snapped at a key moment in the history of US-Mexico relations. At the peak of the bracero program—the 1950s—the Mexican press publicly questioned the benefits of the program. Mainstream weeklies such as *El Universal*, *Todo*, and *La Mañana* published editorials and photographic exposés of the bracero program, lamenting the loss of their compatriots to a foreign power that merely exploited them. In 1949 *El Mañana* ran a four-installment photo exposé about the bracero program titled "El espejismo del dolar" (The mirage of the dollar). Chronicling the life of Manuel García, the article exposed a Mexican middle-class public to the suffering of their fellow countrymen. García stated, "I had to leave my country to shake me from complexes that made me blind. I believe in this I succeeded as did the many others of us who came." As García described program benefits, *El Mañana*'s paternalism superseded his voice to inscribe normative masculinity: "Manuel García is a dry and hard man. He has shredded hands because of his work and eyes that are very fixed and absorbed by the preoccupation that his capacity to labor could be destroyed by the mistake of a fellow worker."[1] Dramatizing García's normative masculinity of *feo y fuerte* (ugly and strong), the exposé is complemented by Mexican photographer José A. del Campo's work. Visually representing and then narrating signs of wear on García's face, hands, and body produced the evidence necessary for a middle-class audience to understand the tragic consequences of the program.

In June 1955, *Todo* ran an editorial, "La liberacion de bracerismo" (Liberation from the bracero program), in which Gustavo Alavos Guzmán argued that because "they leave in search of work, this itself is a sign. They don't know what they are getting into, and they encounter disgrace until the death of their crazy adventure, but they come in the magic name of WORK! . . . This is the formula to avoid much strife and, at the same time, liberate the bracero from our anguish and deprivation with the sad exodus of our compatriots."[2] Part patriotic appeal to nationalism and part paternalism, Guzmán spoke to a middle-class readership by showing how ignorant and blind working-class men were in their chasing of a measly dollar in the United States without understanding the contexts for their exploitation. That disgrace and loss, the craziness of their sacrifices, made braceros a group that the Mexican middle class needed to save from their own devices. This paternalistic attitude was also replicated on the US side in the sense that braceros were infantilized in order to justify their harmlessness, which I discuss throughout the coming chapters.

These photo exposés and editorials in Mexico foreshadowed Nadel's photographic odyssey, which coincided with the 1956 US presidential campaign. His work also came on the heels of 1954 Operation Wetback, the September 1956 report issued by the President's Committee on Migratory Labor, the aftermath of both *Westminster v. Mendez* (1946) and the 1954 *Brown v. Board of Education* decisions, and the growth of the Mexican economy in the 1950s even as the country sent a large percentage of its male workers to the US. All these events shaped a transnational social and economic milieu that made braceros appear to be out of place and out of context, both nameless and nationless, an idea that would prove very central to the critical discourse on and success of the program in the 1950s.

The economic situation and displacement influenced the larger affective sense purveyed by the organization of the Nadel photographic archive and the images themselves, but the local political and social climate in the Salinas Valley in 1956 tells another story. As numerous historians of the program have shown, there were clear divides among Mexican Americans born in the US; longtime residents of the region who still had strong ties to Mexico; braceros themselves, who were temporary populations; the Filipino and Dust Bowl migrants who were increasingly integrated into the permanent settlement of the communities; and the Anglo-, Italian, Portuguese, and Swiss American growers who ran the agricultural industry. Although Catholicism and agriculture were often the only things these ethnic and social classes held in common, the social world of this historical moment suggests a different narrative. For example, in the major growing season, roughly March to September, the community was more densely organized around agricultural production. Social relations and economic interactions were aided and brokered through the produce industry. As a result, farm politics governed the lives of the elite Anglo and ethnic whites, the middle class, and the braceros alike. This shift to growing season as an organizing principle is best assessed through the local press. The *Salinas Californian*, the *Santa Cruz Sentinel*, and the *Register Pajaronian* covered these social fissures caused by economic inequalities and racial inequalities side by side. When juxtaposed with the policies of the Eisenhower administration during his reelection campaign of 1956, those fissures about the economy and processes of creating racial and national difference became transnational issues.

On April 4, 1956, local papers carried the story "Ike Says Farm Bill in Present Shape of Little Aid to Farmer," stating that the presidential primaries had a direct correlation to how farm politics were part of the West Coast campaign tour: "The Chief Executive said he still hopes congress will produce a sensible bill this year but he thought that any benefits from the so-called soil bank would be so late as to be negligible this year. Mr. Eisenhower in a meeting with reporters also expressed gratitude over the heavy vote cast for him in the Wisconsin preference primary yesterday."[3] Local growers, who at this point in California history represented a heavy Republican voting bloc, were watching the election and the farm bill closely. The soil bank, attendant subsidies through Eisenhower's election, and passage of the farm bill all stood to benefit them a great deal. Even though Eisenhower doubted that a "sensible bill" could be passed before the election, he nonetheless strategically linked this concern to the favorable primary numbers in Wisconsin, another agriculture-dominated state. But a conflicted message was documented prior to the convention speech by his office staff. Eisenhower's position outlined the conflicts with the bill in the spring leading up to the convention:

> Situation not changed. Republicans agreed to soil bank. Democrat position is that they have given us money, no authorization. President will take occasion to point out again that he has been urging relief for farmers since the beginning of the year. If asked why administrative tools were not used before, he will say he wanted a good farm bill. He will not say that he personally called Joe Campbell to urge speed in decision as to whether funds appropriated could be used.[4]

Although the public face of the administration drew upon historical tropes of the yeoman farmer to convey to the public that the president was in full support of the bill, the private daily records by his secretary, Ann Whitman, show that he partially supported relief only if it meant farming less acreage and increasing income. The tone suggests it to be a political strategy rather than an actual reality, especially given the split between Democrats and Republicans. In the end, Eisenhower would veto the farm bill on April 16, 1956, weeks before his second presidential nomination, on the grounds that it did not include the soil bank program, which would deter overproduction of farm crops.

Midwest and Great Plains dissatisfaction with Eisenhower's farm policies stemmed from the fact that these areas were the most adversely affected by the soil bank, limiting how and for what their acreage could be used. This is why the 1956 Republican convention was held in California, with a political focus on the very same state. California was the future of agriculture because of the diversity of its production and because it remained without drought at the moment in the way that the plains and Texas were not. This also led to July 5, 1956, preparations in Salinas for the concurrent meetings of the American Farm Economic Association and the Western Farm Economics Association, hosted by the Food Research Institute at Stanford and the Giannini Foundation of Agricultural Economics of the University of California at the Asilomar Conference Center in Carmel Valley. The Republican National Convention had met a week earlier in San Francisco and featured the renomination of Eisenhower and Nixon. With an eye toward positioning California as an agricultural leader, both the Republican National Convention and the Salinas Valley meeting drew attention to what Eisenhower and the local press articulated as the "farm problem."[5] The farm problem was spurred by advances in agricultural technology that led to overproduction in relation to national demand, removing fixed-price supports of surplus crops and encouraging the growth of nonsurplus crops. The Eisenhower administration also pushed for the soil bank, with land use directed at growing trees and building reservoirs versus excessive farming.

To make matters worse, in 1956 much of Texas was facing a severe drought, and eyes turned to California as the site from which to recover the production. As Deborah Cohen has argued, the majority of braceros enrolled in the guest-worker program that followed on the heels of postwar economic and technological prosperity were funneled west in years of drought.[6] Eisenhower's acceptance speech at the convention in San Francisco set the stage for a gathering of agricultural economists. Eisenhower told voters to reject expediency and have patience in national reform:

First, the farm issue. Expediency said: "Let's do something in a hurry—anything—even multiply our price-depressing surpluses at the risk of making the problem twice as bad next year—just so we get through this year." People who talk like that do not care about principle, and do not know farmers. The farmer deals every day in basic principles of growth and life. His product must be planned, and cultivated, and harvested over a long period. He has to figure not just a year at a time but over cycles and spans of years, as to his soil, his water, his equipment, the strains of his stock—and the strains on his income.

And so, for this man of principle, we have designed our program of principle. In it, we recognize that we have received from our forebears a rich legacy: our continent's basic resource of soil. We are determined that, through such measures as the Soil Bank and the Great Plains program, this legacy shall be handed on to our children even richer than we received it. We are equally determined that farm prices and income, which were needlessly pushed down under surpluses—surpluses induced first by war and then by unwise political action that was stubbornly and recklessly prolonged, shall in the coming months and years get back on a genuinely healthy basis. This improvement must continue until a rightful share of our prosperity is permanently enjoyed by agriculture on which our very life depends.[7]

Eisenhower's portrait of the patient yeoman farmer hearkens back to Jeffersonian ideals with a populist core. Much like the shift in the South that bore the Walmart megastores described by Bethany Moreton, "The white periphery could make its peace with joint-stock companies and banks as long as they were local stockholders, hometown financiers."[8] In the case of Republican values surrounding agriculture for the 1956 Republican convention, the "farm problem" and the family-owned farm were the mechanism by which discourse effaces the corporatization of agribusiness. In other words, the 1956 yeoman farmer "has to figure not just a year at a time but over cycles and spans of years, as to his soil, his water, his equipment, the strains of his stock—and the strains on his income. . . . [F]or this man of principle, we have designed our program of principle."[9] Eisenhower concentrated on tradition and intimate knowledge of the soil, experiential learning that is passed down by generation, a male-centered form of practice that valorizes the strain on income and the strains of crop growth that characterize America. Although this nationalism patriotically woos the audience to believe in saving the American farm and the American farmer from the drought of that year through patience and governmental subsidy, it also obviates the correlating labor reality of the time: the bracero program. With increased mechanized production of agricultural products, the invisible labor behind the yeoman farmer emphasizes that they are not "the soil and water" of the nation; rather, they are the equipment. The discourse salvages American agriculture and performs a sleight of hand with regard to economic realities. Eisenhower celebrates the bodies that matter, those of the presumed Anglo-American yeoman farmer, in opposition of those invisibilized bodies of the Mexican bracero.

While preparation for the Republican convention was in full swing, the same July 5, 1956, issue of the *Salinas Californian* reported that the Salinas Valley was preparing for visitors from the "Conducted Tour of Californian Agriculture August 24–26, 1956," which started in Berkeley and stopped in Stockton, Merced, and Salinas.[10] Total attendance for the meeting was 875, one of the largest tallies in the history of the organization to date. Those who took the agricultural field trip paid their way. Touted as a place to discuss "the No. 1 political and economic question mark in the nation, the farm problem," attendees reported on the latest technologies for improved production and the ways to maximize profit in the industry.[11] Those on the tour surely saw the improvements in dairy technology in Berkeley and stopped in Stockton and Merced to see advances in asparagus, cherry, cantaloupe, cotton, grape, tomato, walnut, and almond production. Salinas was targeted for its domination of strawberry and lettuce production. It was no accident that the leading agricultural economists toured northern California farms staffed by braceros or that the meeting followed the Republican convention. Many of those same economists provided data to the Eisenhower administration.

The Salinas Valley remained squarely involved in national Republican politics, so transnational capitalism informed local social and economic relations in myriad ways. On the same day that the *Californian* reported the agricultural economist conference, it announced that rosary services for Miguel Franco were being held later that evening in King City at the Ree C. Grim Funeral Chapel. A fifty-eight-year-old resident of a south Monterey County community, he was a native of Ciudad Obregón in Sonora, Mexico, and his body was to be sent for burial in his hometown after the services. The deceased was survived by a son and seven brothers in Sonora, and his daughter, Mrs. Mario Ramirez, was also a resident of King City. The owner of the Rancho Grande Café in King City, he had resided in the area for thirty years. He was also a labor contractor.[12]

Franco's funeral announcement might appear mundane when positioned next to the Republican convention, Eisenhower's speech, and the agricultural economists' tour, but it does in fact provide intimate details of that communal stratification of Mexicans, Mexican Americans, and Anglos in the Central Coast agricultural communities. First, that Franco's body was to be returned to Mexico indicates that labor was in the US but that home was always in Mexico. Second, that a Mexican, whether naturalized or not, had rosary services in the Ree C. Grim mortuary demonstrates that such services were not segregated like many funeral homes throughout the nation.[13] However, given that Franco was a business owner, a part of the established middle class that had normative relations of economic interchange with the very growers and shippers that had used him as a labor contractor before, shows the exemptions made at these crucial moments of community formation. Finally, that Franco was a labor contractor marks *how* he became a business owner. Labor contractors, especially Mexican and Mexican American ones, often worked their way up the grower hierarchy and were long established in the communities in which they contracted for growers. The contractors were known for playing favorites, hiring their friends, and even accepting bribes. Although Franco's death was clearly newsworthy in the Salinas Valley because of his long-term and established economic climb into a firm middle-class position as a restaurant owner, that legibility as a subject and valued community member was built on the exploitation of braceros. The "farm problem" was not just about patience and a "legacy [that] shall be handed on to our children even richer than we received it," but it was indeed about the invisible racialized and gendered forms of capital exchange that typified the industry. It was absolutely necessary for Eisenhower's rhetoric to coexist with the Mexican-national business owners and labor contractors of the world. The fantasy of the yeoman farmer in national rhetoric was dependent upon men like Franco and upon those he exploited.

If we think of Franco, labor contractor and business owner, as representing the invisible backstory of racialized capital reproduced through the bracero program, we see the costs and benefits of such political absences. When an agricultural worker named Richard Duarte was electrocuted on the job in Delano on July 10, 1956, we get a clearer sense of the human cost of bracero lives as minor in comparison to the behemoth size of California agribusiness profits in that same year. The twenty-eight-year-old Duarte was working on a ranch ten miles south of Delano, near Tierra Bella. The coroner's report says that a "boom he was operating to load baled straw onto a truck came in contact with an 11,000-volt [power] line."[14] This had been a benchmark year for massive changes in power line codes, increasing height of transformer location, service line drop, and line upgrades based on age, but it is obvious that agricultural contexts were secondary to residential spaces in terms of code implementation.[15] Such hazards were common and reflected the desire to increase production levels without considering worker safety. The placement of the power line on the property—on a county-, state-, or federal-maintained road or on private property (the Tierra Bella ranch)—determined where responsibility was placed. Although we do not know Duarte's citizenship status or who was responsible, even if he was a Mexican American agricultural worker, bracero contracts required extra monetary compensation for operating heavy equipment.[16] Given the monetary compensation requirement, it is highly likely that Duarte was a Mexican American working side by side with braceros. The newspaper article reports the facts of the electrocution and not any sort of legal or economic responsibility for the deceased. And, unlike Franco, whose life was celebrated in a memorial service to be attended by the community, no mention is made of any celebration of life or surviving relatives.

Because the California State Crop Reporting Service predicted that alfalfa hay and hops harvest would be larger for 1956, the Duarte electrocution was a by-product of economic demands. With the state's 1956 alfalfa output estimated at 5,668,000 tons, "topping last year's crop by 231,000 tons on increases in both the yield and acreage, [t]he 1,206 acres exceeds last year's plantings by 24,000 acres. The indicated yield of 4.7 tons an acre was up 0.1 tons."[17] Intensified alfalfa hay production meant more harvest and more profit. Duarte's death was part of production costs to meet and exceed the predictions of the alfalfa harvest in California. Because Duarte was functioning as a bodily portal or instrument of capitalism, his coming into contact with a faulty line was a normalized occupational hazard. His precarious life, what Judith Butler would describe as an experience of "heightened vulnerability," exemplified the ways that bodies of agricultural laborers were and continue to be expendable.[18] It also shows the ways that faulty power lines and perhaps even faulty equipment went unrepaired despite the increased demand for the processing of agricultural products. Though not a terrorist body threatening the body politic of contemporary discourse, Duarte and his death by electrocution show the vulnerable brown masculinized subject as labor surplus. As Karl Marx explains, "Labor power or capacity for labor . . . denote[s] the aggregate of those bodily and mental capabilities existing in a human being, which he exercises whenever he produces a use-value of any kind."[19] Use-value then informs racialized forms of capital: Duarte as an expendable form of Mexican (American) labor added to the promise of new technology in 1956, with the heavy-equipment manufacturers of the New Holland Co. Model 77 bailer promising to deliver "1 man + 1 hour = 10 tons of nutritious bailed hay!"[20] The capacity for increased production and efficiency still does not account for power lines not up to code. Technology promised more profits, yet technology failure was placed squarely on the worker, who often got paid by tonnage. This was the very precarious basis by which Duarte became a fatality in the body = machine power dyad. Transnational capital circuits squeezed more value out of labor, both foreign and native born, through ever-intensified exploitation.[21] He glibly provided the energy of the labor force, and his body was a conduit for electricity and profit.

At the same time that the Washington Committee on Migratory Labor quietly advocated for migrant housing reform and human use-value met expendability in the fields of California farms, Spanish speakers in the Salinas Valley were also mounting their own conversation about inclusion, labor surplus, inequality, and precarity through the "Section in Spanish" of the *Salinas Californian*, written by Adolfo Flores. First appearing on July 12, 1956, it again marked the pivotal nature of demographic, economic, and agricultural changes in the Salinas Valley agricultural industry. Flores began with an editorial on solidarity:

> The word Solidarity, which is ancient was used only in legal language, has made all the echoes resonate. Not only in this word is the clasp that closes all official harangues, all social conferences, all calls to set the strikes and to forge the exchanges; but it appears increasingly more like a heading in pedagogy treaties.
>
> Especially, let us unite over the fact that men represent each other to the point of being responsible for each other. Being the United States of North America a country that has given happiness to distinct races of different creeds and to all gives the same opportunity without making any difference(s); in this same way the newspaper from Salinas, California deigns to offering us a special section for all of us; since this is the first time a Spanish column appears in this newspaper.[22]

Although much of the tenor for the historic "Section in Spanish" is religious and legal, soliciting a middle-class, normative readership, Flores nonetheless addresses the audience with *usted* and *los hombres*. Indeed, these forms of address represent universal Spanish-language gender norms of the period, but they nonetheless assume a masculinized reading public. And that reading public is also assumed to be largely religious, interested in law, and invested in community through solidarity, whether through social conference or strikes, as Flores states above. All calls for strikes and the forging of increased wages, he argues, need to be created in solidarity: through universal humanism and the US rhetoric of an assimilationist melting pot that on the one hand makes up the great difference of the nation and on the other hand names that difference as a problem. Flores calls the Spanish section an act of dignity bestowed by the newspaper. Further, when he argues for the idea that "let us unite over the fact that men represent each other to the point of being responsible for each other," Flores evokes brotherhood and a system where Spanish speakers and, by extension, Mexicans in Salinas represent each other and are representative. Understanding the political climate within the city because of the bracero program, Flores discussed how inclusion within US borders was vital to Spanish speakers. Though in stark contrast to the suffering and negotiation of poverty documented in the Nadel bracero photos and numerous histories, Flores's unifying call for celebrating opportunity in difference marked a middle-class, aspirational Mexican American subject position. At the same time, Flores declared a homosocial linguistic world in a rural community, drawing on familiar and acceptable codes of interaction between Spanish-speaking men. Normalized masculine interaction through brotherhood and passionate claims of solidarity also exposes the homoerotic potential of actually answering this call to community.

By drawing on middle-class solidarity, Flores addressed the volatile potential for not having such a political bloc: the middle-class Spanish-speaking community had to account for what braceros were doing and how it was different from their own claims to citizenship in this small rural agricultural town. The "Section in Spanish" was written for those who owned the businesses and provided services to those abject braceros. The class differences, citizenship status, and place of residence (single-family home versus labor camp) of the readership represent stratification among Spanish-speaking Mexicans in the Salinas Valley, stratification that was deceptively subsumed in the use of the Spanish language itself. In other words, this public Spanish-language culture was middlebrow, even if it politely agitated for masculinist brotherhood.

In addition to the homoerotic potential of solidarity and brotherhood launched through the "Section in Spanish," the cartoon that accompanies the column is quite nonnormative and stereotypical of Mexican humor: a smallish Mexican "pancho" serenades a Spanish, Sevillana-dressed, very statuesque señorita from behind bars. If examined closely, the nonnormative nature of this relationship signals several things to the readership: why would a short, lazy, indigenous Mexican peasant (signified through his revolutionary-era Norteño straw sombrero) be serenading a pure-blooded

Española? And what would either of these characters be doing in Salinas in 1956? Their archetypal function as symbol tells the history of racial fantasy, longing, and desire. Hearkening back to the era of Spanish California, when Monterey, a city just ten miles from Salinas, was the capital of Alta California until 1851, the señorita represents the fantasy Spanish-European heritage and bloodline. She seems unadulterated through contact, even though we know that *los moros* (North African Arabs) had come to Andalucía and that there was racial mixture with mulattos and Indians in Alta California, her two-foot height difference over the pancho who serenades represents stereotypical racial aspiration for class-race transgression in sexual desire. That is, the pancho's unwavering pursuit of the Española is marked as an improper, overinflated masculinity that is accounted for in the stereotype of the Mexican macho, marking the scene as nonnormative. Further, that the Española looks directly at him during the serenade also represents a shifting terrain of sexual interest, for she engages the sexual entreaty. But all of this takes place behind bars, whether they are bars on the window of a Spanish open-air patio or the bars of a prison. Either way, the prohibited nature of desire and interaction, even if launched through stereotypes, nonetheless suggests sexual and racial depravity and perversion, visually representing the "Section in Spanish." Whoever drew this image relied on eugenicist pastiche, taking "benign" stereotypes or symbols and positioning them next to depraved remnants of the past that represent the Spanish-speaking community in Salinas during the 1950s. Through this nonnormative visual representation, middlebrow Spanish-language brotherhood supersedes the plight of the bracero out in the field, even though the oddness of both visual repertoires aligns.

Given the Spanish-language male publics established in the Salinas Valley, the 1956 Republican National Convention, Operation Wetback, and Galarza's *Strangers in Our Fields*, a more complex picture appears of the context of bracero migration. Federal policy determined how braceros arrived in the Salinas Valley, but growers facilitated social relations and economic interactions once they arrived. Farm politics therefore dominated both the local and national landscapes at the peak of the bracero program. By legislating their presence in the US, local communities had to cope with not only the split between Mexican Americans and Mexican nationals but also the ways in which grower interests were privileged over the interests of these two populations.

Chapter 10

THE SALINAS VALLEY AND
HIDDEN AFFECTIVE HISTORIES

From Eisenhower's vetoed farm bill to Spanish-language counterpublics of shared intimacy, we can glean the importance of masculinized spaces in 1950s northern California. As evidence of those masculinized public spaces, this chapter looks at a series of photos that were taken during 1956 in a lettuce field that stands five miles from where I grew up in Salinas.[1] Even before the series displays close-ups of the boxes for Cookie Lettuce, this contextual photo (figure 10.1) depicts mechanized labor at a time when lettuce production was considered speculative because of cooling and transporting issues, in addition to the fact that "lettuce prices [were] subject to such violent daily fluctuations" that gluts could cause severely low market prices.[2] Nonetheless, one sees acres and acres of lettuce being packed by hundreds of men. And those hundreds of men, who chose to take on temporary labor, often did so to participate in the project of modernizing the Mexican state, as they too would hopefully become modern through contact with the US and would, as historian Deborah Cohen argues, "no longer [be] considered a source of social or state embarrassment but rather as national ambassadors and future model citizens."[3]

As the thematic unity centers around productive labor for a surplus profit, the bracero is depicted as a rugged, hardworking individual. But the photos also simultaneously produce a national subject of Mexico, one who is primed through mechanized labor to return to his home country as more productive, more disciplined, more modern, and of service to the nation.

FIG 10.1. Davis Road, Cookie Lettuce harvester, Salinas, California, summer 1956. Courtesy of the Smithsonian Museum of Natural History. The Leonard Nadel Collection.

These "labor ambassadors" at work demonstrate how physical bodies served both the US and Mexico with their production. This kind of male subject is presumed to operate within a compulsory heteronormative sphere of existence, but the exceedingly homosocial nature of the work environment (men with men and for men) can render a different set of effects. Even if the men working together do not speak, their indirect contact and the visual field of the photographic series repeat a connection of interaction. That is, the nature of their labor, side by side, in its repetition and in the literal photographic duplication (see figure 10.2), invigorates homosocial bonding and interaction. Although one could argue that such sites of labor "produce men as a dominant class," we still have to attend to the processes of racialization and gender difference.[4] These were brown men performing manual labor, stooped over, both vulnerable and yet a physical force directed at being custodians of agricultural products and not relationships with people. They are, as Luciano and Chen have argued, "turning away from the demand for recognition within the circle of humanity." Their relationship to the nonhuman lettuce is constructed via capitalism and, in many ways, as Luciano and Chen further argue, "asks us to consider the suggestively queer connections between flesh" and lettuce, "between human and non-human."[5] Nadel

FIG 10.2. Bracero performing stoop labor in Davis Road lettuce field while ranch foreman looks on, summer 1956. Courtesy of the Smithsonian Museum of Natural History. The Leonard Nadel Collection.

himself captioned this photo, stating, "Thousands of braceros are brought in to perform stoop labor, a task no machine has been able to replace."[6] A complex form of visualizing invisible forms of labor, the image works against American popular ideas of brownness in the mainstream culture of the lazy peon, bandit, gangster, Latin lover, or macho and thus works against racialized and gendered normativity.[7]

There is excess displayed in the three brown men stooped over as they do a second pass through the field looking for lettuce heads that were suitable for market, but it is not masculinity. As their presumably Mexican American foreman hovers over their contorted bodies, these are debased, brown, and inadequate men in the normative, heterosexual sense, suited for demeaning labor. Rather than masculinizing them in this lettuce-picking context, they are physically subordinate. Nadel was able to document this form of inequality because Salinas Valley Grower Association brokers such as Ben Lopez, born in New Mexico of Mexican ancestry and a former US Department of Agriculture employee, were ideal for negotiating the relationship between braceros and growers because of presumed cultural familiarity.[8] As a bridge between Anglos and Mexican nationals, Mexican Americans had much to gain through their in-between status as citizens and racialized others. That is, the geography of Mexico named braceros as national subjects upon whom the nation's future was built with economic remittances, especially in relation to their Mexican American counterparts. The secondary context of being in the US as racialized and gendered individuals positioned braceros as alien and outside the confines of both normative masculinity, whiteness, sexuality, and the nation. As Nadel stated, "The Bracero, pound for pound, is regarded by many as the finest agricultural worker in the world. Built low to the ground, he is an ideal stoop laborer and his health is usually robust; his stomach is cast iron, his blood defies 120-degree field heat in the blistering climate of California's lowlands."[9] Nadel's hearty description of the bracero body as that of a prizefighter and a weapon in forging capitalism does not escape scientific racism. As he reinscribed the idea that Mexican men, irrelevant of being indigenous or mestizo, were built low to the ground, he used biology to justify their suitability, especially in heat extremities. Moreover, the chiseled-abs-of-cast-iron reference and the well-sculpted bodies wrought of manual labor show that Nadel was indeed paying attention to the bodies and the details of the men he photographed.

Further, for men outside of their context of national origin and without family, wife, or home, the anxiety only mounted, in their perceived inability to act "as properly gendered beings."[10] Growers also advocated for braceros over native-born US workers because "braceros don't have families with them that would have to be housed, are prime workers in good health, inspected before leaving Mexico, and fear to make 'labor trouble' and be sent back to Mexico."[11] To reiterate, the statement codifies how the bracero program itself was a policy agreement with queerness at its center. It assumed normativity in what it disallowed, creating an abject body that must be queer in order to not pose a threat to Anglo-American masculinities or Anglo women. Thus, the position of the migrant was a queer one, neither here nor there, or everywhere and nowhere. Although the scene of agricultural labor is

FIG 10.3. Two braceros stooping to pack a box of Cookie Lettuce on Davis Road, Salinas, California, summer 1956. Courtesy of the Smithsonian Museum of Natural History. The Leonard Nadel Collection.

normative in this region, the brownness of the bracero bodies in their objectification evokes a narrative of queerness and alienation.

Another image from this same Salinas photo series (figure 10.3) lays bare the scale of the production and thus the gendered and racialized power relations embodied therein. In this instance, the analytic of scale allows the reader to perceive the vastness of the geography and the aggregation of bracero bodies into much smaller units. The image represents hierarchies of scale, accounting for the human geographical element within what seems like an endless landscape. Multiple scales interact at once: the body as individual entity, the expansive field as localized production, and the implication of a national market for which the lettuce is being produced, processed, and harvested. Whereas the body and the lettuce partake in a biological realm at different scales, the site of the field and the national market of consumption are socially constructed scales.[12] When we pick apart these scale differences, we see how there was nothing natural or innate about this scene. One might see this image as pastoral, of a bygone era of simple and serene farm or rural life, but the quantity of racialized laboring bodies, as they disappear into the horizon, disrupts any sort of romance that may be depicted in the black-and-white photography of the 1950s. Care is not for the human body; instead, the commodity, the lettuce, is fetishized in the excessive care that is taken to cut, clean, and package it for market consumption. The larger-scale local processing was discreet and only gestures to what is beyond the photo's frame: a market that structures spatial and social organization.

The lettuce field and its harvesting go for miles and miles as the three foregrounded bodies depict a man with a short-handled hoe on his belt moving crates of lettuce, while two others strain to close the box of Cookie Lettuce. A closer look shows one man wearing a straw campesino hat and huaraches while he works, signs of Indianness and markers of central Mexico. In an interview with social scientist Henry Anderson in the 1950s, a grower identified a particular type: "This one is the right size. He's built right. He's a farmworker, you can tell that. He hasn't any big ideas. He's got the right attitude. He's humble, not fresh or cocky. He's an Indian type."[13] The Indian type was not white, not educated, not assimilated, outside of the nation. The denationalized nature of Mexican Indian citizenship made such braceros more malleable, more desirable as ideal workers. Further, huaraches are not "real work shoes" to an assimilated field boss, marking the individual as outside of modernity, a docile laborer, and, by extension, indigenous.

In contrast, his *compañero de trabajo* (fellow worker) wears a baseball cap and appears to be in work boots, suggesting that he has adapted to the work wear of the local farmers. If, as Andrew Herod has argued, "the body appears as a discrete entity depends somewhat on how it is viewed," then the men in the foreground are clearly historically documented as gestalt, a whole entity unto itself.[14] The shape of each man is clearly delineated even though they are all part of a mechanical order. Both men—the denationalized Indian type and the modern subject in a baseball cap—coexist in the same economy of scale. Even though the eye distinguishes agreed-upon racial types and temperaments, the scale of operation in which they function levels out those differences in the name of production. Even though the docile Indian was more ideal according to Anderson, the discourse was nullified through the multivalent ways in which agribusiness output did not distinguish the two.

Nonetheless, it was the fetishized commodity (the lettuce) that dominated the image, reflecting how these anonymous bodies consistently increased the level of geographical and economic development in the region. In creating those commodities, these bodies reflect the "active processes of scale management and coordination at the local and international levels."[15] As one counts what appear to be twenty-seven men stooping to cut lettuce, they seem to disappear into the horizon, as do the boxes of lettuce, off into the marketplace, where the worker is further alienated from his production. Ordered in rows, symmetrical in the positioning of the heads of lettuce and the boxes that will eventually contain them, the workers seem almost out of scale and out of place in the sense that they are disordered in the photograph, randomly moving as their labor necessitates. The fine-grained details of the lettuce overpower the details of their clothes, of Salinas in the distance, of the hats and long-sleeved work shirts worn by the laborers. It must be either autumn or a summer morning at around 5:00 a.m.: a damp and chilly mist hangs in the air. The summer harvest season reaches temperatures of ninety degrees, and it is almost impossible that all the workers would be dressed this way in mid-June. Thinning lettuce was an act of grooming and nurturing, a feminizing of masculinized labor. The care work preparing delicate lettuce crops cannot be overlooked.

In Nadel's image, the work scene's scale demonstrates the totalizing nature of bracero labor and economies. The never-ending panorama of lettuce marks a particular moment in time, space, and place. Yet if one did not know this place intimately (that it is in Salinas, California, on Davis Road) or how to read the signs of place to determine the temporality (long-sleeve shirts, early morning or damp fall harvesting season), and the year when Nadel took these pictures (1956), meaning is lost in a lack of geographical marking or temporal specificity. When meaning is lost and temporality absent, the men in the pictures are further alienated from their labor and represent what Paul Ricoeur has called *human time*, "to the extent that it is articulated through a narrative mode, and narrative attains its full significance when it becomes a condition of temporal existence."[16] If we knew their names, the exact date and time of the photo, they would be seen as agents, rational, thinking human beings attached to a specific history. And although there is no doubt that the braceros are part of a collective history of exploitation and labor histories, the photo does a particular kind of ideological work because it is outside of human time. We also might think of this as queer time, or what Elizabeth Freeman has named the ways in which "queer names a class relation of a different sort from the standard Marxist definition of a relationship between people who own the means of production and people whose biggest asset is their labor power—even as both of these forms of power also involve time."[17] Thus, the claim that such photos mark a disjuncture in time, or rather of the racialized, gendered subject as out of time, reflects the nonownership of the means of production and time itself. The time that belongs to them occurred in other spaces.

The lack of context and having a racialized relationship to capitalism alienated the product of their own labor, reinforcing Galarza's argument about

FIG 10.4. Two braceros packing a box of Cookie Lettuce on Davis Road, Salinas, California, summer 1956. Courtesy of the Smithsonian Museum of Natural History. The Leonard Nadel Collection.

"the degree to which the Mexican alien farm worker, recruited and contracted under the auspices of the governments of the United States and Mexico, actually enjoys the legal, contractual, and civil rights to which both governments have been committed since the inception of the program in 1942."[18] The massive scale of the image speaks to the inability to enjoy the benefits of one's labor and to claim it as such in the public realm. Though rendering invisible the US-Mexican international contracts and individual contacts that brought such men to the US, knowledge of the site of the photograph, the signs of temporality, and seeing the individual bodies as their own sites of scale point to the ideological contradictions of Nadel's photo archive.

And these contradictions seep through in the same series, where Nadel followed, at length, the temporal arch of one man's labor (see figure 10.4). He was in the previous photo; he was the man with the huaraches. Sealing the box with his colleague ensured careful packaging. Although lettuce sold for $.17 for two heads in 1956, meaning roughly $2.50 per box, he appears the more relaxed of the two, comfortable with the fact that his foot on top of the box will not damage the precious heads of lettuce.[19] If we figure a 75 percent profit margin, braceros earned about two cents per head of let-

FIG 10.5. Bracero using row-sized cart to pack a box of Cookie Lettuce on Davis Road, Salinas, California, summer 1956. Courtesy of the Smithsonian Museum of Natural History. The Leonard Nadel Collection.

tuce they packed. Given the argument about the relationship to capitalism through the alienation of one's own labor, it becomes more poignant that we have no idea what the man looks like. His face is hidden under the wide brim of his sombrero. Once the fog burned off at 11:00 a.m., that sombrero was the difference between being moderately tired from heat and heatstroke. He is then pictured (figure 10.5) with his own harvest box. The labor was collaborative, but here the individuated task of filling a box was demarcated by his "row." The boxes behind him leave the trail of productivity: growers were known for paying based on the number of boxes packed, tomatoes picked, or kilos of cotton, for example. Further, the semimechanized nature of the labor (embodied in the cart) increased productivity. The cart sped box movement. Instead of lifting the box each time one moves along the row to cut lettuce and dropping it with a thud and potentially damaging the heads before they reach the market, the lettuce cart moves smoothly down the discrete row, increasing productivity and product quality. Lightning struck, but he was not bothered by it because surveillance loomed; the foreman's truck was closer than it appeared. There is something eerily panoptical about this labor scene, as the openness of the field lends itself to becoming a disciplinary structure. Michel Foucault wrote that the major effect of the panopticon was to induce in the inmate a state of conscious and permanent visibility that assures the automatic functioning of power. Things are arranged so that surveillance is permanent in its effects, even in its discontinuous action; that the perfection of power should tend to render its actual exercise unnecessary; that this architectural apparatus should be a machine for creating and sustaining a power relation independent of the person who exercises it; in short, that inmates should be caught up in a power situation of which they are themselves the bearers.[20]

And though it is important to be aware of the risks of directly and uncritically mapping Bentham's architectural theory in terms of Foucault's reworking of this multimodal vantage point in the middle of prison space, there are ideological similarities between the surveillance in the field and in the prison. First, the grower's truck in the distance was far away yet psychologically present in the consciousness of the worker. For the worker was acutely aware that even though there is a great physical distance between him and the truck, that distance can be made up easily by the truck moving should it appear that one is not productive enough. Second, we are brought back to the question of scale and spatial organization: the rows are constructed as a means of ordering how one interacts on the job. One can't do much else except harvest lettuce, and this fact normalizes physical activity in how it was performed. There is no deviation in movement or activity because the ordered rows provide visual vantage points of observation. Third, I want to make clear that the experience of the field laborer was not that of the prisoner in terms of a direct translation of similar physical punishment, discipline, or labor. However, what remained constant for both populations and their relationship to surveillance was how they were similarly "caught up in a power situation of which they are themselves the bearers."[21] In other words, the bracero in the field reproduces the power structure as much as the surveillance by his boss and the grower truck does. Curtis Marez notes that these technological improvements, "rather than eliminating farmworkers, . . . enabled

FIG 10.6. Two braceros cutting for packing in a Cookie Lettuce box on Davis Road, Salinas, California, summer 1956. Courtesy of the Smithsonian Museum of Natural History. The Leonard Nadel Collection.

agribusiness to restructure and discipline an expanded workforce. Automation enabled the deskilling and downgrading of certain tasks."[22] Thus, the simple technological advances like a box on a cart meant that anyone with the physical strength to lift the cart with a full box could take the job. In later years, as Marez notes, automated packing harvesters were brought into the fields, speeding up harvest, packing, and distribution in a way that the same number of bodies were needed to work the field but using less time.

In Nadel's set shots and chosen subjects, he further reproduced inequality in this measured and calculated sense of self-discipline like Marez mentions: if one wanted to get paid for a day's labor, there were no alternatives. So the lettuce-box cart seemed like an intervention to improve working conditions, but it instead further disciplined the subject as he moved down the rows with speed and precision (figure 10.6).

One has to ask: why do we, as viewers, desire to see the face of the man with the huaraches, toting the box of lettuce down what seem like endless rows? Why does this particular series of Nadel's photos build this desire in the audience? Attached to this mode of visual representation is the imperative to represent him as "the" ideal bracero. There are expectations attached to the image. If we saw his face, we could somehow have a better sense of who he was. However, the reality was that even if we saw the man's face, because there is no documentation we wouldn't know much more except for the ephemeral registers of affect that may or may not satiate our own longing "to know." Even though he didn't engage the camera, there were a number of willing subjects in the background. Anthropological longing to somehow completely know the supposedly transparent could be the focus. But locating this desire to know or be engaged in situating the subject in history is priority. That is, if we somehow knew his name, perhaps his age, his hometown, what company he worked for while in Salinas, we could have a better sense of the larger historical fabric to which he belonged. Further, knowing who he was would allow the viewer to develop an attachment, even if it was with a figure immortalized through photography. What we want from him, as responsible viewers, is to understand his historical context and personal history. Given that Nadel shot these images, we know and want to see suffering. The strategy was to vindicate victims, but the queer reading reveals their desires. As Lauren Berlant has argued, "One's attachments are at best only symbolized in their objects, and that the objects are so charged by our regard for them that they remain enigmatic to us at the same time as they are never fully known."[23] Attachment to the image and knowing the person in it are reflective of understanding that one can never fully know the subject, not as a transparent truth but as a complex being with vast experiences. Because we have none of the accompanying information that might make the man somehow closer to us, the kinds of intimacies and solidarities we might build with him through these "facts" are truly limited.

It is worth spending some time on those ephemeral traces of emotion registered in the face and body. Here, the idea of body as archive and a historicization of the gesture gets at what the ephemeral might tell us. Seven frames later, we finally get to see his face, which is strained and darkened by the sun (figure 10.7). Even though he is upright and pushing the cart supporting a lettuce box, he is in a hurry and a bit hunched over. The cart is actually too small for him to reach maximum speed efficiency. The weight of the box and the speed at which he needs to travel are incommensurate. The performance of such behavior (being in a hurry) was and continues to be unspoken mandates in US labor practices. In particular, in manual-labor settings, the body must mimic normative masculine codes of work: a tense, hard-laboring body, the strained face, and sweat. His eyes look down, not aware of the camera's shutter, concentrating on what he is doing in order to avoid spilling the lettuce, and his mustache is barely visible because of the angle of the face. Behind him is the bounty of a day's labor: eighty-five boxes, each holding twenty-four heads of iceberg lettuce, awaiting vacuum sealing and icing at

FIG 10.7. Bracero pushing row-sized cart of packed lettuce while another stoops to cut fresh lettuce heads for Cookie Lettuce on Davis Road, Salinas, California, summer 1956. Courtesy of the Smithsonian Museum of Natural History. The Leonard Nadel Collection.

the cooling shed. These gestures, whether self-conscious or not, effectively reproduce the demands of patriarchy and capitalism simultaneously, or what Judith Butler would call a "stylized repetition of acts."[24] Given that this photo was taken in 1956, the idea of the farm laborer as "the" Mexican worker type was not yet fully accepted as a normative sign. Although race and racialization alienate normative masculine codes of gender performance in such work and from this man's body in particular, we might also take this criticism a bit further by arguing that it was doing destabilizing work as well. Even as the intertextual nature of the photograph hails other commonly circulating images of bracero suffering, if we dislodge it a bit from this fixed notion of

FIG 10.8. Bracero posing on top of harvester with packed boxes of Cookie Lettuce on Davis Road, Salinas, California, summer 1956. Courtesy of the Smithsonian Museum of Natural History. The Leonard Nadel Collection.

being migrant, Mexican, and male, we may see the space as homosocial and potentially charged with desire and potential homoeroticism.

When we encounter him again in the shot series (figure 10.8), he is on top of the transport truck amid 186 cases of lettuce. In the background, men neatly stack hundreds of boxes into symmetrical rows for easy loading, presumably onto trailers like this one. In the foreground, three men hover, packing the boxes onto the truck, but he is the only one to return the gaze. Unlike the previous image, this one *feels* staged. Unsure whether and how to look busy, he lets his hands loosely rest on a box, just the thumbs pressing the top of the case and the outside fingers slightly balancing it. His eyes express a kind of confusion and longing. It must be good to be desired by the camera, right? Or could the camera be viewed as an extension of surveillance that workers endured on a daily basis? To be important enough for the photographer to take multiple shots of the same man, his face clearly recognizable to anyone who sees this, that must be good. Perhaps Nadel told him that he had taken the other shots and that there was something about his demeanor and mannerism that made him stand out and thus required more photographs, especially if the idea of the bracero photographs was to tell the stories of these men visually. Or the first encounter may have been one of fear, being singled out for being unproductive. The multiple frames signal the desire for varied shots and sustained proximity between subject and photographer. They document desire in all of its forms. That this man returned Nadel's gaze is striking. Eye contact, however unsure, resists the victimization narrative to assert other possibilities of existence and perhaps even an idealized notion of self. In spite of this uncomfortable and unsure look, he chose to look back. The presumed homosocial contracts visualized in Nadel's photographs and the work environment imply a male-occupied sphere. But instead of controlling the homosocial environment, neither the man nor the photographer constructed this environment; they became naturalized and unquestioning participants in the structure of power. Because social relations among men were normalized and sexual ones were not, this photographic interaction between Nadel and the man registered the discomfort of being desired, even if it was for a photograph within a compulsory heterosexual context. His hands are positioned awkwardly on the box, not doing actual work but resting, his eyes aimed directly forward but seeming somewhat vacant. This would suggest that there is little pleasure gained from this interaction. Perhaps it is the sign of a publicly misplaced affect: should he feel pleasure and pride in being photographed?

In the second shot of the same man, we can tell that time has elapsed by the shift in affect and because his body position above the boxes has changed (see figure 10.9). This time he looks wry, body tilted to one side, one hip facing forward, one hand on the box directly in front of his body, the other casually to the side. He seems much more relaxed, and this might indicate a sense of solidarity, further understanding and agreement between him and Nadel: he knew why the picture was being taken and what it is being used for. The reflexive practice of distrust mocks the intentions of the photographer in the first frame.[25] Here, trust makes an appearance in the scene of homosocial contract embodied in his striking a pose. The pose and posing indicate bodily control, intention, and full inhabiting of the self. This

FIG 10.9. Close-up of bracero posing on top of harvester with packed boxes of Cookie Lettuce on Davis Road, Salinas, California, summer 1956. Courtesy of the Smithsonian Museum of Natural History. The Leonard Nadel Collection.

ephemeral moment of transformation shifts the man in the huaraches from being a shy, indigenous, agricultural hand who uses his body as an instrument of labor into a stylized aesthetic subject in this final frame. He participates in his own subject making and aestheticization. The pose's intensity and the hip forward queer the image, a kind of performance that gave Nadel's camera more than it perhaps anticipated. That hip forward and hard return stare to the camera display full self-possession. This pose demands our attention beyond the lettuce cases and humble campesino origins. But Nadel also photographed the same man from another perspective, with him in a scalable image between thousands of heads of lettuce and pushing a box into alignment. Nadel captioned the image as follows: "Thousands of braceros are brought into U.S. farms to perform stoop labor, in the fields, in the hot sun, a task no machine has been able to replace."[26] Thus, the transition from stoop work to actively posing suggests that Nadel wanted to represent an evolution of the man from cog in the wheel of scalable capitalism among nonhuman objects that further dehumanized him to the concept of self-realization. I am not saying that the dialogue of universal humanistic subject formation or the performance of posing hip forward transcends race, class, or gender positionalities; rather, it queers them with that unexpected and delightful form of embodiment.

Chapter 11

HIP FORWARD INTO DOMESTIC LABOR
AND OTHER INTIMACIES

The delight of the hip-forward pose (see chapter 10) offers a counterintuitive alternative to traditional visual productions of bracero national subjects and nationalisms. Fundamental to reading these photos is what critic Gayatri Gopinath contends: most projects of diaspora and nationalism rely on men's experience and their narrativized centrality while simultaneously "demonstrating how female sexuality under nationalism is a crucial site of surveillance as it is through women's bodies that borders and boundaries of communal desires are formed."[1] The shadow text here is the absence of women from these scenes of labor and migration in the US. Instead, men left the gender policing by female relatives behind and traded it for their own surveillance by the Mexican American ranch foremen and growers. What bracero histories do account for in terms of interactions with women while in the US is through their correspondence with female family members, having Mexican American girlfriends, and having relationships with prostitutes and broader publics of women both at the labor camps and in the towns adjacent to where their labor was performed.[2] Lori Flores cites the Salinas Valley in particular as having a male-dominated public sphere, where such in-town interactions were few and far between.[3]

Oral histories indicate a more porous public sphere often linked to labor or commerce. Grace Arceneaux remembered a different set of interactions with braceros that cut against the grain of what most historiographies argue:

> Well when the braceros came I remember meeting them because I was young and single and going to dances. Of course they could have been telling us stories, but mixed in with the poor braceros were one or two young students who came over for the experience. And you could sense that because of their vocabulary, manners, breeding . . . you could tell. I had experiences when I wrote to fellows and they criticized my Spanish and things like that. My brother, Manuel, who lived with braceros, said there were some who had a real good education but they came for the experience, they were going to write about it. Some wanted to pick up on agriculture and really take some information back. That's one type. I think many of those people jumped their contract and just disappeared, mixed in with the rest and never got papers.[4]

Arceneaux's oral history disrupts a number of assumptions made about bracero populations. First, interactions with young men demonstrate that sociality and the possibility of developing friendships and love relationships with US-based men and women were very possible. Second, braceros were highly mobile despite their sanctioned living quarters in camps outside of city limits. Third, not all braceros were poor and illiterate. Many of them were indeed educated, wrote letters, and even had aspirations to become great writers through their migration experience. Fourth, men also saw the experience in the North as a way to bring back the latest and most modern agricultural techniques with them to improve their livelihoods and by extension Mexico. The Mexican state had convinced them that achieving modern knowledge of agriculture was truly possible. Given labor stratification and in-depth historical research, however, it is highly unlikely that many came into contact with such technologies beyond their own bodies. Last and most importantly, Arceneaux highlights the finite stratifications between Mexican nationals and their US-based counterparts. Her written Spanish was criticized despite the fact that she was not a US citizen and her brother, who was born in the US, lived among braceros in the labor camps. Historian Deborah Cohen argues that such camps in California "were older and had often housed both immigrant and domestic workers."[5] The majority of historical emphasis has been placed on what the locals called "nationals," but Arceneaux's oral history reminds us that Mexican Americans also lived in labor camps.[6] Working side by side, internal migrants and Mexican nationals comingled more than one might expect, especially through social outings like the dances that Arceneaux mentioned and the labor camp where her brother worked and lived. These comingled transnational spaces of domesticity and socialization set the stage for hybrid social formations and the shifting of gender roles.

Home Labor

Mexican men who had migrated and had been long established in the community became brokers for growers because they knew the Spanish language but were either permanent residents or citizens themselves. Keeping in mind that male-female sociality structured the bastion of the Mexican family back home whereas male-male sociality structured almost every facet of bracero life, I want to turn to the ways in which the queering of gender socialization emerged in men's domestic labor.

There are countless photos that reflect the modern impulse symbolized by the US and yet were informed by the impoverished living conditions in which the braceros dwelled upon returning from work. But these photos don't make it into the archive of suffering that circulates in reference to the program. Figure 11.1 shows a man washing objects in a basin inside of a makeshift housing unit, and there are hundreds of photos of these interior spaces by Nadel, but we rarely see them in the public realm because they document the domestic labor required for these men to exist. Instead of having wives, sisters, mothers, and female children performing reproductive labor in the domestic space, they did so as migrants representative of global labor market shifts. The domesticated laborer type is again at the center of modernity, for men were retasked with living conditions that did not produce a normative gendered division of labor. I am not referring to a separate-spheres model but highlighting how migration broke down those Mexican national ideologies of male, industrial modernity outside of the home.[7] Here the hip boots used by those who operated and moved muddy sprinkler systems remind the viewer of the ways that the bracero program institutionalized ethnic-racial hierarchies of labor for migrant men who did both productive and domestic labor simultaneously, a queering of gender roles through migration. Though not tasked with creating hearth and home in the historic sense of the idea of domesticity, they were indeed performing the labor of the domestic, private sphere as men, which in turn created a homosocial home, however temporary.

Further, Nadel demonstrated the temporary and unsafe nature of bracero dwellings, often barns that were about to fall down or army barracks that had been condemned, with men crammed into these spaces to sleep and conduct their lives outside of work. In terms of the conventional images we see in bracero photographs, this one is fairly typical: the unnamed man is

FIG 11.1. Bracero washing dishes with gloves and hip boots in dimly lit basin, Salinas, California, summer 1956. Courtesy of the Smithsonian Museum of Natural History. The Leonard Nadel Collection.

engaged in domestic labor, in a substandard domestic space, intently focusing on the task at hand. It also replicated the trope of abjection, especially as it relates to Julia Kristeva's theories, where abject is situated outside of the symbolic order, being forced to face this feminized existence as an inherently traumatic experience. But it also raises more questions: Did Nadel tell this man he was taking the picture? Did he tell him not to look at the camera? How did the man feel that he, not someone else, was selected as the one who was photographed washing objects in his hip boots? Perhaps Sharon Holland's theory of attachment and acknowledgment may be of use here. Racism's preventative grasp limited desire and suspended acknowledgment while the man had his back to Nadel. Positing the subject as photographically desirable, interior shots domesticate what was publicly perceived as an unruly masculine subject. And although this might be read as a humanist positivism at the heart of subject formation, if we consider these notions of desire where "subjectlessness is humanness"—a move to see braceros as non-

FIG 11.2. Wide-angle shot of smiling young bracero in bunkhouse, Salinas, California, summer 1956. Courtesy of the Smithsonian Museum of Natural History. The Leonard Nadel Collection.

subjects—we still have to attend to the engagement with the camera.[8] Thus, interior domestic spaces indicate the domestication of the unruly masculine subject and the forging of same-sex intimacy as a result of discipline.

Along with domestic labor and the domestic space is the notion that interior spaces, or what we could loosely call the home space of the bunkhouse, were photographed extensively to show the humble and squalid conditions of existence in the labor camps. In the same photo series, Nadel has two pictures of the same young man, leaning on his bunk, body half turned, looking at the camera, smiling (figures 11.2 and 11.3). In both images, horizontal and vertical, the young man occupies approximately one-quarter of the space in the right-hand portion of the frame. To his left are seven tightly organized bunks as the far-left corner recedes into the darkness of the unlit room. The

Hip Forward into Domestic Labor 219

FIG 11.3. Side-angle shot of smiling young bracero in bunkhouse, Salinas, California, summer 1956. Courtesy of the Smithsonian Museum of Natural History. The Leonard Nadel Collection.

bunks stand empty, the thin mattresses exposed. They actually appear to be more like mats suspended upon springs, a sarape blanket draped over them, work hats resting on each bed, signaling the end of the workday. In fact, the industry called them thirty-inch cot pads, not mattresses. Local businesses like the Salinas Mattress Manufacturing Company also offered cot pad exchange services, where labor camps could trade up, trade in, refurbish, and return these sleeping pads for cots and bunk beds.[9] Thus, the flimsy materiality of the bunks reflected an economy of cheap, low-quality bedding supplies that dominated the labor camp industry and occupied the rest/leisure world of bracero domestic spaces.

In the dark corner, laundry hangs, blocking the sunlight from the window: white cotton pants, heavier-duty work pants, and long-sleeve shirts. Also, framing the smiling young man, who wears chinos and a long-sleeve shirt, are towels, shirts, and a jacket. As he reclines forward against the bunk, the eye is drawn to his smile, the makeshift nature of the bunk, the cord for the light in the building, and the various jars of pomade and other self-care products that sit on the plank behind him. To his left, a Tide laundry detergent crate doubles as a nightstand, and a box of Fab detergent sits above one of the bunks. The dirt floor, in its loose state, shows a worn and well-traveled path. Although the overwhelming presence of laundry detergent and clean clothes hanging from the walls and makeshift ceiling signals a domestic space that is consumed with cleanliness, the dirt floor disrupts this scene. That is, how "clean" can a space be if its basis is dirt, a building material that signals underdevelopment, instead of materials of modernity such as wood, linoleum, or tile? We must remember that braceros did not choose to live with dirt floors in the labor camps; rather, by 1956, their employers were contractually mandated to provide them with housing, and these floors reflect what growers thought of their workers. Another reading reveals that they were commodities surrounded by commodities. Use value is called into question because of their proximity to other commodities. The photo holds in tension their aspirational desire to be seen in a certain way (smiling and happy) and the photographer's desire to have them seen in a highly particularized way. Nadel's framing shows they were poor, working class, or middle-class Mexican and Mexican American men seeking temporary work in the US, so there was no need to feel any political or social obligation to provide them with clean or modern living conditions. Braceros were responsible for cultivating cleanliness and hygiene on their own, and they did. There was no distinction between living conditions for Mexican Americans and Mexican nationals in the camps, as Grace Arceneaux stated to interviewer Knaster:

> KNASTER: And these were braceros. Yes. And they weren't given very good living quarters or food or anything?
>
> ARCENEAUX: Well, I suppose it was adequate. My brother lived in a camp like that . . . Manuel. It was just a couple of cots, blankets. Always smelled bad. No privacy. Just a huge barn with thirty, forty beds. Showers, cold water.[10]

Replicating the scene in Nadel's images, Arceneaux described the disjuncture between daily experience for all living in the camp and the Nadel photo. Making tidy a domestic space that was simply not conducive to hearth was magnified. Given that Arceneaux remembered how camps always smelled bad and yielded no privacy, Nadel's image tightly organized and contained the representation of bracero domestic spaces and solitariness to cut out the olfactory disgust and true inability to be alone because of the limited frame and scope of the image. As we can see, these rudimentary bunks, dwellings, and their floors represented the vast class difference between the farmer and the Mexican laborers. As Deborah Cohen has argued, growers in this period constructed their public identities as rugged but intelligent and modern harnessers of technology and government resources.[11] According to Nadel, men such as Jack Blas, from the Grower Shipper Vegetable Association, arranged for the "procurement of braceros from Mexico for Association members in the Salinas Valley area. About 10,000 farm workers were imported into this area in 1955 to service about 400 growers. 80 of the growers do the bulk of the work."[12] But these marks of progress and technology were not passed onto the workers, as their mass numbers in 1955 suggest that they were necessary to but not subjects of modernity. Describing them as imports, whether intentional or not, Nadel objectified the men even as he had developed close relationships with his photographic subjects. In this juxtaposition of bracero bodies as premodern forms of labor in the racial capitalist landscape of modern agriculture, their association with premodernity was most clearly represented in the interior spaces of their dwellings.

That the young man is smiling, given the tightness of his space, the clean clothes, and the air of domesticity that surrounds him, tells us several things. Camera engagement with a smile was a nonnormative act, stepping outside of expectations of the abject, and instead, as Gopinath has argued, producing a "range of dissent and non-heteronormative practices and desires that may very well be incommensurate with the identity categories of 'gay' and 'lesbian.'"[13] During this period and even much earlier, overt smiling in photographs was not acceptable. In the context of both Mexican photographic portrait traditions (see the Flores Magón family portraits in part I) and in documentary photo evidence of farmworkers suffering, being disaffected became a modern subject. Mark Overmyer-Velázquez argues that portraiture and the body have an unresolved tension between tradition and modernity: negotiating a smile would be one of these things.[14] The difference between the smile and no smile was distinguishing oneself from the urban and rural underclasses or being a part of them. Smiling was a sign of emotion, a lack of bodily control, and uncouthness.

Thus, the smile returned to Nadel ruptures both class and cultural bodily expectations within the narrative of bracero suffering. Ephemeral emotional engagement amid squalid living conditions performed recognition of the lens with pleasure. Given the exchange between camera and subject, we can argue that the material conditions of the dwelling convey such mutual sentiment and that the latent homoeroticism of the spaces is nonetheless an absent presence. The smile here, perhaps prompted through a joke or a cajoling from the photographer, disrupts the quotidian display of poverty and domesticity, a clear reordering of gender expectations. The smile is a response to being desired. Further, the young man smiles in both photos and playfully turns his face toward the camera while his body is turned away. There is an affective structure of optimistic attachment in this scene. Lauren Berlant might say that it "involves sustaining inclination to return to the scene of fantasy that enables you to expect that this time, nearness to this thing [you] desire will help you or a world to become different in just the right way."[15] The "thing" to be desired could perhaps be happiness, to be desired by the camera, or to revel in a joke among men in a domesticated space that is less than aesthetically or materially pleasing. The smiles, as acts of disruption, stage a different set of expectations about how things could be different. The mere fact that millions of Mexican men left their homes to labor in squalid conditions shows how strongly the attachment to the dream of social and class mobility was: it led men to occupy unfamiliar homosocial spaces that eventually became normalized, in their domesticity, as the reorientation of gendered labor, as bonds of emotional attachment, and as simple expressions of daily life. For men who wanted to conceal their homosexuality from public scrutiny, the bachelor life of the bracero program could easily hide the desire for same-sex intimacies in the privacy away from family members and the social mores of Mexico.[16] This bachelor life was also what allowed Nadel's closeness with his photographic subjects: they could be intimate buddies, permitted by Mexican visual cultures of the 1950s and the bracero program itself.

As part of that Mexican visual genre of the 1950s buddy image, the second set of long-frame shots indicates scale: we see the way the bed is framed (see figure 11.4), which takes us farther into the bracero domestic space, but this time into a space of homosociality, the bunkhouse.[17] The image is quite meta in building abstraction and intent. Unlike the white, middle-, and upper-class gay domestic spaces Stephen Vider analyzes for their "conventional ideals of domesticity [that] structure performances of everyday life," this sphere of domesticity is devoid of class privilege and is almost unimaginable given the ways that such spaces did not circulate in circles of the 1950s "female-centered but male dominant" Anglo social world.[18] Víctor Macías-González has noted that the Mexico-based homophile movement of the same era was critical in considering "how domestic space, households, housework and sociability within private homes provided a homophile identity for middle- and upper-class men."[19] Although men in the bracero program did not have social and political overlap with the Anglo gay domesticity of the US-based or Mexico-based middle-class and upper-class homophile movement, one thing was certain: they were parallel experiences that idealized friendship and intimacy among and between men.

FIG 11.4. Wide-angle shot of three braceros in bunkhouse at leisure, Salinas, California, summer 1956. Courtesy of the Smithsonian Museum of Natural History. The Leonard Nadel Collection.

Nadel's second version, another split-focus shot, further reinforces domesticity. The tightness of the objects organized therein further narrativizes proximity, changing the focus of the lens, which was no accident. Rows and rows of bunks form the frame, with about two feet between them, flanked with a wooden foot locker, a Lakeview Farms lettuce crate for one's belongings, and a zinc washtub placed under the bunk. The shoes below the closest bunk are dress shoes, made for going into town. They contrast greatly with the give in the springs of the bunk, showing the poor condition of both the mattress and the bed itself. Unlike in the previous photo, all three men meet the camera directly with their gaze. One even smokes a cigarette, calmly inhabiting his leisure activity and showing that he can in fact purchase such commodities. His undershirt is somewhat loose, exposing his musculature, his legs spread, his body and position engaging the camera openly. To his right, another man in a button-up denim shirt reclines on his left arm, uncomfortably looking into the camera, engaging in physical acrobatics to avoid touching the body to the left. Meeting the gaze without shame, and even taking pleasure in his physical refusal, he stares beyond the photographer in defiance of being desired by the camera. In front of them is another man reclined fully on his bunk. He looks tired but relaxed, suggesting that he is done with the day. He also seems to be looking off in the distance, farther away than the two men whose faces articulate the sense that they are directly meeting the gaze of the camera. The split shot contradicts meaning and emotion: two men clearly inhabited the homosocial squalor of intimacy while another challenged desire through heteronormative posing and physical discomfort. Contortion of the body, when contrasted with intimate pleasure of physical proximity, disrupts the totality of a queer frame or reading: not everyone in the shot was comfortable with the intimacy. Again, although we cannot know what Nadel told them to do or what he said when soliciting this photograph, that two of the three men enacted a homosocial contract both directly and indirectly shows how comfortable physical intimacy was. All three men previously negotiated their proximity to one another, whether by accident (i.e., assigned bunks) or through friendship and socialization. Both men sat on the bunk, indicating agreement and a desire for camaraderie and physical proximity. Further, proximity and intimacy, even if staged and performed, go beyond positioning on the bunks; they were documented in the photographs.

So then why does Nadel reframe the photo with a horizontal angle (see figure 11.5)? Visual balance is achieved as a kind of indexicality, the time and place of contact or interaction. The notion of desire here, a return of the gaze, provides an aperture for the exchange, which represents homoerotically infused relations between men. Like its peers found in 1950s Mexican cinema that Sergio de la Mora has written about extensively, Nadel's photos also accommodate homoerotic expressions via migration in the visual.[20] Given the ten-hour low-paid days of labor that determined their existence and the fact that many braceros told Ernesto Galarza in 1954 that they "have no names" and are "called only by numbers," the reader gets a clear sense of how both anonymity and wanting to be wanted for something beyond one's bodily output in the fields became crucial points of sustenance. Marking the psychic costs of migration and the impossibility of being wanted in a particular way, because the work made these men feel desirable not in a sexual or social sense but simply for their bodies as laboring entities, this buddy image in leisure was socially acceptable because of the ways that Mexican national cultures via film in the 1950s accommodated homosociality and homoeroticism.[21] The marked psychic costs of migration and the impossibility of being wanted in a particular way made these men feel desirable not in a sexual or social sense but simply for their laboring bodies.[22] The attachment is to the labor the body produces, not the subject or the body itself. Thus, returning the gaze overcame capitalist attachment exclusively to create emotional attachments, however ephemeral. Diaspora, the masculine privileges

FIG 11.5. Narrow-angle shot of three braceros in bunkhouse at leisure, Salinas, California, summer 1956. Courtesy of the Smithsonian Museum of Natural History. The Leonard Nadel Collection.

FIG 11.6. Wide-angle shot of bracero in bunkhouse shower, Salinas, California, summer 1956. Courtesy of the Smithsonian Museum of Natural History. The Leonard Nadel Collection.

of migration, and its documentation in Nadel's photograph track a history of intimacy between these Mexican men.[23]

Intimacy and anonymity in Nadel's photographs fix braceros as a kind of "nearly complete anonymity of all the Mexican citizens who work in the U.S. fields under an agreement between the two nations. During their short stay in this country, the Mexican nationals come close to being nameless men.... [M]ost U.S. citizens are probably not even aware of their existence."[24] Because Galarza's report worked against this notion of men being nameless and objectified in their productive labor by providing individual testimonies and photographs documenting their experiences, one must ask how and why was it that certain Nadel photos reinscribed this objectification, but this time by turning this bracero body into a sexual object and perhaps even a work of art. And even though art has aesthetic value, there is something highly problematic in the exoticization and objectification seen in the next photo sequence. The camera reifies the culture of surveillance, as well as situating the bracero in the visual field of being "looked at," also potentially signaling Nadel's desires. In particular, this series excessively compresses forms of desire and sexual attachments (see figure 11.6).

Hip Forward into Domestic Labor   227

Because the individual was an unnamed and unknowing photographic subject, I playfully refer to him as the Mexican Adonis. This may be problematic to some, but the image recalls classical Greek sculpture of gods, and this man's body is godly in its sculpted nature. Although these images are out of context and indeed objectifying, mostly because of the ways in which Nadel's photo centralizes this quotidian act of showering in squalid conditions (a public and run-down bunkhouse shower), if we take an aesthetic tack in our reading, subjecthood reemerges in what Leo Bersani calls perceptual recognition: "The aesthetic subject, while it both produces and is produced by works of art, is a mode of relational being that exceeds cultural province of art and embodies truths of being."[25] The aesthetic therefore mitigates objectification, creating a relationship between what we see and the subject in the photo. It represents a kind of historical layering or palimpsest in the photographic practice, that of both Greek mythology in the finely sculpted body of the Mexican Adonis and of the bathhouse that we have contemporarily come to know as a space of enacting homoerotic desire. Greek mythology places Adonis at the center of a love triangle between Aphrodite, Ares, and Persephone, and it further describes his youthful beauty and attractiveness as exceedingly notable, creating a cult-like following. On the side of the bathhouse, while this man showers alone, the image, like the bathhouse, is organized with "a sexualized atmosphere that bombards the senses," and from the viewer's perspective, we can imagine that "almost any interaction has sexual potentiality."[26]

But this man seems to be an unknowing Adonis; that is, in the two shots Nadel took of him showering, there was no mutual recognition that he was in fact being photographed. The image also replicates what Macías-González describes about Mexican masculinity, that in the mid-twentieth century bathhouses and bathing were places of modernity, chauvinism, hygiene, leisure, and homosociality.[27] So this raises a question: how does the image broach the ways in which, as Holland suggests, "racist practices limit human desire," in that Nadel may not have seen the photo as a violation of bodily integrity and free will but as an example of abject aesthetics? Sexual possibility exists for us as viewers, for bracero peers who sought sexual encounter, and perhaps in the photographer's pleasure in viewing the naked beauty and simplicity of the stylized body wrought of hard manual labor and not leisure activities such as exercise and bodybuilding, which are primarily middle- and upper-class activities. Instead, the Mexican Adonis was "available" for the camera and thus sexual consumption because he was a subordinate racialized subject captured on film. Because we cannot see his genitals (this is the word that Nadel uses to describe the spraying of men with DDT before they entered the US), there is a stylized nature to the nudity. The image itself is quite penetrating, but it is not a full frontal shot like the ones in the processing center.[28] In this instance, sexual vulnerability is a transparent truth of the photo's objectifying mode. As Nadel remarked in another context, "Most of the time, a photographer has to separate himself from what's occurring in front of him. He has to come away with pictures, no matter how trying the situation may become."[29] If the ethos of separation drove Nadel's documentation, what happened when the photographer was in so deep that there was no separation at all? In the Mexican Adonis photo, spectacle generated potential arousal. And because of that physical proximity and emotional intimacy, the viewer cannot help but be struck by the idea of sexuality and desire, a body and potential sexual practices related to it in the homosocial context, the vulnerability of this body in its unknowingly photographed existence, and the ways in which such notions of desire exist outside of or are produced by the abject nature of bracero diasporic subjects. Such images, even if staged, challenge overly simplistic historicizations of braceros as heteronormative subjects of state reproduction, men who were each "a head of households that included a wife, children, extended family and often unrelated members," according to Cohen.[30]

The version of the Mexican Adonis shown in figure 11.7 is the subject and object of sexual desire for the photo's audience and recalls the latent homoeroticism of spaces such as the bunkhouse and showers in the labor camp. The image documents the permissibility of cross-racial and interracial same-sex desire and intimacy precisely because the interaction is contained in the photos, unbeknownst to the subject in the image. Because the space has ambiguous meaning (a domestic bunkhouse shower), it subverts and perpetuates domesticity as accommodating of same-sex desire and attachment.[31] Further, it reflects what Elizabeth Freeman has called the ways in which "normative masculinity and femininity can only preserve the lost object of homosexual desire in the form of the lawfully gendered subject by evacuating the historical specificity of that prior object." Thus, the absence of normative masculine and feminine contexts or scenarios in the Mexican Adonis photographs generates a text of homosexual potentiality through historical evacuation. The evacuation of historical specificity sutures multiple temporalities: the enactment of homoerotic desires as sexual practice, the capitalist structures of labor, the simple bodily pleasures of showering after a long day's work, and premodernity, given the squalid, underdeveloped,

FIG 11.7. Narrow-angle shot of bracero in bunkhouse shower, Salinas, California, summer 1956. Courtesy of the Smithsonian Museum of Natural History. The Leonard Nadel Collection.

and dimly lit shower conditions and the racialized, gendered Mexican body that inhabits the space. In these multiple temporalities the fragilities of male embodiment and physical strength are rendered visible in the domestic-public space of the bunkhouse shower.[32] The Mexican Adonis, as a photograph, is harder to generalize than the group shots. When someone is not looking at Nadel or desiring to be seen through the photograph's line of sight, the power of looking is emphasized over that of the subject as agent.

Chapter 12

QUEER PRECARIOUS LIVES

The extremely dilapidated conditions of most labor camps became an issue in the Salinas Valley during 1956. After two months of inspections, the Monterey County Department of Health ordered Salinas city officials to perform "major building corrections" or "minor cleanup and repairs." Based on a new ordinance, the county was able to better monitor infractions, including "alleged violations of sewage and garbage disposal regulations" in two north county locations. Given the inconsistency in quality, condition, and services offered in labor camps, one has to ask how grave conditions would need to be in order to become an infraction. And given that most growers did not invest much capital in improving the conditions of labor camps, as the Nadel photos illustrate, it is an open question whether the sewage and trash violations were cited because of bracero health or because of the idea that poor public health conditions might have been brought into the city core of Salinas. We can discern three things from these health citations. First, public health officials for the state office of agriculture, for which there was one employee doing these inspections in the entire state, saw infractions as threats to workers. Second, sewage and trash contaminated groundwater and thus the crops in nearby fields, potentially passing on E. coli to the consumer. Third, judging from the last line of the newspaper article, that the "camps are inspected each spring before seasonal work starts for Mexican nationals brought here under contract," the public health concerns were not for the Mexican nationals but for the extended community, to which these labor camps were marginal, and such violations would increase with population growth during the growing season.[1]

The Salinas Valley had only one physician for braceros, and he was provided by an insurance company. Dr. Stanley Savoy saw about eighty-five men a day in the clinic. According to Nadel, Savoy said the following:

> The men like surgery and look for it...they also want injections because in Mexico they can go into a drug store and pay for it. He said, too, that the most common ailment is backache and that the braceros have a higher incidence of respiratory diseases and appendicitis, it was his opinion that the bad living conditions and unhygienic habits made for upper respiratory illnesses. Medicines, pills and injections are provided to the braceros free and the pills are obtained from the major pharmaceutical firms for free in bulk samples.[2]

Injured bodies and state negligence translated into racist opinions about why braceros sought surgery and pills. Braceros like Ignacio Magallanes Hernández note how their healthcare was included but that most sought care for colds and flu because of the damp conditions in lettuce and strawberry fields.[3] Agustín Bautista remembered that the conditions were very dangerous and prone to cause injury but that the farmers didn't seem bothered by this.[4] Although Savoy clearly stated that the appendicitis and respiratory diseases were most likely caused by toxic chemicals, he didn't rule out hygiene or name occupational hazards: code for racist public health opinions.

The injuries and public health crisis caused by bracero working conditions ramped up when the growing season hit peak production in late March or early April through October. Thus, these infractions from July 1956, along with Savoy's diagnosis, occurred at the point of highest output for lettuce, artichokes, strawberries, and broccoli. And because the citations happened when the workers were at maximum capacity in these labor camps, which produced strawberries or artichokes given their north county location, the citations mark a lack of care for worker conditions and the public health pathogens that could be carried by braceros heading into town on Sunday or by the vegetables produced for sale. However, what is curious is the absence of detail about which growers and which specific camps were cited. Protecting the identities of those who ran the agricultural economic engine, the local press placed the focus on public health. Thus, Mexican nationals were the afterthought to the actual public health risks, showing their vulnerable existence at the same time that they were blamed for contaminating labor camps, the fields, and the communities where they sought services.

The ordinance came on the heels of a labor camp committee meeting the city convened on April 10: "The labor camp problem is caused principally by the increased production of strawberries," which was a communal crisis. The lack of oversight in both the actual management of the occupied camps, coupled with the poor sanitation and lack of uniform construction standards, caused great panic given the probability of "soil disease contamination. . . . [I]t is desirable that large labor camps be located where sanitary sewer connections are available."[5] Implying that workers were urinating and defecating in the fields or that septic tanks were old and faulty exposed structural inequality at the core of work conditions.[6] Yet the committee ruled that camps "should be in or near the general strawberry growing areas." Two logics overlapped in the decision-making process. First, the commission wanted those camps as far away and isolated from the city core as possible. Keeping the camps far away meant less social interaction and an out-of-sight, out-of-mind policy, as if the city would not feel the influx of twelve thousand new workers for the 1957 harvest season. Second, in keeping the camps isolated and advocating for better sanitation, they required growers and camp owners to invest in the infrastructure of these rural and isolated dwellings. The risk of E. coli being transferred to the fruit and vegetables was high, especially if workers passed feces in the fields, not in a bathroom sewage system or portable toilet. Yet the commission ruled that despite being a problem, "labor camps properly constructed and operated are an asset to the community. . . . [C]omplaints come largely from a few camps."[7] I detail the complaints as evidence of latent homoerotic forms of expression meted out through violence elsewhere in these chapters, but I want to focus here on the logic that doubles back on itself.

How could segregation amount to an asset? In other words, why was the segregation of Mexican national workers deemed valuable? With coded language, the committee report ruled that the camps were valuable to the economy, barely mentioning those eight thousand workers who would occupy the camps. Tirso Yepes, who was contracted to lettuce and strawberry growers in González and Soledad (South Salinas Valley) on separate occasions, described the isolated nature of labor camps. Being far away from the towns and Salinas, "the big city," was a form of segregation, even though he did not describe it as such.[8] Further, "the public" was called upon "for cooperation and understanding of the problem to best serve the welfare of the county."[9] The conciliatory tone anticipated mass objection to more labor camps and the bodies that inhabited them. Mass economic growth, increased infrastructure through sewage systems, and higher production outputs outweighed the desires of Salinas residents who objected to the rural "barrioization" of the Alisal industrial zone. Similar problems emerged in neighboring Watsonville, where on April 10, 1956, residents of the Casserly district were "protesting reports that another labor camp for Mexican nationals is planned."[10] Although the Salinas press, the Board of Supervisors for Monterey County, and the Salinas City Planning Commission were careful to never mention Mexican nationals, that was the underlying target population.

A similar incident happened in the small community of Aromas, which borders Salinas and Watsonville. On May 4, 1956, the Aromas school trustees were faced with a vote to approve or deny the building of a labor camp across the street from the schoolhouse. Monterey County Deputy District Attorney Bert Lindsey urged the committee to consider legal aspects of the case, including "whether such a camp would constitute a nuisance or danger to school pupils." Aromas Fire Chief and spokesman for the citizen's group Frank Matthews had similar concerns: "We're not concerned with nationality. We're concerned with the great number of men to occupy the camp and its nearness to the school and Aromas." In contrast, F. V. Birbeck, a grower, spoke in favor of the camp: "I have one labor camp closer to Aromas than the one to be built by Mr. Brown. There have been no complaints about the Mexican nationals at my camp from anyone. They've never created any disturbances, molested anyone, or done anything offensive. There is no finer class of people than the nationals."[11] Lindsey, Matthews, and Birbeck all navigate the conversation away from the negative racialization and sexual demonization of Mexican nationals. After all, these were federally contracted workers. As they walked a fine line between bad-mouthing the bracero program and meeting the economic needs of the growers, community members used children's safety as their linchpin argument. Indirectly, it was not the number of braceros but the fact that those who lived there were unsupervised men who caused a potential danger to children. Pedophilia, while unnamed in the speeches by the fire chief and deputy district attorney, represented the worst-case outcome for placing a labor camp by a school. Although there was no verifiable sexual abuse or violent behavior toward children by Mexican nationals, Colin R. Johnson's research has shown that in rural agricultural America, such nonnormativities and the potential for them could provide the basis of "malicious small-town gossip run amok. . . . [W]e would still learn something important about the manner in which such behavior was understood."[12] Also, potential innuendo and gossip became the basis by which law enforcement officials made preemptive claims

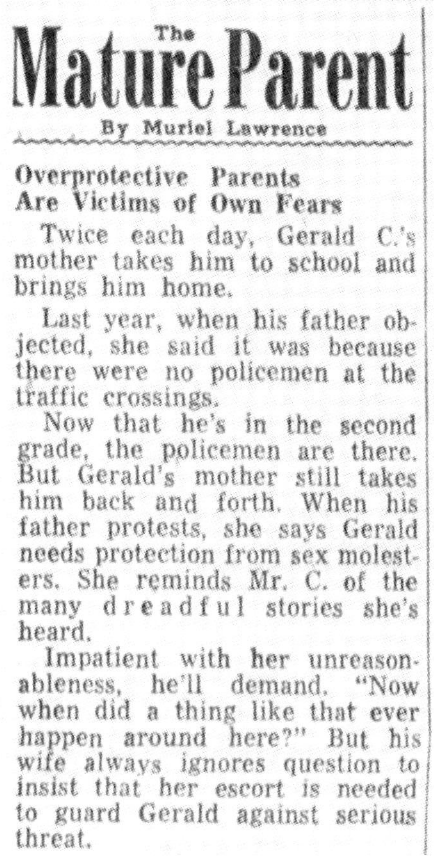

FIG 12.1. "The Mature Parent," by Muriel Lawrence. *Santa Cruz Sentinel*, February 17, 1956.

The Mature Parent
By Muriel Lawrence

Overprotective Parents Are Victims of Own Fears

Twice each day, Gerald C.'s mother takes him to school and brings him home.

Last year, when his father objected, she said it was because there were no policemen at the traffic crossings.

Now that he's in the second grade, the policemen are there. But Gerald's mother still takes him back and forth. When his father protests, she says Gerald needs protection from sex molesters. She reminds Mr. C. of the many d r e a d f u l stories she's heard.

Impatient with her unreasonableness, he'll demand. "Now when did a thing like that ever happen around here?" But his wife always ignores question to insist that her escort is needed to guard Gerald against serious threat.

about the potential for sexual misconduct and public condemnation of such nationals who were in the area without their wives or families.

Fears of sexual abuse certainly pervaded the community. On February 17, 1956, a column in the *Santa Cruz Sentinel* called "The Mature Parent" tackled increasing fears about sex molesters (see figure 12.1). In the column the white mother is the irrational, hysterical woman leading the charge against these men, just like the white women leading the charge against labor camps in Aromas. It is the hetero father who is "the mature parent" whose masculinity refutes the threat of sexual perversion, much like the growers who put down the protest. The spatial expansiveness and inability to contain the rural labor camp deepened the unspoken threat. Braceros like Carlos Villagomes Fuentes viscerally felt this fear and rage directed at braceros. Every time they went from González to Salinas on Sunday he "saw the white people, especially white men, stare at him with disdain when they

Queer Precarious Lives 237

went to buy clothes."[13] To put it more bluntly, innuendo, gossip, and racialized sexual fears became the basis that prevents us from seeing how law enforcement officials made preemptive claims about the potential for sexual misconduct and the potential public condemnation of such nationals.

This particular column built on 1950s stereotypes of aimless gay or unchaperoned men as potential child molesters, with "gay," according to prevailing pathologies of the era, feeding into the idea that being a migrant was a queer sexual-subject position that posed a danger to most children and white women. Historian Nayan Shah has demonstrated how within the legal realm of prosecuting sexual deviance in agricultural California, worker housing yielded spaces for a variety of social arrangements, yet the men in the camps and those in the surrounding communities often "disputed the emergence of sporadic social tolerance for a variety of forms of social intimacy and domestic arrangements."[14] Schoolchildren next to a labor camp pushed the boundaries of social tolerance as a result of grower economic need to house contract laborers. In the Aromas labor camp debate, we see, as Estelle Freedman argues, the inference of a "strict boundary between heterosexual and homosexual males, labeling the latter as violent child molesters." It was the queer potentiality of the braceros living in the camp that made them sexual deviants in waiting: child molesters, irrelevant of sexual orientation, despite the fact that Birbeck states that there was "no other finer class of people than the nationals."[15] Arguing against the potential for child sexual predatory behavior, racial, social, cultural, and national differences balanced capitalist interests with morality.

Examining the Aromas labor camp and the queer potential for nonnormative interactions between nationals and children, when coupled with the April 15, 1956, Salinas City Planning Commission passing of "862: An Ordinance Regulating Labor Camps," raises a secondary set of concerns about what was done in the labor camps by residents and their owners. Ordinance 862 adopted policy measures to control future and existing labor camps in the city, despite the compressed and unsafe potentiality of spaces cited above.[16] Those applying for a license had to verify "whether or not the applicant has ever been convicted of a felony or a crime involving moral turpitude, or the crime of using, possessing, selling, or transporting narcotics or imparting information for obtaining narcotics."[17] And if a camp preexisted the ordinance, the owner had ten days from the date of its passage to file with the city clerk, "requesting the issuance to such applicant of a license to continue to operate and maintain such labor camp."[18] Although there was no strict legal procedure in these small communities to deal with potential pedophilia as a criminal activity, there was indeed a legal precedent for conviction of narcotics possession, use, and distribution. The ordinance framed bracero residents as easy targets for buying and perhaps even vending recreational narcotics. It also suggests that the owner and operator could use the camps as a drug-selling front. Projecting morality-based anxiety onto those living in and operating labor camps cast moral doubt on the tremendous economic gains for having camps near fields.

In the Aromas case, "There is a petition with almost 300 signatures of people who don't want the camp. These people deserve consideration."[19] Small-town fears of sexual violence and drug use near and around children were indeed a psychic reality for those in Salinas and Aromas when contending with labor camp construction. In fact, residents protested that laborers, labor camps, and the Mexican men who inhabited them ultimately forced Salinas housewives to publicly admit that "there was enough trouble with labor camps in 'not being able to walk the streets without being embarrassed by single men.'"[20] Ultimately, the Aromas school trustees rejected the resolution protesting the labor camp, demonstrating how economic interests outweighed Mexican nationals' potential for sexual, moral, or drug-related misconduct around children. The twenty growers in attendance outmaneuvered the three hundred petition signers, the fire chief, and the deputy district attorney in their claims to protect children. The labor camp ruling demonstrated local state actors' inability to view Mexican migrant male sexuality as anything but deviant. And although the public hearing did not discuss gay braceros or sex molesters, the Aromas community and Salinas Valley housewives nevertheless saw bracero behavior and character as transgressive because of their race and foreignness. Bracero presence represented an improper set of attachments and desire for intimacy and proximity to children and white women. Thus, a queer of color critique "makes some sense" of their lives as desiring subjects, which counters the ways in which the community pathologized bracero sexuality as stereotypically opportunistic and perverse.[21]

In Salinas, rulings by the Planning Commission were very contradictory as well. They went on record with the following rulings: (1) favoring new labor camps in the city under controlled conditions; (2) proposing a southern industrial area on Sanborn Road and Harkins Road—the general site for new labor camps to be considered on a case-by-case basis; (3) preparing a checklist for authorizing building permits; and (4) favoring amending the business ordinance so that labor camps would be controlled by health, policing, and appearance. By 1956, the city had nineteen operating labor camps, and officials were primarily concerned with the vast increase in laborers.

The Salinas camps went from housing 1,900 men in 1954 to 4,000 in 1955 to 8,000 in 1956 during the strawberry boom.[22] The total population for the 1950 census of the city was 13,900, which meant that the strawberry boom alone accounted for a total temporary population increase of 56 percent. In fact, the strawberry boom was encouraged with talks by the Salinas Exchange club, hosted by program chairman Joe Wing, in the swank Jeffery Hotel in Monterey.[23] With the town literally being taken over by a migrant labor force for eight months of the year, the profits to be gained from labor camps and an increased volume of laborers were no doubt reason enough to favor and restrict camps. E. J. Raffetto, a produce representative in Salinas, stated that "labor camps are not operated at a profit, which should be taken into consideration if the business license procedure is adopted."[24] Appealing to a necessary evil of spending, Raffetto disabused city planners of the idea that growers were profiting from their camps. Labor camps made growers poor, despite the fact that the laborers who lived in them earned pennies on the dollar through prenegotiated government contracts. Building a labor camp was an act of benevolence and care for workers because the cost to growers was taken at a loss. Yet Grace Arceneaux's oral history about her aunt and uncle profiting from labor camps demonstrates that the physical structure or dwellings of the camps may not have been profitable because no rent was collected but that money was to be made off those who lived there:

> I knew a labor contractor in San Juan after I moved to Watsonville. In San Juan, my aunt and uncle worked for them as cooks in a huge dining hall. So if we went to see my aunt, although she lived in San Juan, she would be out there at the camp working. I knew what they were being fed. Very cheap food. My aunt and uncle made a lot of money. The labor contractor helped them do the shopping. But when they got paid, they had to give the labor contractor the money. Money for having the job. There was graft and corruption all over, exploitation.[25]

It was the services attached to those dwellings, such as a commissary, the kitchen, and/or mess hall, that were the sites where a 100 percent-plus profit margin could be made by overcharging for goods or skimming off the top when money was spent on "very cheap food." Even if Arceneaux's aunt and uncle gave their money to the labor contractor at the end of each month, that very same labor contractor paid them after getting his cut. All these monetary transactions were tax-free, under-the-table payments. Similarly, bracero Agustín Bautista remembered the Morgan Hill strawberry mayordomo (overseer) Cornelio and his family did very well financially by supervising the braceros and maintaining the labor camp.[26] Working-class Mexican Americans could and indeed did become relatively wealthy when compared with the poverty that the braceros they serviced lived in. That graft made the Mexican American middle class entrenched and differentiated them from their Mexican national counterparts, even among their own family. Why would someone share or give up these kinds of privileges if it meant not making "a lot of money?"[27] In busting the myth that all Mexicans in the agricultural industry were equally oppressed, the class stratification in Arceneaux's family demonstrates how her aunt and uncle financially benefited from bracero exploitation by feeding them cheap food.

To further this point, Arceneaux discussed her aunt's deliberate silence about money:

> ARCENEAUX: No, my aunt never talked about it, because she wanted her job. But I knew of them and I knew of it happening. I knew that in many instances they would find something wrong with a worker and not pay him. You know, send him back. Or the contractor, charging, like he'd have his own little store there. And they'd buy cigarettes and they'd buy whiskey and beer and end up not getting any money at the end of the month because they spent it all. Here in Watsonville there were a few families who got quite wealthy in that time, who had labor camps. . . .
>
> KNASTER: Were these Mexican families?
>
> ARCENEAUX: Yes. You can't help but put two and two together because there's not too much money in cooking for men and feeding them unless you have something else to it. If you really cook well for a group of men and they pay you. In those days, room and board was say twenty dollars a week . . . well, yes you can make a lot of money because you work a lot of hours. But you don't end up owning property and putting money in the bank. My aunt and uncle were almost illiterate. My uncle couldn't read or write. My aunt was the brains who could write her name down and keep some form of accounting . . . yet, they made money . . . they were just brought in to cook. They would bring the food and then got paid for doing it. And yet she made money. 'Course they were exploited. In all ways. Washing for them. Ironing for them. Sure it was never done honestly. It's really a shame. Yet they used to say "Well, we're still making money." . . . But labor contractors, . . . they seemed to have the knowledge of how to

get people to work for them.... But they seemed to kind of congregate where the poor people were. And able to get them. Get their licks in.[28]

In terms of racial forms of capital, class and US residency mattered. One group made profit off its contracted Mexican national peers' inability to negotiate capitalist systems on their own terms. And even though Arceneaux's aunt and uncle were under the thumb of the labor contractor, they still made a lot of money, unlike their bracero counterparts, who had fixed, low-wage eighteen- or twenty-four-month contracts. The aunt turned a blind eye to the fact that she exploited braceros despite being Mexican and illiterate herself. In other words, personal economic gain was more important than being in solidarity about poverty and racialized forms of displacement and discrimination. And even though Arceneaux's aunt and uncle were exploited in their mess hall cooking or ironing and doing laundry for extra payment, they nonetheless reaped great benefits from being higher up in the labor chain because they were Mexican Americans. Other Mexican Americans who maintained camps also exploited the labor of Chinese cooks for very low pay, contracting out the intensive manual labor for their own profit.[29] Perhaps exploiting your own people, exploiting other immigrants like the Chinese, and being exploited at the same time was, and continues to be, the winning formula for Mexican Americans to get ahead of their immigrant counterparts both economically and politically.

There was also the informal economy of a contractor charging and having "his own little store there. And [braceros would] buy cigarettes and they'd buy whiskey and beer and end up not getting any money at the end of the month because they spent it all," reifying a predatory practice. The very nature of alcohol and cigarette consumption was tied to maintaining all revenue within the hands of the labor camp owners and labor contractors.[30] Clemente Velásquez Lucio recalled that the *tiendita* (store) run in the Salinas labor camp where he worked in 1956 sold cigarettes, candy, and other small items.[31] In the US, historians such as Monica Perales and Price Fishback have argued that the company store, though outside of external economies of purchase, has been a way for smelters, copper mines, and coal mines to charge exorbitant prices and further entrench exploitative economic relations.[32] In essence, the company store had workers in a state of constant debt, "sign[ing] away their paycheck and their lives."[33] Perales mostly describes the consumption of staples for survival within a geographically isolated smelter town in El Paso, Texas, but Arceneaux's description of bracero consumption indicated that the labor contractor company store focused on purchase for pleasure. Traveling by foot to town after an eight-hour work day was difficult, so the company store filled the gap in midweek leisure and pleasure.

One could argue that the isolated and desolate nature of the camps allowed camp store owners to create a market of scarcity and play upon the notion that Mexican men are of weak moral character and seek pleasure at all costs. Just like Oscar Lewis's influential culture-of-poverty thesis ascribed to Mexicans in Mexico and the US, the "inglorious defects and weaknesses" of the poor determined how braceros were viewed as consumers. Over the years, Lewis's fieldwork was paramount in reinforcing the thrill-seeking, adventurous, and violence-driven Mexican male macho, especially in the second half of Roberto's ethnography in *The Children of Sanchez*.[34] Creating an array of Mexican male types as part of national logic, as McKee Irwin argues, "defin[ing] a macho heterosexual model and another fact that the model was intrinsically Mexican itself," allows the over-performative nature of Mexican masculinity to be read as both a totalizing national discourse and heterosexual.[35] I would beg to differ with the idea that the macho is a totalizing national type, yet this rationale structured company stores and wages, situating the bracero for informal, pleasure-seeking consumption. In Salinas, during a hearing for labor camp construction that was denied, "another woman [said] 'the nationals walk in front of cars and they get drunk,'" reinforcing the idea that braceros not only lacked the civilizing influence of women to care for them but were also prone to poor judgment and did not care much for their lives in seeking pleasure after hard days of labor.[36] Bracero drunkenness summoned the idea of losing self to encourage deviance and even perversion.[37] Clemente Velásquez Lucio remembered that when his peers drank it was often a response to the fact that "nos trataban muy mal" (they treated us very badly).[38] While Velásquez Lucio articulates his comrades' drinking as a response to oppression, the gendered, national, and racial content of bracero character was ultimately understood by white women in the community as a threat to their safety and honor.

As Carlos Decena has argued, we need to "understand the subtleties of [people of color's] presence, participation, and enjoyment in of privilege, [which] demands an analysis that disarticulates consumption and power from a white gay male body and that sets some distance from the 'self'-versus-'other' dichotomy that usually organizes analyses of relations of (sexual) exchange in transnational settings."[39] In the Salinas Valley bracero case, the migrant consumer must be disarticulated from a white male (heterosexual) body. And although sex was not the exact point of consumption in the labor camp store, similar relations of desire were at play in the homosocial Mexican male context of alcohol as communal pleasure seeking. The concrete pathology of masculine excessive pleasure-seeking behavior infantilized Mexican male migrants with their overpriced cigarettes, alcohol consumption, and poor judgment. In *The Care of the Self*, Michel Foucault argues that historically "self-respect . . . [wa]s exercised by depriving oneself of pleasure or by confining one's indulgence to marriage or procreation": anything outside of this rubric was queer.[40] That pathology narrates unnecessary consumptive impulse as nonnormative sexuality, an uncontainable and insatiable desire that is both infantilizing and a response to the displeasure of impoverished living conditions. In other words, consumption, in care of the self, is a surrogate for sexual contact or potentially facilitated sexual contact among same-sex peers.

As Decena has further argued, we should see bracero consumptive impulses as evidence of how even "the subordinated and marginalized in various national and local contexts experience mobility, relative freedoms, and power that are closely tied to the immobility of others."[41] The need for pleasure was enacted in the homosocial space of labor camp or the male-dominated Salinas public sphere with alcohol and cigarette consumption. Their privileges as US-based consumers who were highly subordinated through the very nature of their wage contracts, immigration status, and high interest charged on camp store purchases heightened the erotics of attachment as they were tethered to consumption. Even Mexican periodicals poked fun at how braceros were taught to overconsume in the US. The March 8, 1956, cover of *Todo* depicts a bracero returning home loaded down with consumer goods from the US (see figure 12.2).

The image mocks US consumerism for pleasure, contrasting greatly with Mexican working-class poverty. The frivolity of the image reflects the same capacity to purchase alcohol and cigarettes freely and openly without criticism or the watchful eyes of extended family. Both forms of consumption were liberating in their own right, yet these pleasure-associated goods were charged at high interest rates and against unearned wages, reinforcing the highly immobile nature of the Mexican male migrant. The desire for temporary reprieve from segregated and squalid living conditions was transcended through the homosocial and homoerotic bonding of drinking and smoking in community. Such small pleasures resulted in debt and the complaints of white women who said they were a threat to public safety.

Thus, the freedom to consume and the freedom to seek out pleasure, be it sexual or through purchasing objects, opened up through migration. The alcohol and cigarettes mentioned in Velásquez Lucio and Arceneaux's oral

FIG 12.2. "El retorno del bracero," *Todo: La Mejor Revista de México*, March 8, 1956. Courtesy of the Nettie Lee Benson Collection, University of Texas at Austin.

histories were coupled with wage theft in the camps. Informal economies were dependent on such inherent "weaknesses" of the poor and their geographic isolation. This same logic was deployed in the economic tactics used by labor contractors and camp owners to keep money in their hands. Motivated to contain the somewhat informal nature of the labor camp economic structure, despite government contracts, they relied on the idea that "consumers [were] driven by self-interest to increase pleasure and reduce pain." Given recent economic studies on pleasure and consumption, most notably by economist Daniel McFadden, according to the damning moral accounts of their overconsumption, there was a particular way by which braceros engaged in "hyperbolic discounting ... when individuals systematically underweigh ... future consequences relative to contemporaneous ones, and make choices that gratify now and leave lasting regret, in patterns that cannot be explained by maximization of consistently discounted present value of instantaneous utility."[42]

If public drunkenness was overconsumption, there was a decision-making process where the subject weighed consumption at a much lower rate than its actual monetary or emotional cost. Those future consequences of consumption were moved aside to make way for immediate gratification and utility. Pleasure reaped from drinking and smoking at inflated prices represented "hyperbolic discounting" in an economic system that was already full of regret. Pleasure had a high cost that did not maximize economic value over the long term. Fleeting instances to satiate pain and desire wrought from isolated social, physical, and economic alienation propped up masculinities. Deborah Cohen argues that these consumptive behaviors were tied to how the Mexican government implicitly understood the cultural demands of modernization, with the bracero program "chip[ping] away at ingrained negative behaviors such as alcoholism and poor hygiene, still seen in many migrants."[43] In theory, sending the men away to a more modern lifeworld would correct these behaviors. But without institutionalized Mexican state forms of heteropatriarchy or extended family to contain and police men's consumption behaviors, the braceros were the sole actors, often influenced by homosocial peer contexts, who determined the value of hyperbolic discounting to justify inflated levels of purchase. Sociality clearly heightened the pleasure and risk, creating erotics of consumption. As Nadel noted, "After a hard day's work, there's little else for a bracero to do but rest or seek the companionship of another farm laborer. . . . They feel helpless, isolated and vulnerable."[44] These moments of companionship, exacerbated by isolation and helplessness, forced men to seek solace in one another's company. At the same time, when braceros spent their money on alcohol and cigarettes in the labor camp, it meant that they could not fulfill their heteronormative duty as wage earners who would send remissions back to wives, mothers, and children for survival in Mexico. Lauren Derby has called "consumption . . . a key arena in which anxieties over dissolution of place in the transnational condition are expressed, and the boundaries redrawn."[45] With the bracero case, a distance between place of origin and site of labor shifted consumptive values. One could see the use of alcohol and cigarettes as an enactment of melancholia and loss in relationship to migration, but we must also consider the pleasure derived from being in the constant company of other men and, occasionally, the company of women.

Fleeting pleasure and physical proximity created hyperbolic risks with alcohol and cigarette consumption at inflated prices, but labor camps also became sites of struggle regarding segregation, zoning, and profit. To further this point, on May 23, 1956, the *Register Pajaronian* reported that Antonio R.

Bailleres had applied for a use permit to add a barracks and a new kitchen to a labor camp at 723 Lakeview Road in Watsonville.[46] Though seemingly benign on the surface, Bailleres's petition to expand his labor camp suggests three things. First, Mexican Americans were indeed able to raise the capital to own and expand labor camps. Second, labor camp expansion meant increased profit margins for those who ran the camps and the growers: the Mork family owned the farmland adjacent to the camp.[47] Third, the headline "Labor Camp Plan Will Be Aired" suggests the clandestine nature of such planning, for townspeople often contested and regretted the expansion of camps because of the elements they brought into the geographic peripheries of communities. Fourth, Ballares created the opportunity for braceros to cook for themselves, providing a sense of freedom within the confined space of the camp.[48] Although Bailleres may seem like any other labor camp owner, the fact that he was Mexican American ultimately shows how labor contractors and camp owners' power was so great that their ability to violently wield economic control over pleasure and vice for a profit allowed them to "get . . . their licks in," according to Arceneaux.

Arceneaux and Dr. D. A. Wessels, the commission chair, undermined and contradicted Commissioner Raffetto's argument that growers were poor. Labor camps "represent a cost to the city and have to be policed. 'In other words, they should pay their own way.'"[49] The Salinas city police force averaged forty-five officers plus the commissioner at this time, and the seasonal population increase, coupled with an increase in the policing of square miles, put a strain on city resources despite the fact that agriculture was indeed the major revenue generator for the city.[50] The logic was that no property taxes were generated by labor camps, as they would with single-family homes. Yet Ordinance 862 mandated that the city recuperate its policing expenses by charging a license fee that had to be paid quarterly. The fee schedule was as follows:

— Ten ($10.00) dollars per quarter for fifty or less occupants;
— Fifteen ($15.00) dollars per quarter for more than fifty but not more than one hundred such occupants;
— Twenty ($20.00) dollars per quarter for more than one hundred but not more than one hundred and fifty such occupants;
— And twenty-five ($25.00) dollars per quarter for more than one hundred fifty such occupants.[51]

The labor camp as "policed" space points to the undesirability of the camp and those who occupied them, which manifested in licensing fees. In other words, the fees were a levy tax for the city to profit or at least break even on policing costs at the fringes of city limits, keeping the residents separate from braceros. Without mentioning braceros directly, Wessels criminalized the labor camps, marking them as a drain on city resources: "Labor Camps are being forced into Salinas. Alisal and the county areas don't want them. They're being dumped in our lap."[52] Wessels made an indirect argument for keeping Salinas civilized. The metaphor for forced physical intimacy "dumped in our lap" was highly uncomfortable and overly familiar to predominantly Anglo property and home owners trying to protect their claims to city governance. Wessel's protection of Alisal from becoming a migrant farmworker ghetto was apocryphal, for that part of contemporary Salinas is one of the poorest and most densely populated and Mexican-inhabited zones in the entire United States.[53] Nonetheless, Wessel's ire registers the ways in which city and county officials turned their heads from the mass expansion of labor camps via the bracero program and a production rampup. At the same time, these issues were not new to the community. A. A. Tavernetti, director of the Monterey County Extension Service, argued that there was a much larger historical precedent: "We have got to upgrade these camps. We are an industrial town and have agriculture here and have to live with it. . . . Back in the twenties people couldn't face this thing [zoning and control]. That's why we have Alisal the way it is."[54]

Tavernetti alluded to the "Okies" and "Arkies" who lived in tents and labor camps alongside Filipino and Mexican migrant workers in Alisal during the 1920s and 1930s.[55] By describing the creation of a migrant ghetto by avoiding new restrictions on how people lived in and around the fields, Tavernetti reminded residents that agriculture interests historically dominated local politics and land use. Thirty years later, during the bracero program, those former Dust Bowl migrants and Filipinos from the early twentieth century had carved out home ownership for themselves in East Salinas. The "Okies," "Arkies," Mexican Americans, Filipinos, and their descendants were working in the packing sheds while Mexican nationals remained in the fields.[56] In addition, Alisal became a predominantly ethnic middle-class white community, with agricultural exiles from New Mexico, who migrated in the 1940s after the artesian wells dried up; Tejano farmworkers, who "have a tendency to think they're greater than anyone else" and arrived in the Salinas Valley because of one of the worst droughts in Texas history;[57] and second-generation Swiss, Portuguese, and Italian Americans who were growers in the area. Alisal was not incorporated into Salinas until 1963, but it had historically maintained geographical and ethnic differences from the rest of the city. As Tavernetti asked the City Planning Commission to reckon with its history of excluding laborers who had settled in Alisal, he also mentioned that those voting to stop labor camp growth were "merchants and industry [that] might have overlooked the money workers spend in Salinas."[58] How braceros spent money in local communities is covered in much greater detail in chapter 14, but I want to emphasize that Tavernetti's modernization call for the labor camps references a long history of class inequality and racial segregation as a part of agricultural development and city growth.

Labor camps also furthered the incorporation of land into the city limits: "Between 1950 and 1956 the council began a long series of annexations that brought 43 separate additions to the city, doubling the area."[59] It was also the year when the Nacamiento Dam was completed, bringing more cubic tons of irrigation water to the region than ever before. A total of 120,000 acres were irrigated that year.[60] The prosperity of the postwar boom, the strawberry boom, and the bracero boom grew with each new ounce of water that could be pumped into the fields to increase crop output. The public battle between Raffeto, Tavernetti, and Wessels hinged on the expansion of the Salinas economy and what that economic expansion meant in terms of culture, social class, and racial formations. As local commissions duked it out about land use, they never actually mentioned braceros, the invisible force at the heart of the controversy. What was to become the "industrial zone" in East Salinas had its precursor with labor camps.

The fight in the City Planning Commission came to a head because three building permits were issued to labor camp–related construction. On April 2, 1956, permits were awarded to Jesus M. Arroyo to "erect labor camp. 441 Vertin Avenue $8000. . . . El Sombrero Motel [a rent-by-the-week motor lodge next to the Merrill Farms and Sunkist packing sheds], build 6 additional units, 210 Abbott Street, $12,000. . . . Salinas Motel, build Foundation and Stucco building, 1319 N. Main Street, $1000."[61] Arroyo's application for more labor camps shows how Mexican Americans embedded in racial capitalism had a distinct advantage, especially if they had the liquid assets to build new camps in the strawberry boom of 1956. The approval of an $8,000 construction project, perhaps subsidized by growers, which could house up to two hundred men if packed tightly enough with bunk space, shows the level of Salinas's economic dependency on agricultural outputs. Neuburger described Vertin Road as "an area of truck and bus yards, workshops, yards full of pallets and boxes, and small factories intermingled with whitewashed camp barracks, their exteriors blistered."[62] The full realization of that southern industrial zone in Salinas had become a reality, and Arroyo's labor camp was part of that master plan. In addition, the El Sombrero Hotel still stands in the same location. It has historically been a long-term residency hotel, with kitchenettes and entire migrant groups or families in one room, so the zoning question did not disrupt but actually encouraged hotel commerce. As fears coalesced about the dangers embedded in police reports of "quite a bit of night carousing," these "eyesores" were essential to the city's economy.

Chapter 13

WANTING TO BE LOOKED AT

I want to return to Salinas community leader A. A. Tavernetti's claim in chapter 12 about "merchants and industry [that] might have overlooked the money workers spend in Salinas."[1] Bracero spending is one of the major areas of inquiry that is neglected in the uniform narrative history of suffering and oppression. Upon closer inspection of Nadel's photographs and taking Tavernetti's assertion seriously, we can track the archive of spending on products that made the men look better and feel better. In caring for the self through hair products, face creams, shaving implements, colognes, and the tidy spaces where they kept those objects, we can track the ways in which grooming disrupts the narrative of total suffering, premodernity, poor judgment, and compulsory heteronormativity. As Deborah Cohen states, those drafting bracero contracts included "provisions that gave men access to a primary-school education, skills in English, and instruction in hygiene."[2] Grooming and hygiene were part of the Mexican national project to make braceros into proper subjects, but their assimilation of these beliefs in their squalid living conditions suggests an agenda beyond that of the nation. In many ways, their primping and preening was in line with the 1950s homophile movement tracked by Víctor Macías-González: "The bachelor, who was not expected to locate his sexuality in the consumption of a whole repertoire of new products and technologies promoting masculine glamor."[3] In fact, personal grooming and taking pleasure in grooming recalibrate the history of suffering, diaspora, and the Mexican nation and link it back to Mexico City's epicenter of masculine cultures of modernity. Braceros were positioned as a captive consumer market for grooming products, demonstrating the self-derived pleasures of primping and preening.

Despite the abject state of living conditions, one of Nadel's captioned photographs described the following: "With a huge market available in the bracero camps, modern peddlers make a circuit of the camps in '55 station wagons to sell clothing, lotions, suitcases, etc. at top prices."[4] In other words, the labor of making oneself look and smell good in the company of other men posited the homoerotic and homosocial potential as the obvious audience for the pleasure wrought from such activities.

In almost all of the interior spaces Nadel photographed there are four constants: men in leisure, men performing domestic labor, men reading and writing, and men with their grooming products. These recurrent visual motifs humanized braceros, showing that they were clean, hardworking, industrious, god-fearing, literate, and worthy of protection. And in producing propaganda later used to terminate the program, Nadel captured how technologies of self, according to Michel Foucault, "permit individuals to effect by their own means or with the help of others a certain number of operations on their own bodies and souls, thoughts, conduct, and way of being, so as to transform themselves to attain a certain state of happiness, purity, wisdom, perfection, or immortality." Further, Foucault argues that "concern for the self always refers to an active political and erotic state."[5] Thus, two readings of self-care erotics can be gleaned from Foucault's ruminations. First, transformation and self making allow the individual to attain a state of happiness, wisdom, and perfection through self-care, however ephemeral it might have been. Second, self-care is an act of self-love, a kind of amatory passion that is directed inward but potentially yields outward results. Let me explain this last idea more in depth. As we can assess from the images that follow, bracero self-care was achieved with grooming products and neatness. The evidence of grooming throughout the Nadel photographs coupled with the ways in which the men express desire about wanting to be seen and looked at via his camera places self-care squarely, and with much intention, into the visual field. The erotics of self-care made the men more likely to emerge in Nadel's field of vision—for he had his favorite subjects—but it also made the men potentially appealing to one another and those they encountered on the streets when they left the labor camps.

Nadel settled on four to six photographic subjects (see figures 13.1–13.4). Vulnerability was expressed in this first image, both in the leisure poses of rest that the men inhabit and the fact that some have bare feet. The wood floors of this bunkhouse far exceed those of the majority of camps, which had

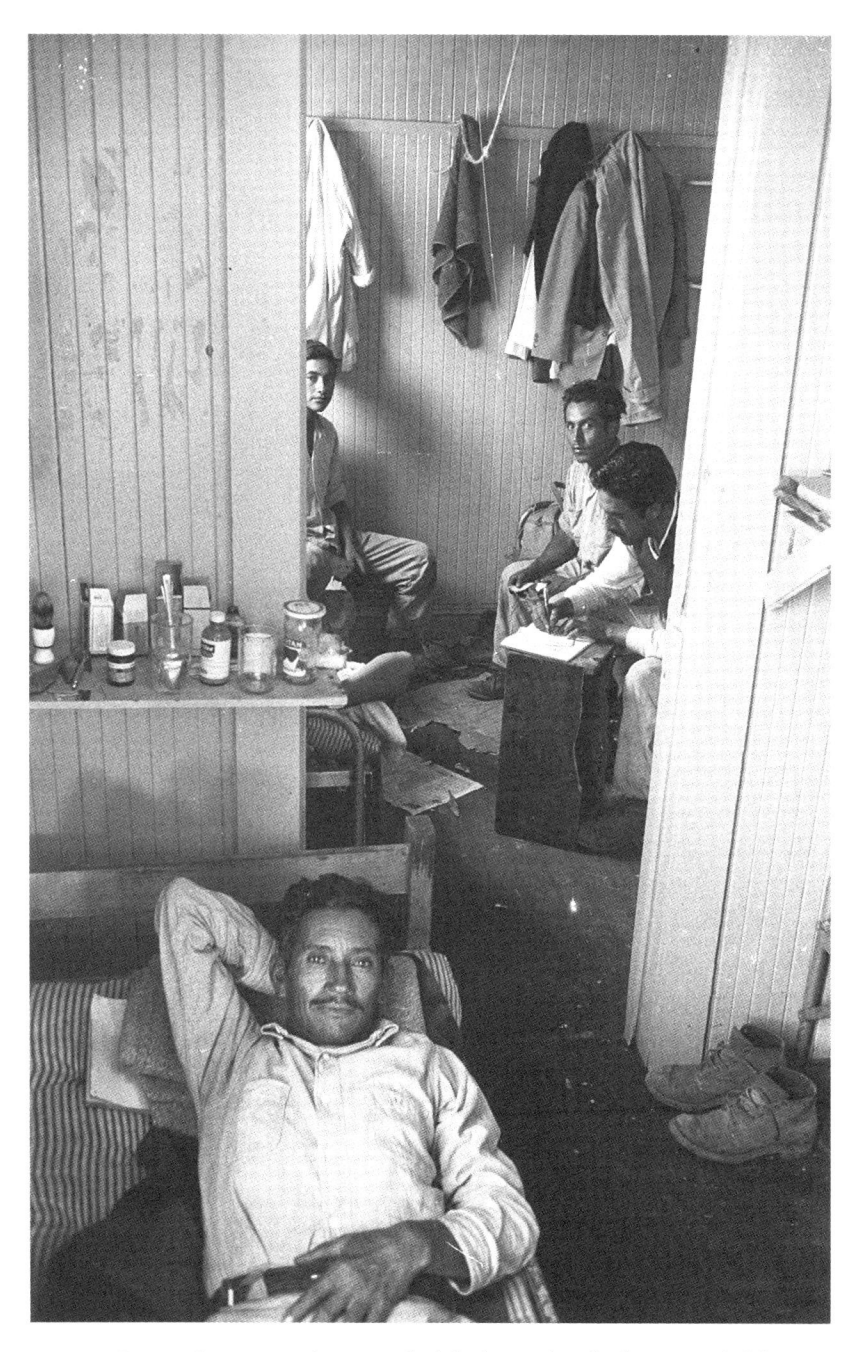

FIG 13.1. Bracero lounging in foreground while three others look on, Gondo labor camp, Watsonville, California, 1956. Courtesy of the Smithsonian Museum of Natural History. The Leonard Nadel Collection.

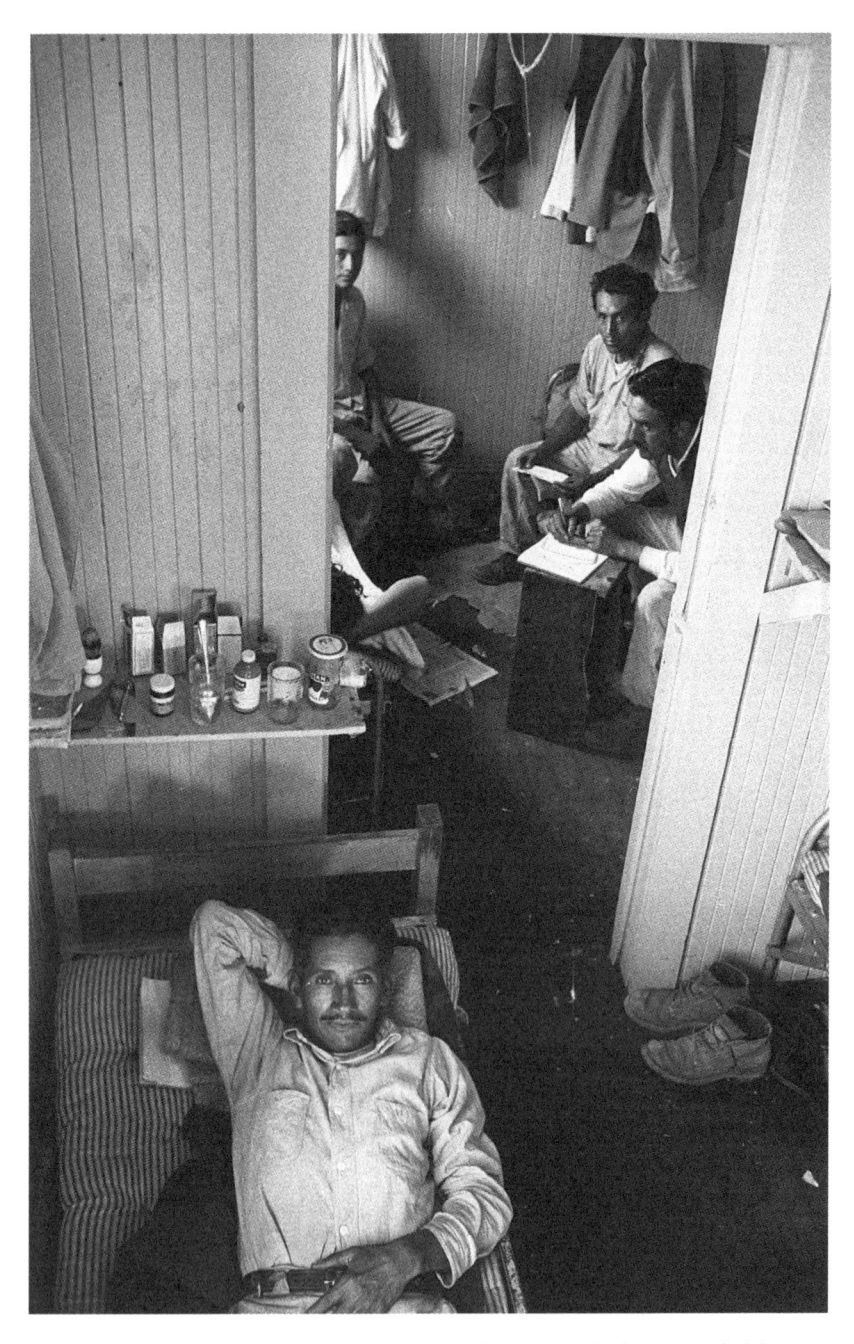

FIG 13.2. Bracero lounging in foreground while three others look on, Gondo labor camp, Watsonville, California, 1956. Courtesy of the Smithsonian Museum of Natural History. The Leonard Nadel Collection.

packed mud for their base. Figures 13.1, 13.2, and 13.3 are close-ups with the reclined medium-brown-skinned man on the left always at the center of the shot and the doorway framing the intimacy and tightness of the space. His mirror image on the back wall never turns from his bunk to be facially present in the shot. Instead, his elbow and top of head remain constant mirror images to the reclined man who was clearly the main object of capture in the image.

In addition, the doorway's hard structure frames the space as orderly and clean, characteristics that were not always mapped onto Mexican nationals in the bracero program. The framing of each photograph with hard natural angles has aesthetic value, argues Derrida, in the sense that it "makes the form more clearly, definitely, and completely intuitable and besides simulat[ing] the representation by their charm, as they excite and sustain the attention directed to the object itself."[6] Thus, Nadel framed to put total focus on the men's bodies and the reclined man to the left in particular. The soft lighting also enhances the frame, taking harshness off their overworked physical forms. Natural light highlights their expressions, even when they are surprised or disapproving as the shutter clicked. Of the six men who come in and out of the frames, the reclined man is at ease, a consenting participant. The soft eye expression and the ever-so-slight adjustment of the hand on his waist fluctuated between rest and active gesture toward what lay beneath the zipper. Perhaps toying with Nadel or fidgeting in discomfort, that readjustment of the hand visually and sequentially cultivates the self in relationship to the torrid zone.

All five men directly engage the camera during various moments of the shot sequence, marking distinct forms of participation. Differential levels of engagement with Nadel, including the hostility in the eyes of the man in the upper-right-hand corner in figure 13.4, express shock in the act of capture. For capturing a photo, if not properly asked for and agreed upon, is an act of violence, even though González-Day argues that all portraiture is an act of violence.[7] Nonetheless, figures 13.1–13.4 also feature grooming products lining a bunk shelf above the head of Nadel's "it" man for the shot series. Pomade, shaving cream brush, razor, shoehorn, four elixir boxes, a glass with a spoon, and a shoe polish rag constitute the implements. They are evidence of self-care and concern for health and impeccable hygiene. That self-care was produced in a homosocial community cultivated the soul and built relationships among individuals, communication, and exchange, and, by extension, institutions, including diasporic Mexican male subjectivities. The circumstances of migration were such that policy undergirded homosocial and homoerotic exchanges for braceros, but it was also what they consumed and whom they consumed with that marked differential consciousness. Enough

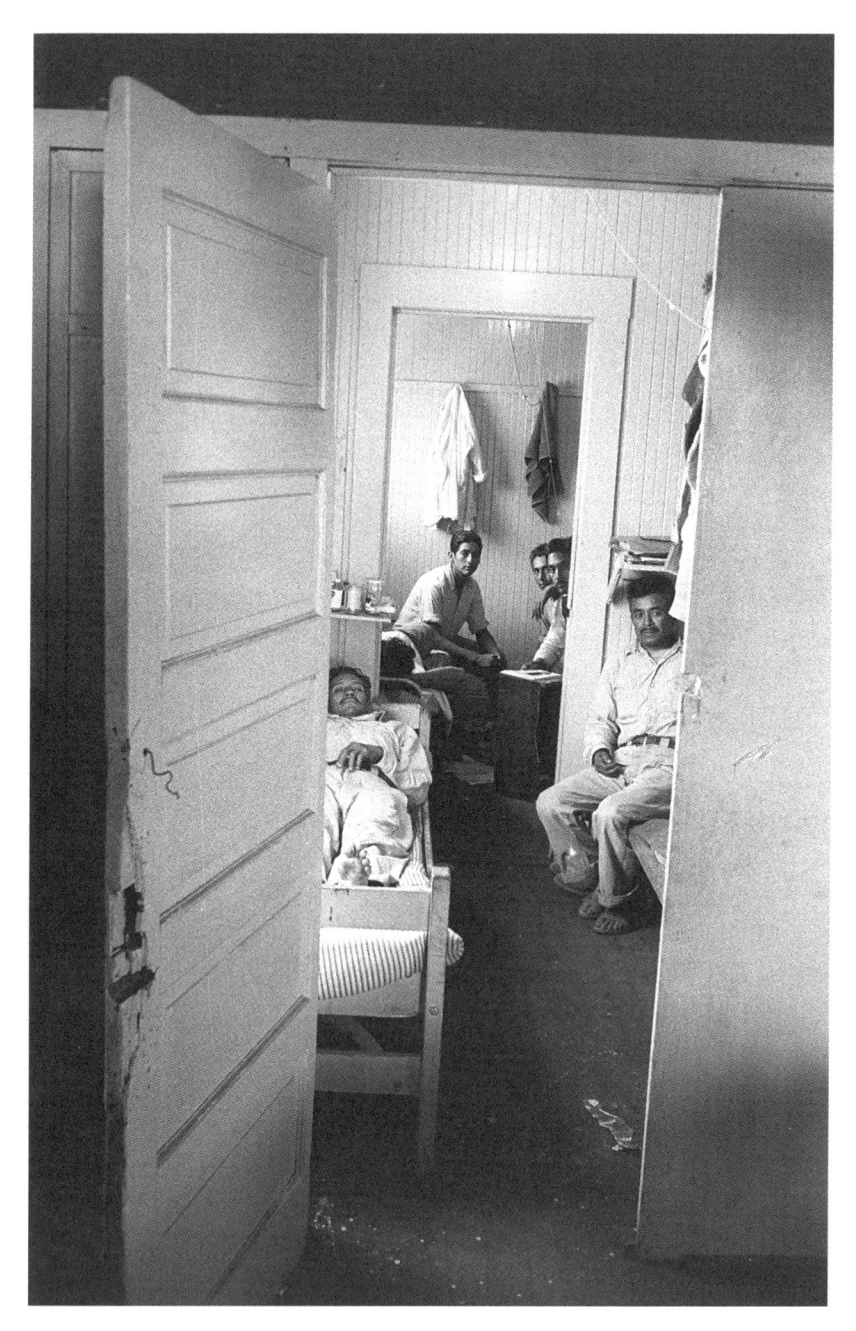

FIG 13.3. Long narrow shot of bracero lounging in foreground while four others look on, Gondo labor camp, Watsonville, California, 1956. Courtesy of the Smithsonian Museum of Natural History. The Leonard Nadel Collection.

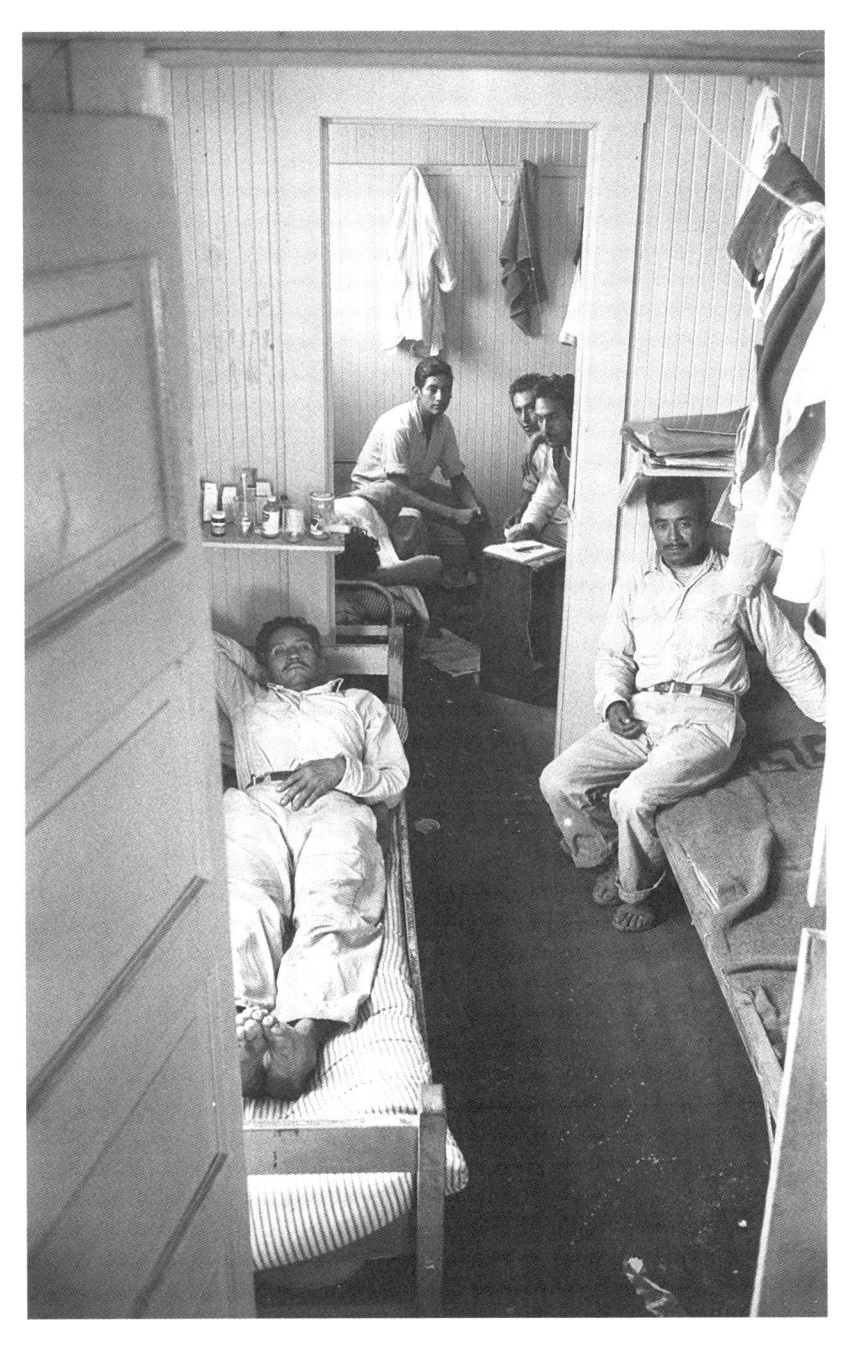

FIG 13.4. Long narrow shot of two braceros lounging in foreground while three others look on, Gondo labor camp, Watsonville, California, 1956. Courtesy of the Smithsonian Museum of Natural History. The Leonard Nadel Collection.

wages were earned to purchase and sustain a level of self-care, even if remittances were being sent back to family members in Mexico. Braceros were demonized as pleasure seeking when that balance between spending time on grooming or, in the case of drinking and smoking, immediate pleasure and self-debasement exceeded that of the heteronormative structures of earning to support families back in Mexico. Grooming products evidence the role of aesthetics in their daily lives, comfort, and subject formation.

Other evidence of diasporic subject formation is represented through the young man who is shown writing in all four shots. He consistently occupied the upper-right-hand corner of the frame as Nadel simultaneously recorded aspiration, longing, and loss. Whether writing a letter home in Spanish for himself or the others sitting with him, taking notes on a book, or practicing English, his representations show literacy and writing as universal benchmarks of the citizen subject. Although braceros were in a contested position as migrant subjects on a temporary contract, writing as leisure portrays them as thoughtful and civilized. It is an act that wins affection, either from Nadel in making the man another focal point in the photo, writing to someone to communicate love, or to that of the American public who would see the tidy photo of men in leisure and literacy, hopefully spurring reform of the bracero program. But literacy could also refer to the aspirational quality of diasporic subject formation in the sense that he could have been one of those whom Arceneaux discussed via her "brother, Manuel, who lived with braceros, said there were some who had a real good education but they came for the experience, they were going to write about it."[8] Writing and literacy were and are a means by which to become a legible subject. Recording bracero experience with the aspiration to be a historian or literary interpreter of migration suggests that the potential for upward mobility in the home country sat on the horizon. Not only would those steady wages or the rite of passage as a male migrant be a key factor in making braceros into modern subjects, but writing practiced by individuals like this gentleman also allowed them to invent, shape, and record modernity in less ephemeral forms.

Writing represents cultivation of the self. As with writing, grooming required access to products. Access occurred in two ways: with traveling salesmen who came to the camps or by going into town. Braceros were most often allowed to "go into town" only on Sundays, and only to designated places. In addition, their confined lives in labor camps also made leisure time extremely restricted to the ramshackle housing that they inhabited. Their contained sphere of leisure was carved out through the specific prisms of race, class, gender, and sexuality, and such limitations become visible in spaces that were not so leisurely at all. When juxtaposed with writing and framed cleanliness, grooming became the means by which to constitute the freedom in diasporic subjectivity, even if solely aspirational.

Nadel's photographs documented the informal economy of grooming, self-care, and diasporic subjectivity in a series of traveling salesman photographs. In this three-shot series, labor camp unknown, two Anglo-American salesmen peddle electric razors, perfumes, hair pomades, vitamins, and facial and body creams. As one white man demonstrates the pleasure and ease of using technology to shave, the other shows the men an electric wand. The razor is a Schick Powershave, which promised to "smooth skin down, guide whiskers, [and] pop whiskers up."[9] His closed eyes suggest two things: either Nadel snapped the photograph while the man blinked or he demonstrates the pleasure of wielding modern technology in the act of grooming. Either way, a sense of awe, rapture, curiosity, and pleasure registered on the braceros' faces during the product demonstration. That sense of wonder might be related to the awe of the electric wand and the razor, but the demonstrators harness technology as a part of the economies of desire. All the men focused intently on the demonstration, for it facilitates proximity to modernity and a groomed, clean, aspirational masculinity.

In terms of the field of vision, close bodies frame the shot. As the men hover, the image recalls Derrida's notion of the "affect of enjoying something, [which] remains thoroughly subjective, we may speak here of auto affection."[10] In giving oneself a present or a pleasure, the subject engages in self-fulfillment. The personal and political dimensions of desire become yoked in the attentiveness to the grooming products. What they desired was in proximity. The furrowed brows, eyes wide open, and perplexed facial expressions mark the ambiguity of desire and the momentary responses (see figure 13.5). To the far right of the frame, one observer drinks a Carta Blanca, suggesting that the traveling salesmen encounter was indeed about leisure and pleasure: the beer intensified the pleasure of voyeurism and product demonstration. The intensity comes from the compactness of the image, the physical proximity, and the varied attitudes about consumption. The man in the foreground holds a dollar bill folded methodically in accordion form, lengthwise, fidgeting as he mulled over an anticipated purchase. As the most assured and prepared of all the braceros, his face registered auto-affection, the experience of pleasure in thinking about the self. With a glimpse of how the individual was realized through acts of consumption, we see that manual labor was not just for remittances. Surplus income could be used for self-fulfillment.

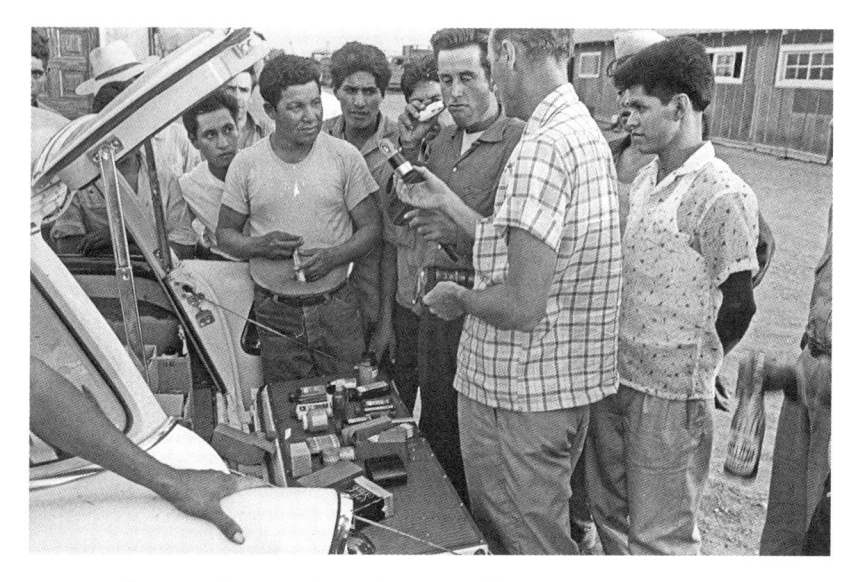

FIG 13.5. Close-up of two traveling salesmen peddling grooming products to braceros in Salinas, California, 1956. Courtesy of the Smithsonian Museum of Natural History. The Leonard Nadel Collection.

As the frames progress, it becomes even more evident that the accordion-dollar man is the real consumer in the scenario. In figure 13.6 he peers more intently as Nadel's angle shifts to the vendors as the center of the frame. In centering an Anglo-driven informal economy of scale, the long shot formalistically locates consumption as the focus, not the braceros to whom they are selling. The shot is almost seamless in its expression of consumption desire until we notice the smallish brown man with an undershirt and sheer short-sleeved button down peering back at Nadel. While others are engrossed with the prospective purchase, the two men, one in the far-left corner and the other in the middle of the shot, skeptically look back to the camera. Bracero ethnic and skin color diversity is captured and codified, for there are as many men with dark skin as there are with light eyes and light hair. Consumptive desire cuts across racial and ethnic lines within the camp: all were a receptive audience. In this frame, desire was multidirectional in acknowledgment of the photographer and wanting to be seen.

Auto-affection worked like a mirror. The young man in the two shirts (one sheer, one undershirt) and khakis breaks photographic convention by rupturing the fourth wall. He too acknowledged being a consumer, but in this instance the consumption and possession occur not through monetary

FIG 13.6. Wide-angle shot of two traveling salesmen peddling grooming products to braceros in Salinas, California, 1956. Courtesy of the Smithsonian Museum of Natural History. The Leonard Nadel Collection.

transaction but with Nadel's lens. The capture is not unassuming. Resetting power relations to document bracero contestation of "capture" in everyday scenarios, they assert personhood. By looking back, being curious, and directly engaging the camera, the man in the sheer shirt disrupts the "naturalness" of braceros in their public communal space. He's impeccably groomed, layering his fabrics and clearly fashion conscious.

In this last frame (figure 13.7), the fourth wall remains intact because of the ways in which the vendors bring the consumers into a product demonstration. As the man who previously held the dollar bill folded like an accordion is now the center of attention as product demonstrator, everyone directs their eyes to his privilege as a potential buyer. In fact, the product demonstration's whimsicality increased desire and proximity as the young men lean in even closer to smell the elixir. Several of them smile intently, and one even leans on his hand, signaling full embeddedness in the product demonstration. While this is not a traditional family portrait, we can nonetheless see the closeness and camaraderie developed through labor camp physical and social proximity. Self-cultivation presented an opportunity to become a market actor when one's labor was bound to producing things for the market. The erotics of pleasure provided enjoyment through proximity versus testing the product

FIG 13.7. Long shot of two traveling salesmen peddling grooming products to braceros in Salinas, California, 1956. Courtesy of the Smithsonian Museum of Natural History. The Leonard Nadel Collection.

oneself. Hetero-affection in a group leading to homo-affection as desire is directed toward one object: the product itself. This consumption and the male-only nature of the bracero program queer the notion of community.

By igniting the olfactory system and curiosity through smell, the vendors facilitated community and homosocial sexual subjectivities to make a profit. Whereas the 1950s marketplace produced desires for a "good close shave," this instance of homosocial bonding also encouraged an all-male audience.[11] It also meant price gouging for a captive audience. Claims by Dr. Savoy that Mexican men were premodern and lacked good hygiene were quelled by the clear indication that the braceros wanted to look and smell good in this photo series. Anthropologist Debra Curtis has documented how "the desire produced in the market [is] intricately linked to the formation and negotiation of sexual subjectivity." Curtis argues for a notion of sexual subjectivity as something produced, and this document of communal elixir smelling is dynamic evidence of bracero sexual subjectivities. In other words, desire extended beyond and through the elixir because it cultivated sexual desirability and desiring subjects among one another and when they ventured outside their community. And although Curtis's fieldwork focused on the demonstration of sex toys at parties for middle-class women, the framework centers performance and demonstration as key elements that command attention to the object and its utility. The smiles and wonderment document how the market shaped desirability and, by extension, sexual practice. The product's effectiveness became more meaningful through the demonstrator's performance, showing how products generate aspirational desire. Desirability, smelling good, and looking good all create consumer satisfaction as the result of a highly profitable informal economy of mobile vending in labor camps. The smiles indicate agreed-upon fulfillment of aspiration through the product: perhaps the elixir would enhance individual sexual success in the marketplace and the pleasure of feeling good because of grooming. As Curtis further argues, "Camaraderie, coupled with romantic and sexual promise, insinuates itself into the consumer's aspirations and sexual-subjectivity."[12] Thus, the compact homosocial nature of the photo imagined the self as a sexual subject and an empowered consumer through the product and the proximity to other men.

The previous scenes of bracero consumption were shot outdoors, but Nadel captures the domestication of Mexican migrant men with interior grooming shots as well. Shaving was again the focus, but I suggest that Nadel's intent is about more than documenting hygiene. Historically, short hair "meant controlled sexuality, and a close shave indicated abstinence."[13] Thus, this also indicates a kind of measured and controlled version of bracero sexuality in the projection of self outward. Whereas the previous photo series was populated by a majority of medium-brown-skinned Mexicanos, this second interior series contrasts greatly by featuring light-skinned mestizos engaged in grooming. These photos demonstrate the grooming practice, suggesting that Mexican racial formation via skin color and whiteness governed why Nadel shot these interior scenes over others. The cuffed Levis mimic typical American fashion trends, in which men wore their pants so many times until they were stiff and stood up on their own.[14] Engaging fashion trends refract the self in figure 13.8, as the mirror highlighted the subject's focus while shaving. This individual close-up crafted the ideal self as clean-shaven and presentable. Soap, shaving cream, a shaving brush, aftershave, and a manual razor mark the technology of hygiene. In this case and particular geographic context, braceros did not worry about the implication that having no facial hair signaled that they were Indian as it did in much of northern Mexico.[15] Instead, grooming and shaving conformed to US notions of modernity and cleanliness and even aspirational whiteness. And these assimilative masculinity standards translated into the ways in which "sexuality—and more generally gender—are major referents in the language of hair," facial and otherwise.[16]

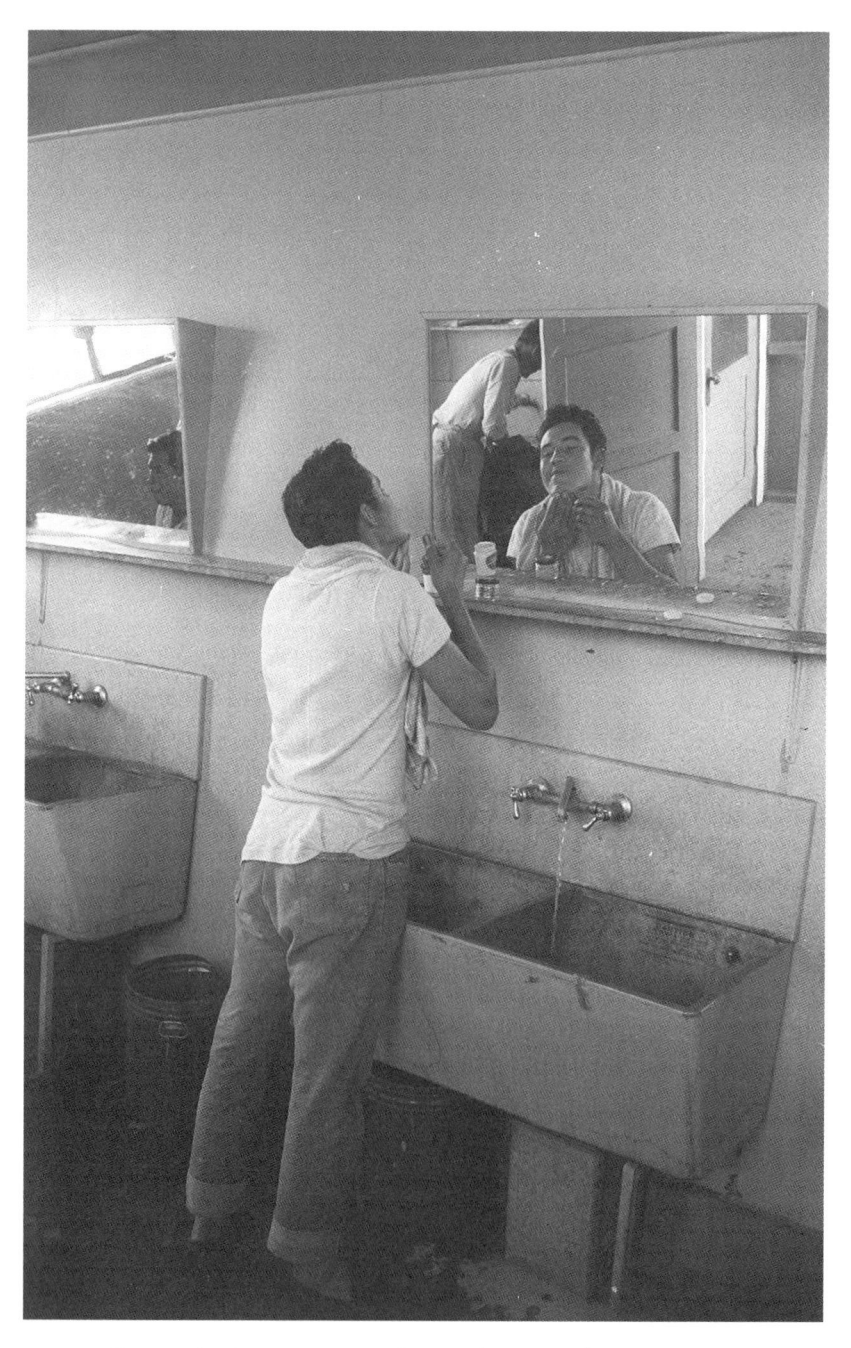

FIG 13.8. Bracero shaving in a mirror, reflecting the image of two others grooming, 1956. Courtesy of the Smithsonian Museum of Natural History. The Leonard Nadel Collection.

FIG 13.9. Three braceros doing laundry in bunkhouse, 1956. Courtesy of the Smithsonian Museum of Natural History. The Leonard Nadel Collection.

A different kind of grooming intersects with the labor of self-care in this domestic photo series. Doing laundry, while seen as women's reproductive labor, here registers a lack of sexual division of labor that makes Mexican men arbiters of hygiene and cleanliness (see figure 13.9). Doing laundry, in the labor camp context, was an extension of grooming because it countered the ways in which, according to Natalia Molina, "medical discourse and public health standards became a dominant way of expressing concern over and opposition to the threat to racial order that Mexican immigration seemed to pose."[17] Multiuse spaces for laundry and grooming within the private sphere were committed to health and self-cultivation. A clearly defined regime was codified in Nadel's photographs, one that ensured optimum health. As a counter to the long-standing fears about Mexicans creating a public health crisis in the US because of their inherent poverty, these subjects constructed the sexual self as contained, hygienic, and concerned with appearance.

In finding another favorite subject in figure 13.10, Nadel returns to the clean-shaven results of the light-skinned man he photographed in figure 13.8, with an additional shaver to his left. Both men examine their cheeks for missed whiskers. On the left, the man in the khakis rubs his face and nose, perhaps checking his whole appearance after a grooming routine. The light-skinned gentleman rubs aftershave between his hands, warming it before the chemical burn that accompanies its medicinal properties. It closely resembles Stag "Pals Deodorant and Aftershave," available at Rexall for $.98, which was "brisk, invigorating with the famous Stag fragrance."[18] Representative of larger trends, studies in 1956 showed that in that year, men were using more perfumed products than women were. Doctor Oliver L. Marton, chief perfumer of Shulton, stated that "men's purchases of fragrance-containing preparations of various types total three times as much as women spend on

FIG 13.10. Three braceros shaving in a bunkhouse, 1956. Courtesy of the Smithsonian Museum of Natural History. The Leonard Nadel Collection.

'perfume, toilet water, bath salts, bubble bath and so forth.'" At the American Chemical Society meeting for that year, the same Dr. Marton told his colleagues that "American men spend more than a quarter of a million dollars yearly on before, during, and after-shaving products alone—exclusive of what they spend for such 'big toiletry items as hair tonics and deodorants.'" If aftershave lotion was measured in gallons versus dollars, it "would be the largest single fragrance market in existence."[19] Many historians have argued that braceros had little disposable income, but given the size of the aftershave market in the US in 1956, we have photo evidence indicating full bracero participation in that market either through shopping at the Rexall or purchasing from traveling salesmen. As the young man checks his whiskers, he engages in self-cultivation that is autoerotic.

"The Berrys," a comic strip that ran in the *Long Beach Independent*, shows the autoerotic effects of aftershave in overdetermining the object of desire (see figure 13.11). In the four frames, a young Anglo man in his twenties puts on aftershave only to find that the smell of romance intoxicates the self with auto-desire. While obviously making a joke about youth, the discovery of one's own sexuality, and not knowing the proper sexual object, the content demonstrates how sexual desire can be misdirected if too internally focused. A perfumed product that is "supposed to make the gals swoon" instead creates

FIG 13.11. "The Berrys" comic strip, *Long Beach Independent*, August 2, 1956.

inward fixation on how good the user smells. The heteronormative pact fails when the young man smelling good for the opposite sex on a date leads him to state that the young woman "didn't get a chance" because the aftershave performed the autoerotic instead of aiding in an external erotic and sexual potentiality.[20] But race is of the utmost importance here. It is perfectly acceptable for a young white man to engage in autoerotic practices: his performance is humorous because of his ethnicity. In contrast, bracero sexualities and mobility were highly regulated, so the practice of auto and communal erotics achieved with grooming needed to be contained and isolated. Such erotics were not funny but threatening. Thus, perfumed grooming is supposed to be for the opposite sex, yet it could "backfire" and then short-circuit heteronormative desire by placing emphasis on the autoerotic and, in the context of both the homosocial Anglo and bracero worlds, create homosocial and even homosexual erotics.

What we also glean from figure 13.10 is that while the handsome light-skinned man cultivates self-desire and projected erotics through grooming, there are two other men in the mirror behind him. His concentration on self, coupled with Nadel's concentration on his subjects, yields a moment of double capture and possession: the two men in the mirror with their backs to the looking glass were directed by the camera's force. That force, while seemingly benign, nonetheless dislodged or "evade[d] both traumatic and heroic rendering of the worker," according to Sara Blair. A space of hygiene and self-cultivation, their mobility, while not through direct eye contact with the camera, demonstrates how one's "own presence or capture in the defining spaces of American modernity puts them within reach of state rehabilitation."[21] Yet Nadel's goal was to demonstrate that men grooming and modeling citizenship through hygiene meant incorporation through capture, through the repetition of hygienic regimens of self-care and their inadvertent pleasures. The pleasures of being seen while grooming and reproducing hygiene ultimately expressed an affective history that was not wholly tethered to victimization and exploitation, but instead it registered ephemeral self-possession.

Social documentation of hygiene, grooming, and their inadvertent production of auto erotics focuses on interior space, but the living social world of braceros occasionally extended into the public sphere. When braceros were taken to town from the labor camps, it was often on Sunday mornings when people were in church. They were tasked with doing their grocery shopping, getting haircuts, and, if lucky, seeing a matinee movie in a segregated theater or one of the theaters dedicated to Mexican and Mexican

American patrons.[22] The main reason Sunday mornings were apt for bracero leisure in public was because most good Americans and Mexican Americans were in church on that day and would not see the workers. The braceros also had to work six days per week, so Sunday was the only free day. Many people in communities in the Salinas Valley were afraid that braceros would rabble-rouse; would drink too much; would transgress sexual and gendered lines by trying to go with white women, Mexican American women, and/or prostitutes; or were simply too dirty to mix with the townspeople. Even in their limited leisure time, braceros were segregated from everyday community people.

As Arceneaux stated, businesses did not cater to braceros despite their disposable income. In the 1950s, after she experienced a bout of tuberculosis and wanted to return to work, she recalled applying for work at Karl's Shoes:

> And as I walked by Karl's shoes he was waiting on some braceros. I walked in and listened. I . . . heard him trying to make them understand what size and this and that. I went over to him and I said "What you need is somebody to work here. Somebody like me who can sell shoes for you." He says "But I can't. . . ." I sold them the shoes, right there. I interpreted it and he sold them. When he was through I told him, "You need me right here in the store because you're losing business all the time."[23]

Arceneaux identified the ways in which Anglo-owned businesses depended on Mexican American women's labor in their stores to translate in order to gain market share. Department stores such as Dick Bruhn in Salinas or Karl's Shoes in Watsonville hired young, bilingual Mexican American women to attend to customers and bring in a new consumer base with their language skills and pretty faces. The braceros had regular but minimal opportunities to meet people outside of the labor camps, much less socialize with potential sexual partners and develop love interests.

Nadel photographed the men in 1956 in Watsonville and Salinas on one of those rare days when they were taken to town.[24] (See figures 13.12–13.14.) During these moments, braceros were immediately and temporarily thrust into mainstream American consumer life and leisure time. They could walk around the somewhat abandoned streets of town on Sunday mornings, window-shopping while consuming goods and services. These Sunday economic boosts to business tapped into a secondary and emerging Spanish-language consumer market. As we can see in the photos, the men loitered

FIG 13.12. Braceros shopping on South Main Street, Salinas, California, 1956. Courtesy of the Smithsonian Museum of Natural History. The Leonard Nadel Collection.

in public space as if it was their own. The photos further demonstrate that the notion of "being with friends" was not equivalent across communities.[25] Such lived experiences of racialized and classed forms of living for braceros ultimately separated them from communities in their leisure time. Their friendships were forged around labor primarily and not necessarily around questions of mutual affiliation. The isolated nature of their communities and Spanish as a primary language (exempting indigenous-language-speaking braceros who were often excluded and discriminated against), according to Flores and Loza, made it so that these were default communities.[26] Although the group of nine men waiting by a taxi stand in figure 13.14 is perhaps a subset of two hundred men who worked at the Gondo labor camp, it nonetheless demonstrates affiliations and gestures of friendship by default.[27]

Curiously, the businesses in these photographs all brandish Spanish names or were perhaps even Mexican owned. Rancho Grande (big ranch), Zacatecana Café (café from Zacatecas, Mexico), and Monterey House (Monterey was the first capital of Alta California during the Spanish colonial period prior to 1848) all indicate that the community either had preestablished Mexican-American families who ran and owned such businesses or Anglos in the community saw the utility of having such businesses to cater to the sentiments and consumptive desires of Spanish speakers. The names signaled

FIG 13.13. Braceros shopping on Main Street in Watsonville, California, 1956. Courtesy of the Smithsonian Museum of Natural History. The Leonard Nadel Collection.

FIG 13.14. Braceros packed into Rancho Grande Café on Main Street in Watsonville, California, while others wait by a taxi stand. Courtesy of the Smithsonian Museum of Natural History. The Leonard Nadel Collection.

Mexico's *bajio* (central Mexico), where the majority of the workers were from. The *Salinas Californian* of June 5, 1956, around the time when these photos were taken, has numerous advertisements for "Spanish food" at the Rancho Grande in Watsonville. Ideologically speaking, there are a number of dissonances registered in the Rancho Grande's Spanish food. First, Spanish food, whatever that might mean for a knowledgeable reader of the expression, is an imprecise North American shorthand for "south of the border," the food of those who are the product of Spanish colonialism in the Americas. Spanish food, in the proper sense, would indicate food from Spain. However, the consumers in such restaurants were Mexican braceros. Second, both Zacatecana and Rancho Grande refer to central Mexican states and rural ranch life, not Spain and European sensibilities. Third, Spanish (*castellano*) was the majority language spoken by braceros and by at least some of the employees in these establishments. Fourth, we can see in figure 13.14 that the Rancho Grande was packed to the gills with braceros, drinking what appears to be beer and spending time with friends. That these establishments would call their food offerings Spanish marks a slippage: owners and workers wanted to differentiate themselves from braceros, especially in their leisure time as consumers. The split between local Mexican families who were US citizens and migrant braceros was an important one for those who tried to justify their incorporation into the daily fabric of American life. Using Spain, Spanish food, Spanish language, and thus whiteness was a way to mark the locals as non-Indian, nonmigrant, and upwardly mobile. Still, this segregated portrait of leisure and consumption has much to say about the race and class boundaries of US life in the 1950s.

Chapter 14

PASSIONATE VIOLENCE AND THEFTS

Grooming and consumption formed an integral part of Nadel's documentation of bracero lives, but we cannot avoid talking about what those passionate attachments and autoerotics also produced in terms of violence and theft. Two laborers—Jesse N. Leyva, age twenty-five, and Alex Ramirez, twenty-seven—were sentenced to prison on May 20, 1956, for robbing two stores on Monterey's Fisherman's Wharf. They were sent to San Quentin after pleading guilty to two counts of attempted burglary, second degree. Ramirez had served sufficient time prior to his court date and did not have to go back to jail after his trial and sentencing. But Leyva was already on probation for a second-degree burglary offense and his sentence was harsher.[1] Contrary to the ways in which the majority of scholars approach the discourse of race in relationship to criminality, no mention is made of Leyva or Ramirez's nationalities or characteristics of racial inferiority. Instead, they are identified by their occupation as laborers, positing class inequity as explanation for their attempted thefts. Further, the fact that they were sent to San Quentin, a maximum-security facility, demonstrates the severity of punishment for theft. Although Monterey was not a site where much agricultural labor was performed, it is possible that they were either hospitality workers in the city or worked in the nearby artichoke fields of Marina and Castroville. A robbery in Monterey, a much more affluent community just minutes from Salinas, Marina, and Castroville, would have yielded a far better score given the kind of old money established through the cannery industry.

In fact, burglaries and petty crimes in labor camps and in the larger community occupied the farming valley. Nadel's bracero photos were staged and snapped to show the workers at their best (in domestic spaces, working hard, or socializing with a smile), but local newspapers tell us of the unrest that made up a part of quotidian life. Between July 14 and 27, 1956, two fights and two thefts were reported at four different labor camps around the Salinas Valley. This was no coincidence, for the third week of July marked "Big Week," when the Salinas California Rodeo doubled the city's population on top of the additional eight thousand braceros who were brought in to work during peak harvest season. Such a toxic configuration of events made this time of year extremely stressful.

On July 14, 1956, the Ice Kist labor camp south of Chular was burglarized, according to the Monterey County Sheriff's office. An "undetermined amount of clothing and money, plus a number of radios was [sic] taken this morning from . . . [the] barracks. Doors of six apartments in the building were forced open after the occupants had left for the fields. The burglary was reported by Bill Bostin, a labor camp employee."[2] Even though postwar prosperity would have bettered living conditions in a region that accounted for 20 percent of the national agricultural output, these labor camp thefts tell us several things. First, unoccupied during the day, such spaces made easy targets for theft. Second, because those radios, money, and clothes belonged to Mexican nationals, the thieves felt a sense of entitlement to their earnings: no one would necessarily punish them for doing so. Third, that an Anglo foreman of the camp, Bostin, reported the thefts to the sheriff's department shows how he defended bracero property rights. Their radios, a connection to the social world; their money, a means of supporting themselves, family, and even leisure activity; and the clothing that they wore were indeed worthy of being protected. This obligation to workers is something we rarely see in the archive of bracero suffering. And although no mention was made of who the victims were, Bostin decided to inform the authorities because of an implied understanding of the braceros' fragile relationship to property and capital in the form of small possessions and money. This also suggested that the robbery was not an inside job. A momentary glimpse of solidarity in the loss of meager resources, reporting the crime against bracero workers defended them in a system that viewed their rights as temporary and not necessarily worth protecting.

On the same day that the robbery was reported, Sr. Flores of "Sección en Español" stated the following: "Being such a big danger, especially in the hands of a juvenile delinquent, the city council passed an ordinary law that will sanction all those who sell or carry switchblades."³ The Spanish-speaking audience felt threatened by the possession of switchblade knives by youths in the community. A city ordinance banning such weapons established another class barrier of difference between the *culto* from the undesirable juvenile delinquents.⁴ Although the Ice Kist labor camp robbery and the call for no more switchblades are not necessarily linked within the narrative structure of the newspaper, they nonetheless simultaneously indicate a crisis of faith in youths who disrupted social norms with violence and theft. A response to class stratification in the community, those brandishing switchblades and those who robbed the labor camp indeed had something in common: a clear sense of wanting access to real property that could be fenced, money that could buy food or other items, and clothes to protect one's body. The camp could have easily been robbed by the hoboes who were seen as a problem in the labor camp discourse of the Salinas Valley, but we still need to account for the fact that theft ultimately expressed economic inequality and an impulse to defy the law.

On the same day, two men "hurt in a fight at a labor camp at 611 Vertin street early yesterday, have been charged with peace disturbance, according to Salinas Police. Both Abel M. Vargas, 33 and Domingo M. Benavides, 34, received abrasions requiring stitches and were treated at Salinas Valley Memorial Hospital."⁵ Again, the workers were not referred to as Mexican nationals, nor did racial pejoratives accompany the fight description. What we do know is that the brawl between two men was so bad, and the wounds so profound, that both needed to be treated at a hospital and receive stitches. The invisible hand of labor—that is, the manager of their camp—took them to the hospital, seeing their bodies as valuable. Disturbing the peace was a rather minor, misdemeanor charge designed to caution the person partaking in violent behavior. Concerns were raised by the US Department of Agriculture about the suitability of the temporary migrant male labor force in the 1930s. As Colin R. Johnson has shown through extensive archival work, labor camps were viewed as sites of "social dangers [in] which a group of womanless men" were thought to "engender under such ill conditions of greater menace." Thus, the homoerotic content of the violent, stitch-provoking fight between Vargas and Benavides expressed the pathologies or homoerotics between womanless men that the State Board of Agriculture feared. Such expressions of violence show the intimate nature of Vargas and Benavides's relationship in that it was worth beating the other up over, be the cause money, women, or affection. Similarly, the power struggle between two men who wanted to and succeeded in physically wounding each other blurred the line between love and hate, rejection and desire, heightened by the fight. And something else might have been going on to prompt the police to issue the disturbing the peace infraction. Homoerotic passion in disagreement is often seen as outside of the realm of policing and institutional control in small rural communities.[6] Given the parity in their ages, the two men were on similar footing in the labor camp. A blip on the radar screen of labor camp history in expressing vice, the fight between Benavides and Vargas shows two men who cared enough about each other to wound violently.

A similar incident happened in neighboring Watsonville, the site of major strawberry production in the Salinas Valley. On July 19, 1956, a man fled after José de La Torre, age twenty-seven, was stabbed to death in a Main Street restaurant. The Watsonville police searched for the assailant, Joe García, "also a farm laborer, who was identified by other restaurant customers as the assailant who twice stabbed de La Torre in the chest. Bystanders were unable to explain the cause of the stabbing."[7] Although the highly limited pathological reading of macho behavior posited by Mirandé in his 1997 study *Hombres y Machos* would describe the scene as an "expression . . . of violence, aggressiveness, and irresponsibility," I propose a queer reading that accounts for the layers of racialized capitalist history and desire enacted in this fight.[8] First, although we do not know the cause of aggression, the anger and rage were so fierce that the fight tracks both a disruption and reproduction of gender roles: there was indeed a dispute so intense that it pushed García to stab de La Torre to death. Second, the wound, as Marion Wells has argued, "put[s] Freud's point another way, figur[ing] an internal *psychomania* resulting from the ego's absorption of the object."[9] Absorption of the object here is meted out in rage upon de La Torre's body, resulting in psychomania's fervor in physical action. De La Torre had taken or withheld something from García, and the public scenario of the attack displayed how power needed to be performed in front of others, perhaps as a message. This was not shame or shaming, but an acting out of aggression and desire in the public realm. The resulting affect, being stunned and surprised (both the victim and bystanders), demonstrated public homoerotic desire.[10] Not knowing the context, unable to explain the stabbing, bystanders had no way to read García's staunch defiance of social norms.

Both de La Torre and García were referred to as laborers and not nationals, Mexicans, or immigrants. The absence of pejoratives represents a cognizant press or an underdeveloped lexicon of ethnic difference as racial difference. That the crime occurred on a Thursday also suggests that the men were in town on a weekday and perhaps not braceros. Yet occupation and the community of witnesses demarcate a lack of proximity and knowledge of the dispute if all the witnesses in the restaurant lived in a labor camp together. They would have been able to identify "the real" Joe García as the assailant. Or they could have protected his identity because they knew him. Clearly, the sociality of the agricultural labor community in Watsonville had to extend beyond labor camps and imported temporary Mexican labor, yet the lack of context could have been a community defense strategy against the Watsonville police. Either way, both interpretations make de La Torre and García all the more ambiguous as figures in the historical record.

Nonetheless, the conditions under which the Watsonville police found the "real" Joe García further cement the interchangeability of Spanish-surnamed laborers and the inability to identify the assailant because of lack of community cooperation. Three days later, José Gonzalez García was "taken from a strawberry field yesterday morning by Watsonville police, but none of the witnesses were able to identify him as the slayer of José de la Torre Duran and he was released. 'The wrong Garcia,' was what Police chief Frank Osmers commented as he ordered the husky Mexican national returned to the Morishima Brothers strawberry field near the airport on Paulsen road."[11] Again, either a lack of familiarity with José García or a direct defiance of law enforcement exposes how the community responded to police presence. Further, the ways in which laborers who had the same name were confused with each other, "the wrong García," according to the police chief, shows a weak investigation and an even weaker sense of distinction between all of the J. Garcías who had to be working in the Watsonville strawberry fields.

But there was another dimension to this history, and that is the role of Japanese American sharecroppers who worked with corporate conglomerates Driscoll farms and the California Berry Growers Association. Because Japanese American property ownership was limited immediately following World War II, families like the Morishima brothers could renew access to agricultural cultivation only through the lease system.[12] Unosuke Shikuma, a Watsonville strawberry farmer and landowner, outlined the sharecropping structure as follows: "It was a 50/50 thing. My dad would provide the land and the plants and the tools and work the ground . . . they would provide the labor. And then when the berries were harvested and marketed, why then we would divide the income. He would get families to sharecrop for him. The children of our sharecroppers, I know they picked strawberries from . . . oh, 5:00, 5:30 before school." These families and their children worked the fields in the late 1950s and 1960s, but Shikuma's father imported young men from Japan to work in the strawberry fields in 1955 and 1956, the same time that bracero numbers increased during the strawberry boom. In essence, his father had Japanese imported laborers working alongside braceros during the berry season. The Shikuma family also faced a crisis with the end of the bracero program: "When they eliminated the bracero program, I immediately cut my acreage down because I didn't know where my source of labor would be."[13] Thus, this multiethnic labor history of power and racialized forms of capitalism were created both through the homosocial labor conditions for Japanese and Mexican national contract workers alongside Japanese sharecropping families.

There was also a long historical precedent of Japanese sharecroppers working in Watsonville prior to, during, and after World War II. Richard Guidotti stated that his father's Watsonville dairy had a forty-acre parcel dedicated to Japanese sharecroppers Harry Maya and Frank Morita in the mid-1960s, when they grew strawberries for Driscoll like the Morashima brothers. Prior to the sharecroppers and during World War II, the Guidotti children labored alongside German chain-gang prisoners who worked in the beet fields, which in turn fed their dairy cows in the Espinosa Slough region of the city.[14] Guidotti recalled being scared of the German POWs because they spoke a different language. Even though the Guidotti children were the first-generation children of Swiss-Italian immigrants, World War II propaganda influenced their fear of German war prisoners and the Japanese American sharecroppers who worked the land twenty years later. Guidotti remembered that they would get close enough to the POWs to hear them speak German and then run away from them in fear because the radio programs talked about them so negatively. As children often do when they are afraid and curious at the same time, they played out the dynamics of racial differentiation and social class (remember that the children were working at the dairy) that were ingrained into the minds of youths during World War II. In other words, their feared response to the German POWs demonstrates the effects of propaganda, even on youths. Overall, Watsonville, as an extended part of the Salinas Valley, had a longitudinal history of sharecropping and indentured labor, with families such as the Shikumas, who owned land, and the Kiyotoki, Hirokawas, Lotsishitas, and Nakamuras, who were sharecroppers in the strawberry industry.[15] They piggybacked their agricultural reintegration on land owned by farmers of Anglo, Swiss, Italian, and Portuguese descent. There had been precedent, setting the stage for the Morishita brothers to profit from José González García being subcontracted to a subcontractor.

Nonetheless, braceros or "husky Mexican national[s]" like José González García actually caused sharecropping profit margins to be greater, expanding both the production capacity and the kind of labor support one could get to man more fields. The strawberry industry in the Salinas Valley had a big year in 1956, and 63 percent of all farm labor consisted of bracero output.[16] Technological advances in California between 1950 and 1954 yielded a crop of more than six tons per acre.[17] That year, a crate of fresh strawberries sold for $2.29, and those for freezing sold for $.16 a crate, with $42,044,960 total profit, or $2,627.81 per acre.[18] The seven-month fruiting season in coastal areas made for more work and more profit. Also, new techniques such as using plastic to encase the base of the plant provided better control of diseases and insects.[19] Someone had to tend to insecticides, plant thinning, the plastic on less mature plants, and irrigation. For sharecroppers, losing a laborer like García meant strawberries rotting in the fields and decreased profits for an already small share of production. The estimated manpower for a 20-acre strawberry field necessitated 2–2.5 men per acre during peak harvest, or 300 men for 6 weeks minimum.[20] At the same time, García's status as Mexican national marks a secondary tier of unequal labor in a disorienting agricultural landscape. So while "the wrong García" might appear as an ironic joke about not being able to distinguish between Mexicans, if that García had indeed been the right one, he could have cost the Morishima brothers one to two months of profit from their strawberries. And that de La Torres's murder remained unsolved furthers the notion that the homoerotics of violence expressed in the stabbing put desire in the public realm without resolution.

In South Monterey County, a similar struggle happened in King City just days after the fights in Watsonville and Salinas and the robbery in Monterey. On July 24, 1956, Sánchez I. Gonzáles, twenty-six, was arrested and charged with beating Marion Pares, twenty, according to the Monterey County Sheriff: "Both victim and suspect are employed at the Joe Silva camp in Soledad Mission District. Pares, who was taken to the county hospital in Salinas with a broken arm and other injuries, told deputies that he and Gonzáles had been in town together and that the latter had borrowed $30 from him and he only returned $25 leading to an argument."[21]

Why was there a preponderance of crime and violence between braceros in July 1956? The answer is quite simple. July is peak growing season and holds Rodeo Big Week, the optimum moment when the maximum numbers of braceros were crammed into labor camps and an influx of tourists came to the area. This was the time of year that the industry depended upon the laborers and tourism for huge profits. The stress to perform and sheer intensified proximity between men contributed to the maximum expression of emotion that could result in violence. Too many hours of work and not enough leisure in a context where the rodeo was about spectatorship and Anglo and ethnic white leisure sent mixed messages.

These aggressions should not be interpreted as pathology; nonetheless, we need to understand that capitalist systems and excessive physical proximity did indeed taint daily interaction. Yet the Nadel photographs never show physical conflict between braceros or violent confrontation with growers.[22] Instead, they show worn-down bodies working or bodies in leisure. Such images mask the overwhelming tensions in the broader communities, in the labor camps, and among laborers, whether because of racial differences (mestizo versus Indian) or language differences, struggles about money, the leisure-labor distribution, or homoerotic sociality through proximity.

Part II

CONCLUSION

Instead of reinstantiating a narrative of braceros as solely victims of labor exploitation, or attempting to reinforce their position in the historical record as good fathers, husbands, and brothers, or suggesting that Nadel held all of the power with his camera, part II documents how the photos of braceros register desire, sexuality, and longing forged through hygiene, consumption, leisure, and labor. We might call this a kind of close reading and historicization of the gestures and desire or affective history in the making of such photographs.[1] Even though we may not know the names and individual stories of these men in the photographs, we can glean the ephemeral nature of what it meant to want and to be wanted in a space and labor situation where they were treated as machines, and try to imagine this as a site where homosociality and emotional attachments were both actualized and managed with policy and policing.

Although historians do not readily question the nature of Nadel's archive, the collection selectively and alternatively emasculates or lionizes the subjects of photography. His widow, Evelyn De Wolfe Nadel, pitched the bracero story as a movie script intended to immortalize the work of her husband because of his heroic ability to document the lives of "humble, docile strangers in our fields."[2] This was a further pursuit of selling the picture story beyond Nadel's lifetime, his intimate knowledge, and what his widow called a "sensitive portrayal" of braceros and their living conditions that provided a deep emotional commitment to political activism about their civil rights and human rights.[3]

By examining the totality of Nadel's bracero archives and the visual representations of them in Mexico, we begin to understand just how dynamic the migration process was in providing the space to explore one's sexuality. And although the lack of privacy and the intrusive quality of the photographs are issues that we cannot deny, the images catalog intimacy, consumption, and physical and emotional attachments. Therefore, such images have to be problematized in their optic even as they recorded local and national disenfranchisement or community formation. The shortcomings of Nadel's archive and underestimating the feelings of former braceros are things I've tried to avoid in my own scholarly interpretation, constantly remembering that these men were indeed subjects of their own making. Moreover, from these images we can trace the makings of shifting gender and sexual ideologies in diaspora instead of compulsive heteronormativity of state policy as represented in the scholarship and photographs. Other scholars, such as Ana Elizabeth Rosas and Mireya Loza, provide a more diverse portrait of these communities, both in the sending nation and the US. In demonstrating how intentionality, autoerotics, and communal erotics in bracero sites of consumption generate pleasure and desire, my work disrupts the thoroughly entrenched notion that Nadel's bracero archive is exclusively an archive of suffering. The visual field acutely demonstrates the role of capitalist compression within the confines of the Salinas Valley's postwar booming agricultural economy of scale. As that was the matrix of modernity, this historical accounting of the braceros' presence posits an alternate modernity in spite of the racial capitalist milieu that negated bracero subjecthood. Their return of Nadel's gaze indicates that the bracero archive is one of self-cultivation, desire, and a long-standing relationship that was interactive.

Conclusion

I cannot separate my own worldview from the ways in which this book was written. In feminist studies we call this "standpoint epistemology," where the author takes responsibility for their positionality. I conclude *Archiving Mexican Masculinities in Diaspora* by outing the motivations behind the project. My goal has been to track migratory subjects in their affective and emotive lives across space and time. This was, in part, inspired, by my own deep emotional responses to the archival materials. As I finished writing the first complete draft, my son, Ausiàs March, was teething and wracked by fever. I had just reread Esperanza Flores Magón's letters to her stepfather, Enrique, who was in Leavenworth, and found myself pausing on all the details about his son, baby Enrique Jr. Esperanza called Enrique Jr. "his baby" because he was her half-brother, indicating emotional distance between her and her stepfather and, by extension, "his baby." Ausiàs March and Enrique Flores Magón Jr. were born a century apart, yet as I read the family's letters, I felt the pain that comes with missing a baby's milestones, like teething. I imagined the deep loss that Enrique Sr. must have felt being away from his child. Enrique Jr. was born in March 1917, just months before his anarchist father was carted off to McNeil Island for the second time. The letters from his elder stepchildren, from his comrades in the struggle, and occasionally from his partner Teresa, as well as the trinkets of affection they shared with him, are permeated with a sense of loss and emotional vulnerability. Enrique, too, wrote often and with much detail, first from McNeil Island and later from Leavenworth. Taken together, his writings and the trinkets recorded that profound sense of loss and emotional fragility, a sense that, nearly a century later, permeates the pages of this book. I wondered if Enrique Jr.'s curl reached his father in prison. My hope was that it did, for the boy's father lived for details. His writing was tactile in its recording of memory, and a curl from his baby boy would have provided an optimistic attachment or hope each time he touched it, smelled it, and imagined the baby crying, teething, crawling, and, eventually, walking and talking.

Having a similar response when slowly turning over Leonard Nadel's bracero photographs for the first time, all I could think was how the relationships were brokered with those whom Nadel photographed. My immediate familiarity with these images of the Salinas Valley was also uncanny. As a person who was raised in the region, I can assure the reader that community members know very little about the bracero program's history in making the area an agricultural powerhouse. There I was, almost seventy years after the bracero photographs that Nadel took, and everything looked the same and still profoundly unequal. In the 1950s it was a landscape littered with boxes, with men packing lettuce for Bud Antle, Church Brothers, or D'Arrigo Brothers. Today, that landscape looks largely unchanged, except that the men and women clean, wrap, and box the lettuce for Earthbound Farms, Fresh Express, and Foxy Lettuce, with fancy packaging directly in the fields, unless it is for pre-made salads. Those shifts in how agricultural labor is performed have to do with technology as much as they have to do with masculinity, for Nadel's images remind of how much the business of agriculture has been transformed over the last seven decades. One thing remains constant over time: the grunt work of agriculture. Few acknowledge that bracero farm labor built the shadow infrastructure of what are now global brands. Few understand how the Salinas Valley was transformed by the bracero program or that braceros were deeply transformed by their experiences with racism, segregation, and sexual and social freedom. The history feels radically different now that I've researched the bracero program so extensively, for the wealthy became wealthier and the Mexican American middle class more stable through the labor of Mexican nationals. In part, this is why Nadel's photographs continue to elicit an emotional response. They are documents of physical proximity and intimacies brokered among and between men. Nadel's images or those on the covers of *Todo* will braceros into hypervisibility. On first glance, they present Mexican nationals as socially inferior, but with closer examination we see how these representations are embedded in a complex social, political, and economic context. The same could be said of this book's cover, as four braceros in a Salinas labor camp negotiate intimacy, community, leisure, and self-care. All framed by the hard lines of a doorway, their cleanliness, grooming products, leisure clothes, and writing instruments tightly weave a narrative of homosocial engagement through Nadel's "picture story." But self-representation was just as vital of an element for these men in that they scripted how they posed. Within the frame, they controlled the narrative of self to some degree even though Nadel is the one who took the pictures. Although some of the photos or magazine covers may make the interlocutor alienated because they are so intrusive, others were and continue to be deeply profound for their capacity to aestheticize suffering, represent the self, and document diasporic community as part of bracero daily life in the Salinas Valley.

As members of the Salinas community protested labor camps and bracero deviance in the 1950s, the legacy of the program transformed into a full-scale movement for farmworker rights from the 1960s onward.[1] When I was a child, we crossed UFW picket lines to shop at the Northridge Mall Safeway store. I could not have been more than four years old, but I remember women picketing at a slow clip with black and red flags in front of the store. According to the April 29, 1979, *Washington Post*, the strike was wilting union enthusiasm, and people had begun to defect and go back to work: "A long strike means that the UFW would broaden its walkout from six major vegetable producers in the fertile Salinas Valley to at least an additional 18 growers. This would throw pickets around half the lettuce in the valley, which produces more than 80 percent of the nation's summer iceberg lettuce crop."[2] Asking my mother what was happening, I do not recall the answer. Because I cannot remember, perhaps I was too small to reconcile the seriousness of the picketers and their children's faces with the answer that my mother provided. Therein lay an early life lesson about the differences and lack of solidarity between Mexican Americans and farmworker Mexican nationals etched throughout this book.

Whereas a lack of solidarity often defined relations between Mexican Americans and Mexican nationals in the Salinas Valley, earlier in the century Mexican anarchist communities in Los Angeles were able to form deep attachments with Mexican Americans. Because of the intimacy between these communities in their agitation for labor rights, they developed political connections that were highly emotive and intimate. What we learn from the changes that occurred between anarchists of the 1910s and 1920s and braceros in the 1950s has to do with how emotional bonds and attachments were forged. As an entrenched Mexican American middle class emerged that was invested in being American, vast social and political differences made them separate themselves from Mexican nationals as a means of defending their rights as citizens. But there was also a shift in the performance of Mexican masculinities that occurred in the California diaspora, and it had to do with social class and citizenship. Because of these shifts, both the archives about Enrique Flores Magón and Salinas Valley braceros required narration against the dominant paradigm of machismo, especially because the topic itself—Mexican male migration patterns and narratives of sociality—can be read so easily, and so reductively, merely as machismo. I turned to gender and queer studies because they problematize masculinity. As researchers, uncovering how migration opened up the possibility for actors to be flexible in their gender performativities is necessary for understanding these pasts as more than cookie-cutter historical and unchanging gender scripts. Those passionate attachments mentioned throughout were the site of gender and emotional flexibility because being in the US allowed Mexican nationals (both anarchists and braceros) the possibility to respond differently than they would in their home country: the supposed promise of political and social freedom made it possible. Such archives of intimacy, where emotion served as currency, create an alternative theory of masculinities formed in diaspora. My hope is that this model for reading and interpretation can be exported to other Latinx and gender and women's studies contexts.

This book has much to offer in recasting our understanding the way that Mexican manhood, masculinity, and codes of male conduct were transformed in the California diaspora between 1900 and 1956. *Archiving Mexican Masculinities in Diaspora* illuminates transnational affective histories of masculine intimacies. Enrique Flores Magón and the braceros were migratory subjects, forged through exile. Most braceros, in their migration, were forced to do so because of monetary necessity. In both cases, migration was a necessity for survival, not a mobility afforded with cosmopolitan luxury. The connections between these two migrant cohorts are that PLM members and braceros challenged ideas of racial and gender normativity through their labor in the US. There are many similarities in how they forged diaspora and survived alienation across a half century. The desire to understand how these men negotiated exclusion and how these migrants made sense of their own lives animates the work.

There is something deeply disturbing about how, in our contemporary US culture and in traditional Mexican American cultures, connections are merely thought of as networks without intensive affective ties. To deny the role of affect is to deny that historical subjects had emotional lives of the mind and heart. Such a denial reinscribes gender normativity as a default position for theorizing masculinity in Mexican diasporic contexts. Therefore, affect is the linchpin between the nonnormative forms of sociality that governed the lives and practices of Mexican male migrants and their families, both chosen and traditional, in the first half of the twentieth century. Experiences of loss and displacement for anarchists and braceros in their migrations became a response to living in the United States as an unwanted "other." Documented in photographs, magazine covers, ephemera, the press, oral histories, and letters, those "emotional, physical, and economic barriers," as Miroslava Chávez-García has described them, transformed diasporic Mexican masculinities between 1900 and 1956.[3]

As *Archiving Mexican Masculinities in Diaspora* demonstrates, policy and policing tried to curtail the innate excesses of feeling, emotion, and critique by Mexican nationals, yet the archives that we have scoured suggest again and again that full containment was never possible. The unruly social and affective histories of Enrique Flores Magón and the Salinas Valley braceros reveal the central role of intimacy in cultivating the self, particularly in the face of intensive exclusion, subordination, and poverty. By highlighting the ways that optimistic attachments were formed, the book foregrounds the role of emotion in creating gender and diasporic possibility. With attachments as a theoretical-historical conceptualization of the worlds in which Flores Magón and the braceros circulated, *Archiving Mexican Masculinities in Diaspora* demonstrates how transnational affective histories of masculinities provide an alternative to ideological and gender-normative narratives of early twentieth-century migration. These differential familial and social formations, created through migration, model subject constitution in spite of—or because of—surveillance and policy. Mexican male subjects in early twentieth-century California navigated intensive regulation and policing through segregation, serving jail time for violating international and local laws, or for simple forms of vagrancy and petty theft.

Even with intensive surveillance, that capacity—to maintain and broaden affective ties and relationships of all kinds even amid absence, to have a life of the mind in lieu of physical and political freedom, to build new social and/or sexual relationships in light of loss—animates much of *Archiving Mexican Masculinities in Diaspora*. I did not set out to write a Mexico-California transnational diaspora story, but the narrative arc was directed by the archives themselves. Evaluating sources in a multidirectional sense and even understanding that subjects lied about their intentions in the historical records they left behind was a hard pill to swallow. In this way, the practice of archiving and the materials collected, or how we read them, must be considered and reconsidered within histories of Mexican male migrations and masculinities during this part of the twentieth century. The life stories are as complex as they are compelling, and they require theory to destabilize our usual understanding of the ways in which masculine subjects were and continue to be produced through their mobility. Flores Magón was certainly privileged—educated, highly mobile—in contrast to the majority of braceros. Yet their common connection is nationality, displacement, how they were desired for labor (both intellectual and manual), and the ways in which racialization, sexuality, and even criminalization limited their mobility as migrant subjects over a fifty-year period.

With theories of affect and masculinity, the seams of conventional historical narratives become frayed, especially when we consider how the visual and discursive convey counternarratives of gender and race. Visuality must be a key component for understanding how attachments are formed and how the histories of Mexican anarchists and braceros have come to life and stayed with us throughout history. Images allow us to examine the what if, the history of gesture, the homoerotic, and the intimacies formed in diaspora. Many might recoil at what might be perceived as my merely suggested or proposed possibilities of masculine intimacies in diaspora. But this is precisely my point. If we cannot extend our analysis outward with interpretative queer of color and transnational feminist frameworks for nongay objects, then those theories have failed us in their lack of expansiveness. There is something specific and universal about these theories, and this is why the role of photography and discourse in the formation of attachments, intimacies, and desires is focused on so thoroughly. To drive home the point of the book's title and cover image, these archived lifeworlds are revealed as exceedingly intricate and complex only through the use of such theoretical frameworks.

As Flores Magón invited us into the iconic photograph from the periphery or anonymous braceros like those on the cover look directly at Nadel's camera, the cultural, structural, sexual, and racial forces that have created the meanings of Mexican masculinities are revealed. The sense that the camera's shutter took possession of the subject as it was being photographed, alongside governmental policy and written responses to oppression, shows how monitoring and policing Mexican masculinities in diaspora was the only way that the Mexican and US nation-states could contain these populations and their critiques, both explicit and implicit, of wholesale inequality. The affective traces of love, loss, camaraderie, and intimacy, under conditions of surveillance and regulation, form part of the visual realm in Nadel's bracero photographs and in the US and Mexican state's surveillance of Flores Magón and his family. Both the visual and the discursive make up a varied history of racialized sexuality and gender that cannot be fully accounted for with a theory of machismo alone. Instead, embedded evidence and traces—evinced in policy and photographs, personal correspondence and prison records, newspapers, magazine covers, and surveillance documents—pave the way for new readings, new knowledge formations, and new histories of Mexican masculinities in diaspora.

Notes

ARCHIVE ABBREVIATIONS

AEFM	Archivo Enrique Flores Magón
AGN	Archivo General de la Nacíon Mexico
EIS	Dwight D. Eisenhower Presidential Library Collection
GAL	Galarza Papers, Stanford University Special Collections
NAD	Leonard Nadel Photographic Collection, Smithsonian Archive of the Museum of Natural History
NARAS	National Archives and Records, Seattle Division
NARASL	National Archives and Records, St. Louis Division
SWE	Swearingen Family Private Collection
UCSC	University of California Santa Cruz, Regional Oral History Project

INTRODUCTION

1 AEFM, Box 3, Folder 1, May 5, 1916, "Letter to Comrade from the Los Angeles County Jail."
2 Hirsch, *A Courtship after Marriage*, 8.
3 Carlos Aniceto Gutiérrez, "Mexican Labor Pacts Bring New Ways of Life," *Sacramento Bee*, April 15, 1957.
4 Hirsch, *A Courtship after Marriage*, 17.
5 Shah, *Stranger Intimacy*, 3.
6 As he explains this notion of refashioning via the homophile movement in Mexico City, Macías-González argues that domesticity was a key element of the negotiations with society. Although this book is not about homophile or queer Mexican men per se, Macías-González's reflections about domesticity provide another avenue to think about migration's capacity to reorder gender roles because of contact with domesticity and the domestic sphere in places such as communes and bunkhouses. See Macías-González, "The Transnational Homophile Movement."
7 Jocelyn Olcott has documented how Mexican men and women have historically moved consistently between households and meeting halls, ignoring the demands of a public-private divide. See Olcott, *Revolutionary Women in Postrevolutionary Mexico*, 5.

8 Historian James Cockcroft was one of the first people to question Enrique's reliability as a narrator of history. In saying that Enrique was "not always a trustworthy or consistent source," Cockcroft raises important questions about how we cannot just take the evidence at face value but must interrogate it fully as we interpret. Cockcroft, *Intellectual Precursors of the Mexican Revolution*, 115.

9 The Smithsonian's traveling exhibit "Bittersweet Harvest" appeared in forty-six cities after its 2009 premiere at the National Museum of American History. It included fifteen freestanding banners with text and images, an audio station, and approximately forty bracero photographs.

10 In his unpublished manuscript, Sergio Chávez's interviews with former bracero workers discuss how migration opened up possibilities for men to explore their sexualities, including same-sex relations with other men. Although many of the braceros were reluctant to discuss these relationships at the time, Chávez's interviews from the last seven years document more willingness to break conventions about compulsory heteronormativity in the migrant stream.

11 I put "histories" in quotation marks here to call attention to the fact that my claim is not about writing official history but rather to provide a historically grounded interdisciplinary analysis of how the archive does not match up to and complicates official historical narratives of the PLM, even if scholars deem these discrepancies minor and uninteresting.

12 See Loza, *Defiant Braceros*, 63–65, where she discusses how journalists and photographers complained that the men brought their questionable morals with them. As Loza notes, when the lights went off in the barracks, same-sex sexual encounters would occur. The men would interact with transgendered women in the camps as well. Such interactions were counterbalanced by traveling priests who came to the camps to say mass.

13 Manuel González Ramírez argues that because Enrique long outlived all of the other PLM revolutionaries, his conferences and talks given into the 1950s were the ones that provided the majority of information about Magonismo during the first part of the twentieth century. As a result, the PLM history is skewed to his designs when Enrique provided the source material to researchers. González Ramírez, *Epistolario y textos de Ricardo Flores Magón*, 238.

14 Hard-core supporters of the idea that Ricardo Flores Magón was the main brain of the PLM vehemently defend the idea that Enrique was of no consequence as a political actor. For example, Nicolás Bernal commented that the biography that Enrique told to Sammuel Kaplan was "un libro que por cierto no tuvo relevancia" (a book that had no relevance). See Bernal, *Memorias*, 37.

15 Marroquin Arredondo, Pineda Franco, and Mieri, *Open Borders to a Revolution*, ix.

16 Berlant, *Cruel Optimism*.

17 Lytle Hernández, *City of Inmates*, 12.

18 Campt provides the notion of diaspora formation in images. See Campt, *Image Matters*, 54. Jane Lydon documents refusal and participation in photography as an expression of skill. See Lydon, *Eye Contact*, 2.

19 Lydon, *Eye Contact*.

20 See Mraz, *Photographing the Mexican Revolution*.

21 MacLachlan, *Anarchism and the Mexican Revolution*.
22 Gómez-Quiñones, "Sin frontera, sin cuartel," 195.
23 Fernández Bravo, *El Ideario*, 23.
24 Muñoz Cota, *Ricardo Flores Magón*.
25 Cohen, *Braceros*, 178.
26 Quoted in Gonzalez, *Guest Workers or Colonized Labor?*, 87.
27 See the Silvestre Terrazas Papers (MB-18, University of California, Berkeley, Bancroft Library), where hundreds of pieces of Ricardo, Enrique, and other PLM members' correspondence were copied, sent on, or completely withheld by the Chihuahua governor and the Mexican military. See also Chávez-García, *Migrant Longing*, where she discusses why analyzing private family letters provides a broader view of how individuals understood themselves as migrants.
28 Guerin-González, *Mexican Workers and the American Dream*, 77.
29 Jacobson, *Whiteness of a Different Color*. See also Molina, *How Race Is Made in America*, 42–43, for descriptions of the court cases that excluded Mexicans and Mexican Americans from legal consideration as white.
30 "At It Again. Women Agitators Incite Mexicans. Ricardo Flores Magon's Wife and Daughter Stir Strife," *Los Angeles Times*, April 24, 1917.
31 Flores Magón, "El fracaso de Abraham Lincoln."
32 Flores Magón.
33 Enrique Flores Magón, "A pesar de todo, nuestros braceros continuan huyendo," *El Universal*, December 14, 1951.
34 Flores Magón, "A pesar de todo."
35 Flores Magón.
36 See Flores, *Grounds for Dreaming*, 76–78.
37 See Macías-González, "The Transnational Homophile Movement," for more on this point.
38 Macías-González and Rubenstein, *Masculinity and Sexuality in Modern Mexico*, 6.
39 Molina Enriquez, *Los grandes problemas nacionales*.
40 McKee Irwin, *Mexican Masculinities*, xxxi.
41 Sifuentes-Jáuregui, "Cuerpos, intelectuales y homosocialidad," 99.
42 Sifuentes-Jáuregui, 101.
43 Sánchez Prado, "Vanguardia y campo literario," 191.
44 De la Mora, *Cinemachismo*, 80. Also, anthropologist Matthew Gutmann charted the rise of these controversies in his book *The Meanings of Macho*, in his essay "Trafficking in Men: The Anthropology of Masculinity," and in his introductory essay in *Changing Men and Masculinities in Latin America*, urging scholars to avoid binaries.
45 Gutmann, *Changing Men and Masculinities in Latin America*, 3.
46 Machismo has historically, and unfortunately, formed the backbone of the majority of scholarship on masculinity in Chicano, Latinx, and Latin American Studies contexts. It also does not help that the media and popular culture have also racialized Latinx and Mexican misogyny from the 1930s onward and called it machismo. While behaviors of exotic, ethnicized hypermasculinity form some

cultural practices in Latinx communities, they are not the only type of masculinity out there, which is what the discourse of machismo would have us believe. In Oscar Lewis's studies of Mexican and Puerto Rican families in the 1940s, early Chicana feminist treatises such as Ada Sosa Riddell's groundbreaking 1974 essay "Chicanas en El Movimiento," Alfredo Mirandé's 1997 book-length study *Hombres y Machos*, and even the attempt to have Latino men speak for themselves in Ray González's 1996 edited collection *Muy Macho*, the scholarship presents a pathological model of an unruptured and often static patriarchal construction of racialized manliness. Benjamin Cowan has argued that this exotic, ethnicized hypermasculinity that fuels the pathology and violence is a bit of a global epithet: a result of social scientific and popular anxieties about immigration, overpopulation, security, race, and public health. See "How *Machismo* Got Its Spurs," 607. Machismo is most notably seen as part of Mexican subject formation. I can think of more than half a dozen key ideas in Mexican cultures and in current scholarship that have been cemented with this line of thought. In no particular order, they are as follows: Machismo is accepted as a proven and undisputed fact of Latino masculine behavior. Much social science literature historically places the blame on men in their reproduction of macho cultural practices. The scholarship often fails to implicate men's and women's dual investments in maintaining a narrative of masculine dominance as a means of access to heteronormative (white) patriarchal power. Machismo and the figure of the macho serve more as placeholders rather than as a sustained engagement with the myriad ways that communities and individuals have defined and redefined a full range of practices that run the gambit from pathological hypermasculine to nonnormative. Early feminist conversations about machismo defined it as sexism (see Alma García's 1992 collection, *Chicana Feminist Thought: The Basic Historical Writings*), an all-encompassing model for understanding Latina and Latin American women's oppression by men, especially in the context of nationalist struggles. Hurtado and Sinha's *Beyond Machismo* marks a shift from this position.

47 Joseph, *Revolution from Without*.
48 Knight, *The Mexican Revolution*, vol. 1; Hart, *Revolutionary Mexico*, 47.
49 There is an abundance of scholarship about Ricardo Flores Magón, to the point that he has become a secular saint in Mexican and Chicano discourses of resistance to hegemony. Because I am not particularly interested in secular saints or resistance in terms of the ways in which they reproduce macro-historical narratives, as a scholar of gender and sexuality I prefer to focus on the minor and what is not said, most notably theorized by Emma Pérez in *The Decolonial Imaginary*.
50 Daniel Flores Magón, son of Enrique Flores Magón Jr., also noted that his father read the letters from Enrique to his children before burning them all in the 1970s. This idea of controlling history through eliminating evidence for personal reasons registers the pain and conflict over what belongs to official narratives and what is private to a family and individual. Personal conversation, January 17, 2019.
51 Kristeva, "Powers of Horror," 230.
52 The scrapbooks at the Smithsonian are not all that revealing of Nadel's intentions. For example, Series 1, Box 1, Folder 2, has scrapbooks from 1956 to 1960. The

clippings are mostly of commercial work that Nadel performed during this time period. Very little is annotated throughout the collection. When it is, the captions and descriptions are generic, which is why a close reading of the images provides a better understanding of Nadel's intentions.
53 Nadel's bracero photographs are actually archived contact sheets, not photographs. He made some prints that make up the archive, but the majority have been digitized via contact sheets.
54 See Luciano and Chen, "Has the Queer Ever Been Human?," 186.
55 Macías-González, "The Transnational Homophile Movement," 535.

PART I. ENRIQUE FLORES MAGÓN'S EXILE

1 *Pearson's Magazine*, March 1908, 237.
2 *Pearson's Magazine*, 241.
3 *Pearson's Magazine*, 241.
4 *Pearson's Magazine*, 237.
5 Jameson, "Third-World Literature," 69.
6 See Sommer, *Foundational Fictions*, for more on this point about heteronormativity and national allegory.
7 For traditional narratives of masculinity in the context of the revolution, see Gonzales, *The Mexican Revolution: 1910–1940*; Knight, *The Mexican Revolution: A Very Short Introduction*; Knight, *The Mexican Revolution*, vol. I; Hart, *Revolutionary Mexico*; and Joseph and Buchenau, *Mexico's Once and Future Revolution*. Olcott, Vaughan, and Cano's *Sex in Revolution* provides the best account of how masculinity was remade through feminist actions and women's participation in the revolution.
8 Lomnitz, *The Return*, 228, 230.

CHAPTER 1. GREETING CARDS, LOVE NOTES, LOVE LETTERS

1 Akers Chacón, *Radicals in the Barrio*, 117.
2 Camic, "From Trashed to Treasured," 81.
3 Flores Magón, "Notas intimas."
4 AEFM, Box 7, Folder 4, May 10, 1899.
5 AEFM, Box 30, Folder 129, Num. Series 3524, 1–2.
6 AEFM, Box 30, Folder 129, Num. Series 3524, 2.
7 Kelley, "Rhetoric as Seduction," 70.
8 McKee Irwin, *Mexican Masculinities*, 119.
9 Gabara, *Errant Modernism*, 144–45.
10 Terrazas Papers, MB-18 Part 1, Folder 8c.
11 Ranajit Guha and Gayatri Chakravorty Spivak, *Selected Subaltern Studies*, 45–84.
12 See Fondo Manuel García Ramos, Tomo 27, Primero Tomado del Archivo de la Secretaria de Gobernación, "Tabla Alfabetica de Enrique Flores Magón," AGN, 00240.
13 Lytle Hernández, *City of Inmates*, 94.

CHAPTER 2. PLM INTIMATE BETRAYALS

1. Pérez, "'A la mujer,'" 463.
2. In a March 12, 1946, article for *El Nacional*, Enrique noted that he received his daily correspondence in 1912 bundled in issues of *Regeneración*, which most likely included letters from Paula.
3. See Pérez, *The Decolonial Imaginary*; González, *Redeeming la Raza*; and Deveraux Ramírez, *Occupying Our Space*.
4. González, *Redeeming la Raza*, 76.
5. Pérez, *The Decolonial Imaginary*, 64–65.
6. Pérez, "'A la mujer,'" 469.
7. In *Peleamos contra la injusticia*, Kaplan states that Enrique married Teresa in 1905 in El Paso. He actually married Paula Carmona in Los Angeles in 1909. In another Kaplan-edited autobiography, *Combatimos la tiranía*, 369, he tells the same story.
8. Officially, and according to the Mexican government, the Flores Magón brothers were precursors: they were the intellectuals who fomented what would eventually become a full-blown revolution in 1910. The term got widely adapted after the publication of Charles C. Cumberland's "Precursors of the Mexican Revolution of 1910" in 1942.
9. Census Schedule, District 19-911, Precinct 2, Dominguez Township, Los Angeles County, Sheet 23A, 1930.
10. Such histories include Gómez-Quiñonez, *Sembradores Ricardo Flores Magon y el Partido Liberal Mexicano*, and another account, sanctioned by the Mexican government, Valencia's *Testimonio carcelario*, says that Paula died while Enrique was in prison. See also Kanellos, "Spanish Language Periodicals." Both cite Paula's existence but don't probe beyond that mere fact.
11. 1902 *Buck's Directory of El Paso*. Jacinto Barrera-Bassols states that Rómulo owned a bookstore on South Stanton Street in El Paso. Archivo Magon, https://archivomagon.net/lugares/301-s-stanton-st, retrieved March 1, 2018. He and his wife, Desideria, filed deeds for lots 11, 12, 13, 14, and 15 of Block 50 Campbells addition in the total of $1,800 on July 25, 1903.
12. *El Paso Herald*, December 18, 1903, 6.
13. Nicole M. Guidotti-Hernández, "Anita Swearingen Oral History," March 14, 2018.
14. Kanellos, "Spanish Language Periodicals," 71.
15. Myers, "The Mexican Liberal Party," 47.
16. Myers, "The Mexican Liberal Party," 54, claims that Trinidad was following Enrique instead of Ricardo. Eugenio Martínez Nuñez states that she was Ricardo's lover and, in another context, his wife. See Martínez Nuñez, *Juan Sarabia*, 127. On page 149, Martínez Nuñez states that Trinidad was the lover of both Enrique and Ricardo.
17. 1905 El Paso Texas City Directory.
18. Myers states that Rómulo left Durango in 1906. See Myers, "The Mexican Liberal Party," 114. Census data indicate they had been in the US much longer.
19. Terrazas Papers, Bancroft Library, MB-18, Part 1, Box 10, Folder 13.
20. "Letter from Rómulo Carmona to Ricardo Flores Magón," Terrazas Papers, MB-18, Part 1, Box 31.

21 "Letter from Rómulo Carmona to Ricardo Flores Magón."
22 Lomas, "Transborder Discourse," 53; Myers, "The Mexican Liberal Party," 113.
23 Taylor, *La campaña Magonista de 1911*, 59.
24 García, *Desert Immigrants*, 176.
25 Bernal states that Rómulo did not meet Ricardo and Enrique until 1910 in Los Angeles, which is false because documentation shows that they communicated much earlier. Bernal, *Memorias*, 124.
26 The descendants of Guadalupe Carmona say that Paula ran away with Enrique, but other descendants, such as Paula's grandchildren, agree that Rómulo brokered their union. Guidotti-Hernández, "Anita Swearingen Oral History," March 14, 2018.
27 "La lista negra del Porfirismo," *El Demócrata*, September 7, 1924. The list is dated October 30, 1906.
28 Mario García and the website magonista.org both make these claims. Rómulo also owned the storefronts 652–660 San Fernando just off the Plaza de los Mexicanos in downtown Los Angeles. See https://sites.google.com/site/magonistaorg/1906-1907-hiding-in-la, retrieved March 1, 2019; and *Desert Immigrants*, 176. This property was located in what was then called Frogtown. Myers states that Ricardo lived with Modesto Díaz while hiding in El Paso during 1906. Myers, "The Mexican Liberal Party," 181. Modesto Díaz, an editor of *Revolución*, had the newspaper headquartered at 660 San Fernando Street, Los Angeles. According to census records, the Carmona home and bookstore were part of the complex where Díaz lived, making it possible that Ricardo went from the Díaz home to the Carmona home when he was hiding in Los Angeles. See *Revolución*, June 8, 1907. By October 26, 1907, the paper's offices had moved to 654 San Fernando Street.
29 Martínez Nuñez, *La vida heróica de Práxedis Guerrero*, 114.
30 Martínez Nuñez, 114.
31 "Carta al Sr. Manuel Sarabia, Douglas Arizona" de Rómulo Carmona, Los Angeles, CA, August 28, 1907, SRE, Archivo Historico Magonismo, LE 928.
32 "Carta al Sr. Joaquin Calvo, 508 Monroe St. South Austin TX" de Manuel Sarabia, August 30, 1920, SRE, Archivo Historico Magonismo, LE 928. This is the same Jesus Rangel who would be held in a San Antonio jail with Robert Kline and eleven others for sedition in 1914. "Carta a Henry Max Morton (Tomás Sarabia) Apartado 58 San Antonio TX" de Manuel Sarabia, August 31, 1907.
33 "Eugenio Alzalde," *El Nacional*, March 4, 1946.
34 Abad de Santillan, *Ricardo Flores Magón*, 58.
35 See Martínez Nuñez, *Juan Sarabia*. However, Abad de Santillan claims that Enrique was in Canada from 1906 to the middle of 1908. Abad de Santillan, *Ricardo Flores Magón*, 53.
36 Librado Rivera's wife, Conchita, and their two children testified about the horrors of being on the run from the law to support the liberation of Mexico from the Díaz dictatorship. Lucía Norman and Job Harriman, the socialist lawyer for the three men, also spoke at the event. "Report of the Meeting at Simpson Auditorium, Tuesday November 26, 1907 8:00 o'clock p.m.," Longley, Hefte and Bagley & Co. Shorthand Reporters and Notaries, Los Angeles, CA, SRE, Archivo Historico Magonismo, LE 1934.

37 Albro, *To Die on Your Feet*, 76–77.
38 "Letter to José María Sánchez, Governor of Chihuahua," Terrazas Papers, MB-18, Part 1, Box 28. Again, on July 27, 1908, Maetus stated that Enrique, according to Ramon Corral, was still in El Paso.
39 In both Kaplan, *Peleamos contra la injusticia*, and a September 2, 1925, article published in *La Demócrata*, Enrique Flores Magón spoke as if he participated in the events. See Duffy Turner, *Ricardo Flores Magón*, 165. Bernal makes the claim about Enrique injuring himself as well. See Bernal, *Memorias*, 129.
40 Martínez Nuñez, *La vida heroica de Práxedis Guerrero*, 168–70.
41 Martínez Nuñez, 130.
42 Lomnitz, *The Return of Comrade Ricardo Flores Magón*, 264.
43 Bernal, *Memorias*, 25.
44 SWE.
45 Rosas, *Abrazando el Espíritu*, 113.
46 Campt, *Image Matters*, 7.
47 SWE.
48 Carmona used a post office box number at Station C, and the *Regeneración* offices were located on Fourth Street. He placed advertisements regularly, taking up a half page, from September 3, 1910, to October 26, 1912.
49 In an October 24, 1946, article for *El Nacional*, Enrique wrote about the torture that Matthew Schmidt experienced while in jail for the bombing of the *Los Angeles Times* building.
50 Given their time in San Francisco with the Schmidts, it is quite possible that Enrique had prior knowledge of and even participated in the planning of the bombing. Bernal says that Enrique had nothing to do with the Schmidts and the McNameras, most likely because Bernal idolized Ricardo and hated Enrique. Bernal, *Memorias*, 36.
51 Kaplan, *Combatimos la tiranía*, 250. Enrique also stated that he started working under the direction of Manuel Arias, his supervisor at the company in 1908. "Añoranzas," *El Nacional*, September 9, 1946.
52 Campt, *Image Matters*, 42.
53 Hudgins, "A Historical Approach to Family Photography," 560.
54 See González, *Redeeming la Raza*, especially chapter 2, "Masons, Magonistas, and Maternalists," where González succinctly outlines how domesticity and proper motherhood were at the core of the PLM's disparate beliefs about women's equality and their oppression.
55 Pérez, "'A la mujer,'" 473.
56 González, *Redeeming la Raza*, 77.
57 Bollinger Pouwels, *Political Journalism by Mexican Women*, 26.
58 *Regeneración*, October 8, 1910. This essay was published two weeks after Ricardo Flores Magón's famous essay "A la mujer," which has been reprinted numerous times within the context of Chicana/o history.
59 Deveraux Ramírez, *Occupying Our Space*, 95.
60 Pérez, "'A la mujer,'" 454.
61 "Solidaridad!," *Regeneración*, January 1, 1912.

62 *Regeneración* announced on March 30, 1912, that Rómulo, using his bookstore alias Pilar A. Robledo, was to open a new location in El Paso to sell books and magazines relevant to the Mexican Revolution, including Cuban and Spanish anarchist texts. The expansion of his business holdings also suggests that he financially benefited from supporting the PLM insurgency by servicing its literate clientele.
63 William C. Owen to Enrique Flores Magón, August 23, 1912, AEFM, Box 5, Folder 53.
64 William C. Owen to Enrique Flores Magón.
65 "Jury Finds Magon and Friends Guilty," *Los Angeles Herald*, June 12, 1912.
66 *Regeneración*, July 13, 1912.
67 González, *Redeeming la Raza*, 76.
68 Rosas, *Abrazando el Espíritu*, 48.
69 *Regeneración*, July 29, 1912.
70 *Regeneración*, December 14, 1912.
71 Rosas, *Abrazando el Espíritu*, 48.
72 *Regeneración*, March 1, 1913.
73 *Regeneración*.
74 This letter from Pedro Rincón Gallardo to Rómulo Carmona, quoted in "Perfiles negros. Los criminales," written by Araujo, accuses the two men of conspiring to use the Casa Obrero monies to buy land and houses in Santa Paula. Araujo refers to Rincón Gallardo as a "veteran of the social revolution" and former comrade who helped occupy Baja California during the 1911 armed revolt. The letter read, in part: "Unos cuantos días después de que apareció 1a noticia 'de que ya había compañeros apuntados en la lista de donantes para que al completo de 200 con $50,00 cada uno, se pudiera dar principió a la compra de la 'Casa del Obrero.' . . . Los $10,000.00 que se reúnan de los 200 donantes, servirán en todo caso para irnos de ésta para Santa Paula, Cal. Ahí hay una persona que me proporciona dos lotes de tierra; construiremos allí nuestras casitas y pasemos una vida feliz. Esto, aquí, nuestro se pueda comprar. Yá te digo, arregla por ahora aquí tu pieza.'" *Regeneración*, June 21, 1913.
75 Lomnitz, *The Return of Comrade Ricardo Flores Magón*, 299.
76 Telegram from "Pilar S. Robledo" to Enrique dated April 19, 1913, quoted in Duffy Turner, *Ricardo Flores Magón*, 282.
77 AEFM, Box 12, Folder 24, June 7, 1913.
78 González, *Redeeming la Raza*, 79.
79 *Regeneración*, June 7, 1913.
80 Gómez Gutiérrez, *La vida que yo vivi*, 205.
81 Barrera-Bassols says that it was Ricardo who specifically decided to end the changes made to *Regeneración* and break with Rómulo and Moncaleano, http://archivomagon.net/obras-completas/art-periodisticos-1900-1918/1914/1914-40, retrieved March 1, 2018.
82 Araujo, "La campana contra Regeneración," *Regeneración*, June 7, 1913. Note: I believe the reference "una mujer fatal" insinuates that Rómulo is talking about Teresa Arteaga.
83 *Regeneración*, June 7, 1913.
84 Gómez-Quiñones, *Sembradores Ricardo Flores Magon*, 50–51.

85 For example, Rómulo donated $4.50 to support *Regeneración* on March 23, 1912.
86 Taylor, *La campaña Magonista de 1911*, 112.
87 "Protesta," *Regeneración*, June 14, 1912.
88 "Protesta."
89 "Otra protesta," *Regeneración*, June 14, 1912.
90 "Paula Carmona," *Regeneración*, June 7, 1913.
91 *Regeneración*, June 21, 1913.
92 "Los 'huérfanos,'" *Regeneración*, February 28, 1914.
93 Bernal, *Memorias*, 125, 127.
94 Duffy Turner, *Ricardo Flores Magón y el Partido Liberal Mexicano*, 28.
95 Bernal, *Memorias*, 125, 127, 283.
96 Valencia, *Testimonio carcelario*, 87.
97 *Regeneración*, July 26, 1913.
98 AEFM, Box 35, Folder 15, n.d.
99 AEFM, Box 35, Folder 15, n.d.
100 Lomnitz, *The Return of Comrade Ricardo Flores Magón*, 438.
101 Vaughan, "Cultural Approaches to Peasant Politics," 285.
102 *Regeneración*, January 31, 1914.
103 Although some might point out that this form of masculine violence is part of the innate character of machismo, Ben Cowan has demonstrated that such a label is anachronistic for the time period. See Cowan, "How *Machismo* Got Its Spurs."
104 "Los 'huérfanos.'"
105 Wexler, *Tender Violence*, 7.
106 "Los 'huérfanos.'"
107 Margarita Roselli lived on Arlington Street in Los Angeles and was the divorced stepdaughter of Carl Tsuruji Nakoshima, according to the census. At this point, her mother, Paula Carmona Nakashima, had birthed nine children, including Margarita and Práxedis with Enrique Flores Magón. According to the family, Margarita and Joe Roselli never divorced and went on to have two boys in 1932 and 1936. Their first son, ironically, was named Henry: English for Enrique. See Guidotti-Hernández, "Anita Swearingen Oral History," March 14, 2018.
108 "Los 'huérfanos.'"
109 "Los 'huérfanos.'"
110 Práxedis Carmona, while listed with no major, appears in the college yearbook as a graduate of the class of 1933.
111 See Lomnitz, *The Return of Comrade Ricardo Flores Magón*, 222 and 513, on Ricardo's public slamming of two PLM lesbians, Juana Gutiérrez de Mendoza and Elisa Acuña, and Enrique's common use of the word *whore* to describe Ricardo's partner María Brousse, known for her promiscuity.
112 Bernal interview, www.antorcha.net/biblioteca_virtual/historia/entrevista_bernal/13.html.
113 Carl Tsuruji Nakashima, California Federal Naturalization Records, 1843–1999, District Court of Los Angeles, 1954 Petitions, Box 0475.
114 Julie Simpson, great-granddaughter of Paula Carmona, email correspondence, March 3, 2018.

115 Simpson.
116 Anita Swearingen, granddaughter of Paula Carmona, noted that Carl, along with their children, were interned during World War II and that Paula stayed behind to maintain their home, property that was purchased in the children's names, their fertilizer business, and the oil royalties for the wells on their property. See Guidotti-Hernández, "Anita Swearingen Oral History," March 14, 2018.
117 Sommer, *Foundational Fictions*, 209.
118 Guidotti-Hernández, "Anita Swearingen Oral History," March 14, 2018.
119 Olcott, Vaughan, and Cano, *Sex in Revolution*, 12.

CHAPTER 3. OUT OF BETRAYAL AND INTO ANARCHIST LOVE AND FAMILY

1 "Border Crossing Card Maria Brousse viuda de Magon" provides a 1904 crossing date into the US with residency in country until 1930. NARA, *Index and Manifests of Alien Arrivals at Nogales, Arizona, July 5, 1905–1952*, NAI: 2843448, Record Group Title: Records of the Immigration and Naturalization Service, 1787–2004, Record Group Number: 85, Microfilm Roll Number: 57. In a 1901 letter to Teresa, María states that she is already in Los Angeles and involved with the junta, and mentions Ricardo and that she will try to visit the family soon. There's a bit of a discrepancy between the dates of María's original arrival in these two documents. AEFM, Folder 52, Box 35, May 10, 1901.
2 James Beleno and Teresa Beleno, Census Place: Los Angeles Assembly District 70, Los Angeles, CA, Roll: T624_81, Page: 1B, Enumeration District: 0272.
3 In a letter to Enrique, written in 1918, Teresa mentioned "a nice song about a young girl walking with her little brother in the snow, and the boy exclaimed there is nothing colder than snow, and she said yes, there is. I feel the cold in my sole [*sic*] than in my feet, for my mother made me marry without my consent." Perhaps a reflection on her own experience and the couple's political beliefs about marrying too young, the letter's lament catalogs the lingering sentiment about what the traffic in young women does: it creates depressed and dependent subjects. Teresa A. Flores Magón to Enrique Flores Magón, July 2, 1918, AEFM, Box 45, Folder 15.
4 Carta de María Brousse a Teresa Arteaga, February 1, 1914, AEFM, Box 52, Folder 34.
5 Pérez, *The Decolonial Imaginary*, 66.
6 In a 1913 letter to Teresa, María speaks of leaving Pedrito with "las compañeros y compañeras, lo quieren porque es un niño muy bueno para nada me molesta. Salgo con mi propaganda y lo dejo con Rosa y queda contento." María Brousse to Teresa Arteaga, January 23, 1913, AEFM, Box 52, Folder 34. The letters are the only mention of a son on María's part, but it also could have been Teresa's son Pedro, who was born in 1910 and would have been three years old at the time. But why leave your youngest child with your aunt who is running propaganda at the border and left her older child with you previously? By this time in 1910, at least for the census, Lucy was living with Teresa, her husband, Santiago (James) Beleno, and the eldest children, Esperanza, Santiago (Jimmie), and Stella. See Census Place: Los Angeles Assembly District 70, Los Angeles, CA, Roll: T624_81, Page: 1B, Enumeration District: 0272.

7 Carta de María Brousse a Adelaida Arteaga, May 10, 1901, AEFM. She addresses the letter to Hermana Querida.
8 Teresa's mother, Adelaida, died in Los Angeles on April 3, 1918, which means she lived with Teresa for part of the time that Enrique was in McNeil Island the second time and then Leavenworth. At a minimum, Adelaida helped to raise Teresa's children amid the transitions between her first husband, her widowhood, and her life partnership with Enrique. But because her mother lived with the family, this also came with the additional financial burden of another adult to support in the household.
9 María Brousse to Teresa Arteaga, January 23, 1913, AEFM, Box 52, Folder 34.
10 Lucía Norman to Teresa A. Villapando, March 20, 1914, AEFM, Box 49, Folder 9.
11 Letter to Teresa Arteaga de Flores Magón from Enrique Flores Magón, AEFM, Box 45, Folder 2, July, 3, 1914, 1.
12 Bernal interview, www.antorcha.net/biblioteca_virtual/historia/entrevista_bernal/13.html, accessed January 10, 2017.
13 Enrique Flores Magón, "¿Fatalismo?," *El Nacional*, October 12, 1946.
14 Mendieta Alatorre, *La mujer en la Revolución Mexicana*, 39. The claim about archives is interesting because it means that Teresa was just as much a collector of family ephemera and Mexican history as was Enrique, if not more so. She sufficiently understood the role of the paper, herself, and her family as historical actors within the PLM's transnational network to state this to people in legitimating her status as a revolutionary precursor.
15 Flores Magón, "¿Fatalismo?"
16 Kaplan, *Combatimos la tiranía*, 289.
17 *Regeneración*, November 28, 1913.
18 Enumeration District 386, enumeration sheet 28 A. He is listed as James. The boys' names are all anglicized (Henry, Pete, and Joe).
19 *Regeneración*, November 14, 1914, notes the address and provides directions via the tranvia for arrival to Sixth and Main Streets, going east and getting off at Fargo Street.
20 Hurewitz, *Bohemian Los Angeles*.
21 Maldonado Alvarado, *La utopia de Ricardo Flores Magón*, 57.
22 Kaplan, *Combatimos la tiranía*, 275.
23 "La oficina de *Regeneración*," *Regeneración*, October 16, 1915.
24 Hurewitz, *Bohemian Los Angeles*, 42.
25 Enrique Flores Magón, "Teddy," *El Nacional*, August 6, 1946.
26 Flores Magón, "Teddy."
27 "¡Muera la propiedad individual!," *Regeneración*, November 14, 1914.
28 Estrada, *The Los Angeles Plaza*, 155.
29 Flores Magón, "Teddy."
30 Enrique Flores Magón, "Colmena *Regeneración*," *El Nacional*, July 19, 1946.
31 Flores Magón, "Colmena *Regeneración*."
32 Letter to Teresa Arteaga de Flores Magón from Enrique Flores Magón, AEFM, Box 45, Folder 2, July 3, 1914, 1.

33 This language was submitted as corroborating evidence in Enrique's deportation file to describe Cresencio López Aguilera's relationship with the widow of Ricardo Bernales. In it, the inspector chastises López Aguilera's immorality, almost accusing him of taking advantage of an emotionally weak widow and being a bigamist. Even within his condemnation, he was asked if the "free love union was consummated" before he was divorced, to which López Aguilera replied "yes." United States Congress, Communist and Anarchist Deportation Cases: Hearings before a Subcommittee of the Committee on Immigration and Naturalization, House of Representatives, Sixty-Sixth Congress, Second Session, April 21–24, 1920, 116.

34 Hernández, "Chicanas in the US-Mexican Borderlands," 139.

35 See Pérez, *The Decolonial Imaginary*, chapter 3, which focuses mostly on party efforts in Texas.

36 Enrique Flores Magón to Teresa Arteaga, AEFM, Box 45, Folder 10, March 4, 1918.

37 Enrique Flores Magón to Teresa Arteaga.

38 Enrique Flores Magón to Teresa Arteaga.

39 Williams, "'Copied without Loss,'" 135.

40 Letter to Teresa Arteaga de Flores Magón from Enrique Flores Magón, AEFM, Box 45, Folder 2, July 3, 1914, 1.

41 Letter to Teresa Arteaga de Flores Magón from Enrique Flores Magón.

42 Hernández, "Chicanas in the US-Mexican Borderlands," 139.

43 Lomnitz, *The Return of Comrade Ricardo Flores Magón*, 218–19.

44 Pérez, "'A la mujer,'" 469.

45 Rosas, *Abrazando el Espíritu*, 114.

46 Campt, *Image Matters*, 50.

47 As recorded in *Regeneracíon*, November 14, 1914, "medicinas para la compañera de Enrique" indicates that Santiago was still alive and that Teresa and Enrique were together as a couple.

48 For example, Librado Rivera was arrested and jailed in December of 1916 for "luring a beautiful young woman to what was declared by the police to have been a free love colony in Edendale." Facing charges in the juvenile court, Rivera was charged for encouraging a Dionicia Hernández to the commune, along with her children, Alfonso, Angela, and Alexander, and contributing to their delinquency. In his defense, Rivera "claimed he intended to marry Mrs. Hernández as soon as he could legally do so." "Luring Beauty to Love Colony Charged to Jailed Man," *Los Angeles Herald*, January 5, 1917. When the case finally went to trial in 1917, Rivera was not convicted because of witness testimony that Hernández was destitute and taken into the colony, and there was not sufficient evidence.

49 AEFM, Box 45, Folder 2.

50 Pérez, "'A la mujer,'" 467.

51 AEFM, Box 49, Folder 14.

52 Lomnitz argues that Teresa's literacy and writing were indeed a stark contrast to Enrique's lettered educational history. Lomnitz, *The Return of Comrade Ricardo Flores Magón*, 242.

53 Pérez, "'A la mujer,'" 474.

54 From December 12, 1914, to October 2, 1915, *Regeneración* published only three issues. In each, editor Enrique Flores Magón pleas with the worker masses not to let the newspaper die. They did not print their financial transparency accounting statements in these issues, demonstrating that things were so financially wrong the editors could not make the information public.
55 "La muerte de 'Regeneración,'" *Regeneración*, July 11, 1914, 2.
56 "The Rangel-Cline Case," *Mother Earth*, June 1915, 111–15. Rangel was a lifelong PLM supporter and diehard liberal who went to jail many times in his support of Ricardo Flores Magón's political agenda. Bernal noted that he was a guerrilla fighter and revolutionary until his death. Bernal, *Memorias*, 60.
57 *Regeneración*, July 4, 1914, 3–4.
58 *Regeneración*, 2.
59 *Regeneración*, 4.
60 Pérez, "'A la mujer,'" 473.

CHAPTER 4. BODILY HARM

1 "Associate of Magons Flees U.S.: W. C. Owen, Indicted with Other Editors of Seditious Paper, Eludes Federal Officers and Goes to England," *Oakland Tribune*, December 1, 1916.
2 See Muñoz Martínez, *The Injustice Never Leaves You*.
3 "Arresto de los companeros Magón," *Regeneración*, February 19, 1916, 2.
4 "Enrique y Ricardo F. Magón fueron aprehendidos en Los Angeles," special telegram to *La Prensa*, February 20, 1916.
5 Enrique Flores Magón to Child, May 24, 1916, AEFM, Box 3, Folder 1.
6 Duffy Turner, *Ricardo Flores Magón*, 299.
7 *El Paso Morning Times*, February 19, 1916.
8 Kaplan, *Peleamos contra la injusticia*, 362–63. This is a bit of revision in the autobiography. Enrique was actually sentenced to McNeil Island and then transferred to Leavenworth because of overcrowding.
9 Berlant, *Cruel Optimism*.
10 Nota a Teresa A. de Flores Magón, AEFM, Box 45, Folder 4.
11 Lytle Hernández, *City of Inmates*, 120.
12 P. D. Noel, "Shall Free Thought Be Throttled?," *Regeneración*, April 1, 1916, 4.
13 "A todos los amantes de la libertad," *Regeneración*, March 18, 1916, 1.
14 "A todos los amantes de la libertad," 1.
15 Lytle Hernández, *City of Inmates*, 1–5.
16 McNeil Island Correctional Facility, Prisoner #2199, Records of Prisoners Received, July 7, 1912, NARAS; McNeil Island Correctional Facility, Prisoner #3155, Records of Prisoners Received, May 21, 1918, NARAS.
17 "Plan Uprising of Anarchists," *Los Angeles Times*, September 20, 1915.
18 Kaplan, *Combatimos la tirania*, 272.
19 "Plan Uprising of Anarchists."
20 "Ricardo Magon Feels Nervous," *Los Angeles Times*, May 9, 1916.
21 May 20, 1916, AEFM, Box 3, Folder 1.

22 Streeby, *Radical Sensations*, 15.
23 "Aun presos," *Regeneración*, March 28, 1916.
24 May 24, 1916, AEFM, Box 3, Folder 1.
25 "Takes No Chance. Anarchist Attends Trial of Magons. Visitors to Court Searched for Arms," *Los Angeles Times*, June 3, 1916.
26 Deveraux Ramírez, *Occupying Our Space*, 132.
27 Kaplan, *Peleamos contra la injusticia*, 367.
28 "Communist and Anarchist Deportation Cases for 1920."
29 This was not a new practice for the brothers. Ricardo had used Lucía Norman and María Brousse's names to publish articles in the *Libertad y Trabajo* newspaper while he was serving time in the Florence (AZ) Federal Penitentiary during 1906 and 1907. Duffy Turner, *Ricardo Flores Magón*, 151.
30 Enrique Flores Magón, "Rosa Mendez," *El Nacional*, March 7, 1946.
31 Carta a Teresa A. de Flores Magón, February 27, 1916, AEFM, Box 12, Folder 9.
32 Teresa V. Magón, "Margarita F. Magón," *Regeneración*, March 18, 1916.
33 Deveraux Ramírez, *Occupying Our Space*, 147.
34 Magón, "Margarita F. Magón."
35 *Regeneración*, March 18, 1916.
36 Rafael De Lara to Enrique Flores Magón, August 28, 1918, AEFM, Box 50, Folder 9.
37 "Communist and Anarchist Deportation Cases for 1920," 109.
38 "No olvidar," *Regeneración*, May 6, 1916.
39 Auerbach, "McKinley at Home," 803.
40 "Ley fuga," *Regeneración*, April 22, 1916.
41 Deveraux Ramírez, *Occupying Our Space*, 152.
42 *Regeneración*, June 17, 1916.
43 Sánchez-Eppler, *Touching Liberty*, 100.
44 Streeby, *Radical Sensations*, 17.
45 May 24, 1916, AEFM.
46 "El jurado falló en contra de los hermanos Magón," *Regeneración*, June 17, 1916.
47 "El jurado falló en contra de los hermanos Magón."
48 For more on the point about radical uses of visual culture in the early twentieth century, see Streeby, *Radical Sensations*.
49 Howard, "What Is Sentimentality?," 65.
50 Rosaldo, "Toward an Anthropology of Self and Feeling," 143.
51 "LA Mexican Editors Get Prison Terms," *Bakersfield Californian*, June 22, 1916.
52 "Leniency: Magons Given Short Terms. Ricardo Gets Year and Day; Enrique Three Years. Judge Squelches Attempt to Assume Martyr Pose. Court's Decision Opens Way for Bail for Twain," *Los Angeles Times*, June 6, 1916.
53 "Discurso de Enrique Flores Magón en defensa de su hermano Ricardo Flores Magón y de él en Julio 1916," AEFM, Box 12, Folder 28.
54 "Address of Enrique Flores Magón in Federal Court, Los Angeles, June 22, 1916," AEFM, Box 12, Folder 33.
55 "Address of Enrique Flores Magón in Federal Court, Los Angeles, June 22, 1916."
56 "Safety First. Takes Steps to Prevent Riots. Outbreak Is Feared When Verdict Is Read," *Los Angeles Times*, June 6, 1916.

57 "Verdict. Pair of Reds Found Guilty. Magons Twice Convicted of Incendiary Utterances," *Los Angeles Times*, June 7, 1917.
58 "Out. Again. Released from Jail. Enrique Flores Magon Succeeds in Securing Bond That Meets Approval of Court—Socialists Cheer as "Red" Gains His Liberty," *Los Angeles Times*, July 3, 1916, 9.

CHAPTER 5. DE LA FAMILIA LIBERAL

1 González, *Redeeming La Raza*, 51.
2 Pérez, "'A la mujer,'" 460.
3 Kathrine Schmidt to Enrique Flores Magón, March 17, 1922, AEFM, Box 44, Folder 19.
4 Kathrine Schmidt to Teresa Flores Magón, June 21, 1919, AEFM, Box 44, Folder 19.
5 "Nacimientos," *Regeneración*, February 19, 1916.
6 "De la familia liberal," *Regeneración*, September 1, 1917, 3.
7 For the Cananea strike, the PLM circulated copies of *Regeneración* among the workers and supplied contact with key players Librado Rivero and Antonio I. Villarreal. See C. L. Sonnichsen, "Colonel William C. Greene."
8 Muñoz Martínez, *The Injustice Never Leaves You*, 9.
9 1910 Federal Census Schedule, Los Angeles County, Enumeration District 137, sheet 11A.
10 Feliciano Macías, "Nuevo grupo, El Monte California. Julio 29 de 1917," *Regeneración*, September 1, 1917, 3.
11 Untitled response to Feliciano Macías from Enrique Flores Magón, *Regeneración*, September 1, 1917, 3.
12 "De la familia liberal," *Regeneración*, February 24, 1917, 3.
13 Paula Nakashima, age twenty-seven, 1920 Census for Long Beach Township, Enumeration District 70, sheet 15A. She had five children with her second husband, Carl Nakashima, greenhouse owner.
14 Mickenberg and Nel, "Introduction," 1.
15 *Regeneración*, March 24, 1917, 3.
16 *Regeneración*, 3.
17 "At It Again. Women Agitators Incite Mexicans. Magon's Wife and Daughter Stir Strife," *Los Angeles Times*, April 24, 1917.
18 Eng and Kazanjian, *Loss*, 2.
19 "Nuestro proceso," *Regeneración*, September 18, 1917.
20 "Celery Growers Sign Up," *Los Angeles Herald*, February 10, 1910.
21 "A 'Register' Man Sees and Hears Big Things in the Region of Big Crops," *Santa Ana Register*, September 21, 1908. In Wintersberg, for example, the Reverend R. R. Raymond owned the store in town.
22 "15 de Septiembre," *Regeneración*, October 6, 1917.
23 Duffy Turner noted that William Randolph Hearst was gifted "hundreds of thousands of acres of land at $.10 cents an acre by Díaz." "Writers and Revolutionists," 31.

24 Duffy Turner, *Ricardo Flores Magón*, 310.
25 June 28, 1917, AEFM, Box 9, Folder 11.

CHAPTER 6. THE SPLIT

1 *Regeneración*, February 9, 1918.
2 In 1917, according to José Ávila, "Enrique left the group because of differences with María Brousse and her son-in-law, Raúl Palma." Carta de José Ávila a Librado Rivera, 2 de enero de 1924. In Sasso, "Librado Rivera y los hermanos rojos," 32.
3 Bernal, *Memorias*, 126.
4 "Aviso," *Regeneración*, March 16, 1918.
5 Fernando Palomares to Enrique Flores Magón, March 18, 1918, AEFM, Box 50, Folder 9.
6 Sifuentes-Jáuregui, *The Avowal of Difference*, 147–48.
7 "An Anarchist Even in Death," *Los Angeles Times*, January 6, 1923, states that the Mexican consul took María a $500 check to cover the cost of Ricardo's corpse's transport back to Mexico City. Not surprisingly, given her belief that the Mexican government colluded to kill Ricardo in Leavenworth, she refused. Enrique's address is confirmed by this article: "Tribute Paid 'Scorpion': Sympathizers with Ricardo Flores Magon Gather at His Bier for Final Act of Devotion," *Los Angeles Times*, November 22, 1922.
8 "Tribute Paid 'Scorpion.'" In *Testimonio carcelario*, 96, Tita Valencia also states his corpse was cared for by Brees Brothers Mortuary.
9 Enrique Flores Magón to Rafael García, December 1, 1922, AEFM, December 16, 1922, Box 50, Folder 11.
10 Bernal, *Memorias*, 98: "Es falso también, que Enrique Flores Magón hubiera tenido algo que ver, pues desde que Ricardo estaba preso, se había desentendido de su hermano, ya no le escribía, y por el contrario, le hizo una atmósfera tendiente a desacreditarlo, por lo que era un verdadero traidor."
11 Enrique Flores Magón to Rafael García, December 16, 1922, AEFM, Box 50, Folder 11.
12 Duffy Turner, *One-Way Ticket*.
13 "Ricardo F. Magon's Body in State Is Seen by Hundreds," *El Paso Herald*, November 27, 1922.
14 Duffy Turner, *Ricardo Flores Magón*, 351.
15 Enrique Flores Magón to Teresa V. Magón, July 21, 1918, AEFM, Box 49, Folder 19.
16 "Prisoner file #12839, United States Penitentiary, Leavenworth Kansas," 5, NARASL.
17 Enrique Flores Magón to Teresa V. Magón, December 16, 1919, AEFM, Box 45, Folder 58.
18 Rafael de Lara to Enrique Flores Magón, August 28, 1918, AEFM, Box 50, Folder 9.
19 Rafael García to Enrique Flores Magón, May 31, 1918, AEFM, Box 50, Folder 10.
20 Kathrine Schmidt to Teresa Flores Magón, June 21, 1919, AEFM, Box 44, Folder 19.
21 Esperanza Flores Magón to Enrique Flores Magón, May 31, 1918, AEFM, Box 1, Folder 5.

22 Esperanza Flores Magón to Enrique Flores Magón, July 13, 1918, AEFM, Box 1, Folder 5.
23 United States Congress, *Communist and Anarchist Deportation Cases: Hearings before a Subcommittee of the Committee on Immigration and Naturalization, House of Representatives, Sixty-Sixth Congress, Second Session, April 21–24, 1920*, 110.
24 William C. Owen to Enrique Flores Magón, October 21, 1921, AEFM, Box 5, Folder 53.
25 United States Congress, *Communist and Anarchist Deportation Cases*, April 21–24, 1920, 93.
26 González Ramírez, *Epistolario y textos de Ricardo Flores Magón*, 239.
27 "Libertad de E. Flores Magón," *Excelsior*, June 16, 1923. The article goes on to discuss the precautions taken with his release, including dispatch of the Mexican National Guard.
28 "Red Labor Czar Released from Puebla Prison. Enrique Flores Magón Granted His Liberty Following Workers Strike Threat," *Excelsior*, June 16, 1923.
29 María B., Viuda de Flores Magón, "Un falso líder: Enrique Flores," *Excelsior*, June 18, 1923.
30 Gauss, "Working-Class Masculinity."
31 National Archives and Records Administration, *Index and Manifests of Alien Arrivals at Nogales, Arizona, July 5, 1905–1952*.
32 United States Congress, *Communist and Anarchist Deportation Cases*, April 21–24, 1920.

CHAPTER 7. THE EMOTIONAL LABOR OF BEING IN LEAVENWORTH

1 "Enrique Magon received a sentence of three years for being associated with his brother Ricardo Flores Magon in publishing the inflammatory articles against the government in their newspaper, Regeneracion." "Four Years Is Carlson Term," *Los Angeles Times*, May 18, 1918.
2 Kaplan, *Peleamos contra la injusticia*, 380–82.
3 Kaplan, *Combatimos la tirania*, 289.
4 Teresa V. Magón to Enrique Flores Magón, July 26, 1918, AEFM, Box 45, Folder 20.
5 Enrique Flores Magón to Estela Flores Magón, September 9, 1919, AEFM, Box 1, Folder 5. In his Leavenworth correspondence, Enrique used "=" to indicate a transition of subject or to indicate he was writing to a different person in the same document. He did so to conserve space and paper. They were scant resources.
6 "Record of Articles Received by Prisoners," No. 12839, Enrique Flores Magon, 1–6, 1918–1920.
7 Enrique explained to Teresa that "como quizas, la quieta lo que recibe, para ahorar espacio, en vez de pronto y aponte usaré dos rayitas" so that she understood why he cut his thoughts so abruptly. For a person accustomed to verbose prose that builds its argument with passion, economizing on words and space was a challenge, all the while recognizing that such a privilege could be snatched away at any moment. Enrique Flores Magón to Teresa Arteaga de Flores Magón, June 1, 1919, AEFM, Box 1, Folder 5.

8 Heatherton, "The Color Line and Class Struggle," 82.
9 Enrique Flores Magón to Teresa Arteaga de Flores Magón, June 1, 1919.
10 Warden's Request Intake Form, Leavenworth Penitentiary, October 14, 1919, NARASL.
11 Rosas, *Abrazando el Espíritu*, 120.
12 Enrique Flores Magón to Esperanza Flores Magón, March 9, 1919, AEFM, Box 1, Folder 5.
13 Esperanza Flores Magón to Enrique Flores Magón, May 31, 1918, AEFM, Box 1, Folder 5.
14 Esperanza Flores Magón to Enrique Flores Magón, August 18, 1918, AEFM, Box 1, Folder 5.
15 Esperanza Flores Magón to Enrique Flores Magón, July 17, 1918, AEFM, Box 1, Folder 5.
16 Teresa V. Magón to Enrique Flores Magón, AEFM, July 2, 1918, Box 45, Folder 18.
17 Teresa V. Magón to Enrique Flores Magón, AEFM, July 26, 1918, Box 45, Folder 20.
18 Deputy Warden's Office, Items for Storage, Leavenworth Penitentiary, August 1, 1920, NARASL.
19 Manuscript from Leavenworth *New Era*, 11–12, AEFM, Box 20, Folder 1, Series 3522.
20 Díaz-Sánchez and Hernández, "The Son Jarocho," 192.
21 September 20, 1899, AEFM, Box 9, Folder 11.
22 Manuscript from Leavenworth *New Era*, 12.
23 Duffy Turner, *One-Way Ticket*, 179–80.
24 Heatherton, "University of Radicalism," 564.

CHAPTER 8. DEPORTATION TO A HOME THAT DOESN'T EXIST

1 Enrique Flores Magón to Rafael B. García, November 25, 1922, AEFM, Box 50, Folder 10.
2 United States Congress, Communist and Anarchist Deportation Cases: Hearings before a Subcommittee of the Committee on Immigration and Naturalization, House of Representatives, Sixty-Sixth Congress, Second Session, April 21–24, 1920, 103.
3 Ngai, *Impossible Subjects*, xix, 5.
4 United States Congress, Communist and Anarchist Deportation Cases, April 21–24, 1920, 104.
5 United States Congress, Communist and Anarchist Deportation Cases, April 21–24, 1920, 103, 110.
6 "May Deport Mexican Red," *Los Angeles Times*, October 12, 1922.
7 United States Congress, Communist and Anarchist Deportation Cases, April 21–24, 1920, 106, 111, 110.
8 United States Congress, Communist and Anarchist Deportation Cases, April 21–24, 1920, 108.
9 "Magon Family Says Adios," *Los Angeles Times*, March 2, 1923.
10 United States Congress, Communist and Anarchist Deportation Cases, April 21–24, 1920, 111.

11 United States Congress, Communist and Anarchist Deportation Cases, April 21–24, 1920, 109.
12 "May Deport Mexican Red."
13 "Why Not Keep Him Longer?," *El Paso Times*, October 13, 1922.
14 "Deportation Trial Ends: Washington Officials to Decide If Anarchist Shall Be Returned to His Native Land," *Los Angeles Times*, October 13, 1922.
15 "Deported Mexican Rebel Unguarded on Trip to Line," *Arizona Daily Star*, March 2, 1923.
16 United States Congress, Communist and Anarchist Deportation Cases, April 21–24, 1920, 120–21.
17 Frank M. Sturgis to Warden, US Penitentiary, Leavenworth, Kansas, October 12, 1921, Enrique Flores Magon (12839) Prisoner File, NARA St. Louis Division.
18 "Deported Mexican Rebel Unguarded on Trip to Line."
19 "300 Listen to Radical Talk from Magon," *El Paso Herald*, March 6, 1923.
20 "300 Listen to Radical Talk from Magon."
21 Olcott, *Revolutionary Women*, 3.
22 Nicolás T. Bernal notes that brother Jesús Flores Magón was not happy with the fact that Enrique had given the Arteaga-Beleno children he adopted the Flores Magón name upon returning to Mexico in 1923. Bernal goes on to say that they were impostors who pretended to be Flores Magóns and benefited socially and politically because of this. See Bernal, *Memorias*, 129–30. In 1946 Enrique also wrote an article in *El Nacional* to dispel notions of impostors using his name to commit fraud: "I have not had more than six kids, with the right to use my last name: Esperanza and Santiago who are now dead, the now doctor Pedro Flores Magón; la señorita Estela Flores Magón; the representative of foreign business José Flores Magón and the Navy Teniente Coronel, Engineer and Mechanic Enrique Flores Magón Jr. I have various grandchildren and great grandchildren, of which only four have my last name; a boy Pedro, that is Eduardo and three from José that are Santiago, Martha, and Maria Eugenia. OTHER PEOPLE WHO HAVE THE AUDACITY TO USE THE FLORES MAGON LAST NAME ARE SIMPLY AND SINCERELY IMPOSTORS THAT HAVE SUPPLANTED MY AUTHORITY." Flores Magón, "Los hongos," *El Nacional*, June 24, 1946. Even here Enrique lied, refusing to name Margarita, Práxedis, and Demófilo Carmona de Flores Magón as his legitimate children. What all of this points to is the cultural patrimony of the Flores Magón name and the capital it embodied in postrevolutionary Mexico.
23 Streeby, *Radical Sensations*, 254.
24 Campt, *Image Matters*, 48, 195.
25 "Several Hurt as Fascisti Battle Red-Black Party," *El Paso Herald*, March 22, 1923. Enrique again discussed a potential presidential run and the need to raise one hundred thousand pesos in order to do so in a letter to Enrique Jr. dated April 17, 1939. AEFM, Box 1, Folder 2.
26 "Man Ordered Out of Los Angeles, Held by Mexican Authorities," *St. Louis Post Dispatch*, June 14, 1923.
27 Enrique Flores Magón, "La tranvia," *El Nacional*, May 21, 1946.

28 Enrique Flores Magón, "Orador obligado," *El Nacional*, March 20, 1946.
29 Enrique Flores Magón, "¿Amargados?," *El Nacional*, August 14, 1946.

PART I. CONCLUSION

1 Duffy Turner, *Ricardo Flores Magón*, 361.
2 Antonio Diaz Soto y Gama, "Ricardo y Enrique Flores Magón," November 10, 1954, unidentified newspaper clipping, Terazzas Papers, University of California Berkeley, M-B 18, part I.
3 Campt, *Image Matters*, 203.
4 Enrique Flores Magón, "¿Fatalismo?," *El Nacional*, October 12, 1946.
5 Sifuentes-Jáuregui, *The Avowal of Difference*, 3.

PART II. THE HOMOEROTICS OF ABJECTION

1 Letter from the office of Dwight D. Eisenhower to Mr. Frank L. Noakes, Chairman, United States Mexico Trade Committee, August 9, 1956, EIS, GF 126-I-1, Follansbee.
2 Galarza, *Strangers in Our Fields*, 8.
3 Galarza, 10.
4 Rosas, *Abrazando el Espíritu*.
5 Loza, *Defiant Braceros*, 15.
6 See Cohen, *Braceros*, where the inset of images is used in a descriptive and documentary manner as a kind of material evidence. See also Street, *Everyone Had Cameras*, 373.
7 Galarza Papers, Stanford University Special Collections (GAL).
8 Bloch, "Considering the Photography of Leonard Nadel," 80.
9 Luciano and Chen, "Has the Queer Ever Been Human?," 186.
10 Barojeck, "The State of Visual Matters," 156.
11 *Los Angeles Herald Examiner*, July 2, 1973, 8.
12 Street, *Everyone Had Cameras*, 373.
13 *Los Angeles Herald Examiner*, July 2, 1973, 13, 16.
14 Street, *Everyone Had Cameras*, 372.
15 Excerpt from a talk given by Leonard Nadel to fellow photographers describing his bracero photographic documentation. "The New Role for the Photographer," Folder 13, Series III, NAD.
16 Street, *Everyone Had Cameras*, 373.
17 *Los Angeles Herald Examiner*, July 2, 1973, 9.
18 Letter to Senora Anzorena, Mexico D.F., November 3, 1956, Folder 1, Correspondence, NAD.
19 *Los Angeles Herald Examiner*, July 2, 1973, 11. Although this statement was a direct commentary about the Mexican American children he photographed in the Los Angeles Aliso Housing Project for the Los Angeles County Housing Authority, the ethos transfers to the entire body of Nadel's work, especially when he worked with subjects of Mexican origin.

20 Barojeck, "The State in Visual Matters," 157.
21 Macías-González, "The Transnational Homophile Movement," 522.
22 Macías-González, 525.
23 Sontag, *On Photography*, 5, 4.
24 Holland, *The Erotic Life of Racism*, 46, 42.
25 McKee Irwin, *Mexican Masculinities*, 185.
26 Freeman, *Time Binds*, 53.
27 Berlant, *The Queen of America Goes to Washington City*, 43.

CHAPTER 9. MAKING BRACEROS OUT OF PLACE AND OUTSIDE OF TIME

1 "El espejismo del dolar," *El Mañana*, August 26, 1949.
2 "La liberacion de bracerismo," *Todo*, June 30, 1955.
3 "Ike Says Farm Bill in Present Shape of Little Aid to Farmer," *Salinas Californian*, April 4, 1956.
4 "Diary, March 6, 1956," 2, EIS, Papers as President of the United States, 1953–1961 (Ann Whitman File), Ann Whitman Diary Series, Box 8.
5 "Farm Economists to Hold Asilomar Session in August," *Salinas Californian*, July 5, 1956.
6 Cohen, *Braceros*, 90.
7 Dwight David Eisenhower, "Republican National Convention Acceptance Speech," August 23, 1956, http://millercenter.org/president/speeches/detail/3359.
8 Moreton, *To Serve God and Walmart*, 29.
9 Eisenhower, "Republican National Convention Acceptance Speech."
10 Cockrill, "Conducted Tour of California Agriculture," 704.
11 "Farm Economists to Hold Asilomar Session."
12 "Rosary Services for Miguel Franco Will Be Tonight," *Salinas Californian*, July 5, 1956.
13 Just twelve years before Franco's death, Private Feliz Z. Longoria Jr., despite being a World War II veteran and the recipient of the Purple Heart, was denied a wake and funerary services by the Rice Funeral Home in Three Rivers, Texas, because the establishment did not serve Mexicans.
14 "Farm Worker Electrocuted," *Salinas Californian*, July 10, 1956.
15 NIEHS Working Group, "Assessment of Health Effects from Exposure to Power-Line Frequency Electric and Magnetic Fields," June 1988, 168.
16 "When higher wages are paid for specialized tasks such as the operation of vehicles or machinery, the work is to be paid the wages assigned to such tasks," "Migrant Labor Agreement of 1951," Article 4.
17 "Crop Service Predicts Smaller Beet Harvest," *Salinas Californian*, July 12, 1956.
18 Butler, *The Precarious Life*, xi.
19 Marx, *Capital*.
20 "Your Haying Costs Cut," Doring Implement Ppt. Ltd. advertisement, Victoria, Australia, 1956.
21 Robinson, "The Great Recession of 2008 and the Continuing Crisis," 193.
22 "La Sección en Español," *Salinas Californian*, July 12, 1956.

CHAPTER 10. THE SALINAS VALLEY AND HIDDEN AFFECTIVE HISTORIES

1. NAD, 0138.20.11–0138.20.40.
2. Griffin and White, "Lettuce Industry of Salinas California," 82–83.
3. Cohen, *Braceros*, 35.
4. Kiesling, "Homosocial Desire in Men's Talk," 4.
5. Luciano and Chen, "Has the Queer Ever Been Human?," 184.
6. Caption 14, Folder 16, Part III, NAD.
7. Marez, "Brown," 117.
8. Caption 21, Folder 16, NAD.
9. Caption 1, Folder 16, NAD.
10. Cohen, *Braceros*, 128.
11. Folder 5, Newspaper Clippings and Articles, *Jubilee Magazine: A Magazine of the Church and Her People*, April 1957, NAD.
12. Herod, *Scale*, 60.
13. Anderson and Levy, *Fields of Bondage*, 26–27.
14. Anderson and Levy, 78.
15. Peck, "Political Economies of Scale," 340.
16. Ricoeur, *Time and Narrative*, vol. 1, 52.
17. Freeman, *Time Binds*, 19–20.
18. Galarza, *Strangers in Our Fields*, 9.
19. Van's Super Market advertisement, *Santa Cruz Sentinel*, May 23, 1956.
20. Foucault, *Discipline and Punishment*, 201.
21. Foucault, 201.
22. Marez, *Farmworker Futurism*, 21.
23. Berlant, *Cruel Optimism*, 138.
24. Butler, *Gender Trouble*, 270–71.
25. Diamond, "Re: *Blau, Butler, Beckett*," 37.
26. Caption 12, Folder 16, NAD.

CHAPTER 11. HIP FORWARD INTO DOMESTIC LABOR AND OTHER INTIMACIES

1. Gopinath, *Impossible Desires*, 9.
2. Cohen, Flores, Loza, and Rosas all document these intimacies extensively in their work.
3. See Flores, *Grounds for Dreaming*.
4. "Grace Arceneaux: Mexican American Farmworker and Community Organizer, 1920–1977," UCSC, 117.
5. Cohen, *Braceros*, 118.
6. Bill Kennedy, "'Not One National in Aromas'; Aromas Board Won't Fight Camp," *Register Pajaronian*, May 4, 1956.
7. Macías-González and Rubenstein, *Masculinity and Sexuality*, 5.
8. Luciano and Chen, "Has the Queer Ever Been Human?," 194.
9. "Labor Camp Bedding Supplies," *Salinas Californian*, July 28, 1956.

10   "Grace Arceneaux," 111.
11   See Cohen, *Braceros*, in particular, where the inset of images is used in a descriptive and documentary manner as a kind of material evidence.
12   Caption 20, Folder 16, NAD.
13   Gopinath, *Impossible Desires*, 11.
14   Overmyer-Velázquez, "Portraits of a Lady," 74.
15   Berlant, *Cruel Optimism*, 2.
16   Macías-González, "The Transnational Homophile Movement," 519.
17   De la Mora analyzed acceptable forms of homosociality and homoeroticism in films with Pedro Infante and Cantinflas in his book *Cinemachismo*. Braceros were in direct contact with these narratives and were influenced by them. Cantinflas appeared in person at the State cinema in Watsonville. The State also screened Spanish-language films on the weekends to segregated audiences. See 2004.0138.29.43, NAD.
18   Vider, "Oh, Hell," 881.
19   Macías-González, "The Transnational Homophile Movement," 521.
20   De la Mora, *Cinemachismo*, 17.
21   Galarza, *Strangers in Our Fields*, 1, 51.
22   I take my cue here on impossibility and desire from Gopinath's *Impossible Desires*, 54.
23   Gopinath, 51.
24   Galarza, *Strangers in Our Fields*, 1.
25   Bersani, "Psychoanalysis and the Aesthetic Subject," 164.
26   Binson and Woods, "A Theoretical Approach to Bathhouse Environments," 28.
27   González-Macías and Rubenstein, *Masculinity and Sexuality*, 35.
28   See #11, 8, and 9, Folder 16, NAD. As Nadel's caption reads, "In close-up shots, the men line up to have their heads and genitals sprayed with DDT. The operator wears a mask but the men are totally enveloped by clouds of pesticide." This caption and the photographs also raise questions about disability, for DDT has long been linked to birth defects, and a study about the children of braceros with birth defects as a result of DDT fumigation should be undertaken.
29   *Los Angeles Herald Examiner*, July 2, 1973, 12.
30   Cohen, *Braceros*, 74.
31   Macías-González, "The Transnational Homophile Movement," 529.
32   Freeman, *Time Binds*, 70, 74.

CHAPTER 12. QUEER PRECARIOUS LIVES

1   Frances Froelicher, "City Law Is Cited as a Model," *Salinas Californian*, 1956.
2   Caption 22, Folder 16, NAD.
3   Ignacio Magallanes Hernández, interview by Laureano Martínez, May 26, 2003, Item #200, Bracero History Archive, http://braceroarchive.org/items/show/200.
4   Agustín Bautista, interview by Mario Sifuentez, May 20, 2006, Item #339, Bracero History Archive, http://braceroarchive.org/items/show/339.

5 "Labor Camp Committee Report Suggests County Ordinance," *Salinas Californian,* April 10, 1956.
6 California code evidence shows that strict sanitation regulations in the fields began in the 1970s.
7 "Labor Camp Committee Report."
8 Tirso Yepes, interview by Angelica Rivera, September 1, 2005, Item #183, Bracero History Archive, http://braceroarchive.org/items/show/183.
9 "Labor Camp Committee Report."
10 "Watsonville," *Salinas Californian,* April 10, 1956.
11 Bill Kennedy, "'Not One National in Aromas'; Aromas Board Won't Fight Camp," *Register Pajaronian,* May 4, 1956.
12 Johnson, *Just Queer Folks,* 117.
13 Carlos Villagomes Fuentes, interview by Ivonne Cachu, May 13, 2006, Item #276, Bracero History Archive, http://braceroarchive.org/items/show/276.
14 Shah, *Stranger Intimacy,* 93.
15 Freedman, "'Uncontrolled Desires,'" 211.
16 "Planners Set Policy on Camps," *Salinas Californian,* 1956.
17 Ordinance no. 862, N.C.S.: An Ordinance Regulating Labor Camps in Salinas, April 15, 1956, Salinas City Recorder's Office, 3.
18 Ordinance no. 862.
19 Kennedy, "'Not One National in Aromas.'"
20 "Citizens Protest: Labor Camp Permits Denied," *Salinas Californian,* March 15, 1956.
21 Hong and Ferguson, *Strange Affinities,* xi.
22 "Planners Set Policy on Camps."
23 "Strawberry Plans Told at Exchange," *Salinas Californian,* April 2, 1956.
24 "Planners Set Policy on Camps."
25 "Grace Arceneaux: Mexican American Farmworker and Community Organizer, 1920–1977," UCSC Regional Oral History Project, 110–11.
26 Bautista, interview. Morgan Hill is in Santa Clara County just north of the Salinas Valley. They are considered part of the same Central Coast–South Bay region.
27 "Grace Arceneaux," 110–11.
28 "Grace Arceneaux," 111–12.
29 Bautista, interview.
30 "Grace Arceneaux," 112.
31 Clemente Velázquez Lucio, interview by Monica Pelayo, Item #392, Bracero History Archive, http://braceroarchive.org/items/show/392.
32 Fishback, "Did Coal Miners 'Owe Their Souls to the Company Store?'"; Perales, *Smeltertown,* 68–69.
33 Perales, *Smeltertown,* 69.
34 Lewis, *The Children of Sanchez,* xxix, 191–93.
35 McKee Irwin, *Mexican Masculinities,* xii.
36 "Citizens Protest."

37 Shah also discusses the ways that drunkenness was often used in court proceedings to dramatize alcohol consumption in its capacity to blur a man's ability to check his desire. See Shah, *Stranger Intimacy*, 70.
38 Lucio, interview.
39 Decena, *Tacit Subjects*, 211.
40 Foucault, *The Care of the Self*, 41.
41 Decena, *Tacit Subjects*, 211.
42 McFadden, "The New Science of Pleasure," 2, 28.
43 Cohen, *Braceros*, 35–36.
44 Captions, page 3, Folder 14, NAD.
45 Derby, "Gringo Chickens with Worms," 455.
46 "Labor Camp Plan Will Be Aired," *Register Pajaronian*, May 23, 1956.
47 "Labor Camp Plan Will Be Aired." Arthur Mork, from Nebraska, had settled in the area to farm. See the 1940 US Census schedule.
48 Bracero Pedro del Real Pérez recalled that the labor camp in Santa María, California, required them to provide and cook their own food. Pedro del Real Pérez, interview by Mireya Loza, Item #152, Bracero History Archive, http://braceroarchive.org/items/show/152.
49 "Planners Set Policy on Camps."
50 The Salinas City Police Yearbook for 1954 listed fifty-one officers and in 1951 listed thirty.
51 Ordinance no. 862.
52 Ordinance no. 862.
53 In a report by Monterey County, the findings for Alisal were staggering in terms of economic disparity: "Census 2000 shows that per capita income in 93905 was just $9,134, representing only 63% of the average personal earnings for Salinas, only 45% of Monterey. Consequently, a much larger proportion of residents are living below the poverty level in Alisal (one of every four residents), more than in other parts of this community (roughly one in five for Salinas, and one in eight for Monterey County as a whole)." Alisal is also home to the county's largest population of undocumented immigrants whose poverty rate is 20 percent higher than the rest of the community. "Building Healthy Communities East Salinas California. Logic Models and Plan Narrative," www.cfmco.org/files/cfmc/Media_Publications/BHC%20Narrative%20-%20March%2018%20-%20FINAL%20DRAFT%20_6_.pdf, 4.
54 "Planners Set Policy on Camps."
55 Salinas Public Library, www.salinaspubliclibrary.org/learn-explore/local-history/city-salinas-history/accordion/1930-1939, 1.
56 Neuburger, *Lettuce Wars*, 108.
57 "Grace Arceneaux," 116. The USDA Agricultural Marketing Service deemed Texas crops "poor" in the Rio Grande Valley and "near failure" in central Texas for July 1, 1956, because of drought, whereas California crops were deemed "good to excellent" during the same time frame. USDA Reg 8876 (2), EIS, White House Central Files, 1953–1961, Box 2, OF1, Folder July 1957.
58 "Planners Set Policy on Camps."

59 Salinas Public Library, www.salinaspubliclibrary.org/pdf/Salinas-History-1930-2009.pdf.
60 Monterey County Water Resources Agency, www.mcwra.co.monterey.ca.us/Agency_data/RecDitchFinal/Ch02_HistoricalConditions," 24.
61 "Building Permits," *Salinas Californian*, April 2, 1956.
62 Neuburger, *Lettuce Wars*, 108–9.

CHAPTER 13. WANTING TO BE LOOKED AT

1 "Planners Set Policy on Camps," *Salinas Californian*, April 15, 1956.
2 Cohen, *Braceros*, 34.
3 Macías-González, "The Transnational Homophile Movement," 528.
4 Caption 23, Folder 16, NAD.
5 Foucault, *Technologies of the Self*, 18. 24.
6 Derrida, "The Parergon," 9.
7 González-Day, "Analytical Photography," 23–30.
8 "Grace Arceneaux: Mexican American Farmworker and Community Organizer, 1920–1977," UCSC, 117.
9 "Schick Powershave Razor Commercial (1950s)," https://www.youtube.com/watch?v=uSsTIN_bGUs.
10 Derrida, "The Parergon," 13.
11 "Schick Powershave Razor Commercial (1950s)," https://www.youtube.com/watch?v=uSsTIN_bGUs.
12 Curtis, "Commodities and Sexual Subjectivities," 95, 98, 101, 102.
13 Bromberger, "Hair," 380.
14 Ramírez, *The Woman in the Zoot Suit*.
15 Jimena Paz Obregón-Iturra documents that in ethnic border regions of Mexico, women of Spanish origin make it a point not to shave their legs to disassociate themselves from their naturally smooth-skinned indigenous counterparts. See "Il s'en faut d'un poil," 129, 164.
16 Bromberger, "Hair," 381.
17 Molina, *Fit to Be Citizens?*, 119.
18 Rexall Drugs advertisement, *Santa Cruz Sentinel*, June 13, 1956.
19 "Men Using More Perfumed Products Than Ladies," *San Bernardino County Sun*, September 29, 1956.
20 "The Berrys," *Long Beach Independent*, August 2, 1956.
21 Blair and Rosenberg, *Trauma and Documentary Photography of the FSA*, 21, 23.
22 The Fox catered to an English-speaking audience, and José Enrique Fredrich's Pajaro Street Plaza Theater catered to Spanish speakers. For more on the Plaza Theater, see Flores, *Grounds for Dreaming*, 98.
23 "Grace Arceneaux: Mexican American Farmworker and Community Organizer, 1920–1977," UCSC, 106.
24 These photos were taken in Watsonville because the same Rancho Grande business was advertised in the *Salinas Californian* on March 23, 1956.

25 Stewart and Floyd, "Visualizing Leisure," 450.
26 In the captions, Nadel noted that the Watsonville camp housed over a thousand men in "inadequate, over-crowded facilities." The Gondo camp was one of the largest in the region. Caption 25, Folder 16, NAD. Flores, *Grounds for Dreaming*; Loza, *Defiant Braceros*.
27 Caption 23, Folder 16, NAD.

CHAPTER 14. PASSIONATE VIOLENCE AND THEFTS

1 "Monterey Laborers Sent to Prison," *Salinas Californian*, July 13, 1956.
2 "Burglars Get Clothing at Labor Camp," *Salinas Californian*, July 14, 1956.
3 "Sección en Español," *Salinas Californian*, July 14, 1956.
4 *Culto* describes the middle-class knowledge of behaving properly with or without being middle class. There is a performative quality to it. *Ser cultuo* or to be *culto*, in this context, means that Mexican Americans (actual members of the middle class or those who performed middle-class social mores) were separating themselves from the violent, undereducated, juvenile members of their community in Salinas.
5 "Two Men Are Hurt in a Fight," *Salinas Californian*, July 14, 1956.
6 Johnson, *Just Queer Folks*, 101, 102.
7 "Farm Laborer Stabbed to Death," *Salinas Californian*, July 19, 1956.
8 Mirandé, *Hombres y Machos*, 70.
9 Wells, *The Secret Wound*, 75.
10 Here I draw upon La Fountain-Stokes's notion of Latino/a antigay shame to address the crowd's stunned affect regarding García's public violence. See "Gay Shame, Latina and Latino-Style," 70–71.
11 "Watsonville," *Salinas Californian*, July 21, 1956.
12 "Sachi Morishima's Saga Continues," *Santa Maria Times*, October 28, 2012, http://santamariatimes.com/lifestyles/columnist/shirley_contreras/kaichi_morishima-s-saga-continues/article_092dea3c-20a3-11e2-8acc-001a4bcf887a.html, retrieved April 3, 2014.
13 "Hiroshi Shikuma: Strawberry Growing in the Pajaro Valley," UCSC, 13, 36, 40.
14 Nicole M. Guidotti-Hernández, "Oral History of Richard R. Guidotti," April 14, 2014.
15 "Hiroshi Shikuma," 13.
16 Flores, *Grounds for Dreaming*, 102.
17 McDowell, "The Economic Impact of Technology on Strawberries," 1787.
18 Wright, "Agricultural Crop Report 1956," 3.
19 McDowell, "The Economic Impact of Technology on Strawberries," 1756.
20 "Hiroshi Shikuma," 39.
21 "National Held after Argument in Labor Camp," *Salinas Californian*, July 24, 1956.
22 For more on the history of these confrontations, see Flores, *Grounds for Dreaming*.

PART II. CONCLUSION

1 Deborah Paredez, "*Day in, Day out*: Lena Horne's Diva Citizenship," unpublished manuscript.
2 "Bracero Movie Script," June 1, 1994, Folder 8, Series III, NAD.
3 "Leonard Nadel Biography," Evelyn De Wolfe Nadel, Folder 9, Series III, NAD.

CONCLUSION

1 See Flores, *Grounds for Dreaming*, and Castro, "The Lettuce Monster," for more on this point.
2 Lou Cannon, "Chavez's Lettuce Walkout Is Wilting," *Washington Post*, April 29, 1979.
3 Chávez-García, *Migrant Longing*, 193.

Bibliography

Abad de Santillan, Diego. *Ricardo Flores Magón: El apostol de la revolución social Mexicana*. Mexico City: Centro de Estudios Históricos del Movimiento Obrero Mexicano, 1978.

Akers Chacón, Justin. *Radicals in the Barrio: Magonistas, Socialists, Wobblies and Communists in the Mexican American Working Class*. Chicago: Haymarket, 2018.

Albro, Ward. *To Die on Your Feet: The Life, Times and Writings of Práxedis Guerrero*. Fort Worth: Texas Christian University Press, 1996.

Anderson, Henry, and Jacques E. Levy. *Fields of Bondage: The Mexican Contract Labor System in Industrialized Agriculture* (1963).

Auerbach, Jonathan. "McKinley at Home: How Early American Cinema Made News." *American Quarterly* 51, no. 4 (December 1999).

Barojeck, Jennifer. "The State in Visual Matters." *Theory, Culture and Society* 27, nos. 7–8 (2010).

Berlant, Lauren. *Cruel Optimism*. Durham, NC: Duke University Press, 2011.

Berlant, Lauren. *The Queen of America Goes to Washington City: Essays on Sex and Citizenship* (Durham, NC: Duke University Press, 1997).

Bernal, Nicolás T. *Memorias de Nicolás T. Bernal*. Mexico City: Centro de Estudios Históricos del Movimiento Obrero Mexicano, 1982.

Bersani, Leo. "Psychoanalysis and the Aesthetic Subject." *Critical Inquiry* 32, no. 2 (Winter 2006).

Binson, Diane, and William P. Woods. "A Theoretical Approach to Bathhouse Environments." *Journal of Homosexuality* 44 (2003): 3–4.

Blair, Sara, and Eric Rosenberg. *Trauma and Documentary Photography of the FSA*. Berkeley: University of California Press, 2013.

Bloch, Stefano. "Considering the Photography of Leonard Nadel." *Yearbook of the Association of Pacific Coast Geographers* 74 (2012): 76–95.

Bollinger Pouwels, Joel. *Political Journalism by Mexican Women during the Age of Revolution, 1876–1940*. Lewiston, NY: Edwin Mellen, 2006.

Bromberger, Christian. "Hair: From the West to the Middle East through the Mediterranean." *Journal of American Folklore* 121 (2008).

Butler, Judith. *Gender Trouble: Feminism and the Subversion of Identity*. New York: Routledge, 1999.

Butler, Judith. *The Precarious Life*. New York: Verso, 2004.

Camic, Paul M. "From Trashed to Treasured: A Grounded Theory Analysis of the Found Object." *Psychology of Aesthetics, Creativity, and the Arts* 4, no. 2 (2010).

Campt, Tina. *Image Matters: Archive, Photography, and the African Diaspora in Europe*. Durham, NC: Duke University Press, 2012.

Castro, Christine. "'The Lettuce Monster': A History of State Violence, Carceral Geography, and Industrial Agriculture in the Salinas Valley." PhD Diss., University of Texas at Austin, 2019.

Chávez-García, Miroslava. *Migrant Longing: Letter Writing across the U.S.-Mexico Borderlands*. Chapel Hill: University of North Carolina Press, 2018.

Cockcroft, James. *Intellectual Precursors of the Mexican Revolution, 1900–1913*. Austin: University of Texas Press, 1968.

Cockrill, Miss Elizabeth. "Conducted Tour of California Agriculture August 24 to 26, 1956." *American Journal of Agricultural Economics* 38, no. 2 (1956).

Cohen, Deborah. *Braceros: Migrant Citizens and Transnational Subjects in the Postwar United States and Mexico*. Chapel Hill: University of North Carolina Press, 2011.

Cowan, Benjamin. "How *Machismo* Got Its Spurs—in English: Social Science, Cold War Imperialism, and the Ethnicization of Hypermasculinity." *Latin American Research Review* 52, no. 4 (2017): 601–22.

Cumberland, Charles C. "Precursors of the Mexican Revolution of 1910." *Hispanic American Historical Review* 22, no. 2 (May 1942): 344–56.

Curtis, Debra. "Commodities and Sexual Subjectivities: A Look at Capitalism and Its Desires." *Cultural Anthropology* 19, no. 1 (February 2014).

De la Mora, Sergio. *Cinemachismo: Masculinities and Sexuality in Mexican Film*. Austin: University of Texas Press, 2006.

Decena, Carlos. *Tacit Subjects: Belonging and Same Sex Desire among Dominican Immigrant Men*. Durham, NC: Duke University Press, 2011.

Derby, Lauren. "Gringo Chickens with Worms: Food and Nationalism in the Dominican Republic." In *Close Encounters of Empire: Writing the Cultural History of U.S.-Latin American Relations*, edited by Gilbert M. Joseph, Catherine C. LeGrand, and Ricardo D. Salvatore. Durham, NC: Duke University Press, 1998.

Derrida, Jacques. "The Parergon." *October* 9 (Summer 1979).

Deveraux Ramírez, Cristina. *Occupying Our Space: The Mestiza Rhetorics of Mexican Women Journalists and Activists, 1875–1942*. Tucson: University of Arizona Press, 2015.

Diamond, Elin. "Re: *Blau, Butler, Beckett*, and the Politics of Seeming." *TDR* 44, no. 4 (2000).

Díaz-Sánchez, Micaela, and Alexandro Hernández. "The Son Jarocho as Afro-Mexican Resistance Music." *Journal of Pan African Studies* 6, no. 1 (July 2013).

Duffy Turner, Ethyl. *One-Way Ticket*. New York: Harrison Smith and Robert Haas, 1934.

Duffy Turner, Ethyl. *Ricardo Flores Magón y el Partido Liberal Mexicano*. México City: Comisión Nacional Editorial del C.E.N., 1984.

Duffy Turner, Ethyl. "Writers and Revolutionists." Interview by Ruth Teiser. Oral history transcript and related material, 1966–1967. Berkeley: Bancroft Library, Regional Oral History Office, 1966.

Eng, David L., and David Kazanjian. *Loss: The Politics of Mourning*. Berkeley: University of California Press, 2003.

Estrada, William David. *The Los Angeles Plaza: Sacred and Contested Space*. Austin: University of Texas Press, 2008.

Fernández Bravo, Vicente. *El ideario de la Revolucion Mexicana*. Mexico City: Talleres de B. Costa-Amic, 1973.

Fishback, Price. "Did Coal Miners 'Owe Their Souls to the Company Store?' Theory and Evidence from the Early 1900s." *Journal of Economic History* 46, no. 4 (December 1986): 1011–29.

Flores, Lori. *Grounds for Dreaming: Mexican Americans, Mexican Immigrants, and the California Farmworker Movement*. New Haven, CT: Yale University Press, 2016.

Flores Magón, Enrique. "El fracaso de Abraham Lincoln." *Todo*, September 3, 1953.

Flores Magón, Enrique. "Notas intimas de la vida de un precursor." *Todo*, November 19, 1953.

Foucault, Michel. *Discipline and Punishment: The Birth of the Prison*. New York: Vintage, 1977.

Foucault, Michel. *The History of Sexuality*. Vol. 3, *The Care of the Self*. New York: Vintage, 1988.

Foucault, Michel. *Technologies of the Self: A Seminar with Michel Foucault*. Amherst: University of Massachusetts Press, 1988.

Freedman, Estelle B. "'Uncontrolled Desires': The Response to the Sexual Psychopath, 1920–1960." In *Passion and Power: Sexuality in History*, edited by Kathy Peiss and Christina Simmons. Philadelphia: Temple University Press, 1989.

Freeman, Elizabeth. *Time Binds: Queer Temporalities, Queer Histories*. Durham, NC: Duke University Press, 2010.

Gabara, Esther. *Errant Modernism: The Ethos of Photography in Mexico and Brazil*. Durham, NC: Duke University Press.

Galarza, Ernesto. *Strangers in Our Fields*. Washington, DC: Joint United States–Mexico Trade Union Committee, 1956.

García, Alma M., ed. *Chicana Feminist Thought: The Basic Historical Writings*. New York: Routledge, 1992.

García, Mario. *Desert Immigrants: The Mexicans of El Paso, 1880–1920*. New Haven, CT: Yale University Press, 1982.

Gauss, Susan. "Working-Class Masculinity and the Rationalized Sex Gender and Industrial Modernization in the Textile Industry in Post-revolutionary Puebla." In *Sex in Revolution: Gender, Politics, and Power in Modern Mexico*, edited by Jocelyn Olcott, Mary Kay Vaughan, and Gabriela Cano. Durham, NC: Duke University Press, 2006.

Gómez Gutiérrez, Mariano. *La vida que yo vivi*. Mexico City: Luz y Vida, 1954.

Gómez-Quiñones, Juan. *Sembradores Ricardo Flores Magon y el Partido Liberal Mexicano: A Eulogy and Critique*. Los Angeles: Aztlán, 1973.

Gómez-Quiñones, Juan. "Sin frontera, sin cuartel. Los Anarcocomunistas del PLM, 1900–1930." *Tzintzun: Revista de Estudios Históricos* 196 (May 2008).

Gonzales, Michael J. *The Mexican Revolution: 1910–1940*. Albuquerque: University of New Mexico Press, 2002.

González, Gabriela. *Redeeming la Raza: Transborder Modernity, Race, Respectability, and Rights*. London: Oxford University Press, 2018.

Gonzalez, Gilbert G. *Guest Workers or Colonized Labor? Mexican Labor Migration to the United States*. Boulder, CO: Paradigm, 2006.

González, Ray. *Muy Macho: Latino Men Confront Their Manhood*. New York: Anchor, 1996.

González-Day, Ken. "Analytical Photography: Portraiture, from the Index to the Epidermis." *Leonardo* 35, no. 1 (2002): 23–30.

González Ramírez, Manuel. *Epistolario y textos de Ricardo Flores Magón*. Mexico City: Fonda de Cultural Económica, 1964.

Gopinath, Gayatri. *Impossible Desires: Queer Diasporas and South Asian Public Cultures*. Durham, NC: Duke University Press, 2005.

Griffin, Paul, and C. Langdon White. "Lettuce Industry of Salinas California." *Scientific Monthly* 81, no. 2 (August 1955).

Guerin-González, Camille. *Mexican Workers and the American Dream: Immigration, Repatriation, and California Farm Labor, 1900–1939*. New Brunswick, NJ: Rutgers University Press, 1994.

Guha, Ranajit. "The Prose of Counterinsurgency." In *Selected Subaltern Studies*, edited by Ranajit Guha and Gayatri Chakravorty Spivak, 45–86. London: Oxford University Press, 1988.

Gutmann, Matthew C. *Changing Men and Masculinities in Latin America*. Durham, NC: Duke University Press, 2003.

Gutmann, Matthew C. *The Meanings of Macho: Being a Man in Mexico City*. Berkeley: University of California Press, 2006.

Gutmann, Matthew C. "Trafficking in Men: The Anthropology of Masculinity." *Annual Review of Anthropology* 26 (1997): 385–409.

Hart, John Mason. *Anarchism and the Mexican Working Class, 1806–1931*. Austin: University of Texas Press, 1987.

Hart, John Mason. *Revolutionary Mexico: The Coming and Process of the Mexican Revolution*. Berkeley: University of California Press, 1997.

Heatherton, Christina. "The Color Line and Class Struggle: The Mexican Revolution and Convergences of Radical Internationalism, 1910–1946." PhD diss., University of Southern California, 2012.

Heatherton, Christina. "University of Radicalism: Ricardo Flores Magón and Leavenworth Penitentiary." *American Quarterly* 66, no. 3 (September 2014).

Hernández, Sonia. "Chicanas in the US-Mexican Borderlands: Transborder Conversations of Feminism and Anarchism, 1905–1938." In *A Promising Problem: The New Chicana/o History*, edited by Carlos Blanton. Austin: University of Texas Press, 2016.

Herod, Andrew. *Scale*. London: Routledge, 2010.

Hirsch, Jennifer S. *A Courtship after Marriage: Sexuality and Love in Mexican Transnational Families*. Berkeley: University of California Press, 2003.

Holland, Sharon Patricia. *The Erotic Life of Racism*. Durham, NC: Duke University Press, 2016.

Hong, Grace Kyungwon, and Roderick A. Ferguson, eds. *Strange Affinities: The Gender and Sexual Politics of Comparative Racialization*. Durham, NC: Duke University Press, 2000.

Howard, June. "What Is Sentimentality?" *American Literary History* 11, no. 1 (Spring 1999).

Hudgins, Nicole. "A Historical Approach to Family Photography: Class and Individuality in Manchester and Lille, 1850–1914." *Journal of Social History* 43, no. 3 (Spring 2010).

Hurewitz, Daniel. *Bohemian Los Angeles and the Making of Modern Politics*. Berkeley: University of California Press, 2007.

Hurtado, Aída, and Mrinal Sinha. *Beyond Machismo: Intersectional Latino Masculinities*. Austin: University of Texas Press, 2016.

Jacobson, Matthew Frye. *Whiteness of a Different Color: European Immigrants and the Alchemy of Race*. Cambridge, MA: Harvard University Press, 1998.

Jameson, Fredric. "Third-World Literature in the Era of Multinational Capitalism." *Social Text* 15 (Autumn 1986): 65–88.

Johnson, Colin R. *Just Queer Folks: Gender and Sexuality in Rural America*. Philadelphia: Temple University Press, 2013.

Joseph, Gilbert M. *Revolution from Without: Yucatan, Mexico, and the United States, 1880–1924*. Durham, NC: Duke University Press, 1997.

Joseph, Gilbert M., and Jürgen Buchenau. *Mexico's Once and Future Revolution: Social Upheaval and the Challenge of Rule since the Late Nineteenth Century*. Durham, NC: Duke University Press, 2013.

Kanellos, Nicolas. "Spanish Language Periodicals in the Early Twentieth Century United States." In *Protest on the Page: Essays on Print and the Culture of Dissent since 1865*, edited by James L. Baughman, Jennifer Ratner-Rosenhagen, and James P. Danky. Madison: University of Wisconsin Press, 2015.

Kaplan, Samuel. *Combatimos la tirania: Un pionoero revolucionario Mexicano cuenta su historia*. Mexico City: Talleres Gráficos de la Nación, 1958.

Kaplan, Samuel. *Peleamos contra la injusticia: Enrique Flores Magón, precursor de la Revolución Mexicana, cuenta su historia a Samuel Kaplan*. Mexico City: Libro Mex Editores, 1960.

Kelley, William G. "Rhetoric as Seduction." *Philosophy & Rhetoric* 6, no. 2 (Spring 1973).

Kiesling, Scott. "Homosocial Desire in Men's Talk: Balancing and Recreating Cultural Discourses of Masculinity," *Language and Society* 34, no. 5 (November 2005).

Knight, Alan. *The Mexican Revolution*. Vol. 1, *Porfirians, Liberals, and Peasants*. Lincoln: University of Nebraska Press, 1990.

Knight, Alan. *The Mexican Revolution: A Very Short Introduction*. London: Oxford University Press, 2016.

Kristeva, Julia. "Powers of Horror: Approaching Abjection." In *The Portable Kristeva*, edited by Kelly Oliver. New York: Columbia University Press, 1997.

La Fountain-Stokes, Lawrence. "Gay Shame, Latina and Latino-Style." In *Gay Latino Studies: A Critical Reader*, edited by Michael Hames-García and Ernesto Javier Martínez. Durham, NC: Duke University Press, 2011.

Lewis, Oscar. *The Children of Sanchez: An Autobiography of a Mexican Family*. New York: Vintage, 1971.

Lomas, Clara. "Transborder Discourse." In *Gender on the Borderlands: The Frontiers Reader*, edited by Antonia Castaneda, Patricia Hart, Karen Weathermon, and Susan H. Armitage. Lincoln: University of Nebraska Press, 2007.

Lomnitz, Claudio. *The Return of Comrade Ricardo Flores Magón*. New York: Zone, 2016.

Loza, Mireya. *Defiant Braceros: How Migrant Workers Fought for Racial, Sexual, and Political Freedom*. Chapel Hill: University of North Carolina Press, 2016.

Luciano, Dana, and Mel Chen. "Has the Queer Ever Been Human?" GLQ 21, nos. 2–3 (2015): 183–207.

Lydon, Jane. *Eye Contact: Photographing Indigenous Australians*. Durham, NC: Duke University Press, 2005.

Lytle Hernández, Kelly. *City of Inmates: Conquest, Rebellion, and the Rise of Human Caging in Los Angeles, 1771–1965*. Chapel Hill: University of North Carolina Press, 2017.

Macías-González, Víctor M. "The Transnational Homophile Movement and the Development of Domesticity in Mexico City's Homosexual Community, 1930–70." *Gender & History* 26, no. 3 (November 2014).

Macías-González, Víctor M., and Anne Rubenstein, eds. *Masculinity and Sexuality in Modern Mexico*. Albuquerque: University of New Mexico Press, 2012.

MacLachlan, Colin M. *Anarchism and the Mexican Revolution: The Political Trials of Ricardo Flores Magón in the United States*. Berkeley: University of California Press, 1991.

Maldonado Alvarado, Benjamin. *La utopia de Ricardo Flores Magón: Revolucion, anarquía y comunidad India*. Mexico City: Univerisdad Autonoma de Oaxaca, 1994.

Marez, Curtis. "Brown: The Politics of Working Class Chicano Style." *Social Text* 48 (1996).

Marez, Curtis. *Farmworker Futurism*. Minneapolis: University of Minnesota Press, 2014.

Marroquin Arredondo, Jaime, Adela Pineda Franco, and Magdalena Mieri. *Open Borders to a Revolution: Culture, Politics, and Migration*. Washington, DC: Smithsonian, 2013.

Martínez Nuñez, Eugenio. *Juan Sarabia apostol y martir de La Revolución Mexicana*. Mexico City: Biblioteca del Instituto de Estudios Historicos de La Revolución Mexicana, 1965.

Martínez Nuñez, Eugenio. *La vida heróica de Práxedis Guerrero*. Mexico City: Biblioteca del Instituto de Estudios Historicos de La Revolución Mexicana, 1960.

Marx, Karl. *Capital Volume I: A Critique of Political Economy*. London: Penguin, 1990.

McDowell, A. M. "The Economic Impact of Technology on Strawberries." *Journal of Farm Economics* 37 (1956).

McFadden, Daniel. "The New Science of Pleasure: Consumer Choice Behavior and the Measurement of Well Being." NBER Working Paper No. 18687, January 2013.

McKee Irwin, Robert. *Mexican Masculinities*. Minneapolis: University of Minnesota Press, 2003.

Mendieta Alatorre, María de los Ángeles. *La mujer en la Revolución Mexicana*. Mexico City: Talleres Gráficos de la Nación, 1963.

Mickenberg, Julia L., and Philip Nel. "Introduction." *Tales for Little Rebels: A Collection of Radical Children's Literature*. New York: New York University Press, 2008.

Mirandé, Alfredo. *Hombres y Machos: Masculinity and Latino Culture*. Boulder, CO: Westview, 1997.

Molina, Natalia. *Fit to Be Citizens? Public Health and Race in Los Angeles, 1879–1939*. Berkeley: University of California Press, 2006.

Molina, Natalia. *How Race Is Made in America: Immigration, Citizenship, and the Historical Power of Racial Scripts.* Berkeley: University of California Press, 2014.

Molina Enriquez, Andrés. *Los grandes problemas nacionales.* Mexico City: Imprenta de A. Carranza E Hijos, 1909.

Moreton, Bethany. *To Serve God and Walmart.* Cambridge, MA: Harvard University Press, 2009.

Mraz, John. *Photographing the Mexican Revolution: Commitments, Testimonies, Icons.* Austin: University of Texas Press, 2012.

Muñoz Cota, José. *Ricardo Flores Magón: El aguila ciega.* Mexico City: Instituto Oaxaqueño de Las Culturas, 1973.

Muñoz Martínez, Monica. *The Injustice Never Leaves You.* Cambridge, MA: Harvard University Press, 2018.

Myers, Ellen Howell. "The Mexican Liberal Party, 1903–1910." PhD diss., University of Virginia, 1970.

Neuburger, Bruce. *Lettuce Wars.* New York: Monthly Review Press, 2013.

Ngai, Mae. *Impossible Subjects.* Princeton, NJ: Princeton University Press, 2004.

Obregón-Iturra, Jimena Paz. "Il s'en faut d'un poil." In *Figures du corps*, 145–65. Paris: Société d'ethnologie / Université Paris X.

Olcott, Jocelyn H. *Revolutionary Women in Postrevolutionary Mexico.* Durham, NC: Duke University Press, 2005.

Olcott, Jocelyn H., Mary Kay Vaughan, and Gabriela Cano, eds. *Sex in Revolution: Gender, Politics, and Power in Modern Mexico.* Durham, NC: Duke University Press, 2006.

Overmyer-Velázquez, Mark. "Portraits of a Lady: Visions of Modernity in Porfirian Oaxaca City." *Estudios Mexicanos* 23, no. 1 (Winter 2007).

Peck, Jamie. "Political Economies of Scale: Fast Policy, Interscalar Relations, and Neoliberal Workfare." *Economic Geography* 78, no. 3 (July 2002).

Perales, Monica. *Smeltertown: Making and Remembering of a Southwest Border Community.* Chapel Hill: University of North Carolina Press, 2010.

Pérez, Emma. *The Decolonial Imaginary: Writing Chicanas into History.* Bloomington: Indiana University Press, 1999.

Pérez, Emma. "'A la mujer': A Critique of the Partido Liberal Mexicano's Gender Ideology on Women." In *Between Borders: Essays on Mexicana/Chicana History*, edited by Adelaida R. Del Castillo. Encino, CA: Floricanto, 1990.

Ramírez, Catherine S. *The Woman in the Zoot Suit: Gender, Nationalism, and the Cultural Policies of Memory.* Durham, NC: Duke University Press, 2009.

Ricouer, Paul. *Time and Narrative.* Chicago: University of Chicago Press, 1990.

Robinson, William. "The Great Recession of 2008 and the Continuing Crisis: A Global Capitalism Perspective." *International Review of Modern Sociology* 358, no. 2 (Autumn 2012).

Rosaldo, Michelle. "Toward an Anthropology of Self and Feeling." In *Culture Theory: Essays on Mind, Self and Emotion*, edited by Richard A. Shweder and Robert A. LeVine. New York: Cambridge University Press, 1984.

Rosas, Ana. *Abrazando el Espíritu: Bracero Families Confront the U.S.-Mexico Border.* Berkeley: University of California Press, 2014.

Sánchez-Eppler, Karen. *Touching Liberty: Abolition, Feminism, and the Politics of the Body.* Berkeley: University of California Press, 1993.

Sánchez Prado, Ignacio M. "Vanguardia y campo literario: La Revolución Mexicana como apertura estética." *Revista de Crítica Literaria Latinoamericana* 33, no. 66 (2007).

Sasso, Acalayga. "Librado Rivera y los hermanos rojos en el movimiento social y cultural anarquista en Villa Cecilia y Tampico Tamaulipas, 1915–1932." PhD diss., Universidad IberoAmericana. 2006.

Shah, Nayan. *Stranger Intimacy: Contesting Race, Sexuality, and the Law in the North American West.* Berkeley: University of California Press, 2011.

Sifuentes-Jáuregui, Ben. *The Avowal of Difference.* Albany: State University of New York Press, 2014.

Sifuentes-Jáuregui, Ben. "Cuerpos, intelectuales y homosocialidad en *Los de Abajo*." *Revista Crítica Literaria Latinoamericana* 33, no. 66 (2007).

Sommer, Doris. *Foundational Fictions: The National Romances of Latin America.* Berkeley: University of California Press, 1993.

Sonnichsen, C. L. "Colonel William C. Greene and the Strike at Cananea, Sonora, 1906." *Arizona and the West* 13, no. 4 (Winter 1971): 351–52.

Sontag, Susan. *On Photography.* New York: Picador, 2001.

Sosa Riddell, Adaljiza. "Chicanas en el movimiento." *Aztlan* 5, nos. 1–2 (1970): 155–65.

Stewart, William P., and Myron F. Floyd. "Visualizing Leisure." *Journal of Leisure Research* 36, no. 4 (2004).

Streeby, Shelly. *Radical Sensations: World Movements, Violence, and Visual Culture.* Durham, NC: Duke University Press, 2013.

Street, Richard Steven. *Everyone Had Cameras: Photography and Farmworkers in California, 1850–2000.* Minneapolis: University of Minnesota Press, 2008.

Taylor, Lawrence Douglas. *La campaña Magonista de 1911 en Baja California.* Mexico City: Colegio de La Frontera Norte, 1992.

Valencia, Tita. *Testimonio carcelario de Ricardo Flores Magón.* Mexico City: Secretaría de Gobernación, 1977.

Vaughan, Mary Kay. "Cultural Approaches to Peasant Politics in the Mexican Revolution." *Hispanic American Historical Review* 79, no. 2 (May 1999).

Vider, Stephen. "'Oh Hell, May, Why Don't You People Have a Cookbook?' Camp Humor and Gay Domesticity." *American Quarterly* 65, no. 4 (2013): 877–904.

Wells, Marion. *The Secret Wound: Love, Melancholy, and the Early Modern Romance.* Palo Alto, CA: Stanford University Press.

Wexler, Laura. *Tender Violence: Domestic Visions in the Age of U.S. Imperialism.* Chapel Hill: University of North Carolina Press, 2000.

Williams, Kelsey. "'Copied without Loss': Michael Field's Poetic Influence on the Work of W. B. Yeats." *Journal of Modern Literature* 40, no. 1 (Fall 2016).

Wright, Percy F. "Agricultural Crop Report 1956." Santa Rosa, CA: Sonoma County Department of Agriculture.

Index

abjection, 24–28, 175–84, 200, 218. *See also* subjects
Aconte Acasio, Francisco, 144
activism. *See* anarchism; direct action; revolutionary ideology
Adkinson, Sam, 117
aesthetics, 8–9, 11, 26, 36, 177, 212, 228. *See also* visuality
affect: anarchist love and, 84, 93; archives and, 35–36; bodily harm and, 113–15; bracero program and, 197–213; deportation and, 164–65; emotional attachment and, 12, 17; exile and, 36; homoerotics and, 27–28, 178; intimate betrayal and, 76; masculinities and, 4–5, 173–74; performance and, 119–26. *See also* emotion
African Americans, 15–17
agricultural labor: affective histories and, 197–213; bracero program and, 185–94; emotional attachments and, 14, 17, 19; homoerotics and, 24–28, 175–84; masculinities and, 2–3. *See also* bracero program
agriculture, 22
Aguirre, Lauro, 48
Alavos Guzmán, Gustavo, 186
Alemán, Miguel, 166
alienation, 157–69, 200–201, 204–5
alien-exclusion laws, 34
Alzalde, Eugenio, 102–3
American Can Company, 54
American Chemical Society, 266
American Farm Economic Association, 188
anarchism: bodily harm and, 107–15; debt and, 102–3; deportation and, 157–59; emotional attachments and, 10–20; emotional labor and, 155–56; gender ideology and, 43–45, 75–76; intimate betrayal and, 56–64, 69, 78–80; love and, 83–105; masculinities and, 1, 5–6, 9–10, 28, 171–74; performing affect and, 119–27; PLM and, 30; revolutionary desire and, 22–23, 31–33; women and, 115–19. *See also* anarcho-syndicalism
anarcho-communism, 86–87, 126
anarcho-socialism, 126
anarcho-syndicalism, 15, 92, 119, 158
Anderson, Henry, 202
Aniceto Gutiérrez, Carlos, 2–3
Araujo, Antonio de P., 49, 64, 70–71, 79
Arceneaux, Grace, 215–16, 221, 240–45, 247, 269
archives, 9–12, 34, 181, 287–88
Archivo General de la Nación, 40
Arteaga, Juanita, 113, 115, 118–19, 123
Arteaga, Teresa. *See* Flores Magón, Teresa Arteaga de
assimilation, 194
atheism, 88
attachments. *See* emotional attachments
authoritarianism, 69–71, 76–77, 79–80, 104, 143
Ávila Camacho, Manuel, 21

Bailleres, Antonio R., 246–47
baroque language, 23, 35, 39–43, 54, 58, 68, 75–76, 90, 96. *See also* poetics
Bartra, Roger, 9
Bautista, Agustín, 240–41
Belen de Sarraga, Maria, 166
Beleno Villapando, Santiago, 44, 80, 84–95, 99, 105, 109, 115
Benavides, Domingo M., 277–78
Berkman, Alexander, 114

INDEX 329

Berlant, Lauren, 9, 184, 208, 223
Bernal, Nicolás T., 50, 80, 85, 139, 141
"Berrys, The" (comic strip), 266–67
Bersani, Leo, 228
betrayal, 43–81, 84
Birbeck, F. V., 236, 238
Blair, Sara, 268
Blas, Jack, 222
Board of Supervisors for Monterey County, 236
bodies: affect and, 122–23, 126; affective histories and, 199; anarchist love and, 92–93; bracero program and, 175–76, 185, 190, 192–93, 199–202, 211–13; domestic labor and, 216–17, 222, 225, 228–31; homoerotics and, 24, 26, 28, 184; masculinities and, 1, 5, 107–15; revolutionary desire and, 21; revolutionary ideology and, 143. *See also* corporeal punishment
Bohemian Los Angeles, 86
Bostin, Bill, 276
bracero program: desire and, 251–73; domestic labor and, 215–31; emotional attachments and, 10–20; homoerotics and, 24–28, 175–84; masculinities and, 2–3, 6–8, 283–84, 288–90; queer precarity and, 233–50; temporality and, 185–94; violence and, 275–83. *See also* agricultural labor; labor camps
brotherhood, 21, 23, 26, 140–41, 194
Brousse, Adelaida, 84–85, 95–96, 143
Brousse, María, 22, 84–86, 92, 115, 141, 144–45, 165–66
Brown v. Board of Education, 186
Bruhn, Dick, 269
Buck, Eugene, 102
Bureau of Mushroom Industry, 99–100
Burns, CWR, 126
Business Week, 7
Butler, Judith, 192, 209

California Berry Growers Association, 279
California State Crop Reporting Service, 192
Caminetti, A., 163
Campbell, Joe, 187
Campt, Tina, 11, 52, 93, 164

capitalism: affect and, 120, 126; anarchist love and, 86–87, 90–91, 95; bodily harm and, 112, 115; bracero program and, 190–93, 198, 203–5, 209, 213; masculinities and, 1, 13, 39, 182; queer precarity and, 249–50; revolutionary desire and, 21–22, 29–34, 38; revolutionary ideology and, 44, 59–62, 67, 70, 102–4
Care of the Self, The (Foucault), 244
Carmona, Desideria, 45–47
Carmona, Margarita. *See* Flores Magón, Margarita Carmona de
Carmona, Paula: anarchist love and, 92, 97; gender and, 101; intimate betrayal and, 43–81; masculinities and, 35–36, 171–74; revolutionary ideology and, 168–69; women anarchists and, 116
Carmona, Práxedis. *See* Flores Magón, Práxedis Carmona de
Carmona, Rómulo, 44–46, 49, 53–54, 60–73, 76–80, 144
Carranza, Venustiano, 119
Casa del Obrero Internacional, 63
Catholicism, 21
censorship, 30, 48, 144
Chacón, Justin Akers, 36
Chávez-García, Miroslava, 13, 289
Chen, Mel, 198–99
children: anarchist love and, 84–85, 87–88, 96; archives and, 36; bodily harm and, 109, 112, 119; bracero program and, 217, 236–39; emotional attachments and, 14; emotional labor and, 147–56; homoerotics and, 180; intimate betrayal and, 65, 70, 72, 76–78; masculinities and, 2, 172–73; revolutionary desire and, 23–24; revolutionary ideology and, 60–62, 143
Church, the, 39, 59, 78–79, 104
Cisneros, José Abraham, 102–3
citizenship: bracero program and, 192, 194, 202, 216–17, 273; deportation and, 157–59; emotional attachments and, 17–19; homoerotics and, 176, 178; masculinities and, 4, 9
civil rights, 204, 284
Clark, Mary E., 216
class: bracero program and, 185–87, 191, 193–95; desire and, 258–59; domestic labor

and, 223; emotional attachments and, 15–18; homoerotics and, 24, 27, 176; masculinities and, 9; revolutionary desire and, 20; revolutionary ideology and, 88, 102–3
Cleveland, Grover, 38
Cline, Charles, 102–3
Cohen, Deborah, 12, 176, 188–89, 197, 216, 221–22, 229, 246, 251
colonialism, 41, 272
Commission on Migratory Labor, 27
communism, 11, 116, 162
communitarian living, 83, 86–100, 112, 118. *See also* Edendale commune
"Como a Nadie" (Flores Magón), 98–99
Constitutionalism, 22
Cookie Lettuce, 197–213
corporeal punishment, 31. *See also* bodies
courtroom dramas, 124–27
Creel, Enrique, 13, 46, 49
Creelman, James, 29
criminality, 162, 275–82
Curtis, Debra, 262–63

dance, 154–55
Daniel, Hurewitz, 86
debt, 83, 100–105
Decena, Carlos, 243–44
Decolonial Imaginary, The (Pérez), 84
de la Mora, Sergio, 225
de Lara, Rafael, 142–43
de La Torre, José, 278–81
del Campo, José A., 185
democracy, 17, 29–30, 114
Democratic party, 187–88
Demófilo, 81
denunciation, 43–45
deportation, 14, 115–18, 143–44, 157–69
Derrida, Jacques, 255, 259
desire: anarchist love and, 83, 89–91, 97; bracero program and, 195, 207–10; domestic labor and, 218–19, 225, 227, 229; emotional attachments and, 13; homoerotics and, 25–26, 177, 183–84; masculinities and, 4, 173–74. *See also* revolutionary desire
diaspora: alienness and, 157–69; bracero program and, 283–84; desire and, 258; domestic labor and, 225–27; emotional attachments and, 10–20; homoerotics and, 24–28, 183–84; intimate betrayal and, 52; masculinities and, 1–7, 9, 174; revolutionary desire and, 33
Díaz, Modesto, 49
Díaz, Porfirio, 1, 4, 20–22, 29–32, 38, 48, 79
Díaz-Sánchez, Micaela, 154
dictatorship, 11, 29–31, 35–36. *See also* Díaz, Porfirio
direct action, 64–65, 113–14, 116, 140, 172. *See also* anarchism
disability, 112, 123, 143, 162
discipline, 181, 206–7
domesticity: anarchism and, 89, 92, 119; homoerotics and, 26–27, 180–81; intimate betrayal and, 56, 77; masculinities and, 6, 174. *See also* domestic labor
domestic labor, 108, 215–31. *See also* domesticity
Dorantes Tovar, Horacio, 15
Driscoll farms, 279
"drybacks," 19, 177
Duarte, Richard, 191–92

economics, 244–50, 260–63, 269, 284–89
Edendale commune, 1, 85–100, 107, 114, 141. *See also* communitarian living
education, 39, 158
"Educators and Warriors" (Flores Magón), 103
Eisenhower, Dwight D., 5, 27, 187–91, 197
El Comillo Público, 123
El Democrata, 48–49, 144
"El espejismo del dolar" (*El Mañana*), 185
"El fracaso de Abraham Lincoln" (Flores Magón), 15
El Grupo Regeneración Bandera Roja, 69
El Grupo Regeneración Feminino Aspiraciones Libres, 69–70
El Hijo del Ahizote, 30
"El jurado falló en contra de los hermanos Magón" (Arteaga), 119–20
El Nacional, 23–24, 144, 166, 169, 173–74, 179
El Paso Morning Times, 108
El Paso Times, 162
"El retorno del bracero" (*Todo*), 245
El Sombrero Motel, 250
Eltinge, Julian, 86
El Universal, 16–17, 23–24, 144, 166, 185

emotion: anarchist love and, 90–91, 93, 97; archives and, 35–36, 40; bodily harm and, 107, 112–13; homoerotics and, 26–27, 178–79; intimate betrayal and, 71, 74, 80; masculinities and, 4–5, 7, 9; performance and, 119–24, 126; revolutionary desire and, 22, 32–33. *See also* affect

emotional attachments: anarchist love and, 83, 90; archives and, 36; bodily harm and, 115; bracero program and, 218; homoerotics and, 26, 28, 177–78, 183; incarceration and, 147–56; intimate betrayal and, 50–52, 56, 71, 74; masculinities and, 2–3, 5–7, 10–20, 173–74; revolutionary desire and, 33

emotional labor: anarchist love and, 98; bodily harm and, 108–10; debt and, 100–101; homoerotics and, 176; incarceration and, 147–56; masculinities and, 173–74; revolutionary desire and, 24; revolutionary ideology and, 60

empathy, 179
empire, 122–23
epistemology, 181–82
Erotic Life of Racism, The (Holland), 183
erotics, 39. *See also* homoerotics
Espionage Act, 116
Estrada, William, 87
ethnicity, 14, 19, 103, 186–87, 217, 278–79
eugenics, 195
Excelsior, 145
excesses, 26, 28, 93, 174, 199
exile, 4, 6–7, 10, 13, 16, 21, 29–34, 36, 157–69

fame, 124–27
family: 45-81, 56–57, 66; anarchist love and, 83–105; bodily harm and, 108, 110, 115; deportation and, 161, 163; emotional attachments and, 14–15; emotional labor and, 147–56; homoerotics and, 176, 180, 183; liberal, 127–38; masculinities and, 1–2, 7–9, 71–174; queer precarity and, 236–41; revolutionary desire and, 20–24, 29–34; revolutionary ideology and, 60–63, 139–46
farming. *See* agricultural labor
fatherhood, 77–78, 114. *See also* parenting; patriarchy

feeling. *See* affect; emotion
femininity: anarchist love and, 89–97; archives and, 40; bodily harm and, 112; bracero program and, 203; domestic labor and, 229–31; emotional attachments and, 13; homoerotics and, 180–81; intimate betrayal and, 52, 56, 71, 78; revolutionary desire and, 21, 24; revolutionary ideology and, 173
feminism, 44, 57, 79, 84, 118–19
Figueroa, Anselmo, 73, 166–67
Filipinos, 186, 248
film, 225
Fishback, Price, 242
Flores, José, 87, 193–94
Flores, Lori, 215
Flores Magón, Demófilo Carmona de, 45, 60, 62, 81
Flores Magón, Enrique: archives and, 35–40; bodily harm and, 107–15; debt and, 100–105; emotional attachments and, 10–17; emotional labor and, 147–56; gender ideology and, 43–45; homoerotics and, 26–28; intimate betrayal and, 46; love and, 83; masculinities and, 1–2, 5–9, 171–74, 288–90; performance and, 119–27; revolutionary desire and, 22–23, 29–34; revolutionary ideology and, 139–46; women and, 115–19
Flores Magón, Enrique, Jr., 85
Flores Magón, Esperanza, 85, 109, 115–16, 124, 143, 148–53, 167, 285, 301n6, 310n22
Flores Magón, Estela, 85, 115–24, 150–52, 165–67, 310n22
Flores Magón, Hortencia, 85
Flores Magón, Jesus, 35, 140, 142, 160, 171
Flores Magón, José Beleno de, 93–94, 115, 139, 165–67, 310n22
Flores Magón, Margarita Carmona de, 45, 53–57, 61, 76–79, 81
Flores Magón, Pedro, 85, 115, 165–67, 199, 301n6, 310n22
Flores Magón, Práxedis Carmona de, 45, 54–57, 61, 79, 81
Flores Magón, Ricardo: anarchist love and, 84–87, 99; bodily harm and, 107–15; emotional attachments and, 12, 15; intimate betrayal and, 46–68, 80; revolutionary desire

332 INDEX

and, 22–23, 30–33; revolutionary ideology and, 139–46, 171; women anarchists and, 115–19
Flores Magón, Teresa Arteaga de: anarchism and, 115–19; bodily harm and, 108–15; debt and, 100–105; emotional labor and, 147–56; masculinities and, 1–2, 35–36, 43, 52, 71, 73–76, 81–105, 171–74; revolutionary ideology and, 139–46
Food Research Institute, 188
Ford City Pickle Company, 15
Foucault, Michel, 206, 244, 252
fragility. *See* vulnerability
Franco, Miguel, 190–92
Freedman, Estelle, 238
freedom, 5–6, 9–10, 17, 38, 97
Freedom Fund, 7
freedom of press, 71
free love, 43–45, 53–56, 76–79, 83, 172–73
Freeman, Elizabeth, 203, 229
free speech, 30, 160
Frick, Henry Clay, 114
Fund for the New Republic, 26, 176, 182–83
Furlong Detective Agency, 40–41, 46

Gaitán, T. M., 64, 67, 70–71
Galarza, Ernesto, 175–78, 195, 203–4, 225, 227
García, Joe, 278–79
García, Manuel, 185
García, Rafael B., 112, 116, 120, 139, 141, 143
Gaytán, Teodoro, 50
gaze, the, 25, 175–84, 251–73
gender: anarchism and, 115–19, 164; anarchist love and, 83, 85, 87, 89–90, 92, 99; bodily harm and, 107, 109; bracero program and, 191, 193, 198–200, 209, 213; debt and, 100, 103–5; deportation and, 166–69; domesticity and, 217, 229–31; emotional attachments and, 20; homoerotics and, 26–28, 180; intimate betrayal and, 45–81; Mexican diaspora and, 1–7, 9–10; migration and, 176; revolutionary desire and, 20–21, 24, 33–34; revolutionary ideology and, 43–45, 172
Giannini Foundation of Agricultural Economics, 188
Goldman, Emma, 84, 102–3
Gómez-Quiñones, Juan, 12

Gondo labor camp, 253–57, 270
González, Gabriela, 44, 57, 65
González, Sánchez I., 281
González-Day, Ken, 255
Gonzalez García, José, 279–81
Gopinath, Gayatri, 183, 215, 222
Gortari, Rosaura, 57
governance, 30
Gran Mitin Internacional, 117
Great Plains program, 189
Greek mythology, 228–29
grief, 93–95, 145. *See also* loss
Grower Shipper Vegetable Association, 222
Guerra, José, 72–73
Guerrero, Práxedis, 45, 49–50, 52
Guevara, Remigio, 117
Guha, Ranajit, 40
"Guide to the Leonard Nadel Photographs and Scrapbooks," 25
Guidotti, Richard, 280
Gutierrez de Mendoza, Juana Belén, 115
Gutiérrez de Mendoza, María, 116

Harriman, Job, 86
Hart, John Mason, 22
Harvester News, 7
Haymarket riots, 166
health: bodily harm and, 107–15; bracero program and, 233–34; incarceration and, 161–62; masculinities and, 1, 20–23, 40, 97; revolutionary ideology and, 143; women and, 119–20
Heatherton, Christina, 155–56
Hernández, Alexandro D., 155
Hernández, Sonia, 89, 92
Herod, Andrew, 202
heroism, 12–13
hetero-affection, 262
heteromasculinity, 28
heteronormativity: bracero program and, 180, 182–84, 211, 222; masculinities and, 8, 12, 33, 56, 66, 114
Hirsch, Jennifer, 2
Hiss, E. E., 100
Holland, Sharon Patricia, 183, 218
Hombres y Machos (Mirandé), 278
homo-affection, 262

INDEX   333

homoerotics: abjection and, 175–84; bracero program and, 210, 222–31; desire and, 251–73; domestic labor and, 215–31; masculinities and, 24–28; precarity and, 233–50; violence and, 282. *See also* erotics; queerness
homosexuality, 20, 25, 223, 229, 238, 268
homosociality: bracero program and, 180–83, 197–98, 211; desire and, 252–55, 262–68; masculinities and, 7–8, 23; precarity and, 244–46; revolutionary ideology and, 140–41, 172; violence and, 280–86 (*See also* queerness)
housing, 7, 193, 238
Howard, June, 123
Hudgins, Nicole, 56

Ice Kist labor camp, 276–77
"Idea," the. *See* revolutionary ideology
identity, 146, 222–23, 279
illness. *See* health
images, 12, 19–20, 52. *See also* aesthetics; visuality
immigration: alienness and, 157–69; deportation and, 115–18, 143–44, 157–69; emotional attachments and, 11, 14–16, 19; homoerotics and, 27, 175–84; masculinities, 6–7; violence and, 279–81. *See also* migration
Immigration Act (1918), 161
imprisonment. *See* incarceration
incarceration: anarchist love and, 96–97; bodily harm and, 109–15; body, 115; emotional attachments and, 10; emotional labor and, 147–56; intimate betrayal and, 62–63, 65, 74–76; masculinities and, 1–2, 10; revolutionary desire and, 23–24, 31; revolutionary ideology and, 49; surveillance and, 41
Indians, 30, 202. *See also* indigenous people
indigenous people, 17, 24, 30, 41, 194–95, 202, 212. *See also* Indians
Industrial Worker, 123
Industrial Workers of the World, 59, 101–3, 114, 123, 164, 166–67
Infante, Pedro, 21
intellectual freedom, 29
intimacy: affective histories and, 197; anarchist love and, 83, 92, 98–99; betrayal and, 45–81; domestic labor and, 215–31; emotional attachments and, 11–13; homoerotics and, 25–27, 177, 180; masculinities and, 2–9; revolutionary desire and, 22–23, 31, 34; surveillance and, 40–41
intimate betrayal and, 49–50
Irwin, Robert McKee, 20, 39, 183, 243

Jameson, Fredric, 32
Japanese Americans, 279–80
Jefferson, Thomas, 125
Jewish people, 166
Johnson, Colin R., 236, 277
Johnson-Reed Act, 158
Joseph, Gil, 22
journalism, 15, 57, 114–19, 166, 169. *See also* publishing

Karl's Shoes, 269
kinship, 92. *See also* emotional attachments; love
Knight, Alan, 22
Kristeva, Julia, 25, 218

La Aurora (bookstore), 47–48, 53–54, 59–60
La Bandera Roja, 48
labor: affective histories and, 200–213; anarchist love and, 87–90, 93; bodily harm and, 113; bracero program and, 185–94; debt and, 100–101; deportation and, 164–66; emotional attachments and, 10, 13–19; homoerotics and, 25, 175–84; masculinities and, 2–3, 9. *See also* agricultural labor; emotional labor; reproductive labor
labor activism, 22
labor camps: desire and, 252–70; domesticity and, 216–21, 229; homoerotics and, 24–28, 175–84, 216–21; masculinities and, 2–3, 7, 286–87; queer precarity and, 233–50; violence and, 276–82. *See also* bracero program
labor exploitation, 16–17, 25–26, 183, 268, 283. *See also* workers' rights
labor unions, 21
"La campaña contra *Regeneración*" (Araujo), 67
Lakeview Farms, 224
"La liberacion de bracerismo" (Guzmán), 186

La Malinche, 78
La Mañana, 185
Lange, Dorothea, 177
"La protesta contra la conducta mezquina . . ." (El Grupo Regeneración Bandera Roja), 69
Lara, Blas, 64, 67, 70–71, 86, 103, 112
La Reforma Social, 48
"La revolución en el sur de la republica" (Guerra), 72–73
law, 275–82
law, the, 5, 8, 11, 119–27, 195. *See also* neutrality laws
Lewis, Oscar, 243
Leyva, Jesse N., 275
liberalism, 127–38. *See also* PLM
Life, 7
Lincoln, Abraham, 15
Lindsey, Bert, 236
literacy, 36, 45–46, 116
Llano del Rio commune, 86
Lomas, Silvestre, 102–3
Lomnitz, Claudio, 33, 64–65, 92, 116, 141
Long, Warren, 159
Long Beach Independent, 266–67
Look, 7, 179
Lopez, Ben, 200
Los Angeles County Housing Authority, 7
Los Angeles Times, 7, 15, 124, 126, 141, 158
Los grandes problemas nacionales (Enriquez), 20
"Los 'huérfanos'" (Flores Magón), 76–79, 150
loss, 23, 33, 74–75, 119, 145. *See also* grief
love: anarchism and, 83–105; archives and, 35–40; bodily harm and, 115; intimate betrayal and, 50–52, 74, 78–79; privacy and, 101; revolutionary desire and, 23, 33–34. *See also* romantic love
Loza, Mireya, 176, 284
Luciano, Dana, 198–99
Lytle Hernández, Kelly, 41, 110

machismo, 4, 20, 180–84, 194–95, 288, 293n46
Macías-González, Víctor, 6, 20, 223, 228, 251
MacLachlan, Colin, 12
Maetus, Fernando, 50
Magallanes Hernández, Ignacio, 234
Magón, Margarita, 35–37, 97, 116–18
Magonistas, 30, 45–46

Marez, Curtis, 206–7
marriage, 45, 53–54, 56, 89–90, 174
Marton, Oliver L., 265–66
martyrdom, 124, 143
Marx, Karl, 192, 203
masculinities: affective histories and, 197–213; anarchist love and, 89–90, 97; archives and, 35–40; bodily harm and, 107–15; bracero program and, 185–94, 283–84; desire and, 251–73; diaspora and, 288–90; domestic labor and, 215–31; emotional attachments and, 10–20; emotional labor and, 147–56; fame and, 124–27; homoerotics and, 24–28; intimate betrayal and, 45–81; Mexican diaspora and, 1–9; performing affect and, 119–24; queer precarity and, 233–50; revolutionary desire and, 20–24, 29–34; revolutionary ideology and, 45, 103–5, 139–46; violence and, 275–83; women anarchists and, 115–19
Masculinity and Sexuality in Modern Mexico (Macías-González & Rubenstein), 20
Matthews, Frank, 236
Maya, Harry, 280
McFadden, Daniel, 245
Mendez, Rosa. *See* Flores Magón, Enrique
mestizos, 20, 24
Mexican Adonis, 228–31
Mexican Americans: bracero program and, 191–95; desire and, 268–71; domestic labor and, 216, 221; masculinities and, 3, 14, 19, 186, 191, 195, 200, 269; queer precarity and, 241–42, 247–49; violence and, 286–87
Mexican Liberal Party. *See* PLM
Mexican masculinities. *See* masculinities
Mexican Revolution, 12, 20–24, 29–34, 36
migration: bracero program and, 186, 195; deportation and, 157–69; emotional attachments and, 10–13, 16, 20; homoerotics and, 26–28, 175–84; masculinities and, 2–9, 102; revolutionary desire and, 23. *See also* immigration
militancy, 146
militarism, 20
mining, 24
misogyny, 40–45, 76–79, 166, 172–73
modernity, 20, 164, 176, 228
Molina Enriquez, Andrés, 20

INDEX 335

Molina, Natalia, 157, 265
Moncaleano, Blanca, 57
Moncaleano, Juan F., 63–66, 68–70
Monterey County Extension Service, 248
Monterey County Department of Health, 233
Mora, Sergio de la, 21
morality, 20, 59, 65–66, 78, 80, 115, 123
Moreton, Bethany, 189
Morita, Frank, 280
Morton, Henry Max, 49
Mother Earth (Goldman), 102–4
motherhood: archives and, 35–37; intimate betrayal and, 78–81; revolutionary ideology and, 56–66, 97, 116–18, 173. *See also* parenting
Mraz, John, 11–12
Muñoz Cota, José, 12
music, 154–55

Nacamiento Dam, 249
Nadel, Evelyn De Wolfe, 8, 283–84
Nadel, Leonard: affective histories and, 197–213; bracero program and, 185–96; desire and, 251–73; domestic labor and, 213–31; emotional attachments and, 11–12; homoerotics and, 24–28, 175–85; masculinities and, 3–8, 283–84; queer precarity and, 233–50; violence and, 275–82
Nakashima, Carl, 80
National Agricultural Workers Union, 175
nationalism: bracero program and, 184, 186, 189–90; masculinities and, 5–7, 10, 15, 28–30, 38, 81; revolutionary desire and, 20–21, 32–33
nationality, 186–87, 191, 195, 200–202, 216–17, 248–49
nation-states, 5, 10, 34, 182, 290. *See also* state, the
neutrality laws, 10, 31, 57, 60, 111
Ngai, Mae, 158
Nixon, Richard, 188
Noon, N. K., 112
Norman, Lucía, 85–86, 115–20, 125, 139, 141. *See also* Norman, Lucille
Norman, Lucille, 159. *See also* Norman, Lucía

Olcott, Jocelyn, 164
On Photography (Sontag), 181
Operation Wetback, 27, 176, 186, 195

optimism, 9–13, 27, 41, 52, 223
Ortega, Margarita, 57
Ortiz, Candelario, 102
Osmers, Frank, 279
Overmyer-Velázquez, Mark, 222
Owen, William, 59, 65, 144

Palma, Raúl, 86, 117, 139
Palomares, Fernando, 140–41
panopticon, 206
parenting, 60–62, 147–56, 237. *See also* fatherhood; motherhood
Partido Liberal Mexicano (PLM). *See* PLM
paternalism, 186
patriarchy: bodily harm and, 109–10; bracero program and, 209; homoerotics and, 180; intimate betrayal and, 44, 76–77, 81; masculinities and, 4; revolutionary desire and, 29–33; revolutionary ideology and, 174
patriotism, 50, 186, 189–90
"Paula Carmona" (Flores Magón), 65–66
Pearson's Magazine, 29
pedophilia, 236–39
Peleamos contra la injusticia (Flores Magón), 81
Perales, Monica, 242–43
Pérez, Emma, 43–44, 84
"Perfiles negros. Los criminales" (Araujo), 64, 70
performance, 119–27
photography: affective histories and, 197–213; desire and, 271–73; emotional attachments and, 10–20; homoerotics and, 24–28, 175–84; masculinities and, 10
place, 185–94
PLM: anarchist love and, 83–89, 98–99; archives and, 39; bodily harm and, 107–15; debt and, 100–101, 103–4; emotional attachments and, 12, 15; emotional labor and, 147–56; gender ideology and, 43–45; intimate betrayal and, 45–49, 53, 56, 59, 64, 66, 69, 75, 79–80; masculinities and, 1, 4–7, 9, 171–74; performing affect and, 122, 124; revolutionary desire and, 22–23, 29–32; revolutionary ideology and, 140–46; surveillance and, 40–41. *See also* liberalism poetics, 32, 35–41, 69, 73–74, 76, 89, 98–99. *See also* baroque language

policing, 1, 6, 8, 13–14, 110, 119, 247–48, 283
Post, Louis F., 163
poverty, 87–88, 112–13, 168–69, 177, 180; revolutionary ideology and, 62
precarity, 233–50
President's Committee on Migratory Labor, 186
private life: anarchist love and, 83, 96–98, 100; bodily harm and, 108; braceros and, 5–7, 13, 27, 217, 223, 265; debts and, 100–105; revolutionary desire and, 32, 34. *See also* public life
proletariat, the, 62, 76, 90, 103–4, 119, 125, 161. *See also* workers
propaganda, 47, 63, 114, 145, 177
property, 38–39, 59, 69, 87
prostitution, 20, 79
Protestantism, 84
public health. *See* health
public life: anarchism and, 83, 92, 96, 100, 108, 120; bracero program and, 223; bracero suffering and, 183–84; debt and, 100–105; emotional attachments and, 11–13; masculinities and, 197; performing affect and, 119–24; revolutionary desire and, 23, 32–34; women anarchists and, 117–18. *See also* private life
publishing, 30, 47. *See also* journalism
punishment, 31, 44, 73–74. *See also* incarceration

queerness, 8, 26, 176–84, 198–203, 213, 233–50, 258, 262, 288–90, 291n6; desire and, 262
"Que luchen" (Carmona), 57–58

race: bracero program and, 186–95, 198–204, 209, 213, 283–84; citizenship and, 158–69; desire and, 258–63, 268–73; domestic labor and, 215–31; emotional attachments and, 13, 15–17, 20; homoerotics and, 25, 28, 178, 180; intimate betrayal and, 80; masculinities and, 2–3, 9–11, 122–23, 126; queer precarity and, 233, 238, 242, 249–50; revolutionary desire and, 21; revolutionary ideology and, 103–4; surveillance and, 41; violence and, 275–82. *See also* skin color; white supremacy
radicalism, 23, 59, 86, 89–90, 119–20
Raffetto, E. J., 149, 240, 247

Ramirez, Alex, 275
Ramírez, Cristina Devereaux, 44
Ramírez, Sara Estela, 115
Rancho Grande Café, 270–73
Rangel, Jesus, 49, 102–3
red scare, the, 14, 121–22, 126
Regeneración: anarchist love and, 84–88, 100; archives and, 40; bodily harm and, 108, 110, 114; debt and, 100–101; intimate betrayal and, 53–74; masculinities and, 173; performing affect and, 121–23, 125; revolutionary desire and, 23; revolutionary ideology and, 139–46; women anarchists and, 115–19
Register Pajaronian, 187, 246–47
religion, 96, 193–94
reparations, 181
reproductive labor, 87, 90, 104–5, 108–9, 165, 176
Republican party, 187–91, 195
Return of Comrade Ricardo Flores Magón, The (Lomnitz), 33
Revolución, 49
revolutionary desire, 20–24, 29–40
revolutionary ideology: deportation and, 160–61; gender and, 43–45; intimate betrayal and, 45–81; masculinities and, 139–46, 171–74
Rickman, J. H., 112–14
Ricoeur, Paul, 203
Rincón Gallardo, Pedro, 64
Rincón, Juan, Jr., 102–3
Rivera, Anselmo, 56–57
Rivera, Conchita, 59, 86
Rivera, Librado, 49, 56–57, 72, 86–87, 142, 166–67
Road, Davis, 198–99
Robledo, Pilar A. *See* Carmona, Rómulo
romanticism, 96
romantic love, 50–52, 65, 74, 83, 90–92. *See also* love
Rosas, Ana, 52, 60, 176, 284
Rubenstein, Anne, 20
Russian Revolution, 161

Salcedo, Trinidad, 46
Salinas Californian, 187, 190, 193, 272
Salinas City Planning Commission, 236, 238–39

INDEX   337

Salinas Mattress Manufacturing Company, 220
Salinas Valley, 197–213
Salinas Valley Grower Association, 200
Sánchez-Eppler, Karen, 120
Sánchez Prado, Ignacio, 21
Santa Cruz Sentinel, 187
Santiago de la Hoz Liberal Club, 46
Sarabia, Juan, 46, 144
Sarabia, Manuel, 49
Sarabia, Tómas, 49
Savoy, Stanley, 234, 262
Schmidt, Kathrine, 54, 143
Schmidt, Matthew, 54
Scott, R. A., 158–59
Secretaría de Relaciónes Exteriores, 40
segregation, 14
Selective Service Act, 159
self-care, 220, 252–59, 265–68, 286
self-making, 7, 26, 33, 44, 52, 244, 258–61
sentimentality, 24, 49–52, 68, 91, 97, 120–23, 162, 172–74
sexism, 4, 77. *See also* misogyny; patriarchy
sexual abuse, 236–37
sexuality: anarchist love and, 83, 86–87, 90–91, 97, 99; bracero program and, 175–84, 195, 200, 215, 283–84; desire and, 262–63; domestic labor and, 227, 229, 231; emotional attachments and, 13, 20, 155; homoerotics and, 25–28; intimate betrayal and, 59, 76–80; masculinities and, 3–10; precarity and, 233–50; revolutionary desire and, 20–23, 32–34; surveillance and, 41
Shah, Nayan, 6, 238
"Shall Free Thought Be Throttled" (Flores Magón), 110
Shapiro, Chaim, 117
Shikuma, Unosuke, 279–80
Sifuentes-Jáuregui, Ben, 21
"Silencio liberticida" (Flores Magón), 103–4
skin color, 9. *See also* race
slavery, 15, 58, 88, 90, 155, 174
Smithsonian, the, 5, 7–8, 25–26, 178, 181
socialism, 114, 126, 166
Soil Bank, 189
Solis, Benito, 50
Sommer, Doris, 81
Sontag, Susan, 181–82
Spanish language, 193–95, 197, 273

spying, 46, 49, 86, 97, 116. *See also* surveillance
state, the: alienness and, 157–69; archives and, 40; bodily harm and, 11, 107, 109, 113–14; bracero program and, 215–16; emotional attachments and, 13; homoerotics and, 27–28, 182; intimate betrayal and, 72, 81; masculinities and, 6–7, 9; nationalism and, 29; performing affect and, 124–26; revolutionary desire and, 23, 31, 34; revolutionary ideology and, 102; surveillance and, 40–41. *See also* nation-states
sterilization, 229
Strangers in Our Fields (Galarza), 175–77, 195
Streeby, Shelly, 113, 157, 164
Street, Richard Stevens, 176–77
strikes, 15, 194
Sturgis, Frank M., 163
subjectivity, 177
subjects: affective histories and, 197–98; alienness and, 147–56; anarchist love and, 89; archives and, 36; bodily harm and, 113; bracero program and, 194, 212; desire and, 251–73; domestic labor and, 215–31; emotional attachments and, 11–13; homoerotics and, 25–28, 177, 180, 182; intimate betrayal and, 52; masculinities and, 20, 173–74; migration and, 6–7; revolutionary desire and, 29–32. *See also* abjection
surveillance: anarchist love and, 86, 92, 97–98; bracero program and, 206–7, 211, 215; emotional attachments and, 10, 13, 17; intimacy and, 40–41; masculinities and, 9, 23, 46, 289–90; performing affect and, 125–26. *See also* spying

Tavernetti, A. A., 248–49, 251
temporality, 32, 177, 185–95, 203–4
terrorism, 192
Texas Thirteen, the, 83, 98, 101, 103
theft, 245, 275–83
"New Role for the Photographer, The" (Nadel), 179
Thompson, J. G., 108
Todo: La Mejor Revista de México, 15–19, 23–24, 144, 166, 185
Torres, Paula S., 69–70
totalitarianism, 111

338 INDEX

Tovar y Bueno, W., 48
trade unions, 41
trauma, 25, 76, 98, 111–13, 218, 268
Trejo, Rafel S., 48
Turner, Ethyl Duffy, 72, 86, 108, 142, 171

"Unavoidable" (Flores Magón), 38
unions, 102–3, 114–15, 145–46, 156. *See also* labor unions
US-Mexico border, 107

Valencia, Tita, 72
Van Vorst Manufacturing Company, 88
Vargas, Abel M., 277–78
Vasconcellos, José, 142
Velásquez Lucio, Clemente, 242–45
victimization, 72, 74, 76, 176, 183, 211, 268
Vider, Stephen, 223
Villa, Francisco (Pancho), 32
Villagomes Fuentes, Carlos, 237
Villareal, Trinidad, 139
violence: anarchism and, 162; bodily harm and, 107, 109–15; bracero program and, 275–83; desire and, 255; emotional attachments and, 14; gender ideology and, 45; homoerotics and, 27; intimate betrayal and, 75–78; nationalism and, 21, 38, 45, 75–78, 109–12, 163–64, 174; sexual, 236–39; surveillance and, 41
virility, 26–27
visuality, 9, 11, 13, 177. *See also* aesthetics; images
vulnerability: archives and, 40; bracero program and, 192, 198; desire and, 252–53; domestic labor and, 229; gender ideology and, 45; homoerotics and, 26–27; intimate betrayal and, 52, 76; masculinities and, 3, 23, 29, 97, 174; revolutionary desire and, 24, 31, 33–34

Walmart, 189
Washington Committee on Migratory Labor, 193
Wessels, D. A., 247–49
Western Farm Economic Association, 188
Westminster v. Mendez, 186
"wetbacks," 16
white supremacy, 122. *See also* race
Whitman, Ann, 188
Williams, Kelsey, 90
Williams, Raymond, 13
Wilson, Woodrow, 119
Wing, Joe, 240
"Wobblies." *See* Industrial Workers of the World
women: anarchism and, 115–19; anarchist love and, 84, 87, 92, 95–96, 99; bracero program and, 194–95, 215–17, 237–38, 244; debt and, 100; desire and, 262–66, 268–69; emotional attachments and, 14; homoerotics and, 25, 180; intimate betrayal and, 57–60, 70, 79–81; Mexican masculinities and, 2–4; migration and, 6; revolutionary ideology and, 43–45, 172–74
workers: bracero program and, 185–95; debt and, 102–4; emotional attachments and, 15–17; revolutionary ideology and, 68–69, 145–46; surveillance and, 41. *See also* agricultural labor; labor; proletariat, the
workers' rights, 15. *See also* labor exploitation
Works Project Administration (WPA), 7

yellow press, 15, 126
Yepes, Tirso, 235

Zapata, Emiliano, 22, 32
Zogg, Zen, 159